VOLUME 294

JULY 1954

THE ANNALS

of The American Academy *of* Political
and Social Science

THORSTEN SELLIN, *Editor*

RICHARD D. LAMBERT, *Assistant Editor*

AMERICA AND A NEW ASIA

Edited by
JAMES C. CHARLESWORTH, Ph.D.
Professor of Political Science
University of Pennsylvania
President, The American Academy of
Political and Social Science

PHILADELPHIA
1954

CONTENTS

BOOK DEPARTMENT   PAGE

The articles appearing in THE ANNALS are indexed in the *Readers' Guide to Periodical Literature* and the *Industrial Arts Index.*

FOREWORD

With the exception of the article by Mr. Tatsuo Morito, the papers in this volume of THE ANNALS are addresses presented at the Annual Meeting of The Academy, April 2 and 3, 1954.

Each of the six sessions of the Annual Meeting was devoted to a single subject—the relations between the United States and a particular country or region in Asia. It was not the purpose of the meeting to air disputes between Asian countries, hence the differences between Pakistan and India, between Israel and her Arab neighbors, between North and South Korea, and between the Republic of China and the People's Republic of China are alluded to but are not elucidated.

Because of the unavoidable absence of Dr. Halford L. Hoskins, his paper was read and discussed by Dr. George A. Codding, Jr., of the Department of Political Science of the University of Pennsylvania.

JAMES C. CHARLESWORTH

The War for the Mind of Japan

By Harry Emerson Wildes

IN this opening article, I want to discuss the impact of the American occupation on Japan and perhaps something about the impact of Japan on Americans.

I want it to be understood that I am not writing either in praise or in condemnation of any individual. The occupation was not one of individuals: the occupation was a joint enterprise, and a joint enterprise not only of Americans and other members of the Allies but also of the Japanese. It is a firm conviction of mine that the success of the occupation was due quite as much to the remarkable co-operation of the Japanese as to the work of the members of the occupation staff—perhaps even more.

Therefore if I say anything in praise of the occupation, it will include praise for the Japanese, and if I say anything in condemnation of the occupation, that, too, must be shared by all of us.

I should like to point out that in the very beginning we entered Japan under difficulties because the Americans and the others who manned the occupation made very little effort to understand the people whose destinies they undertook to govern. Seemingly, we never knew, we never cared to know, the people whom we ruled. Knowing nothing of their customs, their psychologies, their aspirations, we scorned their prejudices as feudalistic; we considered many of their desires as nothing more than a yearning for an outworn ultranationalism. Happily we had passed beyond the point of thinking that Japan was just a land of cherry blossoms and of geisha, but many of us still weltered in the thought that all the Japanese were vicious gangsters. Because we did not know and did not care to know their needs, we alienated many who had been our enemies but who wished to be our friends. And this despite incessant coaching from the sidelines.

Japan wanted us to win this war against the Soviets. But when she tried to help, too many of our occupationnaires suspected insincerity. A few occupationnaires even helped the enemy, though by ignorance, ineptitude, and inadvertence rather than by outright sabotage.

INFORMATION REJECTED

We spurned advice from those who tried to help. The Office of War Information, for example, had marshaled expert anthropologists, psychologists, historians, and other social scientists to study Japan's needs, to study her disciplines, her ethics, her modes of thought. It supplied that very remarkable team with stacks of data and afforded its members a free hand to probe the personalities of the Japanese then living in America.

The result was Ruth Benedict's *The Chrysanthemum and the Sword,* first issued in mimeographed sheets for occupation information, but the occupation threw away its findings as ill-informed and theoretical. Dr. Benedict, the occupation said, had never set foot in Japan.

That sneer was based on truth. Ruth Benedict had worked with Japanese in California and in various relocation camps. She had read widely in the standard works, in manuscripts, and in great heaps of captured documents, but she had never seen Japan. She had, however, analyzed and evaluated, and

1

her disciplined imagination had taken her deep into the Japanese mind.

AMERICA IN JAPAN

Such scholars as Ruth Benedict, by building on petty and often frivolous incidents, would have found many ways to use Japan's convictions as a force for good, but not the occupation. Scorning the scholarly approach, it saw everything in terms of reactionary plots to bring back ultranationalism. The occupationnaires preferred and trusted unskilled and undiscriminating folk who saw all things American as glistening white, all things Japanese as jet black or blood red. College boys and girls, who lived in American billets, who went in American buses to American offices where they worked only with Americans, who spent their evenings at American clubs or at American movies, who read American magazines and listened to American radio programs, and who, on week ends, went off in American cars to American rest hotels—these were accepted as authorities superior to Ruth Benedict.

Those untrained juveniles—I was among them though not a juvenile—who never saw the real Japan because, in truth, they never left America, controlled all phases of Japan's cultural life. By occupation edict, they could not visit Japanese schools or universities, enter a library, a theater, a music hall, or a movie house, patronize a restaurant, a café, or a hotel, nor, unless in special occupation cars, travel legitimately in Japan. The rule was broken, to be sure, and after four years was relaxed, but only after the occupation, in violation of the orders which created it, had made every effort to prevent legitimate association in Japanese cultural affairs.

In consequence, in warring for Japan's mind, we committed grievous errors for which we have only ourselves to blame. We started out with every possible advantage. We had an honest message to deliver. We controlled every avenue of communication. We had a captive audience which, contrary to all precedent, was eager to hear our message. We had in Washington a skilled and successful propaganda agency which offered its staff for occupation purposes.

Yet with all this in our favor, we discarded our trumps, played badly, and allowed our adversary to pile up points against us.

COMMUNIST PROPAGANDA

To put the matter mildly and charitably, poor judgment let the press, radio, and theater get entirely out of control. These, like the movies, pounded Communism incessantly into Japan's ears. We sat idly by, completely unconcerned. More recently, and to the present day, these same mass media are hammering out anti-American themes, representing our boys in Japan as dope addicts, lechers, sadists, criminals, and degenerates. No one within the occupation ranks then or in official position now could possibly be unaware of this wave of Communist propaganda. Our armed forces even on occasion lent their men and their facilities to Red movie makers for such themes. Despite our powerful, though unacknowledged censorship, this anti-American propaganda has swept unchecked over our captive audience. The failure to check it could only have been due to inattention, to indifference, or to unwillingness to stop its spread. An occupation that was so alert to fears of reviving militarism that it suppressed nascent conservatism was strangely reticent and tolerant towards Communism. True, the worst fever burned itself out in time, and on this the occupation preened itself, but the credit lies elsewhere.

The occupation was complacent about our educational affairs. Here the goal was long range, to indoctrinate the adults of tomorrow by instilling democratic principles into the children of today and, as the results could not be known for years to come, we sat by comfortably, assured that all was well. We worried over the contents of textbooks while Communists mobilized the teachers. We deleted harmless ideas that fanned Japan's legitimate aspirations and her patriotic pride, but we allowed the schools to pass out Communist propaganda leaflets. We forced the schools to pole-vault to heights never seen on land or sea, much less in our own school system. The consequence was chaos.

We let the children hear that established law and order was reactionary, feudal, capitalistic, and intolerable but that "progressivism," which many teachers construed as Communism, not only was desirable and democratic but was favored by the occupation.

We crusaded against Communism, but in doing so we committed tactical and strategic blunders. Ignorant of actual conditions, we appealed to Japanese by using the same arguments, often couched in the very words, that we used at home in warning Americans against the Reds.

U. S. FAILURES IN IMAGINATION

Thus, to people who had never tasted freedom, who knew nothing of justice in its Western sense, who had been taught that individualism was evil and that democracy was degeneration, and by whom Christianity was not generally accepted, we warned that Communism periled all those aims.

Japan remained unmoved by revelations of Russian atheism, of Soviet disregard for private rights, of its hampering of representative government, of its suppression of civil liberties—all these abuses so shocking to Americans but for

centuries all too familiar to Japan, left Japan unmoved. Men in military uniform who cherished caste and who, only recently, had plastered Japan with off-limits signs against both Japanese and their own subordinates were ineffective in condemning Russia as undemocratic.

Occupationnaires whose treatment of Japanese officials had been highhanded and whose disregard for Japanese laws and customs had been unconcealed failed to convince Japan that they also would be Russian puppets or to warn against the importation of an alien Soviet culture. Certainly the Japanese were mistaken, but many of them saw but little difference between the Allied occupation of Japan and Russian control of North Korea.

In fact, as Orientals conscious of their Eastern heritage, some of them thrilled at the news that Chinese and Russian armies had driven back American troops. While as Japanese they held contempt for both Chinese and Korean soldiers, the Red victory, however fleeting, proved to them that Asians could stand firm against the whites.

COMMUNISTS EXPLOIT AMERICAN WEAKNESSES

Communist propagandists exploited these opportunities. Pointing to the GI radio programs, to the Westerns, Tarzan, and gangster movies sent by Hollywood for showing in Japan, to comic books, and even to the cowboy suits and toy pistols worn by little boys of the American community, the Reds charged that Americans lacked culture. The arguments would have been laughable had they not been so convincing. The tawdriness, drunkenness, and vice near Army camps, the lack of any real effort to appreciate Japanese culture, the almost insulting assumption that everything American was good and all things Japanese were feudal, worked to Communist advantage.

Not that these accusations were true or that Communists were wholly free from criticism. Soviet soldiers stationed in Japan had been overbearing, grasping, and contemptuous. Their treatment of Japanese employees had been notorious, and their insistence upon Russian superiority had been as constant as it had been loud and boorish. But most of the Soviet soldiers had been withdrawn, and those that remained had segregated themselves. Drunken Russians no longer paraded nightly in the Dai Ichi Hotel corridors chanting "On to Budapest." Red excesses had been forgotten. But GI's continued to stroll hand in hand with pickups on the Ginza or to sprawl, bottle in hand, on cushions of crowded tramcars.

Red propagandists pointed to concrete instances, while Americans preached vaguely about theories unknown to the rank and file of Japanese. We talked of habeas corpus and judicial supremacy, of the Diet as the supreme organ of the state, of equality of opportunity and of the inalienable right of civilians to control the military. But the Reds were quick to point out that we named our housing projects and our movie houses after military heroes and that a huge sign proclaimed that Tokyo's central park was now Doolittle Field, named for the man who had led the firebomb raid on Tokyo.

THE TRAPPINGS OF WESTERNISM

The conservative Japanese strongly resented what seemed to represent the American impact on the Japanese. The fad of Westernism had been indiscriminate; the sense of values was suspended; trappings were more visible than the essentials. To chew gum and drink Coca-Cola, to pet in the romance seats of darkened movie houses, to sing "Buttons and Bows," to wear red shoes and aloha shirts—these seemed important democratic end products.

Aging Diet members and sedate Supreme Court justices sported green paper flowers on Saint Patrick's Day, plodded through square dances, or danced the rhumba at the exclusive Esquire Club. A Turkish bath, elaborate to a degree unknown to Istanbul or Ankara, fascinated businessmen who supposed that attractive lady attendants were also available in American establishments.

A virtually new language arose, a fearsome hodgepodge of several tongues, of antiquated slang, of mispronunciation. *Après-guerre* youth, demanding de-mo-kra-sie hubba-hubba, damme-dammed all the past and asked for skoshi itsy-bitsy hotto-dog and poppu-corn. And yet in all fairness I should add that even this strange caricature was far superior to any Japanese that I could speak.

Neither the olympian occupation nor the stratospheric Embassy could afford to bend low enough to notice the teen-age excesses of the bebop set, but they were singularly silent also in combating Soviet propaganda that the United States was turning Japan into a military base, taking good rice-growing land for baseball fields, mulcting Japan of taxes, and converting free Japan into a colony. None of these charges was true, but we were slow and clumsy in rebutting the untruths.

SOME COMMUNIST BLUNDERS

Luckily for Americans, the Red agents also blundered. They may have been too sure of victory. Had they played their cards well, they might have taken over Japan. General MacArthur was under orders not to interfere with any overturn of government that did not imperil occupation objectives—and Russia was then a full-fledged and equal member of the occupation. But, with incredible maladroitness, Communist leaders, by staging riots and disorders at times when things were running in their favor, sabotaged their own chances. Their encouragement of violence, their plagues of unnecessary strikes, the multiple evidences that Communists who talked so glibly and so convincingly of American colonization were more servile to Russia than loyal to Japan, spoiled their effectiveness as propagandists.

Stupidly, the Reds stressed issues upon which they were at least as vulnerable as the Americans. They ranted against American occupation of Okinawa at a time when Russia held the Kuriles. They raged against American-dictated purges and censorships at the very time the press was filled with tales of Russian thought control. They charged Americans with disturbing the peace while Soviet planes were flying over northern Honshu. They complained of American interference in Japan's domestic affairs at the very time that the Cominform agents were demanding that Japan punish certain Communist leaders for deviationism.

Soviet inconsistencies and blunders, together with the ineptness of Japanese Communist leadership, helped the democratic cause. This was a godsend, since the occupation, by freeing Red leaders and by nursing them into prominence, had given Communists a long head start.

Is It Too Late?

Has that head start been too great? Is the hour now too late? Has Communism won the battle for Japan's mind? Has the occupation's blindness, complacency, and sloth given the Reds a lead that cannot now be overcome?

No one who knows Japan believes that its people favor Communism. The country is not "Red" and does not welcome Red ideas. For more than two centuries it has stood fast against the Russians. It has no love for them today.

But occupation blunders threw Japan into the Russians' arms. We seemed to favor them at first, and though that impression has been clearly counteracted by Washington's more determined stand, we must now, at last, do the work the occupation should have done in 1945 and 1946. We must make clear the fact that democratic policies are not Russian and, for that matter, are not necessarily an American monopoly. We must make clear that the Japanese have also been democratic and not always feudal, an idea that the Potsdam Declaration itself suggested but which the occupation threw aside.

How many occupationnaires made even the slightest use of the magnificent bibliography on Japan's human rights movement which the National Diet Library compiled in 1949? How many even knew that it existed? As propaganda it would have been invaluable, appealing as it did to Japanese patriotism, tradition, and precedent; it won more sympathy than any number of quotations from foreigners of whom the Japanese had never heard. It exerted the same type of appeal as the wartime Office of War Information broadcasts, but was even more effective. Yet the occupation wholly ignored it.

A New Propaganda Line

We must make clear that we do not intend to tell Japan what it must believe. The Russians, whose propaganda has been at least as clumsy as our own, have at least known that they must not force Japan to parrot Soviet slogans. Japanese apologists for Communism believe quite sincerely, however mistakenly, that they can accept Red ideas without losing their own nationality. Americans must convince Japan that her people can be both free-world democrats and Japanese.

We must not condemn everything in

the past as wicked, reactionary, and feudalistic. Much in the past was bad and should be discarded, but much, also, was good. Heretofore we have thrown out the baby with the bath. Japanese customs may have differed from our own and we may not have liked them, but Japan has a right to do her own selecting. No one enjoys being ordered about, and Japan, more than any other great peoples of the world, resents being ridiculed, particularly when the orders and the ridicule are in the name of freedom and the preservation of individual dignity.

Prewar militarist stupidities and post-war American policies somehow unwittingly conspired to identify reform with Russian Communism. The highmindedness that thought it beneath its dignity to notice absurd distortions created a situation where Americanism, capitalism, conservatism, and even liberalism had become synonymous with reaction. Japan is not anti-American, but she is opposed to exploitation, to stagnation, and to militarism, and these, without effective protest from us, have been effectively and unjustly pinned to the Stars and Stripes.

We must strike back with the truth about the Rosenbergs, the Hiss case, the color problem, and our relations with Latin America, and we must do it as forcibly, though honestly, as the Soviets have attacked us on these themes. We have a clean case and a just case, but we have been content to assume that we had no pressing need to defend ourselves. We need effective, forceful, consistent, and, above all, interesting propaganda. To rebroadcast a Presidential speech in English is dignified, but when directed to Japan is all too often ineffective.

We started with advantages which we have tossed into the ashcan. We must begin again under handicaps. We must not sit immobile in an ivory tower expecting the Japanese to bow before the shrine. We must get out into the arena, not as a caste apart enjoying special privileges, but as friends and neighbors. The GI with his candy bar, which, incidentally, was illicit, did far more for friendship than the general before whose car all policemen stood at stiff attention. The American "dependents" who loaded up their cars with neighborhood kids to take them to the Ueno Zoo did more to help America than all the formal press releases rolled together. In every natural catastrophe the Army pitched in and helped Japan. This Japan remembers long after the impressive parades have been forgotten.

NOT AS MASTERS

We must lend aid but not as condescension and certainly not as a bait or bribe. If we must stay in Japan for her protection, as well as for our own, we must not stay as aristocrats and masters; we must not expect privileges we do not give to aliens in America. We may not like the laws in force but we must not override them. We may not like the customs but we must observe them. We must not curl the lip and act as though all Japanese are dirty and immoral.

America is God's country but so, too, is Japan. Their folkways are as dear to them as ours to us. She has a right to make her own mistakes as well as to exercise her own good judgment.

Japan will not be moved by legalistic proof that the Russians do not cleave closely to the laws of international relations. She will not be swayed, though, of course, she should be, by long-winded exposition of what the Soviets have done to Poland or to Latvia, nor will she be alarmed to hear that Russian spy rings have been active in Ottawa or Guatemala. These matters must be pinpointed to Japan's own life.

1952 AND 1953

For this reason it was unfortunate that in 1952 and 1953 we let golden opportunities go down the drain. A Communist who was a Russian spy was caught red-handed and we let the Russians turn the case into a national agitation against the American counterintelligence agency which unmasked him. A Russian ship captain landed spies and saboteurs, but when he was arrested we let the Communists divert the matter into a complaint against interference with his freedom. A Japanese whom Northwestern University had supported for fifteen years came out into the open as a Communist and, clutching his Stalin peace prize, attacked the nation where he had been befriended, but we were loath to brand him as an ingrate. A woman who had been deported from America as undesirable spread news that she had been our friend until our wickedness had disillusioned her. But we held our peace about the facts. A high-ranking Russian diplomat in Tokyo deserted to our side and we all but kept the matter secret.

It is high time that we reversed our course in propaganda. We must be truthful and we must be honest. We must not lie nor twist the truth, but we must cease to play the game that helps the Reds prevail. For nine precious years which never can be recovered we have let the Communists carry the attack to us until the score has piled up in their favor. Let us take the initiative and move back to victory.

Harry Emerson Wildes, Ph.D., is a Philadelphia journalist and writer. He was professor of economics and social sciences at Keio University, Tokyo, in 1924. During World War II he was regional specialist for Japan in the Office of War Information, and between 1946 and 1951 he was in Tokyo with the occupation as chief of the Political and Social Affairs Division, Civil Historical Section, and as a member of the Government Section. He recently served as a Fulbright Visiting Lecturer at the International College of the Sacred Heart, Tokyo, and is author of Social Currents in Japan (1927), Japan in Crisis (1934), Aliens in the East (1937), and Typhoon in Tokyo (1954).

The Place of Japan in a Resurgent Asia

By Sadao Iguchi

IN the conduct of its foreign policy, each nation seeks its own self-interest. To be sure, all nations profess lofty idealism and, indeed, they may be motivated in varying degrees by sincere altruism. But in the very nature of things, in the final analysis, nations have no choice but to act in accordance with their self-interest. Such are the facts of life; such are the realities of international politics.

But in the pursuit of its self-interest, a nation may have a very narrow vision and seek its advantage at the expense of its neighbors, or it may have a broad conception of self-interest and realize that its own advantage can best be attained by contributing to the welfare of neighboring nations and the general welfare of the world. The first of these two alternatives represents traditional power politics, which ultimately defeats its own ends. The second alternative represents the enlightened statesmanship which we must cultivate if the world is to be saved from catastrophe. Modern science has caused the world to shrink, and today no nation can live unto itself alone. It can find its own well-being only by sharing in the general well-being of the interdependent community of nations. Self-interest dictates, therefore, that the nations of the world develop a consciousness of their mutual and interdependent welfare.

I think I can speak with some conviction on this point because of the recent bitter experiences of my own country. But whatever faults we may have, we Japanese are not the people "who learned nothing and forgot nothing." We have learned our lesson. We have acquired the realization that we can find our self-interest only in the common interest of the world at large, and we are anxious to make our proper contribution to that common interest.

It is in the light of this broad concept of common world interest that Japan today views her position in relation to the new Asia.

As we look at Asia, we see that practically all of the countries of that part of the world are engaged in a great striving for national self-fulfillment. We see a tide of resurgence in which the peoples of Asia are throwing off the impediments of the past and struggling to attain a more complete life of national independence, economic well-being, social justice, personal dignity, and cultural richness. Asia is on the threshold of a revolutionary transformation which will probably go down in history as one of the most inspiring developments of all time.

But because Asia is in the midst of such great change, there is also much confusion. All periods of great change are painful; all periods of great change are accompanied by tension and instability. It should be remembered that only three nations of the Far East—China, Thailand, and Japan—were independent and sovereign states before World War II. All the others—India, Pakistan, Ceylon, Burma, Vietnam, Cambodia, Laos, Indonesia, the Philippines, the Republic of Korea—have been recently created as sovereign nations. Such a widespread creation of new nations is a magnificent development, but it is not surprising that the turmoil of creation has not yet all been quieted.

THE ECONOMIC PROBLEM

In this turmoil which besets the new Asia, the most serious aspect, to my mind, is the economic problem. Most of the countries of Asia have rapidly increasing populations which press acutely on the available resources. Modern preventive medicine has reduced the death rates, and the birth rates remain high. Economic productivity has not kept pace with the rise of population. For instance, Asia's production of rice has only within the past few years managed to regain the prewar level. Merely to secure for their people a tolerable livelihood, or even a bare subsistence, entails an almost impossible task for many of the governments of this area.

It has been said that "you cannot teach democracy to a hungry people." Before we can even think of political stability, there must be economic stability; and economic stability requires the attainment of a respectable standard of living by the masses of the peoples of Asia.

Although the countries of Asia are not all at the same stage of economic development—Japan being conspicuously more industrialized than the others—the basic economic needs of all of them are quite similar. All of them must increase productivity and learn to make more complete utilization of their abundant manpower. All of them need more foreign trade—imports to feed and clothe their people and to supply their industries; exports to provide the foreign exchange to pay for the imports. All of them have a crying need for more capital and technical knowledge to develop their unutilized resources.

A CO-OPERATIVE FRONT FOR ASIA

In the face of these common needs, it should be obvious that more can be accomplished by the group working to-gether in co-operation than by each member of the group working independently. Yet very little has been accomplished in the way of co-ordinated planning by the free nations of Asia. Perhaps it is the heritage of a period of colonialism when most of the countries of Asia were separately linked to different colonizing nations of the West. But the fact remains that the more natural intraregional economic relations among the countries of Asia continue to be relatively undeveloped.

Each nation is trying separately to shore up its own economy, to develop its own resources, to educate its own people, and to meet all the myriad other requirements of progress. At the same time, very little consideration is being given to the needs and potentialities of neighboring countries. Except for the United Nations Economic Commission for Asia and the Far East, which is doing some excellent preliminary work directed toward the development of the economy of all Asia, no real attempt has been made to co-ordinate the efforts of the Asiatic nations for economic development.

I think the moral is obvious. The building of a co-operative front among the free nations of Asia is an absolute prerequisite to the successful solution of the problems we have. The co-operation I envisage would involve the defining of common aims and goals. It would include the practical planning of regional economic development, the drawing up of agreements to bring about an expansion of both intra- and inter-regional trade, and the exchange of ideas and knowledge. Of course, all these objectives cannot be attained in a few months, or even a few years. But a start could—and should—be made now.

To such a co-operative common front in Asia, we Japanese believe we can make a useful and constructive contribution. More than any other country in

Asia, Japan possesses industrial technology, managerial experience, and skilled manpower. We have also experience in adapting Western techniques to Asiatic conditions. The industrial economy of Japan is complementary, rather than competitive, to the economics of most of the other Asian nations.

Japan is often called the "workshop of Asia." But we do not believe that the term should be understood in any exclusive sense; all the nations of Asia should be encouraged as rapidly as possible to become likewise "workshops of Asia." But for the present there can be no objections to making full use of what Japan has to offer. Soft goods and utensils made in Japan at prices which the peoples of Asia can afford will contribute to the raising of the standard of living throughout the region. The heavier manufactures of Japan, such as industrial machinery, rolling stock, electrical equipment, and spindles and looms, would help increase the productivity of the underdeveloped areas and would speed the day when all Asia would be one great and prosperous workshop. Food production in Asia would also benefit substantially from the use of Japanese fertilizers, and Japanese agricultural implements have been proved to be particularly suitable for the conditions prevailing in most of the countries of Asia. Japan also possesses many manufacturing techniques, particularly for household industries, which are adaptable to the needs of other Asian countries.

Within our limited capacity, we are willing to export investment capital, although we can only make a small beginning to meet the need. In this connection, the democratic nations of the West could render invaluable help by providing essential developmental capital on the basis of an integrated plan designed to meet the needs of the entire region.

Japan's Needs

In all these arrangements, we naturally hope that, as the other parts of Asia prosper, Japan also will benefit. Like many other countries of Asia, Japan suffers from a large and growing population on very limited land. Even more than other countries, Japan suffers from a lack of natural resources. Industrialization and foreign trade are the only means by which Japan can attain a viable economy.

To maintain a minimum standard of living, Japan must import annually well over two billion dollars' worth of raw materials, food, and other necessities. Japan must export enough goods to pay for these imports. But our present trade balance shows a deficit of almost one billion dollars. So far, the difference has been met by the spending of American military forces in Japan and by special procurements for the United Nations effort in Korea, but this source of income is drawing to an end. We must find a solution through the normal channels of international trade.

To expand our foreign trade, we must bring down our present cost of production; for although many Japanese goods are priced at levels which most Asians can afford, other Japanese goods are priced above the competitive range. To bring down our cost of production calls for the modernization of our industrial facilities and of our production techniques, which will require more investment capital. It will also require access to cheaper sources of raw materials. At present many of our bulky imports—such as grains, sugar, cotton, iron ore, coal, and salt—must be brought at great cost from distant and uneconomic sources because sources closer at hand are not open to us. In this connection, it might be noted that in the past our trade with China used to account for about one-third of our total foreign trade. To compensate for the stoppage of this source, we must find adequate opportunities elsewhere. The expanding economies of the free countries of Asia must provide the solution.

We are, therefore, particularly anxious to sit down with the other nations of Asia to work out agreements to liberate international trade from the artificial obstacles which prevent a healthy expansion in the exchange of goods. Efforts of the United States government toward freer trade among the free nations of the world are most reassuring to us, and I hope that they will soon be enabled to minister better to each other's needs. Incidentally, the integration of Japan's industrial and commercial talents to the task of building up the economy of the rest of Asia would reduce the cost to the American taxpayer of American aid to that part of the world.

I am aware that there will be those who will question Japan's sincerity and reliability. But, as Prime Minister Shigeru Yoshida declared on the day the Peace Treaty came into effect, "Our people know that no nation can live unto itself, that no nation can draw dividends unless it invests in the common welfare of humanity." This statement expresses the principle which has come to guide our national foreign policy now.

ON THE FOUNDATION OF THE PAST

I am also aware that Japan is said by some to be taking a course which they characterize as the "reverse course." They imply that Japan is today bent on reversing the course set by the occupation. It should be apparent to any close observer, however, that Japan cannot reverse the course of history, even if she should wish it. And of course she does not wish it. No nation could have experienced war and defeat, and then

the tremendous impact of the occupation, without undergoing an irrevocable change. Japan is today going through a period of readjustment. After eight years of the occupation during which the Japanese were guided in new ways, they must now learn anew to guide their own steps. Because we had been under tutelage for so long and because our economy had been supported by outside aid, it was only natural that our people should have become somewhat less self-reliant and accustomed to having others make our decisions for us. This is no reflection whatever on the occupation, whose lofty aims and valuable achievements are above question.

It is inevitable, however, that, in the nature of things, in striking out for themselves our people should grope for a while to find their true bearings. They must rediscover themselves in the light of their newly won rights and their new freedoms.

If there are in Japan today certain tendencies which appear to indicate a return to the past, I would suggest that it is by no means a simple return to the past. It is rather a conscious attempt to take our new bearings in relation to our past. The most valuable and effective of the reforms instituted by the occupation were those which were built solidly on the foundations of our past. No nation can survive if it is cut off completely from its historic roots. What we are now trying to do is to verify what was valid in our past, so that we may build upon it in the present, to the end that we may attain our true destiny in the future. If Japan is to contribute effectively to the strength of the free world, she in her own way must shape her own life to fit into her historic pattern—enriched, however, by her new and broader understanding of the universal principles of humanity, equality and justice.

Japan's present commitment to the

ways of democracy is rendered all the more secure by the fact that democracy is no new and alien importation introduced to the Japanese solely by the occupation. Japan has had a representative parliamentary government since 1890 which, although faltering at times, nevertheless developed encouragingly until a notable degree of democracy and liberalism was attained by the middle 1920's. The democratic reforms instituted by the occupation have found ready acceptance because they represent a restoration of a spontaneous indigenous tendency which had been only temporarily subverted.

It will yet take considerable effort before all the neighbors of Japan can willingly trust her. But Japan is making every effort to prove her good faith. For example, she is pushing the negotiations over reparations with the claimant nations with the intention of meeting her responsibilities to the utmost limit possible without wrecking her precarious economy. Japan hopes also to foster mutual confidence by promoting an extensive program of international intellectual exchange. This would involve not only the sharing of industrial techniques but also professor and student exchanges, scientific and business conferences and conventions, exchange of experts in the fine arts as well as in the useful arts, and many other possibilities too numerous to mention. We are confident that if we get to understand each other better, we shall be able to work together more effectively.

THE DEFENSE EFFORT

I have said nothing so far about Japan's defense effort. This subject involves a whole complex of problems which I do not have the time to discuss here. Suffice it to say, however, that Japan is committed to shouldering her due share of the burden of defense

against Communist aggression within the limits of her present very modest economic power.

It will be recalled that under the terms of the Security Treaty between Japan and the United States Japan is endeavoring to "increasingly assume responsibility" for her own defense. A Mutual Defense Assistance Agreement has recently been signed in Tokyo under which the United States will aid in building up the defense establishment of Japan.

It is modeled after similar agreements between the United States and many other nations participating in the mutual security programs, and is designed to facilitate the planning of a defense assistance program for Japan. It is a manifestation of Japan's alignment with the free nations of the world and marks another step forward in the ever closer relations between Japan and the United States.

But we Japanese believe that, vital as military defense is, military measures are not the final solution to the Communist menace. Formidable as is the threat of Communist imperialism on the march, just as dangerous is intellectual subversion by Communists from within. Communism feeds on poverty and economic instability, and if we cannot unite to abolish poverty and economic instability, the Communist doctrine will exert a tremendous appeal to peoples who can see no other hope for the future.

Defense measures cannot be pushed faster or farther than the condition of the economy of the country will permit; otherwise we court the risk of a political or economic collapse, or both. Such a catastrophe would defeat all our aims.

Therefore I feel justified in emphasizing economic co-operation as the basic prerequisite for solving the problems not only of Japan but of the new Asia which is emerging today. The vision of a resurgent Asia is an inspiring one, but before the vision can become a reality, the peoples of Asia must join their efforts to attain their common goal. If they do not learn to co-operate, they will succumb one by one to the threat of Communism which lies in wait. A united Asia is a noble ideal, but even more, it is a practical necessity dictated by the enlightened self-interest of all of the free nations of Asia. To that end, the countries of Asia must continue to have the benefit of active American interest and sympathetic effort. Joined together as close partners in the cause of humanity and peace, we can meet with confidence the challenge of our time.

His Excellency Sadao Iguchi, Washington, D. C., is Ambassador of Japan to the United States. After three years' study in Oxford University (1921–1924) Mr. Iguchi held various posts in the diplomatic service, including several in this country. From 1941 to 1946 he served in the Foreign Ministry in Tokyo, resigning in 1946 to become an executive of the Taiyo Fishing Company. In 1951 he was recalled to government service as the Vice-Minister for Foreign Affairs, and in the following year became Japan's Ambassador to Canada, a post he held until his present assignment.

Relations Between Japan and the United States

By Robert J. G. McClurkin

ARTHUR O'Shaughnessy's Ode, "We are the music-makers," has two particularly famous lines,

"For each age is a dream that is dying,
Or one that is coming to birth."

I have always quarreled somewhat with the use of the conjunction "Or," for in a very real sense each age is both a dying dream *and* a new one coming to birth. A society which has any vitality at all is a complex and continually changing mixture of the old and the new.

Certainly, Japanese society has abundant vitality. Certainly, also, it is a blending of elements from all the social forces—both internal and external, both from the distant past and from the last decade—which have grown from or converged upon the Japanese people. In Japan in the years from 1945 to 1952 the catalytic action of the occupation speeded almost unbelievably the normal processes of social change.

That occupation had to grow out of and build upon the holocaust of war. It was essentially a military occupation, yet in spite of all the difficulties and all the problems, all the excesses and the failures to understand, the net result of the occupation was good.

The political and economic and social recovery of Japan and the place the country occupies in the world today rest upon two fundamental bases—first, the solid and unremitting efforts that the Japanese people have put forth and second, what the occupation did. The Americans of the occupation, partly because of their pride in American ways of doing things, partly because they were not all-wise and made mistakes,

and partly because American ways were the ways they knew and understood, tried to some extent to create a new Japan in the image of the United States. But six years cannot wipe out the memory and the influence of the thousand which went before. Nor can alien ways completely replace those which are rooted in the native soil. So two years after the Peace Treaty came into force, Japanese society is still in ferment as the new laws and customs and ideas brought by the occupation are being reshaped and modified until they match the fabric of Japanese life.

This process was inevitable, and its results are good. The great strength of Japan lies in the vigor and ingenuity of the people, who for over a hundred years had been struggling to throw off the shackles of an authoritarian society. What the occupation accomplished was to free and strengthen the democratic elements in Japanese life, so that neither militarists nor zaibatsu nor a reactionary bureaucracy could hold them in domination.

However, somewhere in the emotional shock of defeat, the strenuous task of reconstruction, and the eager grasping for something new, something different from a discredited past, the Japanese lost a portion of whatever it was that gave unity of purpose to their society. Now that the occupation is over, the Japanese government and the people are reaching back into the past for the added assurance that comes from doing things in the traditional ways. This does not mean that everything accomplished by the occupation is being upset or reversed, but rather that the Japanese are gradually building a new and typically Japanese democratic society compounded of elements from both East and West.

I believe that the "new" Japanese society will continue to be essentially democratic because the Japanese themselves want it to be, and because the events of the last few years have made it possible. I believe also that it will be stronger and better because it will not be entirely new but will incorporate much of the best from the rich heritage of the Japanese past.

PSYCHOLOGICAL TIES

United States relations with the new Japan rest first of all upon something intangible—a set of psychological and emotional ties which are not less real because. they are not susceptible of precise description and analysis.

I suppose that we have always had a special interest in Japan stemming from Commodore Perry's voyage in 1853 and the treaty of peace and unity (Treaty of Kanagawa) signed a hundred years ago. Probably we assume far too much credit for the opening of Japan to the West, for developments within Japan had progressed to the point where the years of ingrown isolation were almost certain to end soon. But it was Commodore Perry's voyage which signaled the end of the isolation, just as it was his voyage which was an early symbol of our own awakening interest in things going on outside the still undeveloped American continent. For both the United States and Japan have been slow to realize the compelling influences of the world around us and to accept the full responsibilities of living in that world.

Recent personal contacts

The psychological and emotional ties between us have grown enormously in strength and number in the past few years because of hundreds upon thousands of individual contacts between Americans and Japanese. Like Brownian motion, which is the never-ceasing, disorderly movement of tiny particles suspended in a liquid or a gas, there is in and between nations a seemingly helter-skelter movement of individuals of all sorts, both shaped by, and shaping, great events. And to carry the simile one step further, just as the motion of the tiny particles can be greatly increased by an outside influence like heat, so the aftermath of the war was a vast increase in what might be called the Brownian motion of individuals between the United States and Japan.

Not all of the contacts were good, not all were friendly and helpful. However, there were a great many contacts, and increasingly as the occupation went on those contacts became wider and more friendly, and the results were better and better. The American soldiers and civilians of the occupation were not concentrated in Tokyo and Yokohama, Kobe and Osaka. They were in all parts of Japan, meeting in daily contacts Japanese farmers and fishermen, miners and textile workers, teachers and local government officials. And still today—two years after the end of the occupation—there are American soldiers and civilians in daily contact with the Japanese. Some of these are United States government officials, some are tourists, some are businessmen and missionaries; by far the largest number are those who are a part of the United States forces stationed in Japan. In the past nine years, more than two million Americans have been in Japan.

Although many of the bad features of American life show up as they always do, perhaps even more plainly, when they are transplanted from the United States, nevertheless this vastly increased contact between the citizens of the two countries has on the whole bred understanding rather than misunderstanding.

I say this in spite of the fact that last summer there was a flare-up in Japan of anti-Americanism, so-called. Actually the Japanese expression for it is idiomatically translated "fed up with Americans." There have been so many of us, for so long, telling them so much, giving them so much advice about how to run their country, that it is small wonder that they feel some sense of surfeit. Nevertheless, the core of truth is that the lasting results of the contacts are good.

Most Americans who have lived and worked in Japan have learned to respect and admire the good qualities of the Japanese character. They have developed an appreciation of Japanese culture. They have built friendships with the Japanese people. Many of these Americans gave all of their energies for a substantial period of time to efforts to help build a new Japan. Thus they have a personal, emotional interest in what happens to the structure which they helped to create.

Intercultural activities

For the belief that this host of individual contacts must have produced a measurable effect upon the United States, there is plenty of evidence. Scarcely a week goes by that the Sunday editions of the *New York Times* or the *Herald Tribune* or the *Washington Post* do not have special articles on Japan. Other examples multiply—the exhibition of Japanese art which toured the United States last year and attracted such large and appreciative crowds, the short stories and articles in the magazines, the movie *Rashomon,* the success of the Kabuki dance group in this country, the best-selling novel by James Michener. All these things are visible evidence of the pattern of interest that exists.

Nor are the movement and the interest one-sided. There are twenty-three well-patronized American Cultural Centers in Japan in major cities. When it appeared that some of the original occupation centers would have to be closed because of budgetary cuts, local Japanese authorities stepped in to help keep them open. United States documentary motion pictures, distributed through Japanese local governments at a cost to them of a million dollars a year, have a cumulative attendance of 20,000,000 a month in Japan. Japan is one of the largest foreign outlets for motion pictures produced in the United States. Portions of the Voice of America short-wave broadcasts are rebroadcast regularly by the twenty-two new commercial stations in Japan. And Japanese come to the United States, many of them. Students, teachers, labor leaders, and political leaders come here under the exchange of persons program. Businessmen and industrial technicians come to exchange ideas and to develop associations with American firms. Mayors of West Coast United States cities visited Japan last year, and mayors of Japanese cities returned the visit and toured the United States.

Perhaps the point needs no further belaboring. There exists a deep, abiding, and fully reciprocal bond of sympathy and understanding between the United States and Japan, and all relations between the two countries rest upon and are governed by this fact.

COMMUNITY OF NATIONAL INTEREST

The private bond which exists is amply reinforced by a community of national interest, one important aspect of which is a common recognition of the danger of international Communism.

For Japan the threat is even more immediate than it is for the United States, because Japan is the primary Communist goal in the Far East. The Communists covet Japan because of its strategic position in the offshore island defense chain, because of its potential military strength, and most of all because of its industrial potential. They believe that if they could bring Japan within their orbit, the whole balance of power in the Far East would shift in their favor, and it would be only a matter of time until the rest of the Far East would fall to them. They may well be right.

Their ultimate aim is domination of Japan—not neutralization but domination—because the Communists agree thoroughly with at least one biblical dictum, "He that is not with me is against me." But they know that they cannot take Japan over immediately, and they believe that once Japan is neutralized, Communist domination will inevitably follow. So for the present they cultivate interim measures aimed directly at driving wedges between Japan and the United States. Almost every day the Peiping radio and Radio Free Japan, the clandestine radio station somewhere in Communist China which is beamed toward Japan, exhort the Japanese people not to accept military assistance from the United States, to throw out of office elected officials who are friendly to the United States, to make the United States forces in Japan go home, to build trade with the Communist mainland of Asia.

When the Communists attacked Korea they were looking beyond Korea to Japan. When they support the Vietminh aggression in Indochina, they are thinking not only of control over southeast Asia but also of the fact that Japan needs to buy food and raw materials from there and to sell industrial products in return. They are thinking about Japan. The manner of the getting is irrelevant to them, but they want Japan.

We do not have to rely on secondhand evidence as to Communist intentions. They are explicit. This is Tokuda, secretary-general of the Communist party of Japan, writing in the *Cominform Journal* in 1952:

. . . we (the JCP) can instigate the people to participate in anti-American and anti-Yoshida movements. . . . In this connection, we must utilize our legal and illegal press to disseminate the spirit of our party's new platform, particularly the concept of armed struggle, so that we can create a public determination to defend peace, independence, and freedom. Now is the time for all the people to think of arming themselves to meet the plot of the American and Japanese reactionaries, who plan to revive militarism for the purpose of aggression.

And this is Malenkov talking to the Supreme Soviet last August, talking about the task of "normalizing relations with Japan":

Serious obstacles are encountered along this path because the United States of America is pursuing a policy of strangling the national independence of Japan, turning it into a springboard for war. The healthy forces of the Japanese nation recognize, increasingly, that it is essential to overcome the obstacles and uphold national independence.

The Communist line in Japan has changed from armed struggle to popular front; but whether it talks about arming the people to seize power or about "healthy forces" which will "uphold national independence," the object in view is the same—full Communist control of Japan.

Japanese defense forces

The Japanese government recognizes that it is not safe to allow Japan to lie defenseless in the face of this Communist threat, and with our help it is now moving ahead with the strengthening of the Japanese defense establishment. Let me emphasize that both we and the Japanese are thinking exclusively in terms of Japanese forces of a defensive character. Because it is so convenient, people have fallen into the use of the shorthand expression "Japanese rearmament," a term which carries unfortunate connotations of a return to the 1930's. It is especially unfortunate since nothing could be further from Japanese intentions or from ours.

Today the Japanese have a ground force of 110,000 men—out of a population of 87,000,000 people—and small naval and coast guard forces. A year from now they expect to have the beginnings of a three-force defense establishment with a total of about 160,000 men. Although our joint thinking has not gone beyond this year's program, our military experts think that Japan's defense requires it to have eventually a ground force of 325,000 or 350,000 men, a navy consisting mainly of small patrol craft, minelayers, minesweepers, and destroyers, and in time a small jet air force of interceptors and medium bombers for tactical support purposes.

U. S. military assistance

We want to bring our own forces home from Japan as soon as the Japanese have developed their own defensive capabilities to a point where Japan will be safe even though our forces have left. Partly to this end and partly to help build free-world strength, the United States is willing to provide certain military equipment for Japanese ground, sea, and air forces on the same terms and conditions as those under which we are providing similar assistance to other free-world countries. That is the whole meaning of the Mutual Defense Assistance Agreement with Japan, which came into effect on May 1, 1954. But despite the assistance we provide and despite Japan's efforts on her own behalf, for the indefinite future in case of an attack upon the Japanese islands

Japan will need naval and air support from the United States in addition to its own defense forces.

I emphasize that United States military assistance to Japan is not a matter of pure altruism—if, indeed, the pure quality exists. Since the safety of one depends upon the safety of all, when we act to help others we are acting in our own self-interest. Nevertheless, the plain fact is that the others are in danger, too. In an excellent speech in New York on March 18 Ambassador Iguchi underlined the common interests of the United States and Japan. He said:

The interests of Japan have come to coincide with the interests of the United States. . . . We help ourselves by helping each other, and by benefiting each other we contribute to the security and peace of the world. . . . In this common endeavor for our mutual self-preservation, Japan is now ready to contribute her proper share.

This clear recognition of the shared danger, which can be prevented only if we act in concert to prepare against it, is another of the factors underlying relations between the United States and Japan.

ECONOMIC RELATIONS

A third set of factors is economic in nature, for the economic relations between Japan and the United States have great importance for both countries.

The war destroyed many of the old patterns of Japanese trade, and particularly those in which Japan had, in a sense, a captive market and captive sources of raw materials on the Asiatic mainland and in Formosa. These trade patterns have not developed anew. So far as Communist China is concerned, Japan has been co-operating fully with the free world in security trade controls and has, in fact, maintained stricter controls than any other industrial country except the United States and Canada, which have complete embargoes. This action on the part of Japan has been a major contribution to the defense of the free world.

However, Japan must import nearly all of the principal raw materials of its industry and 20 per cent of its food supply, and in the postwar period Japan has turned to the United States as a major source of supply. In the calendar year 1953, Japan spent 700 million dollars to purchase products in the United States. Japan was our best foreign customer for cotton and soybeans; our second best foreign customer for wheat, rice, barley, and bituminous coal. For all of these products and for corn, hides and skins, capital goods, automobiles, oil, and iron ore, the United States was Japan's principal supplier.

To look at the other side of the coin, the United States was Japan's best foreign customer, buying a wide variety of products ranging from silk and china and tuna fish to toys and gadgets. But whereas Japan bought from us to the extent of 700 million dollars, our commercial trade purchases in Japan amounted to only 260 million dollars.

Japan's trade deficit

Unfortunately that story is generally true of Japanese foreign trade. Japan, which can earn its way in the world only by buying raw materials and exporting manufactured products, had in 1953 a commercial trade deficit of one billion dollars. The reasons are various. Curiously enough to those who remember the prewar period, the Japanese in many fields of manufacture— steel is one of the most important—are priced out of the market because of obsolescent machinery and outdated industrial techniques, the high cost of raw materials many of which must be hauled long distances to Japan, and in-

ternal inflation. In addition, in spite of the present situation there is sufficient fear of Japanese competition so that many nations are reluctant to allow trade with Japan to develop freely. To some degree, this fear and the concomitant reluctance exist within the United States.

The problem of Japanese trade is one which the Japanese and the free world must face. Fortunately we have a little time, because the expenditures of the United States in Japan, most of which will continue for a while and which result chiefly from the presence of our forces there, have been large enough to cover nearly all of the Japanese commercial trade deficit. But these expenditures will not continue forever. If in the meantime Japanese trade does not develop to a point where the Japanese economy can stand on its own feet, there will be a serious threat of lowered standards of living in Japan and economic collapse. And the inevitable result would be a vastly increased risk of internal Communist subversion.

Even if all controls over trade with the Soviet bloc were removed, and even if it were possible for the Japanese to do business on reasonable terms with the Communists instead of having the business and the trade used as a political weapon against them, trade with Communist areas would make up only a portion of the Japanese trade deficit. So most of the answer must be found elsewhere.

A part of the answer is the responsibility of the Japanese themselves. They will need to call upon all of their own reserves of determination and ingenuity and take those rigorous measures which will be effective in reducing costs of production and improving their competitive position. Their "austerity budget" for the fiscal year which is just beginning is a noteworthy step in this direction. In addition, the creation within Japan of an improved climate for foreign investment would help to overcome the shortage of capital in Japan.

Free world markets

The second part of the answer lies with the rest of us. No matter how great the efforts the Japanese put forth, they will not suffice unless the Japanese are allowed to buy and sell freely in world markets on the same fair and competitive terms as anyone else. One natural trading area for Japan is southeast Asia, and trade with that area has already recovered to prewar levels. But that is not enough. It is only as the co-operative efforts of the whole free world and of the southeast Asian countries produce rising living standards and an expanding economy in that area that the possibilities will be created for southeast Asia to have an expanding and mutually profitable trade with Japan and other free world countries.

However, by talking about Japan's natural area of trade with southeast Asia, the United States cannot shirk its own responsibility. Japan's commercial trade deficit with the United States last year was 440 million dollars, and the United States must do its full part in helping the development of Japanese trade, not only by encouraging others to open their markets to Japanese products, but by giving Japan a fair opportunity to sell its products in the United States.

President Eisenhower, in his recent message to Congress on foreign economic policy, gave special recognition to the necessity of dealing with the problem of Japanese trade with the United States. And in keeping with his message I emphasize the necessity for mutuality in trade relations between sovereign states. The United States and the rest of the free world need Japan as a customer; the United States and the rest of the free world must therefore buy from Japan.

TREATIES AND AGREEMENTS

The prophet Amos asked, "Can two walk together, except they be agreed?" In the world today Japan and the United States are walking together because of a fundamental community of interests. However, the very complexity of the relationships between a nation of 87,000,000 people and one of 160,000,000 makes necessary a full and complete understanding and agreement if the two nations are to continue to walk together in amity and common purpose.

These understandings, so necessary to relations between the United States and Japan, are embodied in many carefully negotiated treaties and agreements. They vary in nature and breadth from the multilateral Peace Treaty to an agreement for the reimbursement of shipwreck expenses. Two of them are concerned with the prevention of double taxation of individuals or businesses who might otherwise be considered subject to both tax jurisdictions. Another one spells out the precise rights and privileges which the citizens of one country will enjoy while sojourning or doing business in the other country. Still another sets the terms and conditions under which military assistance will be provided. And so on and on. These are the ground rules under which the relations are conducted.

A listing of these treaties and agreements in force as of April 1, 1954, reveals something of their scope and variety.

Postwar bilateral agreements between the United States and Japan

1. Fulbright Agreement
2. Security Treaty

3. Administrative Agreement (the detailed implementing agreement for the Security Treaty)
4. Reciprocal Waiver of Non-Immigrant Visa Fees
5. Taxation Relief for Expenditures Made by the United States in Japan under the Mutual Security Program
6. Charter Party Agreement (Agreement re Loan of Naval Vessels)
7. Agreement on Sharing of Claims Costs under Article 18, Administrative Agreement
8. Treaty of Friendship, Commerce and Navigation
9. Civil Air Transport Agreement
10. Copyright Agreement
11. Transfer of Amami Oshima Islands
12. Technical Missions by Japan to Study Production of Defense Equipment and Supplies
13. Mutual Defense Assistance Agreements
   Mutual Defense Assistance Agreement
   Purchase Agreement (with respect to surplus agricultural products under Section 550 of the Mutual Security Act)
   Agreement Regarding Guaranty of Investments
   Agreement on Economic Arrangements

Prewar treaties between Japan and the United States, revived or continued in force pursuant to Article 7 (a) of the San Francisco Treaty

1. Treaty Relating to Extradition of Criminals
2. Supplementary Convention Relating to Extradition of Criminals
3. Arrangements for Direct Exchange of Information Regarding Traffic in Narcotic Drugs
4. Arrangement for Exchange of Information Relating to Seizure of Illicit Narcotic Drugs and to Persons Engaged in the Illicit Traffic
5. Convention and Additional Conventions for the Exchange of Money Orders
6. Parcel Post Agreement with Detailed Regulations

7. Arrangements Relating to Perpetual Leaseholds
8. Convention for the Prevention of Smuggling of Intoxicating Liquors
9. Arrangement Relating to Reciprocal Exemption from Taxation of Income from the Operation of Merchant Vessels

Postwar multilateral agreements to which Japan and the United States are parties

1. Treaty of Peace with Japan
2. Settlement of Disputes Arising under Article 15 (a) of Treaty of Peace with Japan
3. North Pacific Fisheries Convention
4. United Nations Forces Agreement
5. World Health Organization
6. World Meteorological Organization
7. Narcotic Drugs Protocols
   Amending the Agreements, Conventions and Protocols of January 23, 1912, February 11, 1925, February 19, 1925, July 13, 1931, November 27, 1931, and June 26, 1936
   International Control of Drugs Outside the Scope of the Convention of July 13, 1931, as amended
8. International Office of Public Health Protocol
9. Agreement Revising and Renewing the International Wheat Agreement
10. International Rice Commission
11. Amendment of the Constitution of the International Labor Organization
12. International Bank for Reconstruction and Development Agreement
13. International Monetary Fund Agreement
14. Indo-Pacific Fisheries Council
15. Fur Seals Agreement (Research Programs in North Pacific Ocean)
16. Universal Postal Union
17. International Civil Aviation Convention
18. International Whaling Convention
19. United Nations Educational, Scientific and Cultural Organization
20. International Telecommunications Convention
21. Safety of Life at Sea Convention

International organizations set up before or during the war in which the United States is a member and in which Japan has revived its membership

1. Permanent Court of Arbitration
2. International Bureau of Weights and Measures
3. International Cotton Advisory Committee
4. International Council of Scientific Unions and Associated Unions
5. International Hydrographic Bureau
6. International Union of Travel Organizations
7. International Union for the Protection of Industrial Property
8. International Union for the Publication of Customs Tariffs
9. International Wheat Council
10. Rubber Study Group

Bases of good agreements

Fundamentally, all these treaties and agreements have three things in common with all other good agreements. First, every good agreement is a fair bargain. It has advantages and disadvantages for each side. Neither side gets everything it wants. Each side is therefore paying a tangible or intangible price for what it gets. Second, all agreements, good or bad, rest upon consent, every bit as certainly as do the relations between a government and its subjects. Agreements are good as long as the parties have an interest in preserving them and as long as the advantages gained seem to outweigh the disadvantages incurred as part of the bargain. As Machiavelli said:

Not only do princes pay no attention to pledges which they have been forced to give, when that force has ceased to exist, but they frequently disregard equally all other promises, when the motives that induced them no longer prevail.

Third, all good agreements should be written flexibly, so that with the passage of time and the inevitable changes in the specific conditions which existed when they were written, their terms will not constitute a rigid impediment to the peaceful readjustments necessary to meet the changed conditions. This point of view, not new, was developed very effectively in a book written in the 1930's called *War, Peace, and Change*.[1] Unlike many authors, the author of this work subsequently not only had an opportunity to put his ideas into practice in international affairs, but also lived up to the principles he had earlier espoused. The Japanese Peace Treaty, which he negotiated, stands as the living embodiment of those principles.

Nine years ago the United States and Japan were still at war. In the years since, we have developed deep, extensive, and friendly relationships predicated upon a wide range of common interests. I know of no comparable example in the history of nations.

We have many current problems and difficulties, and doubtless we shall find a full quota of new ones in the years ahead. If we can face them with candor and with mutual understanding and respect, the United States and Japan will continue to walk together in international affairs. And if we do so, it will augur well for the future of the world.

[1] John Foster Dulles, New York: Harper & Brothers, 1939.

Robert J. G. McClurkin, Washington, D. C., is Acting Director of the Office of Northeast Asian Affairs of the Department of State. Earlier government service was with the Board of Economic Warfare and Foreign Economic Administration (1942–45), the Aircraft Division of the Office of the Foreign Liquidation Commissioner, as Deputy Director and Director (1945–46), and the Economic Bureau of the Civil Aeronautics Board, as Assistant Director and Director (1946–51).

Japan and the Two Worlds

By Tatsuo Morito

JAPAN, at present, has completely lost her prewar position as one of the "big three" or "big five" powers. She is now a small state just recovering her independence—an imperfect independence, both politically and economically. However, what attitude she will assume towards problems arising from the existence of two conflicting worlds will be significant not only to herself but to the whole world situation.

First, it will be significant because of her position in the balance of power between the two groups of states. It is true, of course, that Japan, like Germany, cannot take the initiative in postwar international politics. Neither can be more than the object of power politics. However, Japan's geographical location at a strategic point and her industrial potential, due in part to her hard-working, trained, skillful manpower, have made the small state very attractive to each of the two worlds. Accordingly, each rivals the other in seeking to win Japan to its side. It has been said that the final aim of the struggle for Korea was to secure Japan.

In such a political situation Japan can no longer remain passive. Now is the time for her to take a definite stand and to play an active role in world politics. Only by doing so can she prove her real worth. The whole world is watching with keen interest to see what stand she will take.

Second, Japan's position as the decisive factor in the balance of the two worlds means not only that of power or strategy but also that of culture and economy—that is, civilization in general. Therefore, her choice will bring about important consequences in international relations.

Third, which side Japan will choose will influence not only international relations but also Japan's own domestic government, and even her fate as an independent state. As is often said, the foreign policy and the domestic government of a state are closely related to and reflected in each other. But in the case of Japan the relation between the two is unequal, the former having far more weight than the latter. This inequality is due, on the one hand, to the degradation of Japan into a defeated and powerless state and, on the other, to the development of world affairs toward closer interdependence, or even unity, of states.

Thus it is not too much to say that Japan's choice of which world to stand by will determine her future course and fate, both internal and external.

JAPAN'S CHOICE

The more important to the world situation Japan's attitude is, the more resolutely as well as prudently must the Japanese people make up their mind. How, then, should the Japanese people solve the grave problem they are confronted with? What solutions are they contemplating?

My opinion is summarized here. In order to realize the peaceful world order which Japan holds as her supreme ideal, the Japanese people must not fail to take into account the reality of international relations, that is, the reality of power relations among states. However, the Japanese people, and perhaps other Asian peoples also, are inexperienced and untrained in seeing the real state of affairs in international politics. Generalization rather than individualization is more familiar in the thinking of Asian peoples in general. Therefore, the old-fashioned utopianism which is now outdated in the Western world of socialism is still popular and influential among peace advocates in Japan.

Since it is difficult for the Japanese to penetrate the realities of international power relations, two theories of peace are often proposed as alternatives instead of close and exact investigation into international politics: one is absolute pacifism and the other, Marxism or economic determinism.

Absolute pacifism

Absolute pacifism is based on the traditional belief in human reason. It derives its basic principle from the idea of liberalism, which regards human reason as supreme and almighty and asserts that once the inherent reasonableness of mankind has been awakened, permanent peace can be brought about immediately. Advocates of absolute pacifism are opposed to the view that a peaceful order can be established only after various obstacles to peace have been removed and conditions of peace fulfilled. In other words, they consider the ideal of peace and nonviolence not only the goal of a peace movement, but the beginning and the method as well.

If we put aside re-examination of the premise, it seems rather easy for Japan to steer her course in accordance with absolute pacifism.

Economic determinism

Economic determinism develops from Marxian dialectic materialism applied to the evolution of capitalist society. It prophesies the inevitable disintegration from within of the capitalist economic structure. On the other hand, Marxian political theory leads not to the peaceful coexistence of the two worlds, but to the class struggle, not only domestic but also international. Therefore, Marxian determinism, it seems to me, indicates the direction not of peace but of world-wide class war in the final stage of evolution of capitalist society. However, detailed discussions about Marxian political theory need not be entered into here.

What I wish to point out is the fact that the evolution of capitalist society seems to indicate a movement toward peace and prosperity rather than toward struggle and disintegration. This fact seems to me to prove the fallacy of Marxian theory. Moreover, Marxism advances no definite criticism of the so-called "backward socialism," a term applied to a half-feudalistic, half-agricultural society, while it presents a very elaborate analysis of advanced industrial society. In a backward society that had not yet been completely released from the feudal regime and accordingly had not fully enjoyed liberalism and democracy, totalitarianism grew influential, and still remains so to some extent even now, as the basic principle of domestic government and world politics. Marxism lacks a clear analysis of the evolution of such a backward socialist system.

Further, it must be pointed out as an evident proof of the one-sidedness of Marxian theory that despite its exaggeration of the warlikeness and aggressiveness of capitalist states neither recognition nor criticism is voiced about the same or more intensified tendencies in the totalitarian camp.

As we have seen above, both absolute pacifism and Marxian determinism present various weak points as the basis of peace and accordingly as a guide of Japan's future international course. However, we must not ignore the importance of human reason as the motive power of historical evolution, nor, at the same time, the contribution of

Marxian theory in analyzing the structure of capitalist economy. What I wish to emphasize here is that neither from the standpoint of economic determinism nor from the standpoint of absolute pacifism is it easy or simple to probe the real international situation precisely and to find Japan's right course in the future.

International realities

Very complicated and difficult though the task is, I do not think it impossible. The antagonism of the two worlds is, in its essence, that of power—of political power in the broadest sense, which is based upon a synthesis of military, political, economic, and spiritual powers. Therefore, it is essential for Japan to analyze correctly the complicated power relations around her and her own political and economic strength, in order to decide which side she should stand by.

We, the people of Japan, are prone to consider the international situation, especially the power relations surrounding Japan, from a single point of view, in other words, to see only the aspect that is hopeful and convenient to us and to ignore the other. Herein lies one grave danger. But there is another danger far more serious. It is the over- or underestimating of Japan's national power by the Japanese themselves.

Such a tendency is more or less natural, even unavoidable, in a state which has undergone an unprecedented catastrophe such as the defeat. Having no exact judgment of the true national power, people make serious mistakes—either having far-reaching ambitions beyond their means or losing their spirit of self-help and independence. In neither way can Japan recover her honorable international status and live respected as a peace-loving, independent state.

JAPAN'S FUTURE COURSE

Various views are advocated as to Japan's future course in an international society divided into two worlds. They can however, I think, be classified into five categories, as follows: (1) Japan should be a member of the group of conservative liberal states; (2) she should be a member of the group of progressive liberal states; (3) she should be a neutral state; (4) she should join the third-power group; (5) she should co-operate with the "peace powers." As applied to the postwar foreign policy and peace movement of Japan, views (1) and (2) insist on "majority peace," that is, Japan's Peace Treaty concluded with the democratic states, while the other three emphasize "over-all peace," that is, a treaty with all states. Such a classification may be deduced not only from the basic theories but also from the line-up of political leaders and peace advocates.

Opinions that Japan should be a member of the group of liberal states are based on analysis of, and respect for, the circumstances brought about by the Japanese Peace Treaty and the United States–Japanese Security Treaty, by Japan's new foreign relations in the political, economic, cultural, and other fields resulting from her defeat and occupation by Allied forces, and by the policy of postwar Japan as contrasted with her prewar course. Such opinions are, of course, to some extent colored by the Americophile and Russophobe national feeling of the Japanese people. Advocates of this view assert that only through membership in the group of liberal states can Japan find the best way not only of achieving her independence and security but also of promoting world peace.

Some assert that Japan should stand by the conservative liberal states. These people put more emphasis on the capitalist system of the liberal regime than on the democratic aspect. Therefore, conservative parties which desire the preservation of the status quo are the main advocates of this opinion.

Those favoring membership in the group of progressive liberal states are opposed to these conservatives. They criticize the status quo both domestic and international as incompatible with justice, and intend to reform it gradually by peaceful means. They recognize the political principle and structure of democracy as the means of achieving reformation, or, so to speak, peaceful revolution. They do not stick to the capitalist regime as an eternal and basic political principle of liberal states. Only through membership in the group of such progressive democratic states, they argue, can Japan secure independence and prosperity. This point of view is opposed not only to the conservative one but also to the other three views. It is most strongly supported by right-wing socialists and democratic socialists.

CAN JAPAN REMAIN NEUTRAL?

The following three views were proposed after Japan's desire for a peace treaty with all states proved to be unrealizable as *Realpolitik*. Therefore they are, it can be said, variants of Japan's insistence on over-all peace, and have both the strong and the weak points of their origin. The feature common to all of the three views is opposition to the liberal-state group, some showing anti-American feeling and others pro-Russian and Communistic tendencies.

The first variant of the insistence on peace with all states was the advocacy of Japanese neutrality. According to this point of view, the best way for Japan to secure independence and peace is to remain neutral, never joining either of the two worlds. The idea was suggested originally by General Mac-

Arthur's denomination of Japan as the "Switzerland on the Pacific." Now, however, it has diverged from its origin. It is accompanied by criticism of the unconditional Americophile attitude of some Japanese political leaders.

Advocates of neutrality oppose the rearmament of Japan on the ground that there is no danger of Japan's being attacked or invaded so long as she remains neutral, not allying herself with either of the two worlds. They argue also that Japan, by keeping herself aloof from the two camps, can be free from the influences of either party, and can go her own way—the third and better way of adopting the advantages and improving on the shortcomings of both worlds. Furthermore, they expect that Japan, through her neutral stand, may keep free from involvement in war even if it breaks out. Thus they conclude that neutrality will bring to Japan peace and prosperity.

It would hardly be possible for the defeated Japanese people to find a more attractive course than neutrality. In reality, however, the neutrality theory is, as is generally known, substantially the conceptual pacifism supported by idealistic liberalists and left-wing socialists or the disguised strategy of Communists and their sympathizers.

SHOULD JAPAN SIDE WITH THE THIRD-POWER GROUP?

The idea of the third-power group is an attempt to get over the utopianism of the neutrality theory and to make it realizable. I may be blamed for using the word "idea," for the theory of the third-power group is no longer a mere conceptual idea isolated from the reality of international power relations. It is a definite *Realpolitik* supported by a group of influential states steering neither the liberal nor the Communist course but a third and peaceful course. Those states are India, as the leader, and other Asian and Arabian countries. The theory of the "third powers" is becoming influential even to some extent, it is said, in the Latin American republics and recently in a part of Western Europe also.

Thus the peace theory and movement of the third-power group are more or less influential in every region of the globe, and Japan is no exception. Advocates in Japan, with ready belief in future peace based on the third road, insist on Japan's affiliation and co-operation with the third-power group, instead of the conclusion of military agreement with or the grant of strategic bases to either one of the two worlds.

JAPAN AND THE "PEACE POWERS"

Since Japan has recovered her independence by concluding a peace treaty with liberal states, Communists and their supporters have recently changed their strategy. Formerly they supported the theory of neutrality or the third-power group, which they utilized as disguised instruments for nourishing anti-American and pro-Russian national feeling. However, they have now abandoned such indirect strategy. They have become critical of the neutrality policy and third-power advocacy and have made their Communistic attitude clear. Their new disguise is the banner of the "peace powers" which the General Council of Trade Unions and other pro-Communist organizations in Japan are flying.

It is natural that the Communistic and pro-Communistic stand should be incompatible with that of neutrality or the third-power group. With the end of the Allied occupation and the increase of Communistic tendencies in the third-power movement in Japan, Communists and their co-operators were unmasked. They have now quit pretending to support neutrality or third powers. However, they still need a disguise, lest they should be exposed to the strong anti-Communist national feeling of the Japanese people, and that disguise is the banner of the "peace powers" which they are deliberately flying.

PRESUPPOSITIONS

Which of these five positions should Japan prefer? The answer will vary according to the ideal society the answerer contemplates establishing and his judgment on the political situation, especially the political relations of Japan at home and abroad. I am of the opinion that we, the Japanese people, should rebuild our new Japan on the basis of democracy, peace, culture, and welfare as the new Constitution definitely indicates, that we should steer our new course on this principle as an independent state in international society.

My conclusion, however, presupposes that the antagonism of the two worlds will not be dissolved in the near future, even though it may be weakened to some extent. If the antagonism could be actually dissolved the situation would be utterly different, and the problem of the choice of position would become meaningless. Nor do I anticipate an immediate revolution of Japan's governmental form and foreign policy. If I did, my conclusion would also naturally be different.

The most essential task for us, I repeatedly emphasize, is to probe correctly the status and weight of Japan in international politics. If we fail to do so, any aspiration or policy, however far-reaching and lofty it may be, will not only be a mere conceptual ideal but will also lead our country in a wrong direction.

UTOPIAN NEUTRALITY

Of these five views on Japan's future course, the most attractive to those who are not practical but yet are eager to pursue peace is advocacy of a neutral

Japan. This is proved by the fact that the theory of neutrality is supported by many young people, women, and religionists. However, more and more people have come to realize that however attractive the image of the "Switzerland on the Pacific" may be, in the twentieth century it can be nothing more than a utopia. The reason may be well understood by considering the fact that there could scarcely be a more difficult task for Japan than to conclude a neutrality pact with both of the opposing two worlds; or, if the pact itself could be concluded, it could hardly be observed because of Japan's strategic importance. Moreover, like the security system, neutrality is already out of date now that an organization such as the United Nations and the idea of world government have appeared before the footlights of the international political scene.

Accordingly the advocates of neutrality have changed their project into the third-power system, such as that of India, or the isolation system such as that of Sweden. But it is very doubtful that the proposal of world peace by a separate state can bear effective fruit in an international situation where the antagonism of the two worlds is so intense that the evolution of world history may be determined by it. If it is considered calmly, everyone will deny the possibility. I, too, feel so, especially in the case of Japan, a state not only defeated and powerless, but also suspected by other states as to the validity of her desire for peace because of her foreign policies in the past. Nothing will more endanger the future of the Japanese nation than to embark on such an unstable neutrality policy.

THE THIRD-POWER GROUP

The theory of the third-power group seems to cover the weak point of the neutrality policy, for there will, no doubt, be formed a third-power group strong enough to meet the power of the United States of America or Russia, if Asian and Arabian states are allied under the leadership of China and India, with Latin American republics and some East and North European states joining in, and if, further, British and French co-operation could be counted on. In fact such a tendency has made its appearance in various regions and to various extents, and even seems to be increasing in strength. These facts, it seems to me, have substituted realizability for the utopianism of the neutrality theory and have inspired it with a new life. In this sense, I have no hesitation in recognizing that the theory of the third-power group deserves our respectful attention as a practical development of the neutrality theory.

We should investigate carefully, not in the light of hope but with a cool head, the plan of *Realpolitik* based on the theory of the third powers. To my great regret, however, there is not space here for a detailed argument, but I shall try to outline the essential points.

It is true that the states mentioned above feel dissatisfaction with the global policies of both America and Russia and have general antipathies to both countries also. Can they then be united in a third group with political power strong enough to check either America or Russia, or perhaps both? Speaking frankly, I cannot help feeling a great doubt in this respect. Can Red China and India, for instance, join hands with each other, breaking away from the Communist group and from the British Commonwealth, respectively, to form ˙a third group? I cannot suppose it. Nor will Great Britain and her dominions, or yet the North European states, leave their democratic league to enter a third camp. The same can be said concerning the Latin American republics.

It may be concluded, therefore, that

as a problem of reality those willing to combine themselves into the third alignment are only the southeast Asian and Arabian states, with India as their head. By themselves alone, can they make an influential third group? The strongest bond between them may be their common antipathy to European and American imperialism. Their inner motive to ally themselves with one another seems not so strong. In addition, the national power of each of them is too weak to cope with the power politics of the two worlds.

Weak points of the contemplated Asian-Arabian third alignment will be understood from remarks of Premier Nehru of India who, being fully aware of the situation of those states, recognizes clearly their lack of power. Further, India herself as a whole will, it can be estimated, remain a member of the liberal group as a member of the British Commonwealth, despite her repeated declaration.

As long as the reality of the third-power group is so uncertain, the peace policy based upon it cannot be stable and reliable.

THE COMMUNIST ALTERNATIVE

Since the peace policy of neutrality cannot be relied upon as practical politics, there is no other way Japan can choose except to stand by the side of one of the two main groups—Communist or liberal. We must abandon the attitude of irresponsible onlookers and have conviction and courage in choosing our way. We must select the practical way, even though it is a next to best, instead of the abstract best.

As a problem of practical politics, Japan cannot choose the way to the Communist group, for it is impossible for Japan to do so. Japan's policies both foreign and domestic throughout prewar and postwar periods prove that Japan is an anti-Communist state. If

Japan with such a historical background should happen to enter the Communist group, it would be necessary for Japan to undergo a revolutionary change in her international and domestic policies. That means a fundamental change not only of Japanese foreign relations but also of her form of government, namely, the abolition of the Tenno rule and the adoption of a totalitarian system in every field, which would entirely destroy, perhaps with violence, the newly born, postwar democratic Japan. Such a drastic revolution of both government and foreign relations can never be easily effected.

Even putting aside these difficulties, conversion to the Communist side is not per se desirable for Japan.

ALIGNMENT WITH THE LIBERAL GROUP

Not only from the viewpoint of her historical background but also from that of the reconstruction of her future, Japan should prefer the liberal group rather than the Communist bloc. I feel that through affiliation with the liberal group Japan is most likely to contribute effectively to world peace as well as to secure her own independence.

The antagonism and rivalry between the two worlds will never cease substantially, I think, as long as the fundamental ideology of Communism remains unchanged. Declarations of peace and coexistence by Stalin and Malenkov cannot be effective in resolving the struggle. The antagonism, however, will not lead to a World War III fought with such destructive weapons as the hydrogen and atomic bombs, so it may be possible to call even such a state of antagonism "peace and coexistence" if people wish to do so. It is lacking, however, in the basic condition of peace, that is, the spirit of mutual understanding, confidence, and co-operation. Therefore, it can be nothing more than a cold peace and accordingly is a cold war.

In such an international situation of cold peace, Japan should stand by the side of the liberal states, strengthen their power, and contribute to promotion of the peace and welfare of mankind. Why? The reasons are as follows:

1. The group of liberal states guarantees far more freedom to member states than the totalitarian group does. It must be recognized, of course, that in the liberal bloc also each member state is obliged to assume responsibilities, large or small according to the circumstances. Surveyed as a whole, however, liberal states can and do enjoy far more freedom than member states of the Communist bloc. This is evidenced by the fact that members of the British Commonwealth, including India, some North European states, and even Titoist Yugoslavia belong to the liberals, and also by a comparison of conditions in Japan and West Germany with those in East Germany.

Economic aid

2. Japan very keenly desires the investment of foreign capital in order to achieve the reconstruction and modernization of her economy, especially her industry, as the accumulation of Japanese capital is limited and poor. Therefore, we must join hands with such a state as will lend the necessary capital, with no ambition, or as little as possible, to hold political sway over our country.

The liberal bloc under the leadership of the United States is, needless to say, superior to the Communist states on the first issue. In regard to the second matter, it may be asserted that the traditional imperialistic policy of advanced Western states has made them less generous than Russia. In respect to this economic foreign policy, it must be observed that a reduction of control over colonies by advanced imperialistic powers is the general tendency of the postwar international situation. Therefore we should be careful not to consider international mutual aids among interdependent countries in the coming world similar to colonial domination in the past.

As for the Russian attitude concerning economic aid to her satellite states, she not only holds political sway over them but also engages in economic exploitation far more severe than that of the capitalist states. East Germany and Czechoslovakia can be mentioned as examples. It is reported that the revolt which took place in Middle and East Europe last year and other social disturbances there were the result of poverty and the lack of freedom caused by the exploitation and suppression of Communistic totalitarianism in its foreign application.

Remarks of the political leaders of Yugoslavia who succeeded in getting loans from both America and Russia in recent years may be worth listening to. They said that the American way of economic expansion is less imperialistic and less exploiting than any other imperialistic policy; especially as compared with the Russian method that of the United States is preferable. They pointed out that the Russian way of exporting capital usually demands the importing state to accept various feudalistic conditions, such as partial military occupation, political control by bureaucratic and police powers, suppression of democratic tendencies, establishment of a puppet government, and so forth. This may be a good lesson in comparing the attitude toward economic aid of both blocs and may explain the term "Red Imperialism."

Dignity of the human being

3. In respect to ideology and culture also I prefer the liberal world to the totalitarian. In the free world the core

of belief and culture is the freedom and dignity of the human being, even if this ideal happens sometimes to be somewhat deformed. On the other hand, in the Communist world the dignity and freedom of the human being are forcibly suppressed under the pressure of technology and authoritarianism. This situation is due to the hurried construction of socialism in a region where the economic system and belief in human rights are backward. People who have once enjoyed human liberty and human rights can never live desirable lives in the culture of backward socialism.

Fears

Preferable though affiliation with the liberal bloc may be, I cannot close my eyes to some possible dangers. They are, as is often pointed out, that Japan, by joining the group of liberal states, may become a munition factory or a source of manpower in the East, and finally become involved in war, or that Japan may degenerate into a colony, enslaved and exploited, or that the capitalist system in Japan may be consolidated and democratization prevented, so that she comes to play the role of agent for suppressing the emancipation of nations in the East.

These may be, of course, extreme fears. But some of them are not groundless and might develop into reality. However, the dangers would be far graver if we entered the Communist camp.

Progressive growth

How could these dangers for Japan be prevented? I assert, by enlightening the liberal states so that they would not remain conservative, sticking to the status quo, but would evolve toward that progressive international society which can and does apply the principle of human dignity and liberty to ever

changing world affairs. I suggest the following five points to promote progressive growth of the liberal states:

1. Each member of the liberal group should have the necessary minimum armament to defend herself and the group against attack and aggression both direct and indirect by other states and, at the same time, should have no intention of aggression toward other states. In other words, we must hold not to absolute pacifism, but to realistic pacifism.

2. Advanced and wealthy states, not adhering inflexibly to the capitalist regime, should promote the realization of that peaceful social reformation called for by the imperative of social justice. Especially is it essential to help the evolutionary development of states into welfare states.

3. The more advanced states must help reform the systems of government in Asian and African countries, adopting a democratic overseas policy based upon the principle of interdependence and international mutual aid. Through such reformation those advanced states should realize, in peace, the aspiration for political revolution of backward people in those areas.

4. In domestic administration, each member state of the liberal group should fulfill the revolution of humanity, that is, the restoration of the human consciousness to a condition of human dignity and liberty—in fine, the perfect observation of the spirit of democracy. The greatest evil of modern civilization lies in the suppression of genuine humanity by the increased pressure and mechanism of materialism and by the concentration of power in a small part of society. This tendency is not a feature of capitalist society only, but is likewise outstanding in Communist society. In other words, it is the deplorable evil commonly felt in regard to both capitalist and Communist society.

5. The structure of the group of liberal states is different from that of the Communistic alignment. The former is pluralistic and dynamic; the latter, unified and totalitarian. The liberal bloc should express the superiority of its composition.

The perfect realization of the above five points will make the liberal bloc superior to the Communist group. More than that, it will make possible political contact and economic and cultural interchange between the two worlds through the channel of the United Nations and other international organizations, or through treaties and agreements. So long as the superiority of free states can be maintained, the position and prestige of the United Nations will be raised, for the liberal camp is always the eager supporter of the United Nations.

A THIRD IDEOLOGICAL POWER

In the world of the liberal states, the progressive tendency is stronger than attachment to the status quo. Accordingly, the liberal world is far more flexible and elastic than the totalitarian world. This results from the difference of composition in the two worlds. I believe it is possible for the free world to adapt itself to new circumstances.

However, some progressive states of the free world seem recently to have interest in, or even to approve, the proposal made by Premier Nehru of India for the formation of a third region, a proposal which is a revised edition of the third powers. I hesitate to agree with such an opinion, for it entails a double danger: on the one hand, it cannot make those states powerful enough to cope with either or both of two giants; on the other, it decreases the strength of the free world. The desirable thing at the present state of evolution of world history is, as I have already pointed out, consolidation of the group of liberal states and increase in their progressiveness; dissolution of the cold peace under the superiority of the free world; and the opening of mutual understanding and co-operation between the two camps, as a first step leading to true world peace.

We, at the same time, sincerely look forward to the rise of progressive states in the Communist bloc also. As such progressive powers become influential, the nature of that side will, I hope, change, and a seed of true peace be sown.

In conclusion, the way Japan should go between the two worlds is neither the way to neutrality nor to the third powers, much less the way to the Communist side, but the way to the liberal bloc, to contribute to the promotion of its consolidation and progressiveness. If there is anyone who wishes to use the term "the third" in advocating a peace schedule to secure Japan's independence and safety, he must use it in the meaning neither of a third power opposing the two giants, nor of a third area playing the role of a neutral zone or a buffer state, but of a third ideological power in the countries on both sides of the two worlds pushing the world they belong to towards peace and progress. I mean here by the term "third" a synthesis of both capitalist and Communist ideologies.

Tatsuo Morito is president of Hiroshima University, Japan. Formerly Minister of Education, he is a member of the Japanese National Commission of UNESCO and attended the conference in Paris last year. He has written a number of books on social problems.

A Brief for Korea

By Robert T. Oliver

THE Korean situation has so often been called "difficult and confusing" that I think I should warn you in advance that in my view the basic issues are inescapably simple and clear cut. In my judgment we Americans have tended to label* the Korean problem as being difficult to understand when what we really mean is that it is difficult for us to handle and that consequently we should like to disengage ourselves from it wholly if we could. This state of mind did not originate after we became involved in an unpopular war in Korea. On the contrary, it has marked our view of Korea from the first.

To the historically minded, of course, "from the first" is an aggravating phrase. How far back into American-Korean relations do we have to go to get our thinking about the problem firmly and properly oriented?

Koreans go back to 1882, when Korea was first persuaded by Commodore Robert W. Schufeldt of the United States Navy to give up the isolationism of its Hermit Kingdom phase and enter into diplomatic and trade relations with the West. In the treaty with Korea which our Senate ratified in 1883 we promised to use our good offices to assist Korea in case any other nation "should deal unjustly" with her. For two decades American business and American missionaries penetrated significantly into Korean life. We built in Seoul the Orient's first electric streetcar system. We developed Korea's gold mines (which produced 3 per cent of the world's gold). Then we became discouraged because of the corruption and inefficiency of the decadent Korean monarchy and because the eager interest of both Russia and Japan in Korea made it clear that we could only maintain an American foothold there at the cost of what appeared to be an unprofitable effort.

Accordingly, President Theodore Roosevelt took steps to relinquish the obligations we had assumed in the treaty of 1883. He sent his Secretary of War, William Howard Taft, to Tokyo to sign a secret agreement with the Japanese Prime Minister Katsura (on July 29, 1904) to the effect that the United States would not oppose extension of Japanese control over Korea, in return for a promise that the Japanese would not attack the Philippine Islands. When Korea's liberal statesmen, Prince Min and General Hahn, sent the youthful reformer Syngman Rhee to plead with Roosevelt to observe the aid provisions of the 1883 treaty, Roosevelt held Rhee at bay with personal graciousness while the Portsmouth Conference proceeded to award Japan a protectorate over Korea. As soon as this was done, the United States was the first nation to close its Legation in Seoul and transfer operations to Tokyo.

TOWARD KOREAN INDEPENDENCE

In 1919, inspired by Woodrow Wilson's promise of "the self-determination of peoples," the Koreans organized a massive nonviolent "demonstration of independence" throughout Korea and elected Rhee (who by that time had received his Ph.D. from Wilson at Princeton) as President of the Korean Republic-in-Exile. For the next twenty-six years (and especially after the Pearl Harbor attack) this government struggled unsuccessfully to win American recognition. The first constructive step toward the restoration of Korea's 4,300-year old nationality was the pledge at Cairo, on December 1, 1943, by Franklin D. Roosevelt, Churchill, and Chiang Kai-shek that "in due course" Korea's independence would be restored.

The close of the Pacific phase of World War II resulted in a series of concessions to Russia, of which one was the "temporary" establishment of the 38th parallel line across the middle of Korea. Within the next few months it became apparent that the Soviet Union had no intention of withdrawing to permit the reunification of the Korean nation under any government except one dominated by Communists. The United States maintained an American Military Government in South Korea for three years, but in another movement of disengagement we persuaded the United Nations to assume responsibility for the establishment of a democratically elected Republic of Korea. Upon the refusal by the Soviet Union to accept United Nations jurisdiction in northern Korea, the projected election was held "in all areas of Korea accessible to" the United Nations Commission. On August 15, 1948, the Republic was inaugurated, under a constitution affirming its sovereignty over all Korea, and with one hundred seats in its National Assembly reserved for members subsequently to be elected for the northern provinces. On December 12 of that year the United Nations General Assembly approved the election which its commission had supervised as being "fair and free" and declared that the Republic of Korea was "the only lawful government" in Korea.

During the next two years the United Nations maintained a commission in Korea "observing and advising" the development of democratic processes and reporting that under the circumstances satisfactory progress was being made. The United States provided economic aid through the Economic Cooperation Administration. The Communists maintained a vigorous program of subversion which resulted in a bloody uprising in November 1948 but which gradually was brought under control and rendered ineffective. In July 1949, the United States withdrew the last of its occupation troops, leaving behind a 500-man military advisory group, which helped develop a constabulary force of 96,300 men but which denied the Korean plea for a regular army on the grounds that an armed force in southern Korea might lead to an outbreak of war with the heavily armed northern Communist regime.

The process of disengagement continued with a speech by Secretary of State Dean Acheson on January 12, 1950, in which he declared that the American defensive perimeter in Asia lay in the island chain extending from the Aleutians through Japan and Okinawa to the Philippines. This process was continued in the form of a directive circulated to American foreign service personnel asking them to prepare to explain the anticipated fall of Formosa to the Chinese Communists, and in a statement by Senator Tom Connally, chairman of the Senate Foreign Relations Committee, that if Korea were attacked the United States could not go to its assistance. On June 25, 1950, the Communists put this policy to the test by launching a heavy attack across the 38th parallel.

WAR BEGINS

President Rhee, in Seoul, had no way of knowing that his government would receive outside aid. He had in mind the example of Poland, which had been promised support in 1938 but which, nevertheless, was abandoned to enemy occupation; and the example of Czechoslovakia, which had surrendered to Communist pressure and which in 1950 was still receiving preferred treatment as a "showplace of Communism." Even so, he did not hesitate, but ordered his carbine-armed constabulary to resist to the full the tank-led Communist attack. Within three days half the Korean defensive force had become casualties and southern Korea was left open to invasion without an established front line.

In Independence, Missouri, President Truman was also confronted with the need for an instant and momentous decision. Concluding that to permit armed Communist aggression to succeed in Korea would be a renunciation of the Truman Doctrine which had worked so well in Greece and Turkey and might mark the end of the United Nations (which had been boycotted for six months by the Soviet Union), he moved quickly to assure United Nations sanction and American military support for a "police action" to defeat the aggression.

The first United Nations reaction, which occurred as an astounding evidence of Allied unity and determination, was deliberately ambiguous. The June 27 resolution of the Security Council called upon all the United Nations members for aid "to restore peace and security in the area"; it made no reference to the 38th parallel line. However, after the success of the Inchon Landing, the General Assembly on October 7, 1950, passed a resolution noting that "the unification of Korea has not yet been achieved." "Recalling that the essential objective of the resolutions of the General Assembly . . . was the establishment of a unified, independent and democratic Government of Korea," it resolved that "All constituent acts should be taken, including the holding of elections, under the auspices of the United Nations, for the establishment

of a unified, independent and democratic government in the sovereign State of Korea." There have been many assertions that the United Nations "never" intended to reunify Korea by force of arms, but the simple fact is that on October 9 the United Nations armies moved across the 38th parallel and headed, with little opposition, for the Yalu and Tumen Rivers.

When the Chinese Communists entered the fighting in November, General MacArthur declared that this marked the beginning of "an entirely new war," and quickly withdrew his forces down below the 38th parallel. The General Assembly of the United Nations again considered the question and decided that its responsibilities had not yet been fulfilled. On February 1, 1951, it adopted a resolution branding the Chinese Communist armies as "aggressors" because of their presence in Korean territory. In subsequent fighting the Chinese Reds were soundly defeated and, on the authority of Generals MacArthur and Van Fleet, were on the verge of collapse. They were rescued, however, by a hint from Yakov Malik, delivered over the United Nations radio facilities in New York, that Russia would welcome a truce in Korea.

Truce Talks

In retrospect there has been almost universal agreement that truce talks ought not to have been undertaken until after the aggressors had been driven from Korean territory. In the summer of 1951, however, a "truce without victory" was welcomed by all the participant governments except the Republic of Korea, which pleaded urgently for a continuance of the war. The "neutralist bloc" led by India demanded a truce on the grounds that Red China had intervened justly to protect its own frontier and that peace in Asia should be sought not by conquest of the Communists but through recognition and conciliation of Red China. England supported the truce on the grounds that she would never "fight to conquer North Korea for Syngman Rhee." The United States was influenced by the the feelings of its allies but was even more fundamentally influenced by the "island defensive perimeter" concept. With South Korea kept free from Communist control, Japan would be safe and the island perimeter could not be breached. No goal in Asia beyond this was deemed important enough to justify a full-scale war with Red China. American observers agreed that the truce was a resounding defeat for the Republic of Korea, but they added that this is just one of the international injustices that have to be tolerated.

The subsequent signing of the truce, the withdrawal of two United States divisions from Korea, and the January 12, 1954, speech by Secretary of State Dulles indicating that American policy henceforth would be developed around the theory of "massive retaliation" (directed at Russia?) rather than the fighting of "Korean-style" local wars, all constitute a further extension of American efforts to disengage ourselves from involvement in Korea.

A partial negation of disengagement was achieved by President Rhee, through his threats to disrupt the truce, in the negotiation of the American-Korean Mutual Defense Treaty. But despite earnest efforts by President Rhee, the United States refused to write into the treaty any guarantee to assist in repelling the Chinese Red aggressors from Korea. In the talks between Rhee and Dulles (in mid-July, 1953) Dulles assured Rhee that the truce did not constitute a "surrender" by the United States or the United Nations. "We still stand firmly by our declarations that Korea must be reunified under its own free and democratic government,"

Dulles told Rhee in emphatic terms, "but we shall achieve that reunification by political negotiation rather than through war." Rhee replied in substance, "I agree, provided you will promise me that if negotiation fails you will then resume the fighting with us."

What would happen if negotiation does not succeed, however, was postponed for later decision. The most to which Dulles would assent was to agree to walk out of the projected political conference with the Republic of Korea, if, after ninety days, there was no substantial progress toward Korean reunification. After that, the United States and Korea should jointly consider what further action they would take. The Communists did their best to nullify the effects of the "ninety-day" clause by refusing to hold the conference on October 28, 1953, as they had promised to do; instead, a new date of April 26, 1954, was finally selected. Meanwhile, the Communists proceeded to violate the truce by establishing military air bases in North Korea and by reinforcing their ground armies in that area.

WHY U. S. INVOLVEMENT IN KOREA?

This historical review brings our consideration of American-Korean relations up to date, but necessarily has omitted a number of important considerations. The most important one is whether the United States has any real reason for being involved in Korean affairs, or whether the whole situation is not merely the result of fumbling failures, to be written off quickly as an unfortunate development. One of the strongest proponents of this view has been Owen Lattimore, who, on July 17, 1949, wrote in the New York *Post*, "The thing to do is to let South Korea fall, but not to let it look as if we pushed it."

The question of whether the United States has vital interests of its own to pursue in Korea breaks down into two major subquestions. Are there negative (largely strategic) reasons for preventing the Communists from controlling Korea? Are there positive (largely political) reasons for assisting the establishment in Korea of a genuine democracy? These questions are of vital import, for they not only help us to understand past developments in Korea but also guide us in shaping our future policies toward that country.

There has been endless debate among the military experts concerning the strategic values of withholding Korea from enemy occupation. When the Joint Chiefs of Staff ordered the withdrawal of American troops from Korea in 1949 and refused to sanction the build-up of a Republic of Korea army, they clearly indicated their judgment that Korea could be "allowed to fall" to the Communists. In my own talks with many of our American officials, I became convinced that they anticipated the fall of Korea through internal subversion and were not willing to make major efforts to prevent this result. Some light is shed on this policy by the fact that the ECA in Korea refused to spend money to build productive resources (maintaining instead a soupline relief program) and in successive years turned back unspent a substantial proportion of the funds voted by Congress to be used in making South Korea economically self-sufficient. The slowness of the development of the current United Nations Korean Reconstruction Agency and United States rehabilitation programs in Korea indicates that this same attitude is still prevalent. In 1949, the policies of withdrawal from Korea were similar in import to the explanations presented in the State Department's *White Book on China* for our stoppage of aid to the Chinese Nationalist government.

Historians have called Korea "the heart of the strategic triangle of North Asia," bounded by China, Russia, and Japan, and have noted that when Japan secured control of Korea in 1905 it was enabled to move on through that land bridge to the conquest of Manchuria and much of China. But in the aftermath of World War II American and European efforts were devoted to finding a modus vivendi with Russia. This led to deliberate efforts in both China and Korea to establish "coalition governments"—presumably on the theory that it is better to join them than to try to lick them.

In Korea, General John R. Hodge, who commanded the American occupation forces, established a Coalition Committee in 1946 and denounced Rhee for his persistent attacks on Communism, which, Hodge felt, interfered with efforts to establish in a reunited Korea a government acceptable to the Soviet Union. A five-year Trusteeship was proposed for Korea, with joint supervision by the United States, Great Britain, Russia, and China. In early March, 1954, this same approach was renewed by Sir Winston Churchill, who proposed that the reunification of Korea be sought under a pattern of joint guarantees by Russia, Red China, the United States, and Great Britain.

Time Is on Whose Side?

Korean spokesmen have pointed out that if they were willing to submit to a government "acceptable to Russia," they could have had it at any time after Japan's defeat. They need not have resisted the Communist attack of June 25, 1950. They could have had that kind of reunification without suffering two million war casualties, having ten million of their people driven from their homes, or having their entire nation laid waste. They cling to the goal which has also repeatedly been stated by the United States and the United Nations, namely, that Korea should be reunited as an independent and democratic nation.

The nature of the strategic dispute involves the basic interpretation of the struggle between the Communist and non-Communist governments of the world. One view is that the totalitarian dictatorship of the Soviet Union is so rotten internally that if the free world can hold a firm peripheral line, preventing the dictatorship from successively handing new victories as sops to its deprived and maltreated peoples, the whole Communist structure will eventually break down. This breakdown might take the form of Red China's becoming "another Yugoslavia." It might consist of disruptive revolutions in Eastern Germany and other parts of eastern Europe. It might result from power struggles among Stalin's successors. In any event, according to this view (which appears to be the one accepted by President Eisenhower) time is on our side and postponement of conflict offers hope of avoiding world war.

According to another interpretation, Communism advances best without "hot war." Operating through an international conspiratorial organization, the Communists seek to disrupt governmental and economic processes in free nations (as in Italy, France, and Indonesia), to arouse resentments against "Western colonialism" (as in Africa, the Middle East, and South America), and to stir up localized rebellions that can be represented as internal civil war (as in China in 1949 and Indochina today). Communist propaganda represents the Korean War as a Communist victory, pictures Communism as "the wave of the future," and depicts the democracies as rich but decadent states intent only on maintaining a status quo which is infinitely to their advantage. Negotiation with the Communists is worse than useless, for they seize upon every concession that is offered, give nothing substantial in return, break the agreements they do make, and count confidently on observance of agreements by the free world because they feel democratic opinion will oppose any violation of agreement as a step toward war. (Our strict observance of the truce in Korea even though the Communists have openly violated it is a case in point.) In this view time is on the side of the Soviet Union, which proceeds systematically to "soften up" the free world while building its stockpile of atomic weapons and awaiting the day when it may feel able to launch the final global attack.

Syngman Rhee is a leading proponent of this latter view. He feels (as do Generals MacArthur, Van Fleet, and Clark) that there is no solution in Korea short of a decisive military victory— limited to the definitive aim of driving the Communists back across the Yalu River. He feels that the truce in Korea was another Munich, which encourages the very aggression it sought to deter. He is convinced that Russia is not yet strong enough to win a global war, and therefore will not fight one now—thus giving to the free world a diminishing period of time in which to reverse the course of the cold war, by improving rather than frittering away our vital margin of military superiority.

The answer, then, to the question of the strategic value of keeping Korea out of Communist possession is not universally agreed upon. Every responsible non-Communist would probably agree that the attack upon southern Korea had to be repulsed to prevent the break-up of the United Nations and to safeguard the "island perimeter." The future will have to demonstrate whether South Korea can continue to stand as a "bastion of democracy" without the integration of North Korea into the Republic of Korea. President Rhee feels that in time the United States will tire of supporting South Korea economically and militarily, and that the Korean people will tire of living on a soup-line economy continually beset by Communist subversion—so that in his view postponement of the issue is tantamount to surrender. The dispute is reminiscent of what was said about China in 1948 and 1949.

Korean Democracy

And that brings us to our second question, for many Americans and Europeans have likened the Republic of Korea to Nationalist China and Syngman Rhee to Chiang Kai-shek. Can we, they ask, properly support a government which is not genuinely democratic? Prime Minister Nehru has gone further and declared that abandonment of Syngman Rhee (presumably even if this meant the communization of all Korea) is required by his view of what constitutes Asian self-determination. Fundamentally the nub of the Korean question is whether the Republic of Korea does actually represent healthy democracy.

This question has many times been answered affirmatively in official statements. The United Nations Commissions in their respective reports have consistently declared that despite difficulties and limitations democracy is being firmly emplanted in Korea. United States Ambassador John J. Muccio, who spent four years in Korea, declared on May 30, 1952, that "a workable form of modern democratic government with the classic checks and balances was being molded [up to the time of the Communist attack] out of the crucible of events as they affected Korea." John Foster Dulles, in a speech on July 4, 1950, explained that the Communists attacked Korea because "the society was so healthy that it could not be overthrown from within."

At the same time, many criticisms from private sources have been made against the Republic of Korea, and these need to be examined. Since space precludes their full discussion here, it may be pardonable to refer inquirers to my book, *Verdict in Korea*,[1] for comprehensive data.

The Constitution of the Republic of Korea grants full suffrage to men and women and contains an elaborate bill of civil rights. Skeptics have pointed out that so do the constitutions of Nationalist China and of the Soviet Union. However, in Korea, every election has been under the close observation of the United Nations. Campaigning is open and vigorous, and there have always been many candidates with differing platforms for every elective office. More than ninety newspapers are published in Korea, and although foreign critics have charged censorship, readers of them find many criticisms of many phases of governmental administration. Executive domination of the legislature is denied by the running feud which has existed between President Rhee and the National Assembly. The report of the United Nations Commission on Korea dated September 5, 1951, highlighted an important fact when it said:

The Republic of Korea has placed no restrictions whatever upon observation within the country by international bodies. . . . This willingness . . . is a sign of a genuine desire to carry out the purposes and principles of the Charter of the United Nations to the best of the country's abilities.

Many of the charges made against the Republic of Korea for alleged lack of democracy ought, rather, to be levied against its poverty, or low level of education, or lack of a tradition of Lockian equality, or the urgent need for defense against Communist infiltration and subversion. Even in the United States,

[1] State College, Pa.: Bald Eagle Press, 1952.

which is infinitely safer than South Korea, the power of the police to ferret out hidden Communist connections has been considerably expanded. The "phenomenal fact" in Korea (again to quote Ambassador Muccio) is that the basic civil rights have been so well maintained.

On the constructive side, democracy in Korea has proved so healthy that an average of 86 per cent of all eligible voters have gone to the polls in all the elections. Education has expanded to the degree that four times as many students are in high school as during the Japanese rule, that thirty-nine colleges are in operation, and that illiteracy has been largely eliminated. Women's rights have expanded enormously, not only through gaining the ballot, but in a decided change of social and economic attitudes. The problem of landlord control of the farm lands has been almost wholly eliminated, as Korean farmers have been granted the right, and assisted by government aid, to buy the land they cultivate. Farm rentals now constitute less than 10 per cent of all Korean farm lands.

Constitutional amendment of 1952

President Rhee came under heavy attack from foreign critics in the spring and summer of 1952, when he forced through the National Assembly a constitutional amendment that transferred the power of electing the President from the Assembly to the entire electorate. Admitedly he had to utilize all the pressures at his command to secure the relinquishment by the National Assembly of this vital power. But there is no question that the people of Korea solidly supported the change. All of the Provincial Assemblies voted for it, and 1,400 local Councils (out of a total of 1,700 in all South Korea) adopted resolutions favoring it. The "pressure" exerted on the National Assembly to

accept the amendment largely consisted of the convergence upon it of committees bearing these resolutions. Those critics who charged that Rhee was "violating the Constitution" overlooked the fact that it was being amended, not violated, and that our own concept of democracy demands the election of the President by all the voters, rather than by the National Legislature. Rhee himself feels that the future of democracy in Korea would not be safe unless the essential power of choosing the chief executive was safely emplanted in the people as a whole.

Korean individualism

The only dependable safeguard of any democracy is the nature of the people themselves. The Koreans have solidly proved their sturdy individualism. The Japanese occupied Korea for a full generation and sought with all their ingenuity to "Japanize" the population—but failed notably. The Russians tried with all the means in their repertoire to rule the North Koreans, but four millions of them managed to escape into the south; and the communization of North Korea had to be accomplished under the leadership of a Soviet citizen, Kim Il Sung, backed by an influx of two million repatriates from Siberia and North China, most of whom were communized during their generation-long fight against Japan. The Koreans have been christened "the Irish of the Orient." Aleš Hrdlička, who was the chief anthropologist for the Smithsonian Institution and who specialized in Korean anthropology, called them "the white people of the Orient." Missionaries have agreed that Korea is "the most Christian land in the Orient." From my own experience among them, I testify with careful assurance that they are a superior people, wholly capable of managing their own destinies and determined to do so. Their determination, high morale, and ebullient individualism under all the hammerings of the war have been noted and praised by a great number of highly competent observers. No such people as the Koreans would endure a despotic government at home any more than they would accept a colonial rule from abroad.

SUMMARY

In a general summing up, then, of the relations between America and the new Korea, a number of conclusions emerge, all fitting together into a rather simple and definite pattern.

1. The United States has been reluctant to maintain close relations with Korea (not wishing to be entangled with affairs on the Asian mainland) but has been forced into recurrent commitments because of the strategic importance of Korea for the defense of our own security.

2. In the Korean peninsula have been planted the seeds of genuine Western-style democracy—a fact which may turn out to be the most important, historically, of all the developments in the Far East in recent years.

3. The war in Korea was an essential defense of the free world against Communist imperialism, and it may prove to be true that we have gravely endangered our own security by our failure to win it.

4. The Korean question was not solved by the truce, but remains one of the crucial issues of the cold war—one that will require decisions in the future fully as momentous as those in the past.

From whatever point of view we may examine the Korean question, its basic simplicity emerges. It is a clear testing ground for the United States and the Soviet Union in the world-power struggle between our antagonistic ways of life. It is a test of the ability of the industrialized Western nations to deal effectively with the emergent nationalism, economic ambitions, and cultural stamina of the Far East. It is a test of the ability of the United Nations to develop a world order based upon law. And finally (remembering the emergence of a massive and modernized Red Chinese fighting force) it remains to be seen whether the Korean War as it was conducted was really a contribution to lasting peace or rather a reproduction of the Spanish Civil War prelude to world war. Any way we look at it, the Korean people are caught in the middle of a vast network of global conflicts. They deserve our sympathy, our understanding, and our help.

Robert T. Oliver, Ph.D., LL.D., State College, Pennsylvania, is head of the Department of Speech at the Pennsylvania State University. During the summer of 1946, he was a guest lecturer in Korea University; he was in Korea as adviser to President Syngman Rhee at intervals from 1949 to 1953 and has also served as adviser to Korean delegations to the United Nations. He is manager of the Washington Bureau of the Korean Pacific Press, editor of the magazine Korean Survey, and author of several books on Korea, including Verdict in Korea (1952) and Syngman Rhee: The Man Behind the Myth (1954).

The Aspirations of Korea

By You Chan Yang

IT is a tragic circumstance that Korea is at this time and has been since the end of World War II an artificially divided nation.

A new and reunited Korea would mean a great deal to the peace of Asia and the peace of the entire world. Our geographical position is one of great strategic importance. The centuries-old unity of our people is another factor. Our record of never having waged aggressive war is still another—in over 4,300 years our people have never attacked anybody, and we have no intention of doing so. All these things add up to the realization that Korea can be one of the most stabilizing elements in a world which desperately seeks stability.

It may seem a singular thing that my country, which was long known as "the Hermit Kingdom," and later, when the Japanese made our peninsula a vast prison camp, as "the Forgotten Nation," should in the past five years see itself the subject of countless headlines, innumerable magazine articles, many, many television and radio programs, and discussions so continual as to defy enumeration. It is saddening that a people and a nation known for centuries as lovers of peace should have had contemporary history record their activities in letters of blood.

All of this means, naturally, that Korea has had a tremendous impact on the rest of the world, and those of us who believe in human freedom cannot but pray that the sacrifices which the Korean people have undergone and the sacrifices that Americans have made on those faraway battlefields shall not have been in vain. For the enemy who produced the war in Korea remains our enemy today. He has but one goal and that is the conquest of the entire world and the subjugation of all free peoples to his concept of mankind as the serf of the state. Our concept, on the other hand, is the one which was given magnificent birth in the city of Philadelphia when this Republic emerged.

The difference in the matter of the two ideologies is as pronounced as day and night. Some way, somehow, one or the other must triumph. For better or for worse we—the war-torn and devastated people of Korea—and you, the great and powerful people of the United States, are in this thing together. Whether or not the issue will be finally resolved in Korea, none can say, but we accepted the challenge first—the challenge of Communist aggression—and we should have been overwhelmed, had you not come to our assistance.

If it is thought that our great President and leader, Syngman Rhee, and his embattled countrymen, who believe in his leadership, have been able to be of service to what remains of the free world, I should like to put my own opinion of that service in capsule form, being a physician. Here it is: They have shown everyone with any knowledge whatever of this crucial period of history the folly of appeasement. In so doing, they have been called upon to pay one of the heaviest prices ever paid by a nation.

Syngman Rhee has been termed a stubborn and obstinate old man. Much of this criticism has come from Communist sources; some of it, I regret to say, has come from sources which have been content to rely on snap judgment, sources which have little or no conception of the profoundly vital issue at stake in my country.

To me, Syngman Rhee is just as stubborn and obstinate as were Benjamin Franklin, George Washington, James Otis, Thomas Paine, and the other great patriots of the American Revolution. Those men knew the issue was very simple. It was freedom versus tyranny. In that long and sometimes hopeless struggle, did they either compromise with the enemy or seek to appease him? Not that I am aware of, and my entire education was in American grade and high schools in Hawaii, and in Boston University on the mainland. No, those men knew that what was morally wrong never could be politically right. And they held to that principle despite the fact that they were confronted by all the might and power of the world's then most powerful empire. Think of it, a little fringe of not more than three million persons strung along the Atlantic coast, standing up and giving battle and finally triumphing over a tyranny able to command the resources and manpower of much of the world. They did not shrink. As a result, people in the United States today are enjoying the privileges of freedom, liberty, and the decencies of life. And that is all our people are asking. Is it a crime to ask for freedom, liberty, and the decencies of life? That is all we want, nothing else. We have no interest in other people's territory.

Syngman Rhee is as stubborn as your early patriots where a moral principle is concerned. That wise old Christian gentleman knows full well and has stated in many of his speeches that "to attempt to compromise with evil is as evil as is evil itself."

A Magnificent Past

Somber thoughts must predominate when one talks about Korea these days.

As you know, and as has been said, the past is prelude to the present, and the present is prelude to the future. The Korean people have had a magnificent past—more than forty-three centuries of it on our peninsula. Protected from the mainland of Asia by rivers and mountain ridges, it was possible to develop down throught the long corridors of time a culture and a way of life that enabled us to grow from a few hundred thousand into a homogeneous nation of thirty million people. No more homogeneous nation ever existed.

We are an inventive people. Before Gutenberg, we contrived movable type. Long before any other nation, as far as we know, we built the first solar observatory, which still stands in Korea today. Lost somewhere in the dim recesses of time is our invention of the magnetic compass for mariners. Nearly five hundred years ago our scholars evolved the first alphabet of the Orient —twenty-four letters, the existing vowels and most of your consonants. In 1592 our admiral, Yisunsin, used an iron clad type of vessel to annihilate the Japanese invading forces. Even today, Japanese Satsuma ware is Korean made, by descendants of the three thousand artisans who were taken over to Japan and put in the southern part, in the island of Kyushu. All of these things we did by ourselves alone.

Now I recount these things not in a spirit of braggadocio, but so that it may known what our past has been, and what we have tried to contribute to the march of civilization. Does not an old Korea of this distinction give some hope of what a new Korea may accomplish?

Under the leadership of our great patriot and statesman, President Syngman Rhee—a man of inflexible purpose —the Korean people are in this fight against Communism to the absolute finish. You wonder why? You of the West have taught us the rights of man.

You have brought Christianity to us. Therefore we want to worship God as you are doing today, and we want to be free men and women. Therefore we are determined to fight the despotism of the Kremlin. We would belie our past and forfeit our future if, in the present, we did not show the qualities that enable us to look backward with pride and forward with determination.

Down through the centuries the Korean people have secured not only a good livelihood out of the soil and fruits of the comparatively small peninsula that is our homeland, but also an over-sufficiency for our needs. Let me give you an example of what our people can do. In spite of all the destruction that has gone on and of all the young men being taken into the army, our farmers were able to produce enough rice last year so that we can export 600,000 tons. It is fantastic—$150,000,000 worth to export. It shows the determination of our people.

KOREA AND JAPAN

Korea, standing as a bulwark against any Chinese advance further eastward in the Pacific and equally as a bulwark against any Japanese advance upon the continent of Asia, lived in peace for many centuries. But our dream of perpetual peace was shattered when in 1905 Japan defeated Russia and moved into our homeland. For four decades thereafter we knew the harsh tyranny of alien rule. Yes, we were then "the Forgotten Nation."

American victory over Japan restored to us our liberties in part of our country, and let me say that America alone won the war in the Pacific. You destroyed the massive Japanese military machine and you did it singlehanded. The Russians were Johnny-come-lately's—one week before the Japanese surrender!

I went to Japan as the Korean chief delegate to sit down and settle all the existing problems between Japan and Korea, to hold hands, make friends, and go forward from there because we have a greater enemy to fight, to protect ourselves and to protect Japan and the whole Pacific. Therefore I tried to talk realistically, but so far we have not got anywhere.

On October 6, 1953, we opened the conference in Japan. On the first day, the Japanese chief delegate made the following five statements:

1. The repatriation of Japanese nationalists from Korea was a violation of international law.

2. The establishment of the Republic of Korea by the United States and the United Nations prior to the Japanese Peace Treaty was a violation of international law. In other words, the Republic of Korea should never have been founded.

3. The Cairo Declaration by the Allied Powers that there existed an enslavement of the Korean people was nothing but war hysteria.

4. The turning over of Japanese property to the Korean government by the United States Military Government was a violation of international law in spite of its being written into the Japanese Treaty, Article IV (b), which clearly stated that Japan had nothing in Korea, and also that Japan made an unconditional surrender.

5. The thirty-six years of Japanese occupation of Korea were beneficial to the Koreans.

Now do not tell me the Japanese were in there for their health. Do not tell me they loved the Koreans so much that they went in there to help them, when they murdered thousands upon thousands of my people under any pretext. I can tell you that they were trying to wipe out Christianity and to transplant Shinto into Korea, and they made our Christians bow before the Japanese

Emperor's picture. Do not tell me that was beneficial to the Koreans.

Think it over, please. I do not mind American aid to Japan, but let us go slow.

Before World War II I used to go around this country telling people, "Japan is going to attack the United States." They said I was a crazy fool. I was not such a crazy fool when December 7, 1941, came around. I was trying to save thousands of your boys' lives at Pearl Harbor. I was operating day and night at the General Hospital there, and thousands of your innocent boys were laid out on the green grass. Think it over, please.

WHAT DOES KOREA WANT?

Uneasy as the present is, we in Korea still yearn and hope to do the things civilized men and women do in other parts of the world. We want to rebuild our homes; we want an opportunity to bring up our children and to educate them without the sound of bombs, shot, and shell. We want to rebuild our schools and our churches. We want to improve our roads. We want—with the extraordinary example of America as an inspiration—to raise our standard of living, to assure every Korean child of the best education possible, and, last but not least, to live in peace. We have proved that we can fight, but we are most proud of our record as a nation of never having committed an aggressive act against any other people. For centuries we have been known as the "Land of the Morning Calm," and our love of peace has been such that the ordinary "hello" and "good-by" and "good night" in Korea takes on an added connotation because we say when we meet a friend or a stranger, "May you come in peace," and when we bid him adieu we say, "May you go in peace." Likewise, when it is time for a good night to visiting

friends, we say, "May you sleep in peace." Yes, we love peace.

Regarding the Geneva Conference which is slated to be held the latter part of April, I should be less than frank were I not to tell you that the Korean people face it with grave misgivings. If the conference should, by any chance, result in a Korean peace and the withdrawal of the Red Chinese from the northern half of our country, we should rejoice. But we have had so many conferences with the Communists, and none has resulted in any agreement. We will never get anywhere with appeasement. In fact, Senator William F. Knowland has, in my opinion, an even better phrase. He calls it "surrender on the installment plan." Meantime, from another appeasement corner you have heard the suggestion that the solution of the Korean War may be found in the "neutralization" of my country. I can assure you that the Korean people will never stand for the emasculation of their nationality. We simply are not made that way. We know the history of neutrality; look at Belgium and Holland as two outstanding examples where, when a great and powerful neighbor decided to overrun their lands, their neutrality perished at once. No, we will never accept the status of an unarmed nation while a madman with tanks, guns, and airplanes is poised on our doorstep.

DEVASTATION AND REHABILITATION

The stench of death still hovers over my country. Put yourselves in our place. Imagine your own community in ruins and silent in the darkness of night. All about you in wreckage. Those who have lived here are gone. The dead remain. Your high buildings are broken skeletons against the light of the moon. Perhaps, if you listen intently, you may hear the cry of a child and if you pursue it—and pursue it you will, for humanity always hearkens to the cry of a child—you will find a tiny waif of Communist cruelty, hungry, ragged, and homeless. Where are his parents? How did he get where he is? What can be done for him? You must, first of all, feed him, then clothe him, and then find a place for him to live—an orphanage set up by your poverty-striken government or by GI's out of their modest pay as soldiers.

In this connection I should like to say that the American GI's have contributed nearly $15,000,000 to save our orphans. Our people are saying, "God bless the American GI." Our Korean people, no matter what happens tomorrow in Korea, will never forget the warm generosity and the kindness of your people and the American GI's. Whether you like it or not, we will always stand by you.

That child we heard is one of nearly 200,000 like him. There are 300,000 war widows in Korea. There are 2,000,000 casualties, civilian and military. Look down, in the moonlight, and you may see a legless man, on stumps, crawling along. We have more than 20,000 of his kind who need artificial arms and legs, or crutches and canes, until they can be fitted for the life of a cripple. Owing to the hardships of war, one-third of our population is afflicted with either incipient or advanced tuberculosis.

Alone and unaided, the task of rehabilitation might overwhelm us, but the American people and their government, as well as other members of the United Nations, have responded with help. In this connection, however, there are some disturbing elements which I feel I should comment on. The bulk of funds expended to date, I regret to say, has been spent to build up the Japanese economy rather than to make our goal of a self-sufficient Korea an attainable goal. Since 1949 we have been asking

for fertilizer plants, which are very essential, power plants, and cement plants, but we still have not got them. Large sums of money have been used to purchase consumer goods in Japan for transport to Korea instead of upon the essential repair and reconstruction of Korean factories so that we might make our own consumer goods. We are asking for help so that we can help ourselves. We do not want to be always dependent upon you or upon anybody else. The sooner we are enabled to earn our own way, the sooner we will cease to be a burden on the American taxpayer. That is our aim: to prove to America that we are deeply grateful by standing on our own feet.

It has never been the policy of America to single out one nation in a world area for such preferential treatment and assistance that the other nations in the same area automatically become dependent on the giant. The American creed, as we know it, is that all peoples, wherever located, should have an equal opportunity to move toward full freedom and dignity.

A FREE AND UNITED KOREA

A new Korea faces a multitude of problems. Foremost among them is the transformation of an agrarian economy to one of industrialization. But there is a hardihood, a stamina, in my people that, ominous as the future may seem at the moment, enables them to hope for a new Korea. In addition, they possess, as they always have possessed, the will to work. They know there *must* be a new Korea, if only for the reason that the old Korea is gone. Modern warfare has virtually wiped it off the face of the map.

But it is inconceivable to any Korean to picture the future of our nation on any basis except complete unity, for north of the hated 38th parallel—hated because it was imposed upon us as a basis of our division—north of the parallel are hydroelectric plants necessary to industrialization, while the south is our food basket. In far southern Korea, for example, many farms are able to grow two crops a year because of the equable climate.

Now one is entitled to ask: Well, what of the future, anyway? My answer must be blunt, a free and united Korea by force of arms if all else fails, or a nation and people destroyed at the hands of Communist aggression.

You must realize, though, that we do not want to fight because we like to fight, but because thousands of our countrymen in the north are the victims of Communist barbarity. They are our flesh and blood. They call out to us to rescue them from banishment to the remote provinces of Manchuria and Siberia in order that their homes and lands may be seized by Chinese Communist colonizers. Other thousands of them are dying of malnutrition and ill-treatment.

Suppose the Communists invaded and held a portion of the United States, uprooting your fellow-Americans and sending them into the jungles of the Amazon or the frozen wastes of Alaska? Would you respond to their calls for help? Of course you would. You have proven on battlefields in many other places what you would do for freedom. All we ask for now is understanding of the steps we feel we may be forced to take.

We Koreans prefer an honorable death, alone if need be, to the dishonor of Communist slavery. We have learned the immortal words of your great patriot, Patrick Henry, "Give me liberty, or give me death!" and we are repeating those immortal words today. I do not think you can blame us for that. Please be patient with us. We do not want any more war if we can help it. But what are we going to do? What would you do? We will go along, and if the Korean issue can be settled by peaceful means, we are more than willing. But we are asking if the peaceful means fail, then what is your alternative plan? What do you intend to do? Throw up your hands and say, "We are defeated," while your boys and our boys are sitting on the hills of Korea to be shot at like ducks when the Communists are ready? What are we going to do?

We are not the first people to prefer death to dishonor. The pages of history recount others, though none more glorious than the annals of your own Revolution. There were many who thought, in that day and age, that the new America of 1776, which preferred death rather than the loss of liberty, might not long exist. But look at this great nation today—the hope of the free world.

That chapter in your history is the most compelling reason for the Korean people, in their hour of trial and adversity, to know that some day there will be a new and reunited Korea.

His Excellency You Chan Yang, M.D., Washington, D. C., has been Ambassador of Korea to the United States since 1951. Educated in Hawaii and in this country, he practised medicine in Hawaii from 1923 to 1951, and in World War II directed a medical unit under the Office of Civilian Defense. Since student days he has been active in Korean independence movements, and has recently developed a plan for rebuilding South Korean schools and training Korean technicians. He took part in the negotiations for the Japanese-Korean peace treaty which went into effect in April 1952 and also in those of October 1953.

The Role of the United States in the Far East

By Arthur H. Dean

WHAT can we do to bring about a lasting peace in Korea and the unification of that sorely harassed land? First we must decide what we mean by "peace" and second what we mean by "unification."

As most of you know, the people of Korea, although not themselves Chinese, were for many years governed by Chinese kings under a mild suzerainty to China. Following the defeat of China by Japan in 1895 and of Russia by Japan in 1905, President Theodore Roosevelt by the Treaty of Portsmouth in 1905 arranged for Japan to have a protectorate over Korea; in 1910 Japan annexed Korea.

One of the major policies of the Allies in the last war was to restore freedom to the long-suffering people of Korea and to bring about its freedom, unity, and independence. The able and gallant leader of the Korean people, Syngman Rhee, has spent his entire life to achieve this end, first against the Japanese and now against the Communists. For purely military considerations after the U.S.S.R. had agreed to come into the war against Japan in 1945, Russian military authorities were invited to accept the surrender of Japanese troops in Korea north of the 38th parallel—a purely fictitious line. Subsequent attempts to bring about the unification of Korea by negotiations with the U.S.S.R. proved futile, and after a plebiscite in the southern part conducted under the auspices of the United Nations, the Republic of Korea, under the Presidency of Syngman Rhee, was set up south of the 38th parallel. A de facto Communist government was set up by the U.S.S.R. in the north.

THE KOREAN WAR

In June of 1950 the Republic of Korea was attacked without warning or justification by forces from north of the 38th parallel, inspired and armed by the U.S.S.R.

Following the adoption of resolutions by the Security Council of the United Nations in June and July 1950, we contributed troops to the United Nations command, along with fifteen other members of the United Nations and the Republic of Korea. The United States took on the unified command of the United Nations' collective effort to put down aggression, and President Truman gave the post to one of our outstanding military leaders, General Douglas MacArthur.

We have reason to be proud of our brilliant achievements in Korea, but after the Chinese Communists came into the war in November and December 1950 we did not unify Korea by military might. Among other things we did prove that armed aggression does not pay, and we stopped the timetable of Red aggression in the Far East.

I shall not dwell on the fighting and the events leading to the signing of the Armistice on July 27, 1953, or on the history of the drafting of Paragraph 60, incorporated into the Armistice Agreement.

THE ARMISTICE AGREEMENT

The Armistice Agreement was signed by military commanders on both sides. One side—our side—is made up of the sixteen members of the United Nations contributing troops and the Republic of Korea. The other side consists of the

Chinese Communists and the North Korean Communists.

Paragraph 60 recommended "to the Governments of the countries concerned on both sides" that "a political conference of a higher level of both sides" be held by October 28 by representatives appointed respectively in order "to settle through negotiation the questions of the withdrawal of all foreign forces from Korea, the peaceful settlement of the Korean question, etc."

As a result of the Cairo Declaration in December 1943, the Potsdam Declaration of July 1945, and the U.S.S.R. declaration of war against Japan, August 8, 1945, the "Korean question" referred to in Paragraph 60 of the Armistice Agreement may be defined as the unification of a free, independent, and democratic Korea. The "withdrawal of all foreign forces" referred to in Paragraph 60 was defined in the Armistice negotiations to mean the withdrawal of "non-Korean forces."

KOREAN GEOGRAPHY

If you will look at the map you will note Korea's geographical propinquity to China and Manchuria on the west, Manchuria on the north, and the U.S.S.R. on the northeast, which surround it like gigantic pincers, and if you will look about 200 miles to the west from Pyongyang, you will find on the Liaotung Peninsula the great naval and industrial warm-water ports of Dairen and Port Arthur, the eastern terminus of the Chinese Eastern Railroad.

To the north of Korea itself are the winding Yalu and Tumen Rivers. North and northwestward lies Manchuria and to the extreme northeast the U.S.S.R. itself fronts on Korea.

The great industrial city of Mukden is about a hundred miles from the North Korean border. South of Mukden and north of the Korean border is the steel city of Anshan. The important industrial and railroad center of Harbin lies about 250 miles to the north. Just 60 miles to the northeast of the island of Chongjin (Seishin) on the northeast coast of Korea you will find the large Russian naval center of Vladivostok, which is also the eastern terminus of the Trans-Siberian Railroad.

Korea, as you know, is a 525 mile long S-shaped peninsula extending southward from Manchuria and Soviet Russia to within less than 120 miles of the island of Kyushu in southern Japan. It is shaped somewhat like Florida but is very mountainous. Its area of 85,000 square miles is approximately equal to that of Minnesota. The area actually available for cultivation is relatively small.

The east coast of Korea faces the Sea of Japan. To the west across the Yellow Sea lies China. To the south is the Korea Strait and approximately 500 miles to the south lies the island of Formosa, now occupied by the Nationalist Government of China and its intrepid leader Chiang Kai-shek, whom we are supporting both morally and materially in his fight against the Communists.

Then approximately 390 miles farther south are the Philippines. On the mainland south of China and some 600 miles or more west of the Philippines are Indochina, Burma, and Thailand. Further south lies Malaya. To the east of Malaya and south and west of the Philippines lies Indonesia, that is, Borneo, Java, Sumatra, and Celebes, and further south, Australia and New Zealand. To the northwest of Burma lie eastern Pakistan and India.

Korea lies some 5,600 air miles from Seattle and 9,000 miles from our east coast, no further apart in time by air travel than many points in the United States by rail.

Thus you can easily see that it would

not be much of a problem for the other side either to invade Korea or to withdraw non-Korean Communist forces into China or Manchuria, a relatively short distance north or west across the Yalu River. But it is quite a problem for us to withdraw our forces.

A DIVIDED KOREA

Although the statement is an oversimplification, for the most part the hydroelectric power, the electrochemical industries, the manufacturing plants of heavy industry, the mines, and the heavy timber are in the North. South of the 38th parallel the people are for the most part engaged in farming—principally rice, beans, or barley—in woodcutting, fishing, or in light manufacturing—textile or foundry work, pottery, and some glass. At present, we are engaged in a great program of rehabilitation in the South.

The people in all of Korea were remarkably homogeneous and united before the attack, and the economy of the entire country was reciprocal. Under the Japanese rule the economy was geared to Japanese needs, and Korea was an outlet for the Japanese market. Now it is rudely hacked into two parts, with an almost fanatical desire on the part of the Communists to unite the economy of the North with that of China and Manchuria. The South has been relatively harder hit, and it will be much more difficult for it to survive without the economy of the northern part.

The problem, therefore, of what we can do to achieve a free, united, independent, and democratic Korea where the people can live happily and carry on their normal peaceful pursuits and how we can obtain the truly effective withdrawal of the Chinese Communist forces from Korea is exceptionally difficult.

Communist reports are very misleading, and generally exaggerated; they conveniently omit statistics or compare statistics for unlike periods. But from present Communist reports it would seem that the Chinese Communists with the aid, or at least promised aid, from the U.S.S.R., East Germany, Czechoslovakia, Rumania, Hungary, and Poland are doing their best to rebuild North Korea and to incorporate and integrate the economic life of North Korea into that of Manchuria and Communist China to the north and west and to prevent the unification of North and South Korea into a free, independent, united, and democratic Korea.

The much harassed and sorely tried people of Korea deserve a better fate than a divided Korea. Their soldiers fought bravely and gallantly by the side of our own and the other members of the United Nations command and they are eager and willing to learn. No people has ever defended itself more bravely or more courageously.

When you see the terrible destruction in Korea and the hard, grinding, unremitting toil which is the daily lot of the Korean people today, and the happy, bright-faced children trooping to school —most inadequately clad for the rather severe Korean winter—your heart goes out to them and you wish that there were some way you could bring an end to their trial, tribulation, and suffering. But how?

THE HOPE OF UNIFICATION

President Rhee believes and advocates that properly supervised elections should be held in the North for the seats in the Korean Parliament that are now vacant. He is confident that in free elections his compatriots north of the 38th parallel will choose proper anti-Communist representatives and that he and his party will get the great bulk of the delegates.

But the Communists have now occupied North Korea since the latter part of 1945. Millions of people have been killed or maimed or have fled southward—and if reports can be believed, many thousands of anti-Communists have been forcibly carried away into Chinese Communist or U.S.S.R. slave labor camps, and Chinese Communist farmers have been moved into North Korea to take their places.

The Communists are fanatical zealots dedicated to their unholy cause, and short of renewing hostilities it is difficult to see what will persuade them to unification. Let us examine the possibilities:

1. Would they willingly allow the government of Syngman Rhee with its well-known hatred of Communism to have complete control of the governmental machinery in the North? Even if we were to offer them abundant economic aid and financial rehabilitation greater than that now offered by the U.S.S.R. and the Communist countries of eastern Europe, what would they gain by it?

2. We certainly do not want a Communist coalition government for all of Korea with Communist ministers et cetera.

3. We certainly do not want to recognize the independence of North Korea.

Chinese Communist desires

The Chinese Communists apparently want at least six things: (1) the complete withdrawal of all United Nations and United States forces; (2) the giving up of our right to station troops in Korea pursuant to our Military Defense Pact; (3) the unification of Korea under Communist auspices or at least the complete retention of the northern part or a coalition government in the southern part; (4) the recognition of their regime by the United States; (5) admission into the United Nations and the expulsion of Nationalist China; (6) the withdrawal of the trade embargo

voted on Communist China and North Korea by the United Nations.

The clear and ringing speech of Secretary of State Dulles on March 29 before the Overseas Press Club, followed up by President Eisenhower's and Senator William F. Knowland's announcements, seems to constitute an effective answer to all of these desires and to indicate that our policy will continue to be one of strong opposition to the Chinese Communist regime.

Coalition government

A coalition government with the Communists is, of course, a fool's paradise, as Jan Masaryk in Czechoslovakia found to his sorrow. The Chinese peasants having received "land distribution" must now give it back to a "cooperative collective." Communist promises have a way of disappearing into thin air. A coalition government would lead to a gradual if not complete paralysis of governmental functions. Neither Korean nor American public opinion would tolerate it—certainly we could not agree to economic rehabilitation of or military aid to a coalition government with Communists.

Unification under appropriate workable and realistic terms is certainly a desirable goal. But we ought not to be confused by words, for unification by coalition with the Communists loses its meaning. Although we should, of course, explore every basis of unification that has a workable chance, we must not surrender the tangible gain of the Korean War for the sake of a so-called "successful conference."

The situation in Korea and on Formosa and in Japan has been changed sharply by the serious difficulties the French and the free Vietnamese face at this truly critical juncture in Indochina where the control of the free world in that area is in so much difficulty.

A Program for the United States

In order to bring about better results and in order to get the complete cooperation of the free world I believe we should do at least nine things in the Far East.

1. We must convince by clear and appropriate action the governments of the Far East, the Communists, and our own sincere friends that we are prepared to deter aggression and infiltration and that we will be able to respond vigorously and ably at places and with means of our own choosing.

2. We must convince them that we are not going to withdraw or become fainthearted or leave our friends in the lurch. This is of vital importance.

3. We must use every means at our command consistent with decent and normal relations between allies, and with due humility on our part, to convince our French allies that it is in their own best interest so to establish the Associated States within the French Union that not only the Vietnamese, Cambodian, and Laotian people but others as well are truly convinced they are independent and are fighting for their own independence and not to preserve some vestige of colonialism.

4. This must be done on a cordial, consultative, constructive, friendly basis with the French, the leaders in Vietnam, and if at all feasible with other leaders in the Far East, so that world opinion will accept the political results as the fundamental concept of true independence for which free men can honestly fight. It will be necessary truly to unite local sentiment behind the government and to deprive the Communists of one of their great propaganda weapons—namely, that we are fighting to further colonialism. We must convince the peoples of Asia we are not trying to prevent a people from achieving independence.

5. We must assure the French and the peoples of Indochina, India, Burma, Thailand, Indonesia, Australia, and New Zealand that we propose to make such efforts as may be necessary to drive the Communists from Indochina on both a political and military basis and that those who are on our side will not be fighting on the wrong side.

6. We must work out in consultation with the French the further training of the Vietnamese army and pave the way for the eventual withdrawal of French forces and their return to metropolitan France.

7. Despite religious and ideological differences, we must do everything within our power to work with the Indians, the Burmese, the Thais, the Indonesians, and others in order to convince them of the terrible dangers of our not being united and of the dangers in a fence-sitting policy.

8. We must work out an economic policy toward this part of the world which is not based on "neocolonialism" but which is unbiased and free from any colonial motive or interest so we can woo them away from believing that Communism is an attractive theory, either intellectually or in practice.

Asian revolution

9. By friendly persuasion and not by domination we must attempt to convince those who disagree with us that we are not completely wrong in our approach to the problem. Prime Minister Nehru, and indeed Supreme Court Justice William O. Douglas and to a lesser extent Adlai Stevenson in his recent Godkin lectures at Harvard, if I read them correctly, believe that the revolution in Asia, of which Communism is but a manifestation, cannot be halted; that Communism must be allowed to thrash about in a somewhat irresponsible manner; that given time, patience, and the right treatment, the revolution

in Asia will flow into constructive channels; and that we must evolve the minimum conditions on which we would be willing to live and let live with the Chinese Communists.

This argument continues that the right treatment is not a show of military strength and opposition, as this will only provoke; that the right treatment is economic and technical assistance on as large a scale as can be provided to overcome the hunger for food and land and to restore to the Asian a sense of pride in his own individualism; that he must be treated not as a mere creature of the West, for such treatment makes the Asian turn to the false, facile, and fleeting promises of the Soviet Union; the wrong treatment is for the West to ally itself with corrupt and discredited regimes and to bolster them with military aid, money, and equipment, until they are attacked by people rising in revolt under Communist leadership and then to provide active support of the attacked against the native people.

In a sense, they are, of course, correct that Asian nationalism can be channeled but not dammed, and that promises of a full stomach, of more land and greater yields, and of the reduction of crop loans and interest payments by the simple expedient of killing the landowner, the usurer, the money lender, and the owner of the rice mills have a great ideological appeal to a poverty-stricken and exploited people. The Japanese slogan of "Asia for the Asians" had a great appeal for these people, yet some of these countries were overrun by the Japanese and in part liberated by the Communists. Today we are supporting the Japanese and fighting the Communists.

But I wonder how far this argument is correct, for after thirty-seven years the Russian Communists do not appear to wish to work with us. To my mind

it is too simple to say we could better solve the whole matter by being kind to Communists.

I do believe that experts in politics, agriculture, plant disease, fishery, agronomy, biology, agricultural marketing, nutrition, and home economics could work wonders. The problem is not just one of more money and more military aid and more industrialization, important though they may be.

Must the U. S. Get Involved in Indochina?

There are undoubtedly those among you who shrug their shoulders and say, "We cannot save the world; we cannot prevent the inevitable from happening; we cannot bankrupt ourselves; and we cannot promise military aid all over the world." Having just fought and at least temporarily put out the great blaze in Korea, why do we wish to get involved in this new great fire in Indochina?

The problem is admittedly exceptionally difficult. If the Communists overrun Indochina, they may in time overrun Burma, Thailand, Malaya, and Indonesia, go north to the Philippines, and attack or infiltrate the Philippines and Formosa from the east. Indochina, Burma, and Thailand presently export more food, particularly rice, than they produce, and if the Communists are in control there they can effectually starve Japan or demand her production and the withdrawal of our troops.

It does not seem to me that we can safely regard this situation as inevitable. For if Communism is so extended, the problems of Prime Minister Nehru and the people of India will be sorely accentuated. The free world may not survive an evolution which might take generations.

The problem and its correct solution concerns you, your children, our future as a nation, and all of our lives.

THE MILITARY SITUATION

Today in the northern part of Indochina the Communist Vietminh forces led by Ho Chi-minh are organized, financed, and supplied by the Chinese Communists and are fighting the French and Vietnam forces in a costly and bloody battle at the garrison of Dienbienphu, located in Tonkin between the Mekong and Red or Tonkin Rivers, west of Hanoi and north of Luangprabang and east of Burma and Thailand. The Communists have guerrilla forces in many places in the rice paddies and jungles. They also are attacking southward in Cambodia, in the regions of Muongsay and Attopeu.

The fighting is to determine whether the forces of freedom or Communism shall prevail. While militarily, perhaps, the battle at Dienbienphu is not of fundamental strategic importance, nevertheless the defeat of the French and Vietnam forces there may cast a spirit of gloom and lessen the will of the Vietnamese and the French to fight the Communists. Defeat may make the path of the Geneva Conference and the future of the French Union exceptionally difficult.

If Indochina were to fall into Communist hands or if there were a coalition or a Communist government for part of it, our own problems in the Pacific would be made immeasurably more difficult.

FRENCH AND VIETNAMESE ATTITUDES

The problem in Indochina is a frightfully complicated one. Many native Vietnamese, who have much to lose if the Communists win, appear either to be supporting Ho Chi-minh or to be fence sitting.

In relation to their population and gross national product, the French in the eight-year war have suffered terrible loss of life and have spent vast sums of money in Indochina; the vision of endless fighting in its rice paddies and steamy jungles is abhorrent. True, the United States has been most generous in financial and military support. But the fact that we have thought it wise to conclude an armistice in Korea, the dissatisfaction caused by our insistence on the ratification of the European Defense Community, and the French fear of the rise of German militarism— all exploited by the Communists—contribute to the general distaste with which French people view the situation. The French have made enormous strides in developing this primarily agricultural nation and bringing it into the French Union, but the problem of satisfying the native people on colonialism still remains.

The Japanese occupation during the war, the quarrels between the Pétain regime and the Free French, the necessity for British and Nationalist Chinese troops to occupy the country in order to disarm the Japanese, the constant propaganda and infiltration of the Vietminh, the presence of Communist China on the north, the obtaining by Burma of its complete independence from the British, the organization of the Indonesian Republic to the south and east, the policy of the United States in granting the Philippines their complete independence, and the friction of Cambodia and Laos with Thailand, exacerbated by the annexation of some territory by Thailand with the approval of the Japanese during the war—all make it difficult to rally the native people in support of Vietnam and the French Union against the Communists.

WHERE SHOULD THE U. S. STAND?

With brains and courage and determination to stand by our allies and see it through, to prevent any further extension of the diabolical forces of Communism in Asia, I am sure we can make a greater contribution to the solution of the problem of our present-day civilization by taking affirmative action than we can by standing aloof and allowing the creeping paralysis of Communism gradually to extend over the Far East and southeast Asia.

We must make it possible for these downtrodden and harassed peoples to be restored to a sense of human dignity as creatures of God. We must enable them to believe that they belong in our society as equals and that we are not interested either in exploiting them or in using them to protect our own sons.

We have recently had a very clear and lucid account from the chairman of the Atomic Energy Commission of the latest explosion of a thermonuclear bomb at Bikini Atoll, of the falling of white ashes on Japanese fishing boats many miles away, and of the subsequent illness of the crew. The papers report that the danger area for the new tests has been substantially increased. Whether or not we understand all of these details, at least we know that another war using such weapons might wipe out or at least threaten to wipe out a large segment of our existing civilization and our highly concentrated industrial life. Indeed, the question arises as to whether we or our opponent could survive another such war; or, if we survived physically, whether we could ever again gain individual freedom as we now know it, or ever again live orderly, normal, human lives.

Perhaps at last we have come to the point where the weapons science has built are so truly terrible that we shall really have peace from physical war. In any event it behooves us to do our level best to think imaginatively and to strive for a realistic peace and to do everything that we can by negotiation to bring about a peaceful and constructive settlement of the world's problems.

Arthur H. Dean, LL.B., New York City, was Special Ambassador of the United States to Korea, 1952–1953. He was admitted to the New York State Bar in 1923, and has since practiced law in New York City. He is a director of various business firms, a trustee of the Carnegie Foundation for the Advancement of Teaching and of Cornell University, a director of the Educational Television and Radio Center (Ford Fund) and of the Japan Society, a member of the School of Law Advisory Board of Fordham University, and a member of the Committee on Studies of the Council on Foreign Relations. He has lectured and written on legal, economic, and financial subjects.

The Soviet-Chinese Complex

By Adolf A. Berle, Jr.

THE United States is once more in an area of high tension and great pressure in the Far East. The Soviet Union in close alliance with the Communist government of China has stepped down somewhat its military aggression in Europe but it has accelerated its military effort in the Far East. Though an armistice has stopped active fighting in Korea, the other branch of the Korean War—aggression against Indochina— has been increased. In substance, the Soviet-Chinese military push has been transferred from Korea to Indochina. There, it is clear, the Soviet-Chinese group believe they will find softer resistance, and they are there playing for an immensely more valuable stake.

The American State Department will meet this problem in full force in the Geneva Conference. It does not seem likely that the Geneva Conference can settle anything, and no hopes whatever should be indulged along that line. It does seem possible that a firm position taken by the country may be of help in creating conditions which will end the aggression later on.

The Department of State can take just as firm a position as American public opinion represented in the Congress will let them. Far too little is being done to inform the United States as to the real dangers involved. The fall of southeastern Asia to the Soviet-Chinese complex would be a disaster rivaling the shift of China from the free world to the Kremlin world.

We can afford no more misunderstandings. American policy towards China is not a giveaway to South Korea or to the French empire in Indochina or to anyone else. It must be based on the cold realization that if the Chinese Communist government in alliance with the Kremlin takes over the Asiatic mainland, the world balance will be definitely shifted away from the West and no "military new look" will be able to change that fact.

But while armies are grinding against each other and while diplomacy is temporarily unable to resolve the questions, it is possible that a bridge can be made to communicating, extraofficially, and to discovering what common ground does exist between Communist China and the West. I think there is an area here which can and must be explored; if this exploration is pursued over the next few years it may be possible to bring the Chinese situation once more into negotiating range.

In the long run, China must either act independently of the Soviet Union, or she must be (as she nearly is now) a Russian province. Her interest is that she shall be independent—and that also is the interest of the United States and of the world. The Chinese problem is peculiarly economic, and it is the kind of problem in the solution of which the United States can assist far more than the Soviet Union. The Chinese choice is much the same as the American: either the problem of world peace will be settled by the force of hydrogen bombs, or it will be settled by the understanding that no nation can be aggressor, seizing other countries by force of arms. This is not a case for eighteenth-century diplomacy or for newly styled negotiation. It is a straight case of convincing the Soviet-Chinese complex that more aggression can only mean war, and that the West can not afford to surrender more territory to an aggressive combination.

These are the conclusions; the reasoning leading to them follows.

THREE YEARS AGO

Three years ago the American Academy of Political and Social Science considered the problem of American policy in Asia.[1] The Korean War was then less than a year old. The Communist point of view was set out by Mr. Juliusz Katz-Suchy,[2] representing the Communist government of Poland. He affirmed that the Communist movement was a part of the "irreversible trend of history," and, quoting the words of Prime Minister Nehru of India, that the New China (meaning thereby Communist China) was "a great power to be dealt with on terms of equality by other great powers."[3] This writer, for his part, disclaimed any revelation as to trends of history. Instead he went through some painful arithmetic, fully accepting the power and importance of China but coming to a grim result:

The United States, and with her the peace of the world, is endangered by the emergence of any major aggressive Asian power if that power is allied in simultaneous aggression with a major aggressive European power.[4]

THE CURRENT SITUATION

In the past three years, nothing has occurred to invalidate that bitter conclusion. The tide of events has tended to confirm it. The Korean War is not at an end: there is merely an armistice. Prospects even of holding a peace conference are dim, and those of negotiating a real settlement of the contest seem at the moment still dimmer. Meanwhile, part at least of the strategic and military resources formerly devoted by China to the Korean fighting have merely been channeled southward and are flowing from China to the war now being conducted in Indochina and somewhat less actively in Malaya.

A secondary adventure, the Communist war to seize the Philippine Republic, carried on under the name of the Hukbalahap rising, appears to be near its end, owing to an apparently decisive military and political defeat of the Hukbalahap faction by the Philippine government under the leadership of President Magsaysay. So, as the score presently stands, Russian-Chinese aggression has been defeated, apparently decisively, in the Philippines. It has been stopped at least temporarily by armistice in Korea. It is proceeding full scale in the larger and strategically more important theater of Indochina.

This is certainly not peace. The United States, whatever hesitation and confusion it may have shown in Asian policy prior to 1950, has recognized the situation as pregnant with grave danger of involvement in global war.

Against this background a diplomatic meeting is scheduled to be held in Geneva on April 26, 1954, at which the three principal West European powers have undertaken to sit down with representatives of the Soviet Union and China. So far as public announcement reveals, neither side has given any ground. On the Communist side, agreement upon the Geneva Conference was the signal for intense fighting, the Chinese apparently hoping to present the conference with a fait accompli. On its side the West has no ground to give. Any concession now would appear to be a one-way ticket to future disaster, just as British concessions to Hitler at Munich in 1938 merely fixed the take-off point for World War II. Actually, the Geneva meeting in April is more dangerous in some ways than was

---

[1] THE ANNALS, Vol. 276, July 1951.
[2] Ibid., pp. 48–59.
[3] Ibid., p. 57.
[4] Ibid., p. 67.

Chamberlain's meeting with Hitler at Munich, for Hitler had not completed his offensive and defensive arrangements with the then government of Japan, while at Geneva the Western powers will be faced with a fully matured East-West aggressive alliance—the Soviet Union and China—in being and fully armed. Concession of any territory to that combination threatens the safety at least of the Western Pacific; to make one could easily determine the date and base lines of World War III. Already the Sino-Russian alliance has caused the rearmament of the United States and has occasioned re-examination of the strategy to be pursued. All in all, it is the grimmest Asian complex of circumstances America has faced since V-J Day.

One word of semantic caution.

A good deal has been said about the "New China." This writer has no knowledge whatever of the internal developments in that country. Unhappily this is the situation in which most American observers find themselves. All of us have been treated to a vast amount of speculation about Chinese evolution and probable development. But such speculation is largely impressionistic, and hardly well enough based to use as a guide to policy. We had best, therefore, try to answer the major questions in terms of such solid information as is available. The questions themselves, of course, are clear enough, though the answers are necessarily incomplete. It is not enough to estimate the probable working out of forces there.

SOVIET-CHINESE RELATIONS

First. What are the true relations between the government of the Soviet Union and the government of China? If information on this subject exists in the United States (which is difficult to believe) it has not been given to the public. But we can state, on adequate evidence, that the Soviet government has steadily moved to support the Chinese Communist regime in all diplomatic matters and that her powerful propaganda machine has unfailingly forwarded the Chinese Communist contentions. We do know that the Soviet government has supplied arms and technical assistance in large quantity to Chinese Communist armies on the march. Thus the Korean War was conducted by Chinese armies with Soviet planes, Soviet ammunition, Soviet armor and artillery, Russian organizing experts, and so forth. We now see substantially the same thing happening in Indochina, where even the pretense that Vietminh troops are spontaneously organized native guerrillas has largely been dropped. The Vietminh forces are large organized armies, supplied from Chinese bases, provided by Chinese transport, using modern Russian-made and Russian-supplied munitions of war, in maneuvering full-scale armed conflict.

There is every reason to assume that, for the time being, the Chinese Communist government is acting in complete concert with the plans and policies of the Soviet Union. The unclear point is whether the Chinese Communist government is in substance a captive of the Soviet government or whether it has attained enough strength to claim a partnership relation.

For what one opinion is worth, this writer would feel bound to proceed on the assumption that the Chinese Communist regime is not Moscow's partner but Moscow's captive. The Soviet Union substantially controls the chief industrialized regions in this "New China"—that at least we do know. Russian organization and Russian forces dominate Manchuria; the Soviet Union has military and naval bases in the Dairen–Port Arthur area and she holds military lines of communication to them.

Without contrary knowledge, it would seem probable that Russian troops are stationed so as to guard these lines of communication and incidentally to exert military pressure on the area should this be expedient. This amounts to an almost complete grip on the slender manufacturing resources and military potential of "New China." The situation may be compared to the situation in which the United States would find herself if the Soviet Union controlled the quadrangle Chicago-Pittsburgh-Buffalo-Detroit and, being located next door to the United States as Canada is, held military lines of communication guarded by armed forces to the principal Great Lakes cities. Actually, no serious move of any kind can be made by the "New China" against the desires of the Soviet Union on pain of economic strangulation. If it be said that the Chinese apparently endure strangulation and starvation without uprising (as they do), it may be added that Russian wishes can open up or shut off the military potential which the "New China" must have either to maintain its internal structure or to carry out any foreign aggression.

I conclude then that for the time being the "New China" is for the moment a huge vassal of the Soviet Union, and that in the light of present evidence it would be imprudent for American policymakers to consider her in any other light.

CHINA AS AN INDEPENDENT POWER

Second. What are the present probabilities of Chinese emergence as an independent power?

Emergence of a really independent China as a great power would constitute a major change in the Asian situation. The reasoning in this paper is based on the assumption that there is an existing Sino-Russian complex, aggressive in nature, and moving together in common

development of policy. Diplomacy to the extent that it can operate at all must therefore treat the area as a unit. Obviously, when the area divides, when the Soviet Union and her interests constitute one factor while China and her interests constitute another, and each can be separately dealt with, the condition of affairs will radically alter.

We are told by some that the situation will change, and that China must be considered as China and not as a part of the Russian complex. Protagonists of this view urge that the Chinese interest in the long run is clearly opposed to the Russian. Also, that Chinese governments have often in history been captured and governed by foreign invaders, as for instances in the time of Genghis Khan and the Mongols, and that always the invading forces have been absorbed, whereupon China has resumed her independent integrity. All this is true. The trouble is that there is no possibility of estimating the time factor. Genghis Khan's conquest of China began in the year 1213. Thirty years later his successor, Kublai Khan, was still operating the complex and Genghis' grandson, Batu Khan, was maneuvering at the head of a Chinese and Mongolian army in Europe, not far from the Iron Curtain line which divides East and West today. It was a matter of eighty years or so before the different elements of the vast empire reappeared as independent factors. It is probably the fact that natural expansion of Chinese population almost certainly will eventually threaten Slavic domination of eastern Siberia, to say nothing of the Slavic grip on Manchuria. But it is one thing to foresee this probability a generation or so from now and quite another to proceed on the assumption that the divergence of interest has reached a point leading China to take any line contrary to the will of the Soviet Union. Unquestionably it would be good American diplomacy to encourage China to do so. It would be sheer folly to assume that the present Chinese regime either can or will strike out on its own in the immediate future. The current evidence is all the other way.

It is rumored that high-level conferences are to take place in Moscow between the leaders of the Chinese regime and Mr. Malenkov and his ministers and that these may reveal the real relationship between the two empires. Even if this is true it is difficult to see that this particular conference will occasion any immediate major change in their relationship. There are plenty of weighty matters to discuss—the mere routine business of running the huge complex is vast and difficult. The economics of the double empire is apparently beginning to be onerous for both countries. The Korean War proved a substantial burden on the resources of the United States, and it must have been proportionately a greater burden on the less developed resources of the Sino-Russian group. The burden was not wholly lifted by the Korean Armistice, since a considerable part of the operation appears to have been transferred to Indochina. It appears probable that the Russian population is beginning to be exigent in wanting consumer's goods. Certainly the Soviet government has been publicizing a policy of giving greater consideration to Russian consumer wants. Quite probably internal considerations may press on Moscow to cut down somewhat on the support she is giving her captive Asian partner. Some vague indications suggest that the total food production of the entire area is deficient and that foodstuffs cannot easily be collected by China and sent to the Soviet Union in barter for armaments and manufactured equipment needed to maintain the Chinese aggressive policy. A fair surmise would be that any conference between the Chinese and the Russians at Moscow will be devoted not to debating differences but to cutting their common coat according to the cloth they have. Divergence of the two powers, this writer believes, is ultimately certain, but not in the foreseeable future.

ATTITUDE OF THE CHINESE PEOPLE

Third. Are not the Chinese people essentially peaceful, well-wishers of the United States, and will they not eventually impose a pacific pattern on their government?

Yes, sometime, but clearly not now. Certainly the Chinese Communist government throughout the year 1953 was quite strong enough to conscript armies, to throw them into the Korean War, and to maintain an extremely determined large-scale attack. There is little reason to believe that they are not still in a position to do this.

A little evidence on the other side was provided at Panmunjom. A very substantial number of Chinese prisoners of war, after surrender to the United Nations armies, made it abundantly clear they were determined not to return within the Communist lines. In China, as also in the Soviet Union, it is sufficiently clear that there are considerable elements in the population who will desert Communist leadership at the earliest practical opportunity. In the Korean War, however, they did not prove strong enough to modify the war plans of the Chinese Communists.

NECESSARY U. S. DECISIONS

The conclusion is simple. We have sound historic economic, ethnic, and political grounds for believing that Soviet domination of the Chinese government, and of its policy and armed action, will not continue forever. These suggest lines along which long-range Western policies may be framed. This huge complex is not a monolith; its maintenance involves plenty of problems. There is not undivided loyalty of Russians to the Soviet regime or of Chinese to the Communist regime, let alone Russian loyalty to Chinese aims or Chinese interest in Russian plans. But, in the year 1954, these weaknesses are insufficient to check the continuance either of Soviet or of Communist aggression, developed according to an agreed-on plan of joint strategy. The plain fact of the matter is that the Sino-Russian impact is able to push armed forces of both countries according to unified strategic plans, and that in Asia the alliance is actually executing a strategic plan of armed aggression now.

The result of that has been to force certain decisions on the United States, and they are in the making at this moment. Because the Russo-Chinese complex has the military initiative, the decisions have to be taken under pressure. They will furnish the bases for the American position at the Geneva Conference. In their implications, they are extremely serious.

In considerable measure they parallel the conditions created in June 1950 when the attack of the North Korean armies forced some very swift decisions on a harried American government. Then it was clear that not to prevent seizure of South Korea would be taken as a plain signal that it had best make terms with the Russo-Chinese force; and the United States, rightly, decided to invoke the aid of the United Nations and to resist. Today an exactly similar thrust on a far larger scale is proceeding in Vietnam and Laos, and failure to meet it almost inevitably entails the ultimate loss of Thailand and a renewed upsetting of the hard-won order which prevails in Burma and Malaya. More than these territories are at stake. The newly won independence of Indonesia has not achieved for that country a solid institutional base. Were southeast Asia

in Communist hands, the fate of that vast archipelago would be in doubt, to put it mildly. Further, control of the strategic materials and the rice production of that area could result in great distress in Japan, to say nothing of its eventual effect on certain needed supplies (notably rubber and tin) used by the West itself. It would be folly to take the view that only some Indochinese territory is at stake here.

Defense of Indochina has devolved on the government of France. This, in the writer's opinion, is a historical accident. If the Vietminh movement had been Indochinese and not primarily Russian-Communist in origin, the problem would have been solved now, just as were the problems of India and Indonesia. But it is one thing to recognize that the time has come to give countries their independence, and quite another to hand them over to an aggressive group seeking world empire. One must remember that the Communist attack is parallel in one respect to the attack of Genghis Khan. He too evolved a doctrine—the Mongolian "Order of God"—which gave the Mongols sovereignty over the entire earth. Resistance was rebellion, not self-defense. Communist dogma assumes that everyone not under their empire is enslaved and that their right is to "liberate" all territories, liberation, of course, being complete when the peoples and lands in question are subjected to their rule. What the French ought to do with Indochina is one question, capable of being resolved. Handing over the territory to the substantially mercenary forces of the Sino-Russian alliance is not a problem for France, but a problem for the entire non-Communist world.

It is, I think, weariness rather than principle that has led the Western world to divide, somewhat, on the policy towards China. France has lost more men and expended more treasure in defending Indochina from her northern neighbor than the United States did in defending South Korea. The British, knowing this, and being uncertain of the American position, have advocated a course of attempting to trade out the problem with Peiping. They have an added incentive to this course in the hope that they may resume their profitable prewar trade with China. They are undismayed by the fact that British recognition of China promptly after the Communist seizure resulted in nothing but a studied series of insults. Britain's associate and our great neighbor, Canada, has indicated through her very able Foreign Minister, Lester Pearson, a considerable sympathy with the British view. The United States has said nothing definitive, though a considerable amount of help in the form of money and weapons and some technical assistance has been delivered to the French and Vietnamese forces and more has recently been promised as a result of General Ely's recent mission. Clearly a tremendous factor here is the American position, and that position is now being outlined.

U. S. political scene

At this point, account must be taken of the American political scene. The country has been alerted to the Communist danger from many angles. Practically all elements in American political life have expressed themselves in favor of resisting the march of Communism. Unhappily the group who have appointed themselves leaders in the anti-Communist drive, the McCarthy wing of the Republican party, have likewise been most vocal in demanding that not an American soldier and if possible not an American dollar should be committed to the defense of overseas territory. Having spotted their dragon, these Saint Georges have leaped on their horses and charged, at full gallop, in the opposite

direction. If their professions are to be believed, defense of the free world must be accomplished by investigating committees, and unhappily this seems to suit the armies of the Sino-Russian aggressors extremely well. Secretary Dulles can go only as far as American public opinion and the American Congress will let him. America's European associates understand that, and being in doubt as to the result may be pardoned if they undertake the lead in proposing solutions.

There is, however, clarifying thought. The United States has a way of exhibiting greatest confusion at the moment when it is on the eve of becoming most resolute. So it was prior to the North Korean invasion in 1950; the immediacy of action and of public reaction came as a shattering surprise both to the Kremlin and to Peiping. For what it is worth, this writer's view is that if the loss of southeast Asia appears imminent, the vast majority of this country will demand decisive action at once. If we are having trouble momentarily in emitting a clear trumpet call, it would nevertheless be folly for the rest of the world to assume that the United States might not react like lightning to more dangerous developments.

So much for background. Let us get at the decisions which the United States seemingly must make as a result of the Communist initiative taken through and by the government of the People's Republic of China.

Demands to be met

For we are faced with certain demands, and all of them have to be dealt with. The Russians and the Peiping radio insist that Communist China should be recognized and admitted to the United Nations. No particular *quid pro quo* is offered: they want it. The French would like either all-out support in the Indochinese defense or American acquiescence in a so-called "negotiated peace" which in practice means a variety of surrender. The British would like to reopen trade with Communist China, hoping that by the combination of recognition and commercial intercourse that country may be won towards a peaceful and law-abiding point of view. The Japanese want larger export markets, knowing that without them the ninety million Japanese in that archipelago will be in serious difficulties. Prime Minister Nehru appears to want Asia left entirely to the Asians, apparently relying on philosophical forces to bring about peace, progress, and order. Mr. Syngman Rhee wants the Chinese out of North Korea. The United States wants a world in which she is not constantly menaced by attack from both Asia and Europe. The Soviet Union wants southeast Asia first, and after that, the rest of the globe to the extent that she can conquer it by the armies of her captive powers, without subjecting herself to attack.

Sorting out these questions, we may tackle them one by one.

RECOGNITION OF COMMUNIST CHINA

First. Should we recognize Communist China?

If the foregoing reasoning is accurate, the answer is no—certainly not at this time. The grounds are rather different from those usually urged.

Nonrecognition, by itself, accomplishes little or nothing. Few countries, especially if they are large, quail or shrivel up because they are not "recognized" and do not send and receive ambassadors. The United States is not materially stronger because it must express its views to and about China through the medium of the newspapers instead of through a direct diplomatic mission. Recognition of a government conveys no expression of approval or disapproval of the internal policies of its government. Most serious practitioners of foreign affairs do not hesitate to recognize a government however much they may dislike its political practices and philosophy—if anything can be gained by recognition.

But in the present case, it seems, nothing would be gained, while something can be lost. Recognition of Communist China implies not merely establishing normal diplomatic relations, but accepting this captive government as one of the controlling powers in the United Nations. Article 23 of the United Nations Charter names the Republic of China as a permanent member of the Security Council. It is absurd to suggest bringing into the peace-keeping machinery of the United Nations a country which has made war against Korea and signed an armistice there, but which has refused to make peace and is at this moment actively prosecuting war in Indochina under the thinnest camouflage.

This is not to say that there should be no recognition at any time, and still less to say that Communist China should not sometime be admitted to the United Nations. Sir Gladwyn Jebb, presently British Ambassador in Paris, recently made a forceful speech which unquestionably set forth his government's position. In his view, United Nations should be universal, and every country in the world should be in it and amenable to its obligations and discipline. If, as seems probable, the Communist regime in China has come to stay for awhile, this theory would include the present government. Sir Gladwyn is right: the bulk of China does belong inside the United Nations, and this would go with recognition. But the present problem is whether a captive China, committed either by her own or by Soviet will to aggression, really means to accept the obligations involved in entering the United Nations. It is one thing to admit a member to an organization, being convinced that the member will join in and forward its work. It is another to admit a tough, or a gangster, who hammers at the door with a gun butt. A Communist government which would join in fostering and maintaining the peace of the world would be welcome. Any government not prepared to do that is no real member of the group, however sanctified by election and diplomatic acceptance.

It follows that recognition, and with it in all probability membership in the United Nations, should only be granted on very clear conditions, to be established in fact and not by words.

The minimum conditions of recognition would have to be immediate, complete, wholehearted withdrawal by the Chinese Communist regime from the Indochinese war, and from North Korea with real liquidation of the Korean question, and registration of the Chinese-Russian agreements as agreement of collective defense in accordance with the provisions of Article 51 of the United Nations Charter. There should also be an understanding that the status quo in Formosa will be preserved for some considerable time to come. But there is not the most shadowy reason for believing, at the moment, that the Chinese Communist government would do any of these things. At Geneva, it is quite likely to demand that the United States pull out of the whole Pacific area. This scarcely leaves any real basis for talking; more harm than good would be done by another negotiation Panmunjom style.

The policy of not recognizing Communist China, nevertheless, ought not to be doctrinaire. As and when anything substantial can be gained by it, there is no reason why recognition should not be extended. The writer surmises that the time will come, in a few years, when recognition may be of positive use. Apparently nothing can be gained by it now, either for the United States or for the peace of the world. But nonrecognition is an expedient, not a principle.

CHINA AND INDOCHINA

Second. A decision must be taken whether the United States will or will not prevent Communist China from taking all or any part of Indochina, either directly through her own armies or indirectly through the subsidized and maintained armies of Vietminh.

This is a massive decision: the military problem of Indochina has, strategically, at least four or five times the magnitude of the Korean problem. Tentatively, we have already decided to join the Indochina defense. The American government has given arms, planes, technical assistance, and financial help to the defending French and Vietnamese forces. The decision, as far as it goes, seems justified. Passive acquiescence in the seizure of South Korea in 1951 would have signaled to all Asia that they had best make terms with the Soviet Union and its satellite China. Acquiescence in the seizure of Indochina would lead to a caving-in of the entire southeast Asian structure. It is a bitter decision to have to make, but I see little escape from applying the Truman doctrine to Indochina.

This does not mean that we commit ourselves to defend the French empire there. Clear-cut independence for the three Indochinese countries of Laos, Vietnam, and Cambodia may well prove a necessary step. It means, quite simply, that we commit ourselves to keeping the Soviet Union, the Chinese Communist government, or any group acting on their behalf, from taking over. Otherwise southeast Asia becomes part of the Russo-Chinese complex, which in turn has the proclaimed objective of smashing the West whenever it can.

And whatever other complaints we may have about the Soviet-Chinese empire, we cannot accuse them of not attempting to carry out their declared objectives.

I do not, of course, forget Dr. Katz-Suchy's words in 1951. He said that the People's Republic of China had at the foundation of its foreign policy the "possibility and necessity for peaceful coexistence with the capitalist world." [5] Only a few months later Communist China formally entered the war against the United Nations. The propaganda words of Communist diplomats, like Hitler's word in 1938 that he meant to stop after absorbing Czechoslovakia, are worth exactly nothing. The fact is that Communist China probably will not attack surrounding territory if she believes that she can and will be successfully resisted. Perhaps the best service that can now be rendered to world peace is to make it plain that resistance can and will be interposed and to make it absolutely plain that a non-aggressive Communist China need have no fear of attack.

This brings into consideration the so-called "New Look" in military policy. It has been indicated that our military policy from now on will rest less on throwing large bodies of troops into a particular area and defending on the ground, and more on the possibility of long-range air attacks to center. Perhaps so. But, as Mr. Walter Lippmann has recently pointed out, there seems no good reason why the United States should make commitments of any kind now as to scope and methods of military action should that be needed—as every right-minded person hopes it will not. A government like that of China or the Soviet Union which enters on acts of aggression in this hair-trigger balance takes all the risks there are.

[5] THE ANNALS, Vol. 276 (July 1951), p. 58.

There is no point in making threats. Still less is there any point in suggesting to any aggressor that its risk can be estimated, minimized, or limited. If and when military action is required, our country will have to take whatever military action then appears wisest under all the circumstances.

BLOCKADE OF CHINA

Third. There is raised the question of continued blockade of Communist China.

This is not a decision which the United States can take by itself. It must obtain the assent of its allies and the neighboring countries. It is clear that in two cases at least—Great Britain and Japan—governments with which we have to act do not favor blockade. They want, and perhaps need, the trade. So also does Communist China.

This is a case for a flexible policy, working with facts as they are. Admiral Radford is reported to believe that an all-out naval blockade would be a real answer to Chinese aggression, eventually compelling adoption of a pacific course on the part of the Peiping government. In case of all-out resistance in Indochina, this probably will come about. In less pressing circumstances, I personally would like to see a situation in which trade in the non-strategic or less strategic materials was opened with Communist China, giving her people an interest in a state of affairs in which that trade could be maintained. Such trade currents ought to be sufficiently controlled so that at the first indication of continued Chinese supply to aggressive operations—including Indochina—the trade could be shut off. Normal economic operations with the world ought to be available to any peaceful country, Communist or non-Communist. Such relations ought not to be available when and to the extent that they assist in carrying on operations of aggression. Operating such a policy is not easy. But it is probably easier than either opening the gates without reserve or closing them on purely dogmatic grounds.

ASIA FOR ASIANS

Fourth. A decision ought to be taken as to the American attitude toward the Indian "Asia for Asians" view.

As has been observed, the great Asian counterbalancing force, if there is one, is India. Indian policy has been obscure, often not well based on fact, and frequently grounded in what appears to Americans an obstinate failure to recognize elementary realities of the present-day Communist governments. We ought, perhaps, to be a little tolerant of the Indians in this respect. Most Americans were quite as obstinately opposed to recognizing the realities of Communist China until the Korean War broke out in 1950. We need not therefore quarrel too much with Indians: their mistake, if it is one, is much like those we made in America from 1945 to 1951.

This is a case where the advice of the Honorable Chester Bowles seems excellent. We had best be friendly and tolerant of the Indian position as far as it relates to India. That vast population will, in any case, go its own way; we could not control it if we wished. We can assist the growth of a strong and vigorous India without swallowing the theories of Indian statesmen—most of which have not stood the trial of events too well in the past three years.

There is absolutely no doubt that the Soviet Union proposes to control India as soon as she can. There is little doubt that the Russian intentions are not to use Communist China as her instrument in India but rather to effect direct organization of an Indian apparatus trained by and controlled from Moscow. Even the Indians will have

to recognize this in time, and indeed some do already. The interest of the United States in India is that it should be Indian and not Russian, just as our interest in China is that it shall be Chinese and not an appendage of the Kremlin. With patience, good will, and good sense, there should be a deepening of the comprehension of common interest. It will take time. But it is a fair guess that we shall have the time.

REALPOLITIK 1954

Thus far we have tackled the problem of Communist China in terms of *Realpolitik* 1954. This is sound: the problems have been presented to us in just that fashion, and both the Kremlin and the Peiping Foreign Offices are *Realpolitiker* to a greater extent than were the Foreign Offices of Hitler and Mussolini. Because they are aggressors, Americans are forced to meet them on their own ground. But the ultimate solution does not lie in *Realpolitik;* the fact is that governments which depend wholly on it have a short run in history. While we are dealing with *Realpolitik* on its own terms, let us remember that any real solution must depend on liberating deeper and more permanent forces.

GENGHIS KHAN'S EMPIRE

In one aspect, the Russo-Chinese complex is following an ancient Asiatic model—the model set by Genghis Khan in the thirteenth century. This empire attained about the extent and substantial power of the Soviet-Chinese complex of today. Some of its doctrines, particularly its almost theological insistence that God and history had given it the earth, are suspiciously close to the theology of Communist extremists now. But the empire created dissolved into fragments in less than a century. Not only did it not leave its organization behind it, but it left only minimal fragments of culture.

THE REVOLUTIONARY PATTERN

A somewhat similar conclusion can be drawn from study of the life history of great revolutions. Characteristically a revolution takes advantage of favorable circumstances; imposes the rule of a small group or class with a strongly held doctrine; emerges as a dictatorship, which in due time becomes a military dictatorship. The power of the central organization strangles the attractive ideas which form the basis of revolution. Presently it becomes a self-perpetuating military-bureaucratic power regime, not seriously interesting the mass of people. Then, historically, it engages in a war, is defeated, and disintegrates. The Communist revolution in Russia is following with surprising vitality this historic graph. The ablest students of the Russian revolution, among them Professor W. W. Rostow of the Massachusetts Institute of Technology, highlight the growing potential of the Russian armed forces and the progressive weakening of ideological motivation—this after thirty-six years of undisputed power. The Chinese revolution is comparatively younger, but on straight historical grounds we should expect to find the same repetition of revolutionary pattern. Whatever we have to fear, it is not the Communist dogma. The Communist governments will strangle that more effectively than anyone else. It is not accident that the French Revolutionary armies were unbeatable at Valmy and the Russian armies could not be conquered by the intervention of European powers in 1919 and 1920, while, on the other hand, the French armies under Napoleon were decisively defeated in 1813, and Russian soldiers deserted by hundreds of thousands to the Germans in 1941–42. The problem is not what will happen in the long run: we can almost forecast that. Both the Russian and the Chinese governments will break up. The problem is to assure that the world does not tear itself to a bloody and unrecognizable pulp as history accomplishes its inevitable result.

NATIONALISM

A third consideration is more profound, but more difficult of general understanding. This is the fact that nationalism—the nurturing and preservation of independent sovereign states—was probably logical in the eighteenth century, extremely useful in the nineteenth and early part of the twentieth century, and in mid-twentieth century is beginning to cease to be logical or even useful for many purposes. Only the largest countries can really attain it at all, and even they can only support it with the greatest of difficulty. A comparatively small country with determination, will, and a devoted population handling its economic life without too much reference to the neighboring areas could, two centuries ago, put enough force into the field to stand off even the more powerful neighbors, and could maintain a cultural life satisfying its people and often contributing brilliantly to the world. But mid-twentieth-century scientific progress has shredded the former situation into its component parts.

A small country cannot by itself satisfy the demands of its population for a tolerable standard of living. Even a large one has difficulty in doing so. A small country cannot maintain itself against armies equipped with modern weapons for more than a few days—if that. No nation can maintain a satisfactory interchange of ideas on a wholly nationalist basis: even today the American attempt to cut off exchange of contact with the Communist world—an effort cordially reciprocated—has clearly led to the slowing up of scientific progress of both worlds. These are only illustrations.

This is not the time or the place to elaborate the emerging principles of what seems to be the order demanded by the second half of our century. Enough to say that each country must apparently be intensely nationalist in preserving certain values assumed by it to be crucial—as in the United States the fostering and developing of individuality and of the unfettered minds and souls of free men appears to be a value without which life itself means little. To maintain its power and right to preserve these values a nation must, it seems, join at least in regional combinations. There must be a regional combination for defense, and some freedom of action must be surrendered to the group. It must join a regional combination for its economic life and health, and some degree of freedom of action must be surrendered to that group too. But the group which must unite in defense may or may not be the same regional group that unites for economic development. To maintain a degree of communication with the rest of the world, a nation must join in still further group arrangements—from the obvious ones which parcel out wave lengths for radio as a condition of any radios being capable of receiving anything to arrangements which permit ships to sail the seas or airplanes to traverse the sky. Finally, if there is ever to be a world at peace, a nucleus of world organization capable of becoming in time custodian of peace and administrator of a degree of law must be built and fostered and maintained— and for this reason if the United Nations were to dissolve tomorrow the world would have to reinvent it.

This means that we need not and indeed cannot be stopped by the perfectly accurate reports of the surge of nationalism in Asia. The accounts of emergent nationalism are entirely accurate as far as they go. The pity is that no one has seriously got to work explaining to the world in general as well as to Asia what nationalism of the twentieth century is and does. Within the American Academy of Political and Social Science are many men capable of doing just that. A first-rate academic statement of the realities of national statehood today would be a powerful force towards the cultivation of peace everywhere, and nowhere more than in the Western Pacific and the Asiatic mainland.

TOWARD COMMUNICATION

Once this is done, or even while it is being done, we can get at the accompanying task of discovering common interest. Terribly, or perhaps hopefully, the Asian nationalist who ties up with a Communist invader has more in common with the United States than he has with the prehensile paw to which he reaches for help. On study it will probably be found that the Asian nationalist wishes to realize personal ambitions as do all politicians; to speak his piece in his own country, to neighboring countries, and, if possible, to the world, as does every American Senator. His less vocal followers want jobs or ready access to substance and a degree of comfort. Americans want the same, and they want it not only for themselves but for others, because exchange with prosperous countries is not only more satisfactory but more profitable. The nation complex wants recognition and participation in the development of world affairs, as do most countries. Probably if a real interchange of ideas on an academic basis were sought instead of inhibited (as current thinking seems to exact) we should be on our way towards a real communication with the great areas of Asia to whom at the moment America and the Western world is a paper dragon conjured up by Chinese and Russian propagandists. Striking is the fact that wherever there has been such communication, notably in the Philippine Republic and to some extent even in Japan, common ground has been found, often against a background of the bitterest hostility.

The People's Republic of China has closed every avenue it can towards common thought or common study. But there are great avenues it cannot close. For one thing, there are powerful Chinese communities all over the Far East outside of the Bamboo Curtain. They begin as far east as Hawaii, on American soil, and run all the way across the East to India. There is evidence that Communist China is in continuous communication with these groups, some of which include the ablest living members of the Chinese race. There is the Nationalist government on the island of Formosa. There are powerful groups in Indonesia. Any general ideology which can be worked out with these groups will, I think, have eventual repercussions on the Chinese mainland and, especially if the search for a common denominator includes other Asian groups as well, we shall begin to find the organizing principles of eventual peace in the Pacific. Few will argue that by passing a magic wand over China any group of Communist revolutionaries has immunized the minds of a very old people to all ideas save those generated in Moscow.

So while we are holding the *Realpolitik* line—as we must—it is time perhaps for universities, economists, students of political theory, and international lawyers to work out and work up methods of communication with their Asian equivalents in those parts of Asia still open to free communication, and for the United States government, perhaps through the United Nations, to assist in transmitting the fruit of that

work. The events of today will be yesterday's newspaper soon enough. The ideas generated will be causative for a long time.

So, at least, the problem comes down from the distant mountaintops of statesmanship to the grasp of an academy of political science. In brief, on both sides of this divided world the diplomats cannot solve the problem, and the soldiers with their hydrogen bombs do not appear to. But in reason and in strength, in tolerance and in charity, in strength and in forbearance, the intellectuals perhaps have their greatest opportunity.

SUMMARY

In brief, the situation stands as follows:

The United States with the United Nations is committed to the defense of South Korea. The United Nations is committed to the defense of Japan and the Philippines. The question is nominally open as to the defense of Indonesia, but at least tentatively American policy has defined itself sufficiently so that that archipelago too falls within the projected defense area. Only tentatively are we committed to assist in the defense of Indochina, but the circumstances are such that the world had best proceed on the assumption that the commitment is definitive.

Clearly, in handling the defense the United States will expect the support of the United Nations. But with or without support defense will go forward in case of aggression.

The method of defense is not definitely settled: it might be by limited war as in Korea; or by naval operations where that would suffice; or by direct attack to center as contemplated by the "New Look." Choice in this matter rests with the United Nations if the United Nations accepts the obligation, otherwise with the United States; it need not be made now. But what has occurred through the discussion of military methods is substantially a statement that an aggressor cannot count on being able to make a limited commitment in a little war, or on being able by taking an aggressive initiative to stake out the place, means, and nature of the ensuing conflict. Perhaps that is as good a place as any to leave the discussion, which from here on out belongs within the council chambers of the Department of Defense rather than the debating halls of diplomatists.

We shall press for liquidation of the Korean struggle and simultaneous withdrawal of Soviet and Chinese support for Vietminh and other aggressive adventures of that kind. Recognition of Communist China must await the actual fulfillment of these conditions, accompanied by at least reasonable cause to believe that they will not be repeated.

A flexible trade policy ought to be worked out, tending to give support to these conclusions.

No encouragement whatever should be given either to the Soviet Union or to the Chinese Communist government; otherwise, this writer believes, the results of any parley at Geneva will resemble the conference which sacrificed Czechoslovakia at Munich in 1938. For that matter we should feel no particular pressure to go into that conference. Politicians like to say that the door of the conference room is the door to peace. Regrettably this writer must testify that on two occasions—the Munich Conference in 1938 and the Hull-Nomura conferences in Washington in 1941—it proved the exact opposite. The conferring parties, in both cases, stepped out of the conference room on to the battlefields.

In both these cases the aggressor governments considered themselves relatively safe in going forward because they thought their prospective victims were unable or unwilling to meet the issue. There is considerable evidence to support the view that had they understood what would happen Germany would not have attacked in 1939 nor Japan in 1941. At this time, a practical, clear-cut position seems to be the line of greatest safety.

Adolf A. Berle, Jr., LL.B., New York City, is professor of corporation law in the Columbia University School of Law and is also engaged in legal practice. He was Assistant Secretary of State (1938–44) and Ambassador to Brazil (1945–46) and has been United States delegate to many Pan American and international conferences. Besides books and articles on corporation law and finance he is the author of The Natural Selection of Political Forces (1950).

The Real China

By V. K. WELLINGTON KOO

IN face of the intense cold war between the Communist and the free world, a war which will probably continue for a long time, and in face of the further fact that the Peiping regime is the most powerful ally of the Soviet Union, what kind of a new China will eventually establish itself on the Chinese mainland is necessarily a matter of great concern. Its bearing and effect upon the safety and future of the United States is bound to be far-reaching. Before I proceed to analyze the situation, survey the possibilities, and draw a conclusion as to what would serve the best interests of America and the free world as well as the welfare and freedom of the Chinese people, it will be useful to say a word about the present condition of Asia as a whole.

China, by virtue of her vast population, immense territory, long history, and highly developed civilization, has always played an important role in the development of the Asiatic continent, especially in eastern Asia from Korea and Japan in the north to the Philippines, Indochina, Burma, Thailand, Malaya, and Indonesia in the south. In considering the role which a new China can play in Asia and the degree of her importance to America we must take into account the condition of Asia today.

THE DANGEROUS BACKGROUND

What then is the existing condition of Asia? It is clear that while two-thirds of its territory and more than half of its population are already placed under Communist domination behind the Iron Curtain, the remaining third of the Asiatic continent is divided in policy and outlook. India, Pakistan, Afghanistan, Burma, Indonesia, and Ceylon have recognized the Communist regime at Peiping and, with the exception of Pakistan, are all pursuing what is known as the policy of neutralism and cultivating the friendship of Communist China.

The free countries of Asia are unorganized as a group, and the relations among some of them are still hampered by suspicion and distrust born of the past. Some of these countries, having only recently attained their full sovereignty and independence, are preoccupied with their domestic problems of consolidation and development. They are also highly jealous of their rights and exceedingly sensitive in their dealings with the outside world. Few of their statesmen appear to be sufficiently seasoned to take a far-seeing and long-range view of the present menacing situation in Asia created by militant Communism. Their attitude unwittingly plays into the hands of Communist China and the whole Communist camp headed by the Kremlin. It facilitates Communist fishing in the troubled waters of Asia and makes more difficult the task of the free world to check the Communist threat in the whole Asiatic and Pacific area.

It is against this fluid and dangerous background of the Asiatic continent that I propose to discuss more directly the question of America and a new China.

FORMOSA AND MAINLAND CHINA

Now, first of all, it is necessary to know what is meant by a new China. On the surface there may appear to be two Chinas: one the Republic of China with its temporary seat on the island of Formosa, and the other the so-called People's Republic of China on the main-

71

land, which, as I shall presently show
you, is not China at all. Some of you
may think it difficult for me in my official capacity to discuss them impar-
tially and even delicate for me to discuss them at all. But let me assure you
that I shall endeavor to make my analysis of them as objective as possible. It
should not be too difficult to bring out
the facts so that even he who runs can
see.

TOTALITARIANISM OF THE PEIPING REGIME

Communist China is ruled by the
Peiping regime, which is euphemisti-
cally described by its sponsors as a
democratic dictatorship. This is a self-
contradictory term. It, in fact, consists entirely of dictatorship and not at
all of democracy. As is known throughout the world, the Chinese Communist
party, aided and abetted by the Soviet
Union, seized political power over the
country by force of arms. There have
been no elections of any kind, and absolute political power is wielded by a
Politburo of the Soviet pattern.

Indeed, the fundamental laws setting
up the regime recognize as citizèns only
those people who are Communist party
members and those deemed to be its
sympathizers and supporters. All other
people, including landlords, the former
bureaucratic class, and the so-called
"Kuomintang reactionaries" and their
"henchmen," are not recognized as citizens but merely as subjects without any
political rights. The whole system is a
totalitarian rule of the most despotic
kind. It is a reign of terror, and the
Communist rulers maintain their power
by a policy of terrorism carried out in
the form of periodic purges of the people and the party itself.

The American Federation of Labor,
after a wide survey of the situation,
found that at least ten million Chinese
were enslaved in labor camps and com-

pelled to work against their will. Mr.
Walter Robertson, Assistant Secretary
of State for Far Eastern Affairs, recently stated publicly that at least fifteen million Chinese have been killed
by the Communist authorities. In fact,
arbitrary arrests and imprisonment of
people by the secret police, mob trials,
mass slaughter, forcible transportation
to outlying regions, and confinement in
labor camps are ordained by the Communist rulers on the mainland as standard methods to keep the people under
subjection and control. The time-honored Confucian classics are banned from
the school curriculum, and 86 per cent
of all the books published in China in
the past half century were ordered to be
burned. The cherished institutions of
the family, filial piety, religion and an-
cestor worship, and mutual devotion of
husband and wife are tabooed as medieval ideas, while the first duty prescribed
for every man, woman, and child in the
land is to bow to the will of the Communist party and obey the orders of
the Communist authorities.

From this brief outline of its nature
and policy, it can be readily seen that
the Chinese Communist regime is anything but Chinese either in its conception and origin or in the policy and
methods which it employs to rule the
people and perpetuate its own power.
Although it is called the People's Republic of China and officially described
as a democratic dictatorship, it is alien
to the Chinese both in spirit and in
action. It maintains its control over
the people only with the help of the
Communist army, the secret police, and
the vast hordes of so-called Soviet advisers, who are, in reality, gauleiters
watching Chinese Communist leaders
on behalf of the Kremlin.

FOREIGN RELATIONS

In its foreign relations the Peiping
regime has followed the ruthless Com-

munist pattern, and the free world has gained some enlightening, albeit painful, experience.

Take the United Kingdom, for example. At the beginning of 1950, shortly after the Chinese Communists set up their regime in Peiping, Britain rushed forward and was actually one of the first countries to accord recognition, in the hope of safeguarding her investments in China. British diplomatic representatives were sent to Peiping to negotiate with the Communist Foreign Minister for the purpose of establishing embassies and exchanging ambassadors. Obviously the move from London was meant to be a gesture of good will to Peiping and to induce a feeling of appreciation conducive to the advancement of the British interests in China.

But what has been the reaction of Peiping? What is the outcome? After four years of waiting, the British representative in Peiping has to this day not been received by the Communist Foreign Minister, and no envoy of any kind has been sent to London by the Peiping regime. Many of the British investments on the mainland, such as docks, warehouses, mines, factories, and newspapers belonging to British nationals, have been confiscated. British firms have been arbitrarily closed by the Communist authorities, and British subjects have been seized and imprisoned or expelled from the mainland. Even though many British proprietors of enterprises in China have been able to leave the country after suffering varying periods of maltreatment in the forms of house arrest, imprisonment, and payment of fines, they are still required by the Communist authorities to remit money to Communist China, ostensibly to pay their Chinese staffs, but in reality to increase the steadily dwindling foreign exchange reserves of the Communist treasury. The arrogant attitude of the Peiping regime toward

the British and its adamant policy of subjecting them to humiliation and brutal handling caused the British Foreign Secretary, Mr. Anthony Eden, in the characteristic English style of understatement, to declare in the House of Commons not long ago that the British relations with Communist China have been most "unsatisfactory."

The United States has always refused to accord recognition to the Chinese Communist regime, and of course its citizens in Communist China have fared no better. American property, both official and private, has been confiscated, and thirty-two Americans are still pining away in Communist jails on the mainland. Besides, the American people have come to learn something of the nature and policy of Communist China through their experience in Korea. By valiant efforts to implement the principle of collective security consecrated in the United Nations Charter, the United States, together with its allies, has repelled the Communist aggression in Korea. But Communist China has insisted from the outset that her soldiers fighting in Korea were volunteers, and this deception was at first naïvely believed by the West. Yet she is the real aggressor, masterminded and supported by Moscow. In fact, the aggression of Communist China in Korea has been more than once denounced by the General Assembly of the United Nations. The Korean War was a part of the Communist plan to conquer Asia as a step to world dominion. It has levied a toll of half a million casualties, with the United States alone suffering 32,000 dead and over 100,000 wounded.

PRISONERS OF WAR

The cruel treatment of United Nations prisoners of war by the Communists was shocking to the conscience of the free world. Stories of mass slaughter and burying alive are too gruesome to recount here. Although the bulk of the prisoners taken by the Communist side has been repatriated, over 7,000, including 944 Americans, are still reported to be unaccounted for. The obstinate refusal of the Communist authorities to give further information regarding the fate and the whereabouts of these prisoners illustrates their callous attitude toward human life and their utter disregard of international law and the principles of justice and mercy.

Those who have lived under the Communist rule in China and served in the Chinese Communist army should know the truth. The fact that 14,000 Communist soldiers captured by United Nations forces, constituting 75 per cent of the total number of prisoners of war, deliberately chose not to return to Communist China but to go to Formosa under the government of the Republic of China gives the lie to Communist propaganda that a Communist-ruled country is a paradise.

Thus we can see clearly that the regime on the Chinese mainland internally is a totalitarian dictatorship of the most ruthless type while internationally it pursues a policy of flagrant aggression and constitutes a menace to peace in Asia.

THE NATIONAL GOVERNMENT, FORMOSA

Now let me say a few words about the real China, which is represented by the National government with its temporary seat on the island of Formosa.

This government is the only legitimate and lawful government of China. It is headed by Generalissimo Chiang Kai-shek as the President of the Republic of China. He was first elected to that office in 1948 in accordance with the Constitution adopted by the National Assembly of people's delegates elected throughout the country by direct and secret popular vote. The term of office of the President is six years, and two weeks ago the National Assembly re-elected President Chiang for another term of six years.

The Executive Yuan, equivalent to the Cabinet in the West, exercises the executive power of the government and is responsible to the Legislative Yuan. The Control Yuan is a constitutional body elected by the provincial legislatures on the basis of regional representation; it exercises the power of supervision and impeachment of delinquent officials. The Legislative Yuan, whose members are also elected by popular vote, exercises a power very similar to that of the Congress of the United States. It makes laws for the Republic of China and approves the national budget submitted by the government. It also has the power to summon the Premier and his Cabinet colleagues for interpellation on questions of national policy or on specific cases relating to the conduct of government officials.

Local self-government prevails in Formosa. Not only the mayors of cities and towns but also the members of the Provincial Assembly of Formosa and those of the city and town councils are all elected by the people. In contrast to the dictatorship of the Communist regime on the mainland, democracy is in full operation on the island of Formosa under the government of the Republic of China.

Now and then we hear criticisms of the National government in Formosa by some politically minded Chinese abroad, to the effect that the process of democratization carried out by the government of the Chinese Republic has not been rapid enough and that greater results could have been obtained in this respect. Of course, to criticize the government is one of the rights guaranteed by our Constitution to every Chinese citizen. Indeed, it is nothing surprising, as we see political criticisms made by opposition parties in every democratic country.

But in the case of the Chinese government in Formosa, it seems fair and reasonable to point out that this island, together with all the outlying islands under its control, is constantly threatened with invasion by armed Communist forces from the mainland. A state of war exists in Formosa because of this threat. Indeed it may be said to be in the firing line all the time, as the Communist regime at Peiping has repeatedly proclaimed its intention to attack and seize Formosa. Under these circumstances impartial observers, both Chinese and foreign, have often expressed their wonder and amazement that, in spite of the state of war, so much progress has been achieved by the Chinese government toward establishing and developing representative government and democratic institutions in Formosa.

Overseas nationals

I think it is important to add that, besides the people in Formosa, some twelve million Chinese nationals who live overseas in southeast Asia, Australia, the United States, Latin America, Europe, and Africa support, with few exceptions, the government of the Chinese Republic in Formosa. Indeed, even the people on the Chinese mainland wish the same government well and are eagerly looking to it as the only hope for their own liberation from the yoke of the ruthless Communist rule under which they are now groaning and suffering.

THE POLITICAL DEPARTMENT

Criticism is sometimes directed against the existence of the Political Department of the Chinese Ministry of Defense in Formosa. At first sight this setup appears to be unusual, and there is no precise counterpart in the defense establishments of the Western countries. But in the light of what happened to the government armed forces on the mainland in the struggle against the Communists, this department has been found necessary, especially at the present juncture.

Its work comprises many kinds of duties. One of them is counterintelligence. Another is education, instructing the personnel of the armed forces as to the nature of the Communist menace and the supreme duty of everyone in the armed forces to guard against Communist infiltration, to prepare themselves wholeheartedly to recover the Chinese mainland and liberate their fellow-countrymen from the Communist rule.

Another duty of this department consists of efforts to promote the spirit and morale of the armed forces by attending to the comforts, recreation, and entertainment of the soldiers, sailors, and airmen and to the welfare of their families. These activities take the forms of athletic meets, ball games, theatricals, motion picture shows, and visits to their families. Much of this work in other countries, such as the United States, for example, is done by separate agencies like PX (Post exchange), USO (United Service Organization), the Veterans Administration, and other public bodies; the work itself has been found to be equally essential.

Another important function of this department is to make periodic loyalty checks of the rank and file of the armed forces and to report security risks to the higher authorities for consideration and action. This line of activity has been found indispensable because of the discovery in the past few years of several serious cases of Communist infiltration and espionage involving even some high-ranking officers.

In considering the existence of this

department one must again take into consideration the fact that a state of war prevails in Formosa, which is constantly threatened by the possibility of Communist invasion from the mainland. The necessity of safeguarding the security of the island calls for vigilance and the making of loyalty checks. In other countries the fundamental idea of safeguarding security is not much different. It underlies the practice, in the United States for instance, of checking with the Federal Bureau of Investigation before making or confirming the appointment of a person to a public office in the government or to a military post in the armed forces of the country.

MILITARY STRENGTH

As to its military strength, the Chinese government on the island possesses an armed force of approximately 600,000 men, including a large number of army units, a fair-sized air force, a modest navy, and a marine corps. The personnel of these different branches of the armed forces have been thoroughly retrained and to a large extent re-equipped with the aid of the United States in recent years. There is an American military mission stationed in Formosa, headed by Major General William C. Chase, which has been rendering valuable assistance in the training and reorganization of the armed forces, as well as in teaching them how to handle American equipment.

AMERICAN AID

Economically the United States Foreign Operations Administration maintains a China mission in Formosa with an efficient staff to study, discuss, and work out with the Chinese authorities the most essential programs for utilizing the economic aid granted to the Chinese government by the United States. It is gratifying to know that the pattern of close and fruitful cooperation which has been developed in Formosa between the Chinese government and the various bodies of American representatives to ensure that every dollar of American aid is spent honestly and effectively has been regarded by our American friends as a good example for other recipient countries of American aid in Asia to follow.

These satisfactory results have been obtained because it has been the determination of the Chinese government in Formosa, no less than that of the United States, that the generous aid given by this country to China should be made to produce the maximum benefit toward ensuring the security of the island, maintaining a sound economy, and promoting the welfare of the people. These are not my personal observations alone. They are also embodied in the published official reports and statements made by various diplomatic, military, and economic representatives of the United States in Formosa and have been confirmed by the statements of eminent American Senators and Congressmen and radio and press representatives who have visited Formosa. For example, Senator H. Alexander Smith, chairman of the Subcommittee on the Far East of the United States Senate Foreign Relations Committee, who visited Formosa and other parts of eastern Asia last November, said in a report to the Committee:

As compared to the situation two years ago, we found a marked improvement in political stability and in economic conditions on Formosa. If this progress continues, the Nationalist government will become an increasingly important factor in encouraging disaffection from the Mao Tsetung government among the Chinese on the mainland. Formosa can serve as a rallying point for their discontent as well as a powerful psychological base for a counter-offensive of Chinese democracy.

He went on to characterize Formosa as "a kind of show place for democracy in the East."

INTERNATIONAL RECOGNITION

Internationally, by far the greater part of the free world continues to recognize the government of the Republic of China, whereas the Peiping regime is recognized only by the Soviet Union and its satellites and a few European and Asiatic non-Communist countries. It is encouraging to note that no freedom-loving country in the Western Hemisphere or on the African continent has followed the example of the Soviet Union in recognizing the Chinese Communist regime. Of the sixty member states of the United Nations forty-three continue to recognize the government of the Republic of China. And the maneuvers and protests of Soviet Russia and her satellites to unseat the representatives of the Chinese Republic in that world organization and its various subsidiary organs in favor of the Peiping regime on more than two hundred occasions have invariably been defeated.

COMMUNIST CHINA—PRO-SOVIET, ANTI–UNITED STATES

Here then is the whole situation: the Communist regime at Peiping controls the life and liberty of the Chinese people on the mainland. The leaders of this regime are Chinese by race, but their thoughts and ideas and methods of government and their outlook are no more Chinese than those of the thousands of so-called Soviet advisers who now overrun the country.

The Communist authorities on the mainland are doing everything possible to destroy Chinese civilization and Chinese culture. They officially proclaim the Soviet Union as their welcome teacher, and the people are exhorted and even ordered to worship the Soviet pattern and learn from the Communist Russians. Every important pronouncement from the Kremlin is echoed at Peiping, and every turn and twist of the Soviet policy regarding Asia and the Far East is endorsed by the Peiping regime. The views expressed by *Pravda* and *Izvestia* on important international questions have never failed to be echoed in the Chinese Communist official organ, the *People's Daily News* of Peiping, and in other newspapers under Communist control.

The Red regime, although manned by the Chinese, is tantamount to a branch of the Kremlin. In fact, the Far Eastern Bureau of the international Cominform has its headquarters in Peiping and carries out its schemes of infiltration, subversion, and war in Asia under the general direction of Moscow. Because the Soviet Union regards the United States as its arch enemy in the world and at every international gathering concentrates its attacks on this country, Peiping has organized and proclaimed its so-called "Hate America Campaign." In the schools, in the theaters and press, on the radio, on public platforms and at the officially sponsored mass meetings, the United States is assailed as a warmonger and archimperialist. Everything American or of American origin is condemned as tainted with the evil spirit of American imperialism. Hundreds of American-educated Chinese who refused to denounce the United States as ordered by the Communist authorities have been arrested and jailed as agents and spies of American imperialists.

In order to force the people to join in this vicious campaign, literally hundreds of the so-called Sino-Soviet friendship societies which have been established throughout the country also take a hand in organizing meetings and supplying speakers to malign the United States, as well as to eulogize the Soviet

Union. The artificial hysteria engendered by the Peiping regime in trying to make people believe that the United States had resorted to germ warfare in Korea was one of their transparent attempts to arouse mass hatred of America.

Communist China may be treated with greater consideration by Moscow than any of its European or Asiatic satellites, but it is not a free and independent political entity. At best it is only a junior partner of the Soviet Union in the Communist world. To further the Kremlin's plot of world domination Peiping has not hesitated to engage in aggression openly in Korea and covertly in Indochina.

REPUBLIC OF CHINA—INTERNATIONAL RELATIONS

In contrast with the Peiping regime, there is on the island of Formosa the government of the Republic of China which thinks of the sufferings of the people on the mainland and ponders daily over the supreme task of recovering the mainland and effecting their liberation. While working hard to ensure the security of the island, it has also been exerting its efforts to establish representative government and develop democratic institutions. In thought and action it cherishes the Chinese tradition and fosters the virtues and teachings taught by Confucius and other sages through the centuries.

In its relations with other countries, the Chinese Republic steadily pursues a policy of peace and friendly co-operation to advance the cause of peace. It is a charter member of the United Nations and contributed its part in the writing of the Charter at San Francisco. It is a staunch and consistent supporter of the United Nations, and its delegation has taken from year to year an active part in the proceedings of that world organization. A strong believer in the principles of collective security,

it has not failed to offer its assistance to implement this principle, though such offers have not always been accepted by the United Nations.

In regard to the traditional relations of this real China with the United States, it is a notable fact that throughout the 110 years of official intercourse between the two nations there has always existed between them peace and friendship. While every major power in the world in the past century committed aggression or waged war against China, the United States, like China herself, to our great appreciation and gratitude, has always pursued a policy of peace and friendship toward her. In the two world wars in which the United States was involved, China joined in the conflict to be its ally and co-operated with it closely as allies should. Today the United States, as the leader of the free world against actual and potential Communist aggression, finds the Republic of China pursuing a strong and determined anti-Communist policy in close co-operation with Washington.

Although it might seem that there are two Chinas, there is, in fact, only one legitimate, true China, represented by the government in Formosa. It is a reasonable conclusion from what I have outlined that the continued friendly and co-operative relations between China and the United States can be maintained and developed only with the true and new China which has her temporary capital in Formosa. The Republic of China not only enjoys the support of the eight million Formosan people and twelve million overseas Chinese but also represents the hope of the enslaved 470 million people on the Chinese mainland for their liberation from the Communist rule.

THE GENEVA CONFERENCE

With the Geneva Conference, called to discuss the question of Korea and

Indochina, public interest is growing and speculation is rife as to the attitude of the participating powers and the possible outcome of the gathering. Will the Communists show a change of heart on the part of their governments and make a sincere effort to reach reasonable and fair settlements in the interest of world peace and justice? What will be the attitude of the countries of the West? Will they enter the conference with the firm resolve to defend the cause of freedom and uphold the principles of international justice and peace? Or will they be influenced by considerations of expediency and seek a compromise by means of appeasement? Whatever the result of the conference, it will be of far-reaching consequence, as it will determine the future course of events in Asia and eventually in the whole world. It is no exaggeration to say that much uneasiness and apprehension prevails in many countries of eastern Asia. They are anxiously awaiting the outcome of the conference.

My country's attitude toward this conference has been stated by Dr. George Yeh, Chinese Minister of Foreign Affairs, on February 19, 1954. In the view of my government, because of its inclusion of Communist China condemned by the United Nations as aggressor, the conference sets a dangerous precedent, constituting a negation of the principles of the Charter of that world organization. The Chinese government and people cannot recognize the validity of any decision affecting their interest which may be reached at such a conference.

The position which the United States government would take at Geneva was clarified by the Secretary of State, Mr. Dulles, in a timely and forceful speech before the Overseas Press Club in New York on March 29. He warned in clear and unequivocal language against any further attempt on the part of Commu-

nist Russia and her Communist Chinese ally to impose their political system upon southeast Asia. With equal clarity and emphasis he reaffirmed the opposition of the United States government to recognition of Red China and her admission into the United Nations and gave some very cogent reasons in support of this stand.

In this connection I must also refer to the welcome statement of Senator Alexander Wiley, Chairman of the Foreign Relations Committee of the United States Senate. In an address before the Masons of New York State last week he, too, spoke against recognizing Red China and giving her a seat in the United Nations. His declaration, like that of the Secretary of State, obviously reflects the sentiment of the American people, who, true to their tradition, are strongly opposed to aggression and appeasement of the aggressor.

It is heartening to the freedom-loving peoples of Asia to take note of these authoritative statements of United States policy. They are reassuring, and they will go far to clear the atmosphere of doubt and speculation as to what the stand of the United States will be at the forthcoming conference. They will, I hope, discourage any wavering on the part of other Western powers.

But the policy and attitude of other participating countries on the side of the free world remain a mystery and give rise to much uneasiness. As a student of international affairs I cannot refrain from expressing the view that, in the light of past experience, any attempt to sacrifice fundamental principles of justice and peace and appease the Communists in the hope of getting their promises of good behavior in Indochina and Korea would be a grave mistake of statemanship. Communist bad faith is notorious. Their record of performance in regard to the Yalta, Tehran, and Potsdam agreements constitutes an important lesson and a serious warning to the free world.

U.N. Membership for Communist China?

It is conceivable that Communist China, in order to secure the immediate advantages of diplomatic recognition and membership of the United Nations, will not hesitate to deny her sinister intentions toward Indochina and Korea and to sign agreements with the representatives of the free world. For it is a part of Communist strategy in dealing with what they call the capitalist world to launch economic, military, or diplomatic offensives to further their objectives according to circumstances prevailing at a given moment. It may be that the Communists are counting upon the fruits of a diplomatic offensive at Geneva. But Peiping's pledged word can no more be relied upon than Moscow's. In the speech referred to above, Mr. Dulles cited a series of violations of international agreements by the Communists. Stalin himself once said to the representatives of a Soviet satellite that "a treaty is worse than a scrap of paper because you cannot write on it."

Moreover, the Peiping regime, it will be recalled, was denounced as the aggressor in Korea by a formal resolution of the United Nations General Assembly. To admit it into this world organization would be tantamount to putting a premium on aggression and rewarding the aggressor. It would be difficult to imagine an act which would have a more demoralizing effect on the hopes of millions and millions of enslaved people on the Chinese mainland and upon the spirit of the freedom-loving peoples in Asia. In addition, it would further weaken the United Nations, the effective functioning of which has already been greatly impaired by the policy of nonco-operation and ob-

struction on the part of the Soviet Union and its satellites.

It is sometimes claimed by apologists for the Peiping regime that the United Nations must observe the principle of universality and admit all countries into it without regard to their political ideology. Evidently those who advance this thesis forget the basic requirements for membership prescribed in the United Nations Charter. To be admissible a state must be peace-loving and able and willing to carry out the obligations contained in the Charter. Could Communist China, in view of its flagrant aggression in Korea and of its aid to the Communist forces in Indochina, be considered as a peace-loving country?

As to Peiping's record of observance of its international obligations, the Secretary of State disclosed in the address already referred to that it has committed at least forty violations of the Korean Armistice Agreement.

In some quarters it is stated that it would be better to have Communist China in the United Nations, so that its conduct could be more easily watched and it could be called to account in conference and discussion. If this is the reason for giving the Peiping regime a seat in the United Nations, it is only wishful thinking. The Soviet Union is a permanent member of the United Nations. Has this fact prevented it from instigating Peiping to launch a war of aggression against Korea and to conspire against the French and Vietnamese in Indochina?

Those who advocate Peiping's admission into the United Nations seem to be satisfied that this world organization should serve only as an international forum, unmindful of the fact that the primary objective of the United Nations is to maintain international peace and security through the organization and application of collective security. The Security Council, whose primary responsibility it is to carry out this duty, has been paralyzed by the obstructionist attitude of the Soviet Union. If the United Nations is to be generally only a debating society, then the taxpayers of the member states would have a good reason for complaining that its maintenance is too costly, especially since it now provides as much a forum for Communist propaganda as for others.

TRADE WITH COMMUNIST CHINA

There are people who urge recognition or admission of Communist China into the United Nations in the hope of doing more trade with it in the vast Chinese market, as if the principles of peace and security and the cause of freedom should be evaluated in dollars and cents and bartered away for economic and financial gains. Those who place trade above all other things must be aware of the fact that the immutable aim of international Communism is nothing short of world domination; it is determined to seek its attainment by all means at its disposal.

It must also be realized that the policy of the Chinese Communist regime today is to consolidate its power at home and build up its prestige abroad. While pursuing its policy of expansionism in the neighboring countries of east and southeast Asia, in Burma and Nepal as well as in Korea and Indochina, it is also pressing forward its program of industrialization, so as to increase its war potential. Any move to lift the embargo on strategic goods and promote trade relations with it would be helping its policy of consolidation and industrial development. Once the Peiping regime succeeds in entrenching itself on the Chinese mainland, not only would the hopes of millions of the enslaved Chinese people be dashed to the ground and the supreme mission of the government of the Republic of China to liberate them frustrated, but the task of saving Asia from the Communist grip would become impossible.

The fundamental objectives of United States foreign policy, as I understand them, are peace, security, and freedom throughout the world. Indeed, these constitute the only sound basis for working to raise the standard of living of all peoples and promoting the welfare of humanity. If this understanding is correct—and I venture to believe it is—then every effort must be made to rescue Asia from Communist conquest and domination. For the Communist leaders from Lenin and Stalin down to the present rulers in the Kremlin have always regarded the conquest of Asia with its tremendous manpower, immense resources of food supplies and strategic raw materials, and military bases as indispensable to the success of their plot of world domination. The success of the Communists in consolidating their power in China would portend an omnious future for the whole of Asia, as demonstrated in Korea and Indochina.

HOPE FOR A NEW CHINA

To check this calamitous trend and save Asia for the free world, the government of the Republic of China must be encouraged and supported in its determination to carry out its supreme mission of recovering the Chinese mainland and liberating the Chinese people. Whatever fighting, whatever sacrifices, may be necessary will be enthusiastically undertaken by the Chinese government and people in Formosa. The armed forces under its control today may not be large compared with the Communist army on the mainland, and the population of the island, even with the support of the reservoir of manpower from overseas Chinese, may be limited. Yet the real potential strength of the Republic of China exists among the millions and millions of the people on the mainland. It is sincerely believed—and intelligence reports invariably confirm this belief—that when the army of liberation lands on the coast of the mainland and establishes a beachhead there, not only the anti-Communist guerrillas but the people of the mainland will gladly rally to its banner and join in the fight to overthrow the hated Communist regime.

Once that is done and the government of the Republic of China moves its seat back to the mainland and starts to build up and develop democracy there, as it is doing in Formosa, a true and new China will have arisen: true because she will be faithful to the Chinese tradition and reflect the spirit of the Chinese people, and new because her democracy will be based not only upon the foundation of time-honored Chinese society but also upon the pattern of the United States. It is only that China which the American people can soundly and rightly contemplate and work with for mutual interest. It is only that China which will be in the future, as she was in the past, a loyal friend and faithful ally of the United States, to co-operate in the common task of building a world of peace, security, and prosperity.

His Excellency V. K. Wellington Koo, Ph.D., LL.D., L.H.D., Washington, D. C., has been Ambassador of the Republic of China to the United States since 1946. Before this appointment he was Ambassador to Great Britain (1941–46) and Minister and Ambassador to France (1932–41). In China, he was Minister of Foreign Affairs (1922–24), Finance Minister (1926), and Prime Minister and Minister of Foreign Affairs (1926–27), and he has represented his country at many international conferences, including the San Francisco Conference. Dr. Koo was chairman of the Chinese delegation to the first session of the United Nations General Assembly.

Present United States Policy Toward China

By Alfred le S. Jenkins

IN recent years we have often heard it said that more heat than light has been cast on the China question. I am not surprised at the heat, nor do I object to it, provided there is also sufficient light. The fate of one-fourth of the world's population is not a matter which can be taken lightly, and the addition to the Soviet bloc of China's vast material and manpower resources is a matter involving not only the security interests of the United States but those of the entire free world. I do not see how one can help feeling strongly about these matters. We need not apologize that our thinking about China is charged with feeling. National policies are an expression of national interests concerning which there is naturally much feeling, and our policies are an expression both of what we are and of what we want. We are a nation of free people. We want to remain free to pursue in peace our proper national destiny, and we want the same freedom and rights for others.

We do not believe that the Chinese Communist regime represents the will of the people it controls. First capitalizing on the natural desire of the Chinese people to enjoy full recognition and respect for their importance in the world community, the regime then proceeded by its "lean-to-one-side" policy to betray the powerful Chinese longings to stand up straight. It has followed slavishly the leadership of the Soviet Union and attempted to emulate it in all its ways. With the aid of thousands of Soviet advisers it has set about methodically to change the entire fabric of traditional Chinese culture, substituting Communism's materialistic, atheistic doctrines, wherein the state is the be-all and end-all and the individual its pawn.

The regime at first attracted considerable support, principally through its sponsorship of a land redistribution program, but is now, after establishment of the prerequisite police-state controls, taking the land away from the owners in the same collectivization process which is familiar in other Communist countries and which invariably has brought suffering in its wake. China's much advertised "new democracy" is, of course, in reality "old Communism."

Soviet-Chinese Relations

From its inception the regime has proclaimed a lean-to-one-side policy in foreign affairs and has left no doubt about its dedication to the proposition of world Communist revolution under the leadership of the Union of Soviet Socialist Republics. While its leaning to one side has not brought it to the position of complete prostration to one side characteristic of the Eastern European Soviet satellites, there is not the slightest evidence that this indicates any separatist tendencies. The difference in status of Peiping in its relationship with Moscow (as distinguished from that of the Eastern European satellites) is due rather to its having come to power without benefit, except in Manchuria, of Soviet army occupation; to the prestige of Mao Tse-tung, arising from his long history of leadership of Chinese Communism and his literary contributions to theoretical communism; to China's assumption of the role of leadership in the Communist program for Asia; and to the geographical position, size, and importance of China itself. This relationship has been characterized as that of junior partner, and the association has every mark of being a willing, determined, and close one.

Although Soviet officials previous to the Chinese Communist assumption of power were protesting that they did not know what "those independent agrarian reformers" were up to, there was already close co-operation between Mao and Moscow. Despite the Treaty of Friendship and Alliance between the Republic of China and the Union of Soviet Socialist Republics signed on August 14, 1945, which specified that Soviet "support and aid . . . be entirely given to the national government as the central government of China," the Soviet Union a few months later turned over to the Chinese Communists the Japanese equipment it received in Manchuria. The Union of Soviet Socialist Republics instituted diplomatic relations with Peiping only two days after the regime's establishment, and five Eastern European Soviet satellites followed suit within the week. The North Korean regime, the East German Communist satellite, and the so-called People's Republic of Mongolia also established diplomatic relations with the new regime during the first month of its existence.

The Sino-Soviet Friendship Association, a mass organization whose aim, according to the Communists, is "to found and consolidate fraternal friendship and co-operation between the Chinese and Soviet people and to develop the interflow of knowledge and experience of the two great nations" was founded in Peiping only four days after the establishment of the so-called "People's Government."

Treaties and agreements

The Mao regime has since concluded with the Soviet Union and other Communist states various economic, military, and cultural treaties and agreements. Strong ideological ties bind Moscow and Peiping, and a number of Chinese Communist leaders are Moscow trained. The Chinese Communists also feel the need for close association with the Soviet Union to develop their military strength and striking power. They need Russian military supplies and equipment and Russian technicians and economic aid for the development of heavy industry, which they view as a necessary base for a large military establishment. In exchange, China can furnish the Soviet Union with needed raw materials and foodstuffs and offer the use of the warm-water ports of Dairen and Port Arthur. The Union of Soviet Socialist Republics does not want a strong, independent China on its Siberian border. It is naturally interested in the survival and growth of a Communist China (so long as it does not grow too strong and independent), and in alliance with a Communist China it is in a far stronger power position than it would be otherwise. The close co-operation and interdependence between the Chinese Communists and the Soviet Union in the Korean aggression is well known.

Communist China's attitude toward U. S.

As a corollary to Communist China's "leaning" to the Soviet side, she has unceasingly heaped vituperation and all manner of abuse and insult upon the free world in general and the United States in particular—over the radio, in newspapers, at the conference table, and in numerous periodicals in many languages (even including Esperanto), which are sent all over the world.

Aside from the serious implications of policy in this performance, such conduct somehow seems especially shocking coming from the Chinese. For well over a century Americans have had a deep interest in and sincere friendship for the

Chinese people. Our record in supporting China's territorial integrity and political independence is a well-known one. It is a source of deep concern and regret to us that for more than four years we have been cut off from our accustomed close association with the great majority of the Chinese people.

U. S. POLICY ON RECOGNITION

There are some who feel that this unfortunate situation could be remedied if we were to recognize the Peiping regime and if it were accepted as representing China in the United Nations. Actually, even if we considered such action to be morally justifiable, there is not a shred of evidence to indicate that we could expect reciprocity on any satisfactory basis or that it would lead to a renewal of our association with the Chinese on the mainland. During the few months preceding and following the establishment of the so-called People's Government in Peiping, Chinese Communist authorities jailed or otherwise maltreated a number of our official representatives and never recognized their official status. Finally, when the situation became intolerable, we withdrew all of our official representatives, requesting the British to represent our interests. The British have tried to do this to the best of their ability. They are hampered in this endeavor, however, for while they have recognized the regime and have diplomatic and consular officials on the mainland, the Communists have not seen fit to establish diplomatic relations with the British and have refused to accord full accreditation to British officials. The British, and indeed others with fully accredited representation in Peiping, have in vain attempted on our behalf to secure the release of some hundred Americans held in Communist China against their wishes, thirty-two of whom are in jail now, held incommunicado, without trial, and without even a statement of the charges against them.

The Peiping regime has followed no recognized standards of international conduct. It has repeatedly violated the terms of the Korean Armistice Agreement. It has disregarded international rules on the care of prisoners of war. In order to secure sorely needed foreign exchange to carry on its aggressive adventures and its subversive activities in other countries it has engaged in narcotics trade throughout the world, and has directed an extortion racket against overseas Chinese whose relatives on the mainland are at its mercy. In addition to its aggression in Korea and its defiance of the United Nations itself, it has supplied the Communist Vietminh armies with equipment and advisers and trained Vietminh troops on Chinese soil. It has swept aside traditional local autonomy in Tibet and has carried on an active program of intimidation and subversion throughout southeast Asia.

Internally, the Mao regime is a ruthless police state with all that that implies. Millions of Chinese have been murdered or have committed suicide in connection with the phoney land reforms and the campaigns against alleged irregularities of private businessmen. Property of both Chinese and foreigners has been confiscated without compensation. Personal liberty is a thing of the past. The "justice" of the so-called people's courts is subservient to state policies. Movements of individuals are closely controlled. There is forced labor on a large scale. Children are trained and forced to inform on their parents and friends. There is not even freedom of silence, since all must be vocal in support of Communist policies. Mass "brainwashing" is a continuous process through daily study groups and all media of communication. The family unit has become a special target of the Communist system. The Communists have rewritten history, and attempted to make religion the handmaiden of politics.

In view of all these considerations it is hardly surprising that the firm policy of the United States government is one of strong opposition to the Chinese Communist regime. We cannot recognize this regime, and we shall continue vigorously to oppose attempts to accept it in any United Nations organization as representing the Chinese people. We earnestly solicit the support of the entire free world in these policies. We would view with deep concern a "creeping acceptance" of the Peiping regime by the world community of nations.

We further consider that recognition and acceptance of the Peiping regime would have the effect of substantially weakening the will to resist Communist expansion on the part of other Asian people. The nations and people near the Chinese mainland might under such circumstances erroneously tend to view Communism as "the inevitable wave of the future" and more and more incline their political leanings and economic activities to accommodate this this conviction. If the Chinese Communist regime were the only China to which the twelve million overseas Chinese could look, the Communists would have an important, ready-made "fifth column" throughout southeast Asia and in many other nations of the world. They already have the support of some of these Chinese, but their following among them has fallen off markedly since the extortion episode and as the nature of the regime's excesses has become increasingly apparent.

Those who favor recognition of the Peiping regime beg the question by urging us to "recognize reality." We do recognize reality, and much of it we do not like. But it is not in the American tradition to confuse the *real* with the *immutable*. We recognize with concern an increase in the incidence of cancer in recent years, but we refuse to recognize cancer as "the inevitable wave of the future."

U. S. MILITARY POLICY

So much for our political policy toward the Chinese Communist regime. On the military side it is the view of the United States that the way to deter aggression is for the free community to be willing and able to respond vigorously at places and with means of its own choosing.

EMBARGO AGAINST COMMUNIST CHINA

On the economic side we follow a policy of total embargo against Communist China, and our ships are forbidden to call at Communist Chinese ports. It is realized that every kind of merchandise cannot be considered to be directly helpful on the battlefield. We have felt, however, that the maximum possible economic pressures should be applied against an aggressor engaged in fighting and killing the troops of the United States and other free countries. The aggression in Korea, so far as Communist China is concerned, will not be considered over until its troops are all withdrawn. The Armistice in Korea only stopped the shooting—doubtless because the Communists found the fighting unprofitable—but we have seen no indication so far that the Mao regime has abandoned its aggressive policies. If the time should come when the consideration of lessening economic controls appears appropriate, we shall still bear in mind the effect of such action in regard to Communist China's plans to build a large war potential and its avowed intent to "liberate" all of Asia and eventually the world.

THE GENEVA CONFERENCE

We have been committed since signing of the Korean Armistice Agreement last July and the passage of the United Nations General Assembly Resolution last August to seek a Korean political conference. We have patiently sought since early September to arrange for such a conference on terms consonant with the Armistice Agreement and the United Nations Resolution. The Berlin Conference laid plans for a multipower conference at Geneva on April 26 to consider a Korean settlement. This will not be, as the Communists are claiming, a five-power conference. Communist China, far from attending the conference as a great power, will not in our view even attend as a government. At Berlin we secured Soviet agreement to the following statement:

It is understood that neither the invitation to, nor the holding of, the above-mentioned conference shall be deemed to imply diplomatic recognition in any case where it has not already been accorded.

The time, place, and composition of the Korean political conference are entirely as we wanted. We do not fear this conference. As Secretary Dulles has said:

There is . . . no reason why we should refuse to seek peacefully the results we want merely because of fear that we will be outmaneuvered at the conference table. . . . Our cause is not so poor, and our capacity not so low, that our nation must seek security by sulking in its tent.

We will not be prepared at Geneva to allow the aggressors to achieve at the conference table what they failed to achieve in battle. This applies not only to territorial considerations but to any "deal" which would, as has been suggested in some quarters, trade a United Nations seat and an end to the trade controls for an agreement by Communist China to stop supplying the Vietminh. As a recent *New York Times* editorial put it, "There is neither logic nor profit in paying a bribe to the Communists to get their worthless promise not to do again what they had no business doing in the first place."

Whatever the Communist attitude, we will go to Geneva in good faith and do our best to achieve just solutions to the Korean and Indochinese problems. There is the bare possibility that Soviet Russia and its Chinese Communist ally may be sufficiently preoccupied with plans for internal development to cause them at least to desire a period of relaxation in both areas on an acceptable basis. Meanwhile, we are keenly sensible to the Communist habit of waging war by cease fire, and we do not discount the possibility that they might use a cessation of hostilities merely as an opportunity to build up for renewed attacks. In our view, any settlement in Korea or Indochina would have to provide effective guarantees against such a possibility.

U. S. POLICY TOWARD THE REPUBLIC OF CHINA

Certainly we do not contemplate any action at Geneva or anywhere else which would damage the cause of the government of the Republic of China. Our policy is to extend moral and material support to the Free Chinese, and we have no intention of letting them down. This government has been constant in its opposition to lawless imperialism. We do not forget that the government of China under President Chiang Kaishek, during the long years of its lone stand against the Japanese invader, had several opportunities to reach a seemingly advantageous accommodation with the invading power, but refused to do so. The Chinese government early recognized the true complexion of the Chinese Communists and refused to compromise with them. Just as we view the unswerving friendship of the Chinese government with gratitude, we also view its growth in material strength and political appeal with satisfaction. We are prepared to lend our continued support to these ends, but we cannot ourselves fashion them. This, of course, is primarily a Chinese responsibility. The military and economic progress which has taken place on Formosa during the past four years has been heartening. We hope and are confident that the progress being made there will stand in increasingly favorable contrast to the regimentation and oppression of the mainland regime.

We will continue military and economic aid to the government of the Republic of China. We will continue to recognize it as the government of China, and we will support it as the representative of China in the United Nations. We are convinced that even though it is cut off from the mainland, it is far more representative of the will of the Chinese people than is the Peiping regime. It has conducted itself in the United Nations ably, responsibly, and with dignity. The free world can deal with this government on mutually understandable terms. It does not employ the upside-down vocabulary of the Communists.

THE CHINA PROBLEM

International politics, like domestic politics, is in the last analysis an art of the possible. I do not mean by this that a solution to "the China problem" is impossible. I mean that the solution is not likely to be easy or quick. Time, however, *can* be on our side. The greatest thing the Communists have to fear is truth. This fear erected both the Iron Curtain and the Bamboo Curtain. There is nothing new about Communism, and we know that it is by no means "the inevitable wave of the future." It has been tried for a long time and has proven itself totally incapable of making good on its promises. We are resolved to remain strong in order to have the time to demonstrate, beyond the power of curtains to hide, the simple truth that the systems fashioned by free men can tap the energies and meet the needs of their peoples incomparably better than can a materialistic and cynical system of coercion and regimentation. This truth must yet make millions free who are now enslaved, including the Chinese on the mainland.

The course which we are now pursuing with respect to China may not be easy or quick, but we must never for one moment doubt the possibility of reaching our objectives with honor and with a full sense of our responsibility to this and to future generations. In this let us not seek the counsel either of the timid or of the foolhardy. We feel strongly about the China problem because it affects not only our security but the very values by which we live. If we stand honestly on those principles which have brought us thus far, we need not fear that we shall have to stand alone.

Alfred le S. Jenkins, Washington, D. C., is Officer in Charge of Political Affairs in the Office of Chinese Affairs in the Department of State. Previous to his present appointment he was vice consul at Peiping, Tientsin, and Hong Kong, second secretary and consul at Taipai, Formosa, and international relations officer in the Office of Chinese Affairs.

Paradoxes in the Indochinese Dilemma

By Lauriston Sharp

THE war in Indochina—a colonial war to throw off French imperialism, a struggle to contain a dangerous thrust of Communism, a local trouble become global—frightens the West as it threatens to develop into another Asian situation gone out of control. While the two world colossi flex their thermonuclear muscles, men seek some settlement to end these bitter hostilities which came to Indochina with the coming of peace in the Pacific in 1945 and which marked the return of the Free French among the Indochinese peoples who thought themselves free.

The war has been fought so far with conventional weapons, but it is a highly unconventional war carried on in an unconventional manner. The background, development, and issues of the conflict are so disordered and complex that it is small wonder the public is confused, seeing only a blurred or oversimplified picture taken in the capitals of the nations most concerned through lenses of censorship, propaganda, and inadequate news coverage. This picture aroused little interest among most Americans until about 1950, almost a century after the French began to develop their nation's interest in the area, following the example of other European powers in China. From December 8, 1941, Americans generally have been aware of Indochina's strategic importance in terms of its location, its modern capital equipment and services installed by the French (but since badly damaged by American bombings, scorched earth tactics, or misuse), and its realized or potential resources in agricultural and mineral wealth, hydroelectric power, and one of the most industrious populations in southeast Asia. Only recently, however, have many Americans realized not only that they were being involved in Indochina by containment and economic aid policies, but that developments there were beginning to have very important repercussions on the whole scheme of American strategy in Europe and at home as well as in Asia.

POLITICAL AND RACIAL DIVISIONS

From the point of view of the West, the 28,000,000 people of Indochina are now technically divided among three independent but "Associated States," that is, states associated with France in the French Union: the kingdom of Laos in the northwest; the kingdom of Cambodia in the southwest; and the state of Vietnam which is neither kingdom nor republic although about half of its 22,000,000 population is theoretically ruled, without the aid of a legislative body, by a "majesty," Bao Dai. The Laos are a Thai people culturally akin to the Siamese and, like them, Southern Buddhists, but uninterested in political affiliation with Thailand. The Cambodians, whose ancient kings ruled from Angkor a vast empire, speak Khmer, wholly unrelated to the Thai languages, but share with their old enemies the Thai many cultural traits, including Southern Buddhism. Culturally distinct from either the Thai or Khmer, the Vietnamese, originating in southeastern China and subject to that state from late Han times to the tenth century, are largely Sinicized. Historically, however, the Vietnamese have devoted much of their energy during the past millenium to gaining and maintaining political independence of China.

89

Included in none of these states but centrally located on the borders of all of them is a vast plateau or mountain region inhabited by a million or two aboriginals governed, like a native reservation, under direct French administration. Little is said by the French government regarding the future political status of this region which has some economic and considerable strategic importance.

The complicating factor in the Indochinese situation, of course, is the existence of the Democratic Republic of Vietnam, which was established in August 1945 and a half year later was recognized by the French government as a "free state." This is the political entity of some 11,000,000 Vietnamese controlled by Vietnamese Communists led by Ho Chi-minh, recognized since 1950 by the U.S.S.R., by People's China, and by satellite countries as a legal state. It is a government whose people the French call "Vietminh," or more simply, "Viets," and define as being in rebellion against what the free world considers the legal State of Vietnam, developed under French sponsorship after 1948.

As if postwar Indochina were not complicated enough, the situation has been made more complex by the creation by fiat from Peiping in 1953 of a "free Thai state," whose territory comprises a region populated largely by Thai-speaking peoples, including a large section of northwest Indochina or Laos, the southern corner of Yunnan in southwest China, a bit of northern Thailand, and parts of northeast Burma. So far, such a state exists largely as a plan to which might be attracted anti-Vietnamese Thai tribesmen, Laos, Siamese exiles who now have no one to turn to except Peiping, and some of the dissident Shan (Thai) and Katchin leaders from Burma. Presumably such a state would attempt to build on the Thai pannational interests so widely heralded by the Bangkok regime during the war, but which have been little mentioned since Thailand allied herself with the West in the postwar period. This move perhaps gives some hint of a Communist hope eventually to divest Vietnam of some of its non-Vietnamese and south China of some eight or ten million non-Chinese, who might then be lumped together with other peoples, including possibly the numerically weak Cambodians, to form a new, preponderantly Thai state centering on the rice-rich valleys of the Chao Phraya and Mekong rivers between Burma and Vietnam.

For the present, however, the world's interest in mainland southeast Asia centers on the military stalemate and the resulting political dilemma in divided Vietnam. Some of the realities which lie behind the complex Vietnamese situation and which are frequently too little appreciated may be introduced by listing a number of paradoxes which must strongly influence the outcome in Vietnam.

ANTI-CHINESE SENTIMENTS

First. Vietnamese culture includes strong, traditional, and well-entrenched anti-China and anti-Chinese sentiments; yet a Vietnamese government controlling half the population is now allied with China and many Vietnamese must collaborate directly with dominant Chinese.

A unique combination of an original southeast Asian type of culture with Chinese civilization created Vietnamese culture over a period of more than two thousand years. But in the process Vietnamese governments and people fighting for independence from China developed a hearty antipathy for the Chinese and an active fear of political domination by the enormous neighbor to the north. In this situation the Vietnamese, from north to south, from top almost to bottom, developed a nationalist spirit long before the arrival of the French.

Apprehensions were intensely revived during the nine months following the war, when Kuomintang Chinese troops were sent into northern Vietnam by the Allies to supervise the surrender of Japanese forces there. The Chinese stayed on to loot the country and terrorize the populace, until it became a major aim of both French and Vietnamese to get rid of them. Partly for this end, Ho Chi-minh in March 1946 made a number of concessions to the French, whom he had fought so ardently for so many years; and when compatriots accused him of too easy collaboration, Ho, who had lived long in China, replied that it was better to smell the feces of the French for a little time than to eat Chinese excrement all of one's life.

Since political domination of the Vietminh by China still looms above the fine talk, it may be doubted that the present Vietminh co-operation with China is either enthusiastic or popular among Vietnamese in general, although it is probably rationalized among the collaborators by saying that Communist China is a "new" and different nation which, at least in its relations with the Vietminh, it may well be. However, the paradox still remains of China-fearing Vietnamese being forced to work with China, not necessarily because they fear the Chinese less but because they hate the French more. And the danger remains that the West will assume that a dominant Communist China and a Communist-nationalist Vietnam are inevitably and eternally one in attitude and action. This assumption seems implicit in our willingness to negotiate at Geneva with Moscow and Peiping, which can only force the Vietminh into continued subordination and subservience to these capitals.

FRENCH APATHY

Second. Although the French move into Indochina beginning almost a century ago was exceedingly unpopular with large segments of the French population, it was nevertheless accepted as a means to provide bases from which French influences could be brought to bear on China; yet China is in a position now to bring what may be overpowering influences to bear on the French, who are still unable to muster much popular support at home for the current Indochinese operations.

Nothing could better exemplify the reversal of the power situation in east Asia during a century's time than this present state in which China is a major threat to the French in Vietnam rather than the French being a threat to China. Formerly, even in the face of the French people's continuing apathy or opposition, French governments could go ahead with their ventures in Indochina, but now it is a question whether they can continue a colonial course without stronger popular metropolitan backing. The French people have never had the direct interest in colonies that was common in England and the Netherlands: for one thing, they tended to put their savings into banks, letting the banks invest their funds at home, in the colonies, or elsewhere; for another, proportionately fewer French would emigrate or make their lives in the colonies. Few were impressed with the promises of national prestige and the wealth of China in treasure or in souls which were to follow the "adventures of the admirals" (the early French administrators in Vietnam), the little wars, or other incidents which created the *faits accomplis* which first involved French governments in the Far East. Even though these developments involved no threat to their own or the nation's interests, the French public would complain. It is no wonder that now they should complain more after supporting alone for years a war which is "militarily hopeless, politically a dead-end street, and economically ruinous" and which brings them face to face with the massive threat of a powerful China.

IDEAS VS. PRACTICE

Third. France helped educate a Vietnamese elite in the technical businesses of Western culture and in the doctrines of the French Revolution, including the ideals of liberty, equality, and brotherhood; yet before the war no serious consideration was ever given to the possibility of eventual independence from the strong control wielded by Paris in governing Vietnam, formally or informally. Civil liberties and economic opportunities were limited for Vietnamese, while French colonials were supported in preferred positions and in larger numbers relative to the native population than in other colonial areas.

Vietnam was organized by the French into the two protectorates of Tonkin and Annam and the colony of Cochinchina, with the native government reduced to a shadow. Native inhabitants of the two protectorates had the civil status of protégés, while those in the colony and the larger cities were subjects. Only 2,600 of the entire indigenous population, a minute per cent, were admitted to French citizenship before the war and thus received the political, if not the social, rights and privileges enjoyed by Frenchmen. Opportunities for responsible service in the middle and higher levels of business, government, and the armed forces were practically limited to Frenchmen or natives of other French colonies. No new opportunities were provided to Vietnamese for the practice of democratic representative government (although citizens have fewer such opportunities in France itself than in some other countries). Indeed, various "representative assemblies" were purely advisory bodies whose suggestions could always be vetoed by French officials.

Capital improvements made in Vietnam, of which the French are justifiably proud, although paid for in part from Vietnamese revenues, provided little profit or convenience to the Vietnamese except for small numbers of the elite. Agricultural and mineral production were increased under the French, but so was population, the increase in people about keeping pace with the increase in goods and low-paid jobs. Industry and hydroelectric power were left largely undeveloped. Modern consumer goods and services were imported almost wholly from France, which had first call on exports. While the country itself was thus enriched and developed, it can hardly be demonstrated that the living standards of the peasant or coolie were improved. Under the French many Vietnamese became acquainted with Western practices, doctrines, and ideals, but had little opportunity to express or achieve these for themselves. During and after the war the French have been reaping this Western whirlwind which they helped sow, as it was inevitable they sometime would.

PARTIES OF REFORM

Fourth. Of many small Vietnamese parties organized for revolution, reform, or gradual amelioration, the Indochinese Communist party was the one hardest hit by the French administration and police from the time of its founding in 1929; yet this meant that during the war they were the native party best equipped by clandestine organization, experience, and motivation to serve the purposes of the Allies in Vietnam and thus to receive their support, and to get themselves into a position to dominate the power vacuum created there at the end of the war.

The small educated elite in Vietnam were the first organizers of parties or associations which sought to change the colonial relationship between France and Indochina either by force or by political action. During the 1880's revolts might be led by mandarins of the old native bureaucracy trying to maintain the status quo. But after the turn of the century trouble for France came primarily from those educated under French and, later, Japanese or Russian tutelage and oriented to Western political concepts. These leaders attempted to organize from the top down, but only on rare occasions, as in 1930, for example, were they able to guide large mass uprisings from the rice roots— revolts that proved ephemeral, in part because of the efficiency of the French *sûreté*, which was probably more ruthless than were contemporary British or Dutch colonial police.

The Vietminh

Communist parties, with both Stalinist and Trotskyist leanings, entered the scene in the '20's. The former was led, chiefly from outside Indochina, by Nguyen Ai Quoc, traveled son of an ex-mandarin, who after World War I went from socialism in Paris to Moscow to Canton, where he founded the party among Vietnamese exiles and visitors. Briefly in the open during the Popular Front period, the party in 1939 was again forced underground; as Indochina passed under Japanese and Vichy control and uprisings in 1940 and 1941 proved unsuccessful, its members tended to gravitate to southern China. Here in the spring of 1941 Nguyen organized among the Communists and other splinter parties the League for the Independence of Vietnam, the "Viet Nam Doc Lap Dong Minh Hoi," or Vietminh

for short. Pressed by local Chinese Kuomintang generals, the Vietminh collaborated for a time under another Chinese-sponsored Vietnamese group organized to work against the French and Japanese in Indochina. During this period the Chinese even threw Nguyen into jail as a "French spy." The rival Vietnamese group, however, proved ineffective. Nguyen was then released from prison and in 1943 under a new name, Ho Chi-minh, received Chungking's blessing and financial and military support for underground work in Vietnam.

While other Vietnamese political leaders lolled in China or collaborated with the Vichy French and Japanese in Vietnam, Ho and his Vietminh League linked up with the guerrillas of Communist Vo Nguyen Giap in north Vietnam, recruited new members, and established new contacts in the country, and soon proved themselves the only pro-Allied Vietnamese group capable of eluding the French and Japanese and of promising effective aid in sabotage, espionage, and the rescue of Allied airmen. While they may have done little useful work, it was nevertheless Ho's Vietminh, sponsored and subsidized by the Chinese Nationalists and the American Office of Strategic Services, which at the end of the Pacific war found itself well organized, well armed, and in a position to use quickly the circumstances which permitted it to take over from the Japanese (who had removed and immobilized all French the previous March) by organizing a de facto government, the Democratic Republic of Vietnam.

THE DEMOCRATIC REPUBLIC OF VIETNAM

By the end of August 1945, though still opposed by some Vietnamese parties, this government was firmly established and seated in Hanoi. It was the apparent heir of a Vietnam declared independent of France and united during the previous six months under the Emperor Bao Dai with the collaboration of the Japanese; for it had received Bao Dai's blessing as he abdicated to become a private citizen (better that "in an independent state than emperor of a subjugated country") and to collaborate with it for a time as "Supreme Councilor." It was supported by and included representatives of a fairly wide range of Vietnamese nationalist interests, including Roman Catholics, some of whom still support the Republic. It was led by "Uncle" Ho, rapidly acquiring a wide and popular, almost magical reputation as "the" nationalist leader. By November this government was in such a position that the French General Leclerc could say: "The best thing to do in order not to lose face is to make a 'military promenade' up to the Chinese frontier. Then we should re-embark as many as possible, and get out. There are no other solutions." And the government of the Republic was guided in the name of the Vietminh by members of the Indochinese Communist party who said nothing of Communism and were soon to "dissolve" the party which the French for almost a generation had done their best to destroy. And the Vietminh itself, to top the paradox, had got its start and developed its position originally under the auspices of the exact forces which are now opposing it.

THE MARCH 1946 AGREEMENT

Fifth. Urged by a combination of events and pressures, France and the Hanoi Vietnamese government represented by Ho as President signed on March 6, 1946, a formal agreement recognizing the Democratic Republic of Vietnam as a "free state." Yet exactly ten months later, without making any attempt to "capture" or isolate the Communist leadership of the Vietminh-dominated government of the Republic, France announced its complete repudiation of the agreement, stating that Paris could deal only with the "authentic representatives" of the Vietnamese people.

France, itself recently freed from an occupying power, returned to Indochina with every expectation of reoccupying the territory, of re-establishing the status quo ante and of discussing only then the minor concessions of a reorganization plan for the region hastily announced in March 1945, after the Japanese had suddenly taken over control from the Vichy French. But before French forces could arrive in Indochina, Kuomintang Chinese troops had moved in north of 16° latitude, and British troops south of that parallel, to accept the Japanese surrender and care for prisoners of war as arranged at Potsdam by the Allies in July. The Chinese in the north did not dislodge the government and armed forces of the Republic; indeed, they allowed it to strengthen its situation. In the south, however, the British chased the Republic's representatives out of Saigon and a bitter guerrilla warfare began, soon to be taken up by French forces under Leclerc, the British troops being withdrawn early in 1946.

The agreement of March 1946 was signed in a context including the following elements: The French were established in a few urban centers and held some communication lines in the south. The Republic was established in the north and some forces under its control were fighting in the south. The Chinese were slow in carrying out their assignment, were neutral as regards the Republic, but were ravaging the countryside of the north—both French and Vietnamese wanted to get them out. Many French hostages were in Vietnamese hands. The United States, while aiding the French in France, had announced an official "hands off" policy in Indochina; but during the war, it was rumored, Roosevelt had stated his opinion that Indochina should be placed under an international trusteeship and not returned to French control and more recently American journalists and Office of Strategic Services personnel had apparently urged Ho and the Vietminh to stand firm for the independence of Vietnam, so that the French felt their position threatened by the United States. Ho announced that the Republic would continue to fight against all French forces unless France promised independence, but the Republic had received no international recognition and was weak. The French public was little interested in Indochina and less in fighting to hold it; the French hoped to use the early March high tides to move troops into the north.

In this situation, France was ready to push for the withdrawal of the Chinese and to recognize the Republic as a free state within the Indochinese Federation and the French Union, stipulating that the north (Tonkin), central (Annam), and south (Cochinchina) regions should decide by popular referendum whether they would be included under the authority of the Republic. The Republic, or rather the top leadership of the Vietminh, for there was strong opposition, was ready to sign such an agreement and to accept French troops in the north peaceably. Details were to be worked out in conferences. But in April Saigon began to speak of indigenous demands for a separate "Cochinchinese Republic" and on June 1, 1946, the French civil administration in Indochina recognized such a government headed by a majority of Vietnamese French citizens!

THE AGREEMENT REPUDIATED

In spite of this inept move to retain a maximum of French power in the south, France welcomed President Ho with the highest formal honors as a chief of state when he arrived in Paris shortly thereafter to discuss—quite unsuccessfully for the Republic of Vietnam —details arising out of the March agreement. This treatment could hardly allay the increasing widespread Vietnamese suspicion of French sincerity, heightened by dirty fighting on both sides in the guerrilla warfare which continued in the south and by constant friction and morbid incidents between officials and other French and Vietnamese in the north. Ho returned to Hanoi, still honored by the French (he told reviewing troops he had seen their mothers, wives, and sweethearts in Paris, who hoped for their quick return, as did the Vietnamese), but accused by many of his compatriots of playing the role of a French dupe in still publicly expressing his hopes for a satisfactory peaceful settlement. Starting in Haiphong and Hanoi in November and December 1946, general and open warfare broke out; the government of the Democratic Republic of Vietnam fled its capital, Hanoi; and in January 1947 France repudiated its agreement of the previous March. Many observers feel that Vietnam was lost to France and the Western democracies during 1946. Whether or not it could have been saved had the French made prompt moves toward unity and real independence while taking key Communists into camp is still a question for the historians to argue.

WAR THAT WAS NOT A WAR

Sixth. With negotiations broken off and fighting become general, France entered upon a war which was not a war, and was supported by the United States without being supported by the United States.

France could not at first admit that

the "rebellion" in Vietnam was a "war" for several reasons: such an admission would tend to affirm the legal status of the Democratic Republic of Vietnam; it would open the way for action before the United Nations with possibly dangerous results in North Africa, Madagascar, or other trouble spots in the French Union; certainly for most Vietnamese it would violate the new constitution of the French Republic which states that France will "undertake no war with a view to conquest and will never employ force against the liberty of any people"; and it would require the adoption of rules and conventions of warfare which both sides have chosen largely to ignore in a war of little quarter, few prisoners, Vietminh grenading of Saigon civilians, and French "strategic" bombing of peasant villages.

The United States accepted the French definition of the struggle in Vietnam as an internal, purely colonial problem, not a "war" with which the United Nations or other nations might properly be concerned. The United States thus maintained officially a neutral attitude. This was apparently a bitter disappointment to Vietminh leaders who were naïve in the ways of international law and who had been so encouraged by some individual Americans or by wishful thinking to believe that aid would be forthcoming from "anticolonial" America that they formally, if fruitlessly, addressed long, serious letters arguing the Vietminh case to Senator Capper, President Truman, and others.

But while technically neutral, aiding neither side, the United States felt it necessary to get rid of quantities of surplus military equipment and supplies in metropolitan France and North Africa, and to do this quickly. Much of this American material soon appeared in Indochina, as was to be expected. This led to accusations by Vietnamese, as well as by Indonesians, Burmans,

and Indians, that America was in fact aiding the imperialist powers in their attempts to regain colonial territories by reconquest. The "reservoir of good will," of which Mr. Willkie had spoken, had begun to ebb.

COMMUNISM AND THE FRENCH POLICY

Seventh. The goal of French policy in Indochina from 1947 on was to decrease or eliminate Communist strength; yet the means used in implementing this policy did just the opposite.

The fear of Communism and of the top Communist leaders of the Democratic Republic of Vietnam was a major consideration in the French decision not to deal with, and certainly not to grant independence or make other concessions to, the Republic. Yet they neither offered nor promised any alternative to the Republic which would attract the vast bulk of the Vietnamese people who were either non-Communist or, in smaller numbers, actively anti-Communist, but who at the same time were strongly anti-French in their nationalist desire for independence for Vietnam. The Vietnamese who would not collaborate with the French or sit on the fence could turn only to Ho and his Republic, and many did, thus giving the Communists added strength.

The French, confronted in the country by stubborn guerrillas and uncooperative partisan peasants and finding themselves in the cities on the receiving end of the Republic's brutal terrorist tactics, could see the Republic's power only as coercion and force, to be countered by military action. So Paris voted the military credits (with the help of the French Communist party, which abstained when it could have defeated the bills by voting against them) that put over 115,000 men in the field by late spring of 1947. But military operations against the Republic's forces seemed only to increase their numbers and stiffen the resistance of Vietnamese who felt themselves fighting for Vietnam against foreigners.

In the early years of the struggle Uncle Ho and his government were not defined by the Vietnamese as Communist or even pro-Communist except among the few who were more knowing. The Soviet-type organization of the civil administration and the army meant little to most Vietnamese. For the majority in those years the Republic was an expression of their own patriotic fervor and its chief goals were the total elimination of the French, unification of the country, and then eventually the improvement of the common man's lot. Just as the French were quite unprepared for the realities they found on their return to Indochina at the end of the war, so they were slow in recognizing the potent magical effects worked by the term "independence" as pronounced early in 1945 by the Emperor, aloof and now absent, so that the magic had become firmly associated with Uncle Ho, who might walk barefoot into the village at any moment through the bamboo fence which proverbially kept the Emperor out.

Bao Dai

Eighth. After later attempts to counter the Vietminh leadership with other opposing leaders or groups, none of them having a strong policy, the French turned finally to the former Emperor, Bao Dai; yet this abdicated royal person was from the start clearly not a figure who could rally a wide, enthusiastic, or loyal following behind him.

The Emperor at best had occupied a rather secondary position in the power structure of modern Vietnam under the French. As for Bao Dai himself, he was already compromised by an appar-

ent willingness to collaborate equally with the prewar French, the Vichy French, the Japanese, and the Vietminh, whom he dropped early in 1946 in disgust, moving to Hong Kong. This highly secular Emperor would receive little respect either from the many modern Vietnamese who had repudiated monarchical institutions, or from the more conservative who saw in Bao Dai's abdication and the rise of the Vietminh a clear indication that he had lost the "Mandate of Heaven" without which he could hardly rule. Even though Bao Dai, as chief of state, has stood firm since 1948 in his demand for a unified and completely independent Vietnam, he has been unable to win many away from Ho, who made this demand first.

Hesitation and Fear

Ninth. In recent years both France and the United States have feared that any major intensification of the conflict in Vietnam would correspondingly limit French action in the organization of European defense; yet hesitation born of this fear has actually prolonged and thus intensified the war in Vietnam with a result that French action in Europe has indeed been practically paralyzed.

France and latterly the United States have not been willing to commit to Vietnam a striking force sufficiently large and well equipped to ensure putting a quick stop to the conflict there. This decision may have kept China from more active sudden participation in the war, but it has not prevented the struggle from dragging on with a gradually increasing intensity and an always greater commitment of men and more elaborate equipment on both sides. These developments, of course, have kept the French in a position of weakness and indecision in relation to their European situation.

THE EXPLOSIVE PRESENT

Tenth. French hopes for a military decision which would permit negotiation with the Vietminh from a position of strength have led only to an equal expansion of strength on either side; but since this equality of strength has now been extended from the conventional and local level up to the H-bomb and international level, a negotiated political decision appears to be inevitable even though it can be satisfactory to no one.

In an earlier and simpler situation limited to Indochina a political decision could have been reached, at least before 1950 and the Chinese Communist victory, with a good deal more freedom and more room for maneuvering on either side than is possible now. The expansion of the situation, the increase in the parties and forces concerned, has served only to decrease and contract alternative political solutions, while increasing immeasurably the danger of explosions both political and physical.

Through it all at the bottom of the increasingly charged spiral are the Vietnamese people, more divided than ever before and more unhappy.

Lauriston Sharp, Ph.D., Ithaca, New York, is director of the Southeast Asia Program of the Department of Far Eastern Studies, professor of anthropology, and chairman of the Department of Sociology and Anthropology at Cornell University. He was a fellow of the Australian National Research Council, North Queensland Expeditions, and lecturer in anthropology at the University of Sydney (1933–35). Associated with Cornell since 1936, he taught during the war in the Army Specialized Training program and was acting assistant chief, Division of Southeast Asian Affairs, Department of State (1945–46). He has done field study in many areas, including Thailand (1948–49, 1952–53), and has published studies on Thailand and Indochina.

Our Common Stake in Indochina

By Pierre Millet

I DO not think it is an exaggeration to say that today the problem of Indochina is foremost in the preoccupations of the free world. For example—every week dozens of letters come to my desk from young Americans asking the Embassy if we can help them to fight for freedom in Indochina. Of course, the only thing we can do is to thank those men for their generous spirit and for their courage, well in the American tradition, and explain to them the reasons why we cannot answer their request favorably. But this fact proves beyond any doubt that the concern about Indochina is not now confined to governments, chanceries, politicians, or journalists—that it is the concern of the man in the street. As far as the American government is concerned, the position of the United States towards Indochina has been made quite clear during the last weeks, especially by the President and by the Secretary of State, Mr. John Foster Dulles, in the speech before the Overseas Press Club of New York.

It is not for me, in any case, to define the American position in this matter or to underline what is at stake for Americans in Indochina. I only wish to mention what comfort and what inspiration we get from the fact that once more in a great moment of history, when the eternal values of mankind are again in peril, the United States and France stand together. Indeed, if it were not for American help Indochina would most probably have been lost today to the Communist imperialists.

Nevertheless, if recently the American position towards Indochina has been made quite clear, I feel that many would see more clearly still if they knew, surely, where France stands in this matter. They would see more clearly not only as far as Indochina is concerned, but also about the other problems of the Far East—because at this moment all the problems are closely related: the battle of Dienbienphu, the negotiations in Paris about the status of Vietnam in the French Union, and the prospects of the two conferences in Geneva about Korea and Indochina.

FRANCE IN INDOCHINA

I hope that my readers will forget that I am an official. I know that like my compatriots Americans have a tendency to question the judgment of the government they, and we, have freely chosen. But so far, whether we like it or not, there have not been any substitutes for governments in the conduct of public affairs. I will tell you what we —the French—are doing today in Indochina, what are our intentions for the future of that part of the world, and how we envisage Franco-American relations in the solution of this problem with special reference to the conference in Geneva.

In this statement, I will not try to conceal the mistakes my government may have made in Indochina since 1945. Only totalitarian governments think they are always right—and I hope that, in exchange, it will be recognized that we have, on the whole, accomplished a great task in that part of the world since the Japanese surrender. And if this appears to be the case, I am only asking for your judgment, not for your praise. Only history will tell whether or not France was equal to her duty in Indochina. This is not the time for recriminations but for action, and I find that these words of Winston Churchill in his memorable speech in the House of Commons on June 18, 1940, are relevant to this occasion, "Of this I am quite sure, that if we open a quarrel between the past and the present, we shall find that we have lost the future."

First of all, what is the present situation in Indochina? What is France doing there at the present time?

We are defending the newly acquired independence of the three Associated States and in doing so we are defending the whole of southeast Asia against Communist enslavement.

On this second object, I will not expand. Mr. Dulles, in New York, did it far better and far more eloquently than I could ever dream of doing.

INDEPENDENCE OF THE ASSOCIATED STATES

As to the independence of the three Associated States, from 1947 until the present time France has been negotiating agreements to give these countries full independence within the French Union. If this has not always been apparent to the eyes of foreign observers or to the local populations, it is because at the same time France has been engaged in Indochina in a fight against a Communist rebel which has prevented those observers and the local populations from seeing the true extent of the independence which had been granted by France; that war obliged France to limit the exercise of the newly acquired freedom. But, believe me, that independence is not only written in the agreements the French government has signed; you will find it engraved in the hearts of the overwhelming majority of my compatriots. Colonialism is a thing of the past in my country. Frenchmen

at the very time I write are dying in Dienbienphu for the liberation of Indochina and only Communist propaganda can make people think otherwise. If at one time some doubts were possible on this subject, I think it is out of the question since July 3 of last year, when France reaffirmed the complete independence of the three Associated States, opening the way to new and final agreements.

On October 22, 1953, a treaty of association and friendship was signed between France and Laos, in the spirit and in the letter of the Declaration of July 3. A few weeks ago, negotiations were started in Paris between France and Vietnam to reach a similar agreement. Negotiations with Cambodia will follow. But already, through previous agreements, the three Associated States of Indochina have nearly all the attributes of internal and external sovereignty. This fact is still too little known.

In the field of foreign affairs, the three states now enjoy the rights of full sovereignty. They have been recognized by more than thirty countries, and they are free to have diplomatic relations with the governments of their choice. They are members of international bodies, most of them under United Nations control, and in certain cases they belong to organizations—the Colombo Plan, for instance—where France is not represented. May I remind my readers that as far back as September 1951 the three Associated States, through their own representation in San Francisco, signed the Peace Treaty with Japan? The agreement of the President of the French Republic is not requested for the credentials of the diplomatic representatives of the three Indochinese states abroad, nor is it necessary for the accreditation of foreign envoys in Indochina. In this respect the French Union is more liberal than the Commonwealth.

PURPOSE OF THE FRENCH UNION

I have just written, "French Union." Some people say: Why a French Union? Cannot those Asian peoples be left alone? Why should they be associated with a European country eight thousand miles away?

Our answer is this: The reason of such an association lies in the interest of these states. That interest is the cement of the French Union.

The present age has shown the importance and the advantages of great political and economic entities, such as the British Commonwealth of Nations, the Pan American Union, and the North Atlantic Treaty Organization, not to mention the United States of America and the Union of Soviet Socialist Republics. In the same spirit the nations of Western Europe are now attempting the political, military, and economic integration of that part of the world. In these concepts and creations, the smaller states have found advantages. This is the raison d'être of the French Union, and in the case of Indochina that association has been so far for France more of a burden than a highly profitable enterprise. The French Union, like the Commonwealth, is not a prison. Freedom is its purpose. To prove my point, allow me to read the definition of the French Union as you find it in Article 2 of the recent treaty of friendship and association between France and Laos. The French Union is "an association of independent and sovereign peoples with freedom and equality of rights and duties in which all the associates (and France is but one of them) place in common their resources in order to guarantee the defense of the Union as a whole."

At this very moment, the Vietnamese delegates are trying to find in Paris a formula which will underline the fact that they have freely adhered to the French Union. In this I feel they are right, and perhaps the French Constituents in 1946 exaggerated the prefabricated aspect of the French Union. One does not like to live forever in a prefabricated house; it is only a temporary dwelling until the real house is built. That house, the French Union, is being built, and its walls will be all the stronger if its tenants have all helped in building them.

To go back to the internal status of the Associated States, they have already —in this field—all the attributes of full sovereignty. The only limitations are those imposed by the war now raging in their countries; for instance, military police and censorship.

There were some restrictions concerning rights of jurisdiction over French and Chinese citizens. For them, mixed courts were created like those existing some years ago in Egypt. Today, this distinction is about to become a thing of the past, and negotiations are taking place to that effect between France and Vietnam. They have already been completed for Cambodia and Laos.

Two figures will illustrate the change in Indochina: in 1939, there were more than 28,000 French civil servants in Indochina; today there are only about 2,000, and they are nearly all serving in the administration of the three Associated States and depend on the local governments, not on France.

NATIONAL ARMIES OF THE ASSOCIATED STATES

And, finally, the three states have now their own national armies, symbol and guarantee of their independence. I shall merely mention Cambodia and Laos, these countries which, until recently, were not involved in the war to the same extent as Vietnam; nevertheless, they have now a regular army of about 20,000 soldiers each.

In Vietnam, the progress has been

striking. France, with far less means than the United States, has been trying to do what your country has done in Korea.

In 1949, the Vietnamese army counted only a few battalions. Today, it is over 200,000 strong. At the end of the present year it will be about 300,000. The Chief of that army is Vietnamese, and there are about 1,000 French officers and noncommissioned officers as instructors or on the Vietnamese general staff.

While I am on this subject of the national armies of Indochina, I think I should deal with the question of the training of those forces. During the last few weeks it has often been said and written in the United States that this training by the French was inadequate and that the French High Command should accept the dispatch of an American training mission to Indochina. Surprise and regret have been expressed, too, at the reluctance of the French authorities to agree to such a plan.

We do not deny that the training of the national armies could be improved, and we do not refuse the help of American experience. But certain factors must be kept in mind. (1) As I have said, to build up a Vietnamese army from a few battalions in 1949 to 300,000 men at the end of this year is not a poor achievement, and I know that many competent American observers think that no other government could have achieved that result in Indochina. (2) The Korean War is vastly different from the war in Indochina. In Indochina there are mostly "guerilla" operations while in Korea there was a regular war with a well-defined front. (3) For the last eighty years, France has had experience with the local populations. The question of language—among other things—plays an important part. (4) So far, the responsibility for the conduct of the war in Indochina is the responsibility of the French High Command. Such a responsibility cannot be shared —or if it is to be, then the conduct of the war must assume a very different character. It must not be forgotten that in Korea, if the Korean army was trained by the Americans, the Americans too were fighting and dying on that field of battle. I am not suggesting, and my government has never asked, that it should be so in Indochina. I am only stating a fact in order to make you understand the reaction of the French High Command.

The French Expeditionary Corps is now over 160,000 men strong, with about 80,000 French metropolitan soldiers and officers. To date, the losses of this Corps have been over 136,000 in killed and wounded. The losses of the metropolitan French alone are over 60,000 (of whom more than 1,500 French officers have been killed or are missing). Since 1951, the losses of the national armies have been over 20,000.

Going back to the degree of independence which has been granted to the three Associated States, I am sure that many readers will wonder why, if what I have just said is true, war is still raging in Indochina.

Many will wonder, too, why the French did not grant to Ho Chi-minh in 1946 what they have given since 1947 to Vietnam, Cambodia, and Laos.

Those are pertinent questions. I will try to answer them as best as I can, and, as I have said before, in doing so, I will not try to conceal the mistakes we may have made since 1945.

WHY WAS INDEPENDENCE DELAYED?

First, why did we not grant independence to the three Associated States after the Japanese surrender just as the United States did for the Philippines and as the British Government did for India, Pakistan, and Burma?

In answering that question, I will point out that the American government spent twelve years in the process of granting independence to the Philippines and that Britain had been for two or three decades in the process of freeing from British rule the three nations just mentioned.

The French were asked to do in a few months for Indochina—and at the very moment that these areas were themselves reasserting their independence—what the United States and Britain had had years to prepare for. On this point, I will admit our responsibilities. It is true that the French administration before and during the war did not foresee the explosion of nationalism which was to take place after the hostilities and did not in consequence take the necessary measures to prepare the independence of the three states of Indochina. There were, of course, large sections of French opinion which were in favor of such measures, but, as you know, France has had since the war coalition governments—too many of them at that—and those governments were formed by representatives of various parties which did not see eye to eye as far as the solution of the Indochinese problem was concerned. On this subject, I will remind you that even the Communists were represented in French cabinets until April 1947.

From that situation resulted the necessity of compromise towards many problems—the problem of Indochina among them—and what was easy for the British government, a one-party government towards India, was impossible for our government in the case of Indochina. This is not an excuse. It is a fact—which I personally deplore as many of my countrymen do.

FRANCE AND HO CHI-MINH

As to the other question, Why did you give Bao Dai in 1949 what you refused to Ho Chi-minh in 1946 or, rather, why did you give Bao Dai more than the Vietminh leader asked for in 1946? This question is related to what I have just said.

In 1946, the French government was not prepared and French public opinion was not ready to give off hand to Ho Chi-minh all he was asking for. The main reason is that we knew better than anybody else except Moscow the Communist past of Ho Chi-minh and some of his associates and that we wanted to be sure that their national aspirations—quite legitimate—did not cover Bolshevik designs.

Anyhow, in spite of these misgivings and suspicions, and in spite of the unrealistic attitude of some quarters of French opinion, we did recognize Ho Chi-minh and started to negotiate with him. Those negotiations were broken off by Ho Chi-minh's attack in Tonkin in December 1946.

In the years which followed, we realized in the hardest way possible—through war—the true character of Ho Chi-minh and of the Vietminh. We realized that they were part of a vast Communist conspiracy, the results of which were to be seen in Central Europe, in China, and in Korea. What would be happening today in southeast Asia if we had accepted Ho Chi-minh in 1946 as the master of Indochina? So we went on working for the independence of the three states of Indochina and we refused to deal with Ho Chi-minh. We had to fight against him.

That is why since 1946 French policy in Indochina has been difficult for many foreign observers to understand. On the one hand, we say that we want the independence of that part of the world, and on the other, thousands and thousands of our boys remain there to fight.

They fight for two reasons. First, they fight to defend the independence of the three Associated States against

Communist subversion—against what Marshal de Lattre de Tassigny called in Washington "Communist colonialism." Second, they fight to defend southeast Asia against the same enemy, a point which was made quite clear by Mr. John Foster Dulles in his speech last Monday.

U. S. AID IN INDOCHINA

The United States government recognized the basic character of the conflict in Indochina when continental China fell to the Communists. When the Mao Tse-tung regime started to give increasing help to the Vietminh, and above all when Communist aggression in Korea took place, the United States government decided to help the French and Indochinese governments with money and matériel.

So the year 1950, which is remembered mostly because of Korea, is also the year when the United States began to take direct interest and an active part in the "new Indochina."

Four years have elapsed since then. The anti-Communist forces have not been able to achieve a decisive military success in Indochina, and at the French request it was agreed at the Berlin Conference in February that the problem of Indochina should be discussed in Geneva at the end of April.

FRENCH LASSITUDE

The present feelings of my countrymen towards the Indochinese problem are characterized by a growing lassitude. This lassitude, as expressed in the French Parliament and in the French press, has four main sources: (1) military developments in Indochina; (2) the political evolution of the three Associated States, particularly Vietnam and Cambodia; (3) the effects of the Indochinese conflict upon France's position in Western Europe; (4) the Armistice in Korea.

The military situation

After more than seven years of fighting, the French see no prospect of a quick ending of the war. If it had not been for American assistance, I think we should have had to give up the fight. The French people, like the Americans in regard to Korea, naturally want to see the boys back or at least an end of the fighting. Some people in my country say also, If the fight in Indochina is a fight which is of direct concern to the free world, why are we alone, with the Indochinese, to shed our blood for it?

I know that in the United States some people say: Why do not the French pay the price for achieving a decisive victory, as we did in Korea, and send more men—their conscripted men, for instance? Why do they not have a more aggressive and realistic strategy? To that I answer: We have heavy commitments in Europe and in Indochina, we are paying the price, and in that respect we have been living above our means for years. Anyhow the solution of the problem is not to send more French troops to Indochina, although we did it last year in a small way.

The Indochinese conflict is not an ordinary war—like the one in Korea—it is a politico-military struggle and basically a civil war. A civil war to be won in Indochina only by French troops would have achieved no result. That struggle has got to be won mainly by the local anti-Communist armies if the local governments are to win their ideological fight against Communism, that is, to prove that they are fighting for their own independence and not to maintain colonialism under a different name. That is why France, with extensive American help, is building up the national armies. That enterprise may have started too late—but it takes years to achieve such a goal. You may form a soldier in a few weeks; you need years to form a general staff.

A more aggressive strategy? This is the case with the so-called Navarre Plan, but that plan expects important results only eighteen months from now, mostly because it is based on the formation and instruction of new local forces. Will French opinion keep patient until then? And will Communist China tolerate a defeat of the Vietminh?

Political developments

The second cause of French lassitude is to be found in the political developments in Vietnam, and to a lesser extent in Cambodia. In Vietnam, there is no doubt that the resolution of the national Vietnamese Congress which met in Saigon last October created a very unfavorable impression among my compatriots. This Congress, which met only for a short period, which did not represent exactly the distribution of opinion in Vietnam, and which was led by the most extreme nationalists, passed a motion declaring it was opposed to the inclusion of Vietnam in the French Union. The majority of the Congress promptly realized that they had been outmaneuvered and canceled that motion, passing another saying that the Congress was not in favor of the participation of Vietnam in the French Union in its "present form."

But, as far as French public opinion was concerned, the harm, a very great one, had been done. The reaction of the majority of my compatriots was, Why should we go on being killed for people who do not want to stay with us? This is a very human reaction. After all, what do we expect in Indochina? Certainly not more than the American position in the Philippines. In short, a guarantee of our economic and cultural interests when we go.

The feeling of lassitude is all the stronger because there are doubts in certain quarters about the dynamism of some Vietnamese leaders. Vietnam needs inspiration from them. The United States can provide the money and the matériel for this war. France can give her men—but men, money, and matériel will be of little help without that inspiration. Around the battlefield of Indochina, there are too many spectators on the fence who have not been brought to realize that the match is a match to be fought between local teams.

France and EDC

The third reason for the lassitude of French public opinion must be found in the effects of the Indochinese conflict upon France's position in Western Europe. You are well aware of the important part France must play in NATO and in the organization of the defense of Western Europe. You know too about the European Defense Community plan. In spite of the fact that the French government initiated that project, there is a very strong feeling in France against it. A great number of my compatriots, who have not forgotten German aggression, are afraid that because of France's military commitments in Indochina, where we have the equivalent of ten French divisions, Germany will assume the military leadership in the EDC.

Armistice in Korea

The last important reason for French lassitude towards Indochina is related to the Armistice in Korea. Quite a number of people in France think that if the United States did not refuse to talk to the Sino-Koreans and sign an armistice at Panmunjom, she cannot logically object to the French talking to the Vietminh and eventually to the Chinese who help Ho Chi-minh.

THE PROSPECT OF ARMISTICE

Thus I come to the question of the prospect of an armistice in Indochina and the problems which such an armistice create for the French and the United States governments.

In Berlin, last February, the United States government agreed that the problem of a solution of the Indochinese conflict be discussed at the Geneva Conference, parallel to the Korean discussion. I know that opinion in the United States is not too happy about this decision, fearing that recognition of the Peiping regime and a lifting of the embargo on Red China may be the price of a promise by the Chinese Communists of a settlement in Indochina. I should like to remind you what the French Prime Minister said in the National Assembly on January 8:

We want peace, but not at any cost. We must know, as was the case in Korea, how to go on fighting without becoming discouraged as long as is necessary to arrive at a settlement. We shall never lose sight of the fact that France's aims are the independence of the Associated States and the defense of the world on the southeast Asia front.

A short time after the end of the Berlin Conference M. Laniel, with reference to M. Nehru's truce proposal, made quite clear in the National Assembly the conditions on which the French Command and the Associated States would insist for a cease fire in Indochina. These conditions showed quite clearly that France and her Indochinese allies did not contemplate any armistice which would imperil the position, military and political, of the three states.

The difference of opinion between France and the United States on this problem—and it would serve no purpose to conceal that there is such a difference—is that while both governments are of the opinion that the military operations must go on, the French government thinks that at the same time no occasion must be neglected to ascertain if a solution can be found by negotiation. In this respect Geneva will be the testing ground of Communist intentions.

IF WAR MUST GO ON . . .

If it appears in Geneva that there is no hope of finding a solution of the Indochinese conflict by peaceful means, then there is no doubt about it, the whole conduct of this war will have to be reconsidered by all the parties concerned on the anti-Communist side. Having in mind, among other things, the problems of European defense, any government in Paris will have to find out what alternative there is. We shall have to ask our allies by what practical means they can lighten our heavy burden and how the limits of "joint action" are to be defined. As you probably know, Communist propaganda has adopted the slogan, "The Americans are ready to fight to the last Frenchman in Indochina." I well know the odious character of such a slogan, but its effects must not be underrated.

Do not forget that the failure in Geneva to find a solution or the beginning of a solution in Indochina would mean the return to the same kind of long, indecisive war for many months to come, at least until 1956. Let us not be led astray by such formulas for victory as Give the Indochinese the feeling they are fighting for themselves and not for French colonialism. In this respect the limit has been reached, and the French troops in Indochina know already that whether they win or lose, France will be out of Indochina. Still, even with that knowledge, the men of Colonel de Castries in Dienbienphu fight and die day and night.

Do not forget that apart from the

United States no other nation since the war has been fighting more relentlessly against Communism at home and abroad than France, while she had at the same time to face a colossal task of reconstruction and rehabilitation in many fields.

We welcome the criticisms, we ask neither for praise nor mercy, we know we are fighting the good fight for freedom in Indochina. But there, France is fighting not only against Ho Chi-minh, but against Communist China, the Soviet Union, and its satellites.

The men, Indochinese and French, who are fighting and dying now at Dienbienphu are fighting the war of freedom, but should not the responsibilities be shared more equally if what is at stake now in Indochina is not only the freedom of that country in southeast Asia but freedom itself?

Pierre Millet, Washington, D. C., has been Counselor of the Embassy of France since 1950, in charge of its Far Eastern affairs. He has been in the diplomatic service since 1938: in the French Embassy in China, chargé d'affaires in Thailand, and head of the Division of Southeast Asian Affairs in the French Foreign Office. He was a member of the French delegation at the San Francisco Conference.

The Indochinese Question Mark

By Philip W. Thayer

AS this article is being written, the new Indochina is a question mark. With approximately half of the country and a like proportion of the population under control of the Communist-inspired Vietminh forces, torn by a fluid war of uncertain outcome, no one can say with assurance what the future may hold for the newly created states of Vietnam, Laos, and Cambodia. In the troubled picture which presents itself one thing is nevertheless sure: the question of the preservation of Indochina is a fateful one for the entire free world.

Indochina constitutes a connecting corridor between China and the countries to the south and west. Burma and Thailand are immediate neighbors, and the Malay peninsula stretches beyond, separated by no great distances from the islands of Indonesia and of the Philippines. Throughout this immensely rich and promising area the vital need of the people is time; time in some instances to consolidate the unfamiliar fruits of sudden independence, to consider the numerous and complex problems which have been attendant on an abrupt transition from colonial to sovereign status; and time in all cases to re-establish and develop their economies in the aftermath of the retarding and often disastrous consequences of wartime occupation by the Japanese. Preoccupied with these questions, the countries of southeast Asia are in no position to withstand powerful forces of external aggression. For Indochina to fall into hostile hands, therefore, would mean inevitably the loss of Burma, Thailand, and Malaya, probably of Indonesia, and conceivably of India, Pakistan, Ceylon, and the Philippines.

The present situation, in which there is the gravest danger that the Associated States of Indochina may be overcome by the Communist-inspired troops of the Vietminh, poses problems far exceeding in critical magnitude those of Korea.

Since the surrender of the Japanese, developments in Indochina have been characterized on the one hand by the efforts of the French to recapture their former position of dominance, although on a substantially modified basis, and on the other by the growth of a spirit of nationalism which has been capitalized by Ho Chi-minh for other purposes. Ho Chi-minh has posed as a patriot and a nationalist leader. He has fooled and continues to fool a great many people, chiefly among his own countrymen. Actually, however, there is not the slightest doubt in the minds of those familiar with his personal background and with the record of his past activities that he merely has been making very clever use of prevailing anti-colonial sentiments and legitimate nationalist aspirations to play the Communist game. The familiar pattern of Communist techniques is clearly discernible in all that he has done. Indeed, since the success of the Communists in China in 1949, there has been little attempt to conceal the real nature of Vietminh propaganda. Speaking at the inauguration of the Lao Dong (Workers) party in 1951, Ho Chi-minh was on orthodox ground in referring to Americans as "leaders of the world's imperialists and reactionaries," and in sprinkling his remarks freely with such terms as "lackeys" and "running dogs." The following year he characterized Comrades Stalin and Mao Tse-tung as "the most clear-sighted, the most worthy elder brothers, friends of mankind." Even Ho's own people are beginning to see through his nationalist pose. The ruthless tactics of oppression and destruction used by the Vietminh in the areas under their control have been opening many eyes.

THE FRENCH IN INDOCHINA

The French for their part, returning after the war to bring peace to the country and to protect their own interests, have found themselves forced gradually into a position where they have become guardians of one of the most important bastions of the free world. This is a position which they did not seek and for which they have no particular liking. There is little doubt that the French have made mistakes during the last eight years. At a time when we are more concerned with the present and future than with the past, it would be futile to labor these. Mention should be made, however, of the failure of France to appreciate the full extent of nationalist feeling in its desire for independence and sovereignty. At no point apparently had French plans for Indochina envisaged anything approaching the status of Burma or even of the countries within the British Commonwealth. At the most, they looked toward a limited freedom of action under French leadership. It is noteworthy that all matters affecting the interests of France or of more than one state were subject to review by boards in which France had the right to block or to veto. Similarly, France kept a tight control over foreign affairs, foreign trade, justice, and finance. When concessions have been made, they unfortunately have had the appearance of following on the heels of French reverses. The declaration of July 3, 1953, for example, indicating that France was prepared to transfer to the three Asso-ciated States various functions hitherto under French control, was not issued until after the unhappy campaign of 1952–53. Even the original agreements of March 8, 1949, taking the first steps toward a limited self-government in Indochina, came at a time when the struggle with Ho Chi-minh was not going favorably and when the Communists were on the verge of triumph in China. In the result, instead of getting credit for magnanimity, France has fallen under the odium of acting only under compulsion or force of circumstances.

Like observations would be pertinent in regard to the French conduct of military operations. It could be noted, for instance, that the final decision to expand the Vietnamese army was a belated one, and that the French have been remarkably persistent in keeping officer control down to the noncommissioned level.

Notwithstanding these comments, sight must not be lost of the fact that the situation of France in Indochina is closely tied in with her political position in Europe. However clear-sighted her military commanders and statesmen may have been in facing up to the realities of the fighting in Indochina, they have been at all times severely handicapped by the constant play and counterplay of sensitive forces in the home government. Recent pronouncements from Paris and developments within the French Cabinet are a powerful reminder of the ease with which an ever delicate balance may be disturbed.

It also must be remembered that France has an overwhelming stake in the economic life of Indochina. The French own all the shipping, all the mines, and all the rubber. In addition, they control almost all the banks, practically all industry, and about two-thirds of the rice. Confronted thus by both political and economic factors of a remarkably complex and far-reaching nature, it is not surprising if the French have found difficulty in making decisions.

VIETNAMESE DISTRUST

The ordinary Vietnamese, sitting in the midst of these conflicting claims and interests, with a phony patriot on one side and a grudging savior on the other, perhaps may be pardoned if he has failed to understand the score. Circumstances have combined to make it exceptionally hard for him to determine, if he is a friend of nationalism and independence, whether his aims would be better achieved by fighting with or against the French or by remaining on the sidelines. Of one thing he is sure: that he has had enough of colonialism and wants no more of it. In his mind the French have been and continue to be identified with colonialism, a fixation to which the French themselves, in the persons of too many of their countrymen resident in Indochina, unfortunately contribute by their treatment of the Vietnamese as an inferior race. In the final result therefore the common people of the towns and fields are likely to view the spectacle of the French in shining armor with some distrust and to be disinclined to give them active support. This attitude is exemplified in the lack of conspicuous success which has attended the development of the so-called "light battalions" (*khin quan*) among the Vietnamese. These battalions, numbering at present about sixty, were conceived as forces easily mobile, able to meet the enemy on his own terms, and useful in pacifying conquered territory. In the event, however, they have seemed apathetic and notably deficient in the fighting spirit which is essential.

As stated earlier, the preservation of Indochina is of the utmost importance to the free world. The question therefore is, how can that objective be accomplished in the light of present conditions?

BASES OF A NEGOTIATED SETTLEMENT

Since the date of the Korean Armistice there has been persistent talk of a negotiated settlement in Indochina. Only a glance is necessary to note the complete dissimilarity of circumstances. Inasmuch as Premier Laniel himself has indicated the possibility of such a move, it is nevertheless worth while to explore the suggestion, particularly in the light of the conference at Geneva. A negotiated settlement would appear to involve bases either of partition, of coalition, or of an over-all nature bringing in general Far Eastern questions. Although partition offered a natural solution in Korea, the nature of the conflict and of the interests involved makes it entirely impracticable in Indochina. A line of demarcation was readily at hand in Korea which represented more or less accurately not only the fighting line but also the distribution of population. This has not been true at any time in Indochina. The fighting has been of an extremely mobile and opportunist character. So great has been the ability of the Vietminh forces to appear at unexpected places, to disappear when opposed in strength, and to reappear elsewhere, that the French have seemed often to be combating an army of ghosts. No particular section or sections of the country have been consistently involved. Territorial acquisitions have been for the most part of an ephemeral character. Given positions have been one day in the hands of the Vietminh and on the next day back in the camp of the French, with no sureness at any point as to the real sentiments of the inhabitants. Partition on lines of any logical or satisfying significance appears therefore to offer problems of the utmost difficulty.

Coalition is equally implausible. As

matters now stand, it is difficult to conceive of a coalition government in which Ho Chi-minh and his supporters would not be represented either directly or indirectly. Such a development would be fatal and hence unthinkable.

Finally, should a negotiated settlement take the form of a local arrangement within the framework of a general Far Eastern picture, problems arise of an even more perplexing nature. No settlement of this kind presumably could be effected without a *quid pro quo*, and a *quid pro quo* in this connection inevitably would mean a concession. Could consideration be given, for example, to the recognition of Communist China as the condition for a satisfactory settlement in Indochina? Or to the withdrawal of aid from Formosa? Or to a like cessation of aid in Indochina? Any or all of these possibilities, as well as others equally unpleasant, are almost sure to receive mention at Geneva. Their mere recital is enough to demonstrate the dangers inherent in this type of settlement.

PROLONGATION OF FIGHTING

There remains for consideration the question of continuance of the present armed struggle. Previous forecasts concerning a successful outcome and the time element involved have not been so accurate as to inspire much confidence in current guesses. It will be remembered that as long ago as 1951 eighteen months were mentioned by General de Lattre de Tassigny as the outside limit for triumph. During the intervening years the French have enjoyed an overwhelming preponderance of material advantage. They have had virtually complete control of sea and air, they have held the principal cities and ports, have kept access to the principal producing areas, and have enjoyed the use of greatly superior combat equipment. Numerically, it has been estimated that the French and Vietnamese forces have outnumbered the Vietminh by as much as five to three and have inflicted approximately five times as many casualties. Notwithstanding the favorable inferences which might be drawn from these facts, the fluid character of the fighting, already described, has postponed a clear-cut decision. It may be assumed that the contributions which so far have been made by this country, the recent promise of an additional $385,000,000 (bringing the figures to a point where the United States is paying roughly sixty per cent of the over-all cost of the struggle), and current conversations looking toward further assistance, indicate definite hopes of a not too remote success. In any event, it would appear from present trends that at the very least a continuance of the war will improve the bargaining position, that even a stalemate has the elements of victory, and that the conclusive defeat of the Vietminh is not beyond belief. Local engagements, such as the present struggle at Dienbienphu, should not be permitted to distort this picture. Dienbienphu does not necessarily have great over-all significance. It is doubly unfortunate, therefore, that the situation should have been so built up in the popular mind, possibly as a bargaining point at Geneva, that the moral effect of victory or defeat may be out of all proportion to the actual significance.

Successful prosecution of the fighting, however, presupposes a change of attitude on the part of the majority of the Vietnamese, a change from the hesitancy, the indecision, the apathy, even, which have been so marked in the mass of the population. Only the French can accomplish this transformation, for it involves implanting in the minds of the Vietnamese a clear conviction that the French are in earnest when they talk about independence and are not merely trying subtly to perpetuate their former position. Undoubtedly, France is more in a mood for sincerity at this moment than she has ever been. It is devoutly to be hoped that the negotiations now in progress in Paris may accordingly result in an agreement which will bring genuine independence to Vietnam and not merely a hollow semblance. The hour, however, is late, perhaps even now too late.

COURSES OF ACTION

The foregoing observations have attempted to set forth the gravity of the situation which confronts the free world in Indochina and to enumerate the possible courses of action which may be suggested by way of solution. It is manifest that no one of these courses of action carries with it the assurance of success; on the contrary, all of them leave much to be desired. As tensions mount, however, and as the time approaches when pressures will be increasingly applied in the light of such tensions, clear thinking on the basic issues becomes of paramount importance. Only by firm adherence to principle can the United States remain faithful to its avowed purpose of assuring to the three Associated States the opportunity to develop their rich potentialities along lines freely chosen by their peoples. If, as has been emphasized, the French should relinquish full sovereign rights to the Associated States and leave Indochina, as the British have gone from Burma and the Dutch from Indonesia, this does not mean that the members of the free world should stand idly by while they are driven out by the forces of Communism. No effort, no sacrifice, would appear too great to carry the present struggle either to the point of successful conclusion or to a stage where satisfactory settlement may be possible. In the words of Secretary of State Dulles, if we wish to avoid the greater risks of tomorrow, we must be resolute today.

Philip W. Thayer, LL.B., Washington, D. C., has been dean of the School of Advanced International Studies of The Johns Hopkins University since 1948. From 1920 to 1931 he was in the Far Eastern export-import business, and for part of this period was also research supervisor on foreign trade at the Harvard School of Business. He has been professor of international commercial law at the Fletcher School of Law and Diplomacy (1933–42), acting assistant chief of the Division of World Trade Intelligence in the Department of State (1941–42), special assistant to the United States Ambassador to Chile and cultural relations attaché (1942–45), and expert consultant on legal affairs to the Secretary of the Army (1948). He was editor of Southeast Asia in the Coming World (1953).

Ups and Downs in Indo-American Relations

By NORMAN D. PALMER

THE Republic of India and the United States of America are today respectively the most populous and the most powerful of the democratic states of the world. Each came into existence as a result of a long struggle against British rule. The leaders of the Indian National Congress gained encouragement and inspiration from the American example, and from the stirring words of the Declaration of Independence and other great documents of American freedom. Many Americans followed the course of the Indian independence movement with sympathetic attention, and read the writings of Tagore and Gandhi and Nehru with absorbed interest.

Until 1947, however, relations between the United States and India, on both official and unofficial levels, were for the most part remote and indirect. Since 1947 Americans and Indians have discovered each other. Unfortunately this period of discovery has been an uneasy and trying one, and Indo-American relations have been inescapably colored by the course of world events and by internal as well as external complications. During this period, for obvious reasons, the United States has been forced to concern itself with the defense of the free world in the face of real and present danger, while India has been primarily concerned with the improvement of conditions within her borders and with other grave problems of survival. Basically, because of the similarity of interests and goals, relations between the United States and India have been fairly good; but Americans and Indians alike are distressed by the many points of friction which have

arisen between their two countries, and their feelings toward each other have gone up and down like a Yo-yo since 1947.

Many times in India I was asked why Americans have suddenly taken such an interest in Indian affairs. Sometimes this question seemed to reflect suspicion of American intentions, but more often it seemed to be asked simply out of curiosity. The answer to this question is, I think, quite clear. Until 1947 India was a part of the British Empire; her foreign relations were controlled by the British government and largely by Englishmen, and the states of the world had few formal diplomatic contacts with her. Until World War II the United States was not heavily involved in Asian affairs, and her Asian interests, to the extent that they existed, were concentrated rather in the Far East than in the Indian subcontinent. World War II marked the end of the long period of European dominance of Asia; it ushered in a new and troubled era in Asia, in which the growing aspirations of countless thousands of people whose life conditions are among the worst in the world and the survival of many new independent states are threatened by pressures from without and from within and by the generally unhappy course of world events.

The war also projected the United States into a conspicuous position—one might say an embarrassingly conspicuous position—on the world's stage and saddled it with interests and responsibilities which encompass the globe. For better or for worse, the United States is involved in Asian affairs at a time when Asia is becoming an increasingly important factor in international relations. In the new Asia, India is playing a major role. "If India fails," said Mahatma Gandhi shortly before his death, "Asia dies." The United States clearly has a vital stake in India's efforts to improve the lot of the masses of her distressed people and in her survival as a democratic state. Thus the great interest of Americans in India is a reflection of the new position of both India and the United States.

MUTUAL MISUNDERSTANDING

Any American who visits India is impressed on the one hand with the staggering misconceptions and distortions of America and the suspicions of American policies and intentions and on the other hand with the friendliness and good will which the Indian people show toward Americans personally and with the lively interest in the American scene. Any Indian who visits the United States can testify to the existence of the same attitudes towards his country and his fellow-countrymen. Much of the mutual misunderstanding is based on an ignorance of each other's history and values. This ignorance is understandable, if deplorable; but the time has come when India and America must try to learn more about each other. Americans have a special responsibility in this respect, for they are largely a literate people and they can no longer take refuge in the belief that what they do not know cannot hurt them. One does not have to subscribe to the "East versus West" fallacy to assert that the world looks quite different when viewed from different parts of it and through the eyes of people whose life conditions, cultural values, and experience differ greatly.

"It is probably true," stated Robert Trumbull, veteran correspondent of the *New York Times* in India, in a recent article, "that the Indians understand the United States somewhat better than

Americans understand India." In view of the vast differences in educational and material progress between the United States and India, this statement may startle many Americans, or perhaps even make them indignant. But it is indeed "probably true," and it should serve as an incentive for us to make amends as quickly as we can. We must realize at long last that the history of the world is not synonymous with the history of Western civilization; it never was, in fact, and it will become increasingly less so in the future. There are marked differences between Western civilization and Hindu civilization, as Arnold Toynbee and others have pointed out. India is the home of one of the oldest and most advanced of civilizations; as a continuous civilization it dates back some 5,000 or 6,000 years. The excavations at Mohenjo-daro in Sind and at Harappa in the western Punjab have demonstrated, in the opinion of no less an authority than Sir John Marshall, that "India must henceforth be recognized, along with Persia, Mesopotamia, and Egypt, as one of the most important areas where the civilizing processes were initiated and developed." [1] Well before the beginning of the Christian era India had produced great rulers, great lawgivers and statesmen, great works of art and literature, and some of the greatest of epics.

WORLD UNKNOWN

How many Americans are in any way familiar with the *Mahabharata* and the *Ramayana,* the great Hindu classics? How many have even read the *Bhagavad Gita,* a work which has had a profound influence on Indian life and thought for many centuries? A few months ago a considerable controversy raged in some Indian newspapers over this question: Who was the greater,

[1] Quoted in Jawaharlal Nehru, *The Discovery of India* (New York, 1946), p. 59.

Kālidāsa or Shakespeare? The question was obviously a silly one, and the judgment of the correspondents would in no way detract from the recognized greatness of both writers. But how many Americans could discuss such a question intelligently? In fact, how many have even heard of Kālidāsa? Yet Kālidāsa, who probably lived in the fourth century A.D., has often been called the Indian Shakespeare—or perhaps it would be just as appropriate to call Shakespeare the English Kālidāsa!

Coming to more recent times, how much do Americans know about modern India, say of the past century or so? Aside from Tagore and Gandhi and Nehru, what other Indian names are familiar to them? What do they know of Ram Mohan Roy or Vivekananda or Aurobindo or Tilak or Gokhale or Mrs. Naidu or scores of other great figures in modern Indian life? In fact, aside from Nehru and his sister, Madame Pandit, what living Indian political leaders are known to them?

The general lack of knowledge of India's history and culture is obviously a great handicap for Americans who are seeking to understand India today, and especially for those in policy-making positions who need to have a profound understanding of present conditions and trends and of the mainsprings of Indian behavior and attitudes. Another difficulty comes from the magnitude and complexity of India, and from the many facets of Indian life. As Arnold Toynbee has said: "India is a whole world in herself; she is a society of the same magnitude as our Western society." And, as has been pointed out, it is a complex and different society. "The fissures in the Indian soil," wrote E. M. Forster, "are infinite." No visitor to this bewildering country can hope to do more than gain some insights into the complex pattern of developments and attitudes which characterize the Indian scene. Even persons who have lived in India for fifteen or twenty years or more admit that they cannot fathom many aspects of Indian life and thought. In fact, Nehru himself, who has probably seen more of his country than any other living person, is frank to confess that much of India eludes him. There are depths within depths in Indian society which make it at once intriguing and baffling.

PROBLEMS FACING INDIAN GOVERNMENT

A few months ago a well-known Indian magazine asserted that "all American reports on India, official or nonofficial, have been results either of wishful thinking or superficial observation." I believe that there is at least a measure of truth in this assertion. Most of the information we get on India is probably misleading to a certain degree, and even if it is accurate in itself it may be difficult to place it in proper perspective. Most of the reports from India are either overly optimistic or overly pessimistic. There is danger from both kinds of distortion, but I think we should beware especially of the glowing reports. Certainly it is easy to be pessimistic about India's present conditions and about her future. It is by no means certain that she can cope with her vast problems, the full dimensions of which have to be seen at first hand to be appreciated, or can survive as a democratic state. The threat of political disintegration or of a lapse into extremism of the Right or the Left is real. The political situation is confused and uncertain, and the great unanswered question of "After Nehru—who?" haunts the minds of all who are thinking of the future. Many unhealthy forces and pressures are operating in the Indian scene. Americans, I fear, do not appreciate the gravity of these forces and pressures, or how much they circumscribe the actions of the government.

The magazine from which I have quoted holds that

The threat to democracy in India grows out of the cultural tradition and the prevailing intellectual atmosphere. . . . by and large the cultural tradition of India remains mediaeval and authoritarian. . . . we have in India a formally democratic government, but it is neither good, nor efficient, nor stable.

This magazine refers specifically to the rapid growth of unemployment, the absence of popular support for the Five Year Plan, the deterioration of the administrative machinery, corruption and inefficiency, and "the indifference of the middle class to the democratic values of life." "The siren call of Communism," it declares, "reaches the Indian masses through the educated middle class." The problem of the educated unemployed is often mentioned as one of the alarming problems in India, for a discontented and unemployed educated group is always a danger, especially so in a new and still politically unstable democratic state.

Not long ago the most important newspaper in India, which is generally a supporter or at worst a friendly critic of the government, referred to "the difficult food situation, the disquieting rise in unemployment, the soaring cost of living, the hunger for land, the failure of the Five Year Plan, the educational morass"; and it charged that instead of bending its best efforts to coping with these tremendous problems the Indian National Congress was concentrating on internal squabbles, "with the sickeningly familiar charges of nepotism, corruption, and maladministration." "In other words," stated this newspaper, "the Congress is out of touch with reality. It does not know what ails the people, what their real problems are, and how best to tackle them."

Criticisms of this sort are commonly heard in India today. One can easily paint such a gloomy picture of present-day conditions and prospects. I cite some of these charges not for the purpose of criticizing the present government of India, for I believe that on the whole it is a good government and that almost any conceivable alternative would be infinitely worse, but rather to remind you that such criticisms are commonly heard in India today and that they do raise some questions about the present situation and the future. We should ignore these danger signals and warnings at our peril.

PROGRESS IN INDIA

Fortunately there is another and brighter side to the Indian picture. Dr. Paul Appleby, an American expert who made a special study of public administration in India, declared about a year ago: "What the government is trying to do here is, I think, the most important effort in the world today." And great progress has been made. Indeed, a friendly outside observer will probably be more impressed with the record of genuine progress under adverse circumstances than he will be with the criticisms which he will hear on all sides. The partition of India, less than seven years ago, was accompanied by economic, social, and political dislocation, by riots and massacres, by one of the greatest refugee problems in this century of the homeless man. India has made great progress in dealing with the problems attending partition, although thousands of refugees still live like animals in the cities and although relations with Pakistan are still strained.

Within a few months after independence, thanks largely to the efforts of Sardar Vallabhbhai Patel, some five hundred Indian states were integrated into the Union of India. Less than two and a half years after independence, India became a Republic, under a new Constitution. The work of constitution making is an epic in itself. In late 1951 and early 1952 India held the first general elections in her history, and the largest democratic elections ever held in any country. Some 106,000,000 valid votes were cast. The elections were free and passed off without violence. In a country which had never known nation-wide free elections and where more than 80 per cent of the electorate are illiterate, this was a tremendous achievement. In 1951 the Five Year Plan was launched, and it was made final in December 1952. It is now well under way, and in spite of many criticisms and a disturbing lack of popular support it is helping to transform the face of India. Unfortunately, even if its goals are realized, India will not be much better off than it was when the plan was launched, for each year nearly five million new Indians come into the world and the resources of the country do not permit of the kind of effort that is really needed.

But India is making real progress in increasing the food supply, in providing water and land to the people, in developing its mineral resources, in industrialization, in health and social welfare, and in many other ways. The community development projects and the great multipurpose river valley development projects are truly exciting experiments in India today. In spite of all the propaganda about the progress in China since the Communists gained control, it is probable that the Indian record of actual achievement is more impressive—although less well publicized. Furthermore, this progress has been made in a democratic way and has not been imposed by a ruthless totalitarian regime at great cost of human life and human freedom.

These are impressive achievements,

and they tax the resources of India to the limit; but India must make even greater strides if she is to develop the bases of a tolerable existence for the masses of her people. Even if her leaders were less addicted to their policy of "independence" or "nonalignment" and even if there were greater realism and less escapism in popular attitudes toward life in general and world affairs in particular, India still would not be able to be a bulwark of strength in any co-operative military alliance. The United States should realize that India and the other nations of the uncommitted world cannot be expected to enter into the kind of relationship for the defense of the free world which is represented by the North Atlantic Treaty Organization or by the Rio Treaty or various bilateral security arrangements. This does not mean that these uncommitted countries are pro-Communist in orientation or are any less concerned than the United States and its "allies" in the defense of freedom. For in this respect all non-Communist nations are "allies," whether they associate themselves in formal defense arrangements or not.

India's Contribution

A more realistic attitude for the United States to take toward a country like India was suggested some time ago by H. Stuart Hughes:

In certain border areas the United States need not require ideological uniformity or a full alliance from those nations to which it gives economic aid and which it regards as its friends. Indeed, to do so would be to undermine their value to the Western coalition. . . . Within the United Nations the existence of a loyal opposition . . . offers the only convincing answer to the allegation that that organization is nothing more than a screen for United States policy. This sort of opposition India, under Nehru's leadership, provides. If Nehru did not exist it would be necessary to invent someone resembling him. Only through some such formula as his will there be even a remote chance of reconciling the leaders of Asian nationalism with the former colonial powers. To push Nehru hard, to try to force him to adhere more closely to the American line, is to invite disaster. Americans need to appreciate more fully Nehru's problems at home and the pressure he is withstanding from the more extreme anti-Westerners among his own followers. The policy he is currently pursuing is oriented just about as far West as he can safely go. If Nehru, through too close an adherence to the Western line, should succumb to his own extremists, then surely we should have lost our best hope not only for a reconciliation between Asia and the West, but also, ultimately, for the peace of the whole world.[2]

We show a complete misunderstanding of the Indian temperament and of present Indian foreign policy when we criticize Nehru and other leaders of the government of India for their lack of appreciation of the crisis of our time and for their refusal to make specific commitments to programs of mutual defense. The best we can hope for from India is that she will survive as a free state and will gradually gain vigor and unity so that she will be better able to cope with any emergency, from within or from without. Chester Bowles, former American ambassador to India, expressed this point of view very effectively in his inspiring book, *Ambassador's Report*, a book which every American should read. Mr. Bowles wrote:

If I were given a single wish for the future of our relationship with India and Asia, I would wish to see India and the other new nations of Asia succeed in achieving economic and political stability within the framework of freedom, regardless of what they may think of America.[3]

[2] "Containment Reconsidered," *The Nation*, December 11, 1950, pp. 564–66.

[3] *Ambassador's Report* (New York, 1954), pp. 233–34.

George V. Allen, Mr. Bowles's successor as American ambassador to India, expressed a similar point of view in these words:

America's interest, in one sentence, is that India, which has achieved full sovereign status, shall retain that status completely, and that the faith which the vast majority of the Indian people have in democracy's ability to give them a better and fuller life be sustained and fortified.[4]

FLUCTUATIONS IN INDO-AMERICAN RELATIONS

The ups and downs in Indo-American relations have been particularly marked in the past eighteen months, although I fear there have been more downs than ups. For the sad fact is that these relations have deteriorated sharply in this period. This was particularly true early in 1953, at about the time the Eisenhower administration came into power, and unhappily, after some evidences of improvement last year, the relations are now at a low ebb, due largely to the announcement of American arms aid to Pakistan.

Some of Eisenhower's statements during the presidential campaign, notably his reference to "liberation" and to "Asians fighting Asians," were widely misunderstood in India and caused real alarm. These alarms increased after the Republican victory in November 1952. Many Indians seemed to believe that Republicans were more warlike than Democrats, and they took a dim view of a professional military man in the White House. Toward the end of 1952 rumors that the United States was trying to persuade the nations of the Middle East and Pakistan to join in a Middle East Defense Organization and a very unpopular Anglo-American resolution on Kashmir adopted by the Security Council of the United Nations

[4] Address to the India League of America, New York, April 1, 1953.

had adverse effects on Indian attitudes toward the United States. Some of the early statements of Eisenhower and Dulles after the Republican administration assumed office on January 20, 1953, added to Indian apprehensions.

The recall of Ambassador Chester Bowles was another unpopular move. During his eighteen months in India Mr. Bowles scored a great personal and diplomatic success. At a difficult and delicate period in Indo-American relations he promoted the true national interests of his own country and contributed mightily to friendly understanding between the United States and India. He liked India, and Indians liked him. To Indians he represented the best traditions of the America they admire and respect, at a time when they sometimes wonder whether America is living up to her own best traditions. His recall was a matter which many Indians could not understand. It was useless to try to explain that when a new administration of another party comes into power in Washington, the top diplomatic representatives in most countries, especially the political appointees, are usually changed. Mr. Bowles's recall was regarded by many Indians as another evidence that the Eisenhower administration was not truly concerned with Indo-American understanding.

The reduction-in-force program of the new administration eliminated a few of the ablest members of the American mission in India, greatly lowered the morale and reduced the effectiveness of those who remained, and seriously curtailed some of the most effective programs which the United States was carrying on in India. The transfer of the technical assistance program from the Department of State to the new Foreign Operations Administration, largely for purposes of more efficient administration and co-ordination with other

foreign aid programs, seemed to confirm the suspicions of many Indians that the United States was interested in aid to underdeveloped countries solely as a part of its efforts to combat Communism and to provide for the military defense of the non-Communist world.

U. S. MILITARY ASSISTANCE TO PAKISTAN

Now, on top of these and many other unpopular moves, the United States has decided to give military assistance to Pakistan. While this decision can be justified on many grounds and is in keeping with the policy of the United States to help those free nations which seek American assistance in their efforts to strengthen themselves in a dangerous world, it is bitterly resented in India and has imposed new strains on Indo-American relations. Prime Minister Nehru has warned that the United States–Pakistan pact will have the opposite effect of Washington's intention and will create "a wave of uncertainty" and increase tensions between India and Pakistan. Last year Secretary Dulles declared that closer relations between India and Pakistan were a prerequisite to the strengthening of anti-Communist defenses in Asia. Now the United States has embarked on a policy which will increase the tensions between the two new nations in the Indian subcontinent and which will thereby probably weaken rather than strengthen this part of the non-Communist world.

Apparently it is hard for Americans, even those in high places of responsibility, to realize the gravity of relations between India and Pakistan or the effect of a move such as this upon those relations. Feeling on the Kashmir issue in both countries, and particularly in Pakistan, is strong and bitter; and as long as responsible political leaders as well as other molders of opinion in Pakistan continue to speak so belligerently on the Kashmir issue, it will be impossible to convince Indians that substantial military aid to Pakistan does not increase the danger of military action against India, thereby forcing India in turn to divert even more of her limited resources to unproductive purposes of defense.

FAVORABLE DEVELOPMENTS

Fortunately not all of the developments of recent months have contributed to a worsening of Indo-American relations. Many of India's worst apprehensions of the Eisenhower administration have proved to be groundless. The President's great address of April 16, 1953, in which he expressed the genuine American interest in peace and called for steps to lessen international tensions, had a salutary effect in India. The truce in Korea gave the lie to those critics who maintained that the United States had to keep the Korean War going because it was geared to a war economy. Eisenhower's dramatic proposal to the United Nations General Assembly for an international atomic pool was hailed in India, as elsewhere, as a constructive step. The agreement of the United States to participate in the recent Berlin Conference on Germany and in the Geneva Conference on Korea and Indochina indicated that the American government had not closed the door to negotiation with the Soviet Union and that its policy was less inflexible than many of its critics charged.

The interest of the Republican administration in India was shown by the visit of Secretary of State Dulles and Director of Foreign Operations Stassen in May. This visit by two key figures in the new administration was greatly appreciated, and both Mr. Dulles and Mr. Stassen made a fine impression. Mr. Dulles' report on his trip to that part of the world showed that he had gained a greater apprecia-

tion and understanding of problems and attitudes in the countries he visited. The visit of Adlai Stevenson to India shortly after Messrs. Dulles and Stassen left was also helpful. If Indians had decided the American election, Mr. Stevenson would now be in the White House, and they were happy to welcome him as an unofficial ambassador of good will. The more recent and official visit of Vice-President Nixon also had a good effect. Mr. Nixon was roundly cheered when he told members of the Indian Parliament that when he returned to the United States he would "inform doubters in the United States that any impression that India is leaning toward Communist ideology is completely erroneous." On the occasion of Mr. Nixon's visit Prime Minister Nehru told American newspapermen that there was "no basic chasm" between India and the United States, and "no ill will by the Indian people toward the American people." These reassuring words are, I believe, far more than polite phrases or diplomatic platitudes. They suggest that in spite of all surface differences relations between India and the United States are basically good. As Nehru told the United States Congress in 1949: "Friendship and co-operation between our two countries are . . . natural." This is the rock on which I think we should stand when we attempt to appraise the state of Indo-American relations.

DIFFERENCES IN WORLD POLICY

In the January 1954 issue of *Foreign Affairs* an Indian writer who signed himself simply "P" warned that "there is a growing difference between South Asian opinion and the United States in matters affecting world policy." On three issues, in particular, the differences are great and disturbing. These issues are: (1) ways to peace, (2) the seriousness and reality of the Soviet threat, and (3) policies toward Communist China.

Ways to peace

We may assume, I believe, that Americans are just as interested in peace as Indians, although many Indians do not appear to accept this assumption. But the American people cannot be blind to the facts of life in this atomic age. Reluctantly and only after sincere efforts to co-operate with the Soviet Union the United States has been forced to conclude that in this dangerous world it must keep its defenses strong and must negotiate from strength and not from weakness. It has therefore placed emphasis upon national security and collective security arrangements, of which NATO is the outstanding example. This policy is viewed with real alarm in India, and the alarm is shared to some extent at home as well as abroad. George F. Kennan, for example, in a lecture at Princeton University in late March 1954 declared that many Americans have now become "wholly absorbed with power values to a point where they were impatient of any discussion of international affairs that tried to take account of anything else—inclined to dismiss references to any other problems as frivolous and inconsequential." Yet these "other problems" are precisely those which the countries of the uncommitted world regard as paramount and pressing.

In a two-day debate on foreign affairs in the Indian House of the People on March 23 and 24 Prime Minister Nehru made two significant restatements of India's approach to world problems. He blamed both the United States and the Soviet Union for the unhappy state of international relations. "Each side," he said, "is afraid of the other. . . . Because of this fear, armament is going on in both countries. . . . If this process continues, the world is heading toward disaster." He charged that the emphasis of the United States on collective security arrangements has created "insecurity, uncertainty, and instability" in Asia. He said that there were "two approaches to the question of war and peace": to consider war inevitable and to prepare for it; or the course he chose to follow, to consider that war "must be avoided if not at all costs, almost at all costs." India, he explained, was determined to remain aloof from power alignments and to continue in her policy of advocating "any step to avoid war." "There is no question," he declared, "of India leaning to this side or that."

The Soviet threat

It is obvious, therefore, that while India and the United States are both seeking ways to peace, their approaches to this goal differ fundamentally. Part of the difference may be explained by their varying interpretations of the Soviet threat. Most Americans, mindful of the bitter lessons of the past decade and before, do not need to be convinced that this threat is real and serious. A recent report of a special study mission of the Foreign Affairs Committee of the United States House of Representatives, which traveled some 30,000 miles to investigate the situation in the Far East, summed up the prevailing sentiment in this country in these words: "The Communist danger cannot be overestimated." Contrast this view with that voiced by "P" in his article in *Foreign Affairs:*

Why, then, this difference of approach to the external menace of Communism? Primarily, it is because India is not satisfied that there is such an external menace. . . . We may be stupid or completely blind, but where we do not see the menace, we cannot pretend to do so, merely because we are so advised by no doubt wiser people. . . . It may sound strange to American ears, but nonetheless it is a fact that the leaders of India and Burma, and perhaps of other South Asian countries (excluding Siam), do not feel themselves threatened by Communism.

This does indeed "sound strange to American ears," and it may in fact sound strange to some Indian ears as well; but it does reflect a basically divergent appraisal of the nature of the contemporary world crisis.

Policies toward Communist China

The differences of viewpoint regarding Communist China are well known. India was one of the first non-Communist nations to recognize the new regime in China and has been the leading advocate of the admission of that regime into the United Nations. Dealing with the Central People's Government on the great issues in which that government was involved, declared Mr. Nehru on March 23, was "not a question of liking or not liking," but of "facing facts." The United States, on the other hand, has refused to recognize Red China, or to forsake the remnants of the Nationalist regime on Formosa, and it is opposed to the admission of the Central People's Government into the United Nations or any other international organization. This position was emphatically restated in late March in the report of the Congressional study mission to the Far East and again by both President Eisenhower and Secretary of State Dulles.[5]

Americans should give serious thought to the attitudes of other free peoples, but it does not necessarily follow that when they find themselves in the minority they are wrong. Possibly they exaggerate the nature and extent of the Soviet threat; misunderstand the nature of the relationship between Communist China and the Soviet Union; place too much emphasis on "containment," "building situations of strength," "collective security," and "mutual defense"; rely too much on their own strength; do not give sufficient consideration to the feelings and attitudes of other peoples; and so tend to exacerbate the very evils they seek to avoid. But, on the other hand, it is by no means certain that their interpretation of the Communists' motives and intentions is wrong, or that any other policies than those they have supported would secure better results. It is possible that whereas they exaggerate the nature of the Soviet threat, others may underestimate it; that whereas they tend to take too harsh a view of the Chinese Communists, others may be too lenient and in their desire to promote friendly relations with the "New China" may serve as dupes and tools of those to whom friendship as they conceive it has little meaning.

Americans have good reason to take exception to one prevalent Indian attitude. Chester Bowles, in his answers to questions by Indian journalists on the eve of his departure from India in March 1953, defined this attitude and his reaction to it:

Americans are puzzled and disturbed . . . when some Indians who are personally devoted to democratic ideals, refer to the present unfortunate world conflict as a "struggle between two power blocs, each bent on world domination." . . . any implied charge of a "plague on both your houses" seems to us not only wholly unwarranted but also dangerously unrealistic.

This thesis of two power blocs, both equally bad, is a dangerous and misleading one, but it is the stock in trade of many Indian foreign policy analysts. That it is still prevalent and finds expression in high places is indicated by the following excerpts from a special dispatch to the *New York Times,* dated New Delhi, March 24, 1954:

The United States and the Soviet Union shared equally today in an assessment by

---

[5] For a particularly strong statement of this same position, see the article by Alfred S. Jenkins in this issue of THE ANNALS.

Prime Minister Jawaharlal Nehru of the blame for current world unrest. . . . Considering the expression of the Indian Parliament as a whole, the United States has come out on the short end again.

It should be pointed out that many Indians deplore this tendency to equate the United States and the Soviet Union, and to speak in terms of two "power blocs." Writing in *The Statesman* (Calcutta and New Delhi) in January 1953 in criticism of a resolution on foreign policy adopted by the Indian National Congress, Mr. A. D. Gorwala, a respected public figure in India, declared:

To talk in these circumstances as if it was a question of a dispute between similar contending parties is to be not only unrealistic but also immoral. And the immorality is emphasized when it is noticed that . . . it seems to make no difference at all that the aggressive side consists of some of the cruellest and most despotic though efficient police states the world has ever seen, while on the defending side are ranged real democracies, paying in their daily conduct, except for very occasional lapses, due respect to freedom, the rights of the individual and the rule of law. The disintegrating power of fear can seldom have seen to better effect than in this spectacle of a professed democracy equating wrong with right, tyranny with freedom.

Shared Aspirations

We should not allow honest differences of opinion to make us forget the fundamental beliefs and aspirations which the United States and India share; nor should we forget that by giving sympathetic understanding and concrete assistance to India we are promoting our own national interests and enhancing the prospects for peace and freedom in

the world. Fortunately the leaders of the United States, after a considerable amount of blundering and hesitation, are giving signs that they have at last reached the solid ground of common interests. The Assistant Secretary of State for Far Eastern Affairs, Mr. Walter S. Robertson, recently stated:

I feel that nowhere more than in Asia, where so many are struggling against such heavy odds for one-hundredth part of the rewards we take for granted, will assistance from us be productive of important returns for all mankind.[6]

And in his report to the American people on June 1, 1953, after his trip to the Middle East and South Asia, Secretary Dulles said:

These peoples we visited are proud peoples, who have a great tradition and, I believe, a great future. We in the United States are better off if we respect and honor them. It profits nothing merely to be critical of others. President Eisenhower's administration plans to make friendship—not fault-finding—the basis of its foreign policy.

These statements suggest that the spokesmen of the Eisenhower administration have found the right words; now let us hope they will find the right policies. One can ask no more than that the present government of the United States will make a renewed effort to live up to its own promises and to the best traditions of the great country whose destinies it is now guiding. In these efforts, I believe, it will have the support of the American people and the appreciation of freedom-loving peoples everywhere, including the citizens of the Republic of India.

[6] Address to the English-Speaking Union, New York, February 18, 1954.

Norman D. Palmer, Ph.D., Philadelphia, Pennsylvania, is professor and former chairman of the Department of Political Science at the University of Pennsylvania. He was visiting Fulbright professor at the University of Delhi in 1952–53. He is the author of The Irish Land League Crisis *(1940) and coauthor of* Fundamentals of Political Science *(1952) and* International Relations *(1953). He and Mrs. Palmer have written a book based on their experiences in India, to be published in September.*

India and the United States: Democracy East and West

By Gaganvihari L. Mehta

RELATIONS between different countries are of vital importance in the world today. Without a harmonious relationship not only peace but economic development is impossible. Such relations are determined by a country's conception of its own interests and its immediate and distant objectives. Until the beginning of this century, what mattered most was relationships between different countries of Europe, many of which had far-flung empires with sources of raw materials and markets abroad. The United States of America was preoccupied with its own economic development and with preventing interference and domination by European countries on the whole of this continent. It was only after the emergence of Japan that the existence of Asia came to be realized; and it was not until after the two world wars and the attainment of independence by several Asian countries that the importance of Asia as a factor in world politics began to be gradually, if somewhat reluctantly, recognized. While the problem of the relationship between the Asian continent and the United States is of vital importance in the present conditions, the maintenance of amicable relations between the United States and India is a matter of the highest significance.

Two Big Democracies

America and India are both large countries, although India is only about one-third of the size of the United States; they are practically on opposite sides of the globe. Each has a large seaboard and is richly gifted by nature —with minerals and metals and a variety of agricultural products. No doubt, India's resources have yet to be fully developed or even completely surveyed, but there is little doubt that, given a period of peace and stability and the application of co-operative endeavor, organization, and technical skill, India's economy has the capacity for immense development.

India is an ancient land with a historic tradition and a cultural heritage that go back to 3,000 years before Christ. The United States is a modern nation. And yet, in a certain sense, India is also a young country. Her political independence was achieved less than seven years ago. We observed the centenary of our railway system last year and our textile industry celebrates it this year. The steel industry in our country is less than fifty years old. But India has for centuries had domestic and cottage industries and handicrafts for which she is justly famous. Nevertheless, as a united, democratic state with a national economy in the modern sense, India is in the initial stages of development.

Incidentally, in one other sense also there is a similarity between the two countries. India, like the United States, has a conglomeration of several races and communities with different religions and creeds. But just as the United States has been welding this large concourse into a national entity, so too through the cultural unity of ages, the framework of a national Constitution, and the elements of an industrial structure, India is also a united nation today.

The United States is the largest

124

democracy in the West (population 161,000,000) while India is the largest democracy in the East (population 360,-000,000). They have different systems of representative government but the essence and the spirit are the same. Both our countries believe that governments must be based on the consent of the governed; that no man should be punished except after due process of law; that economic well-being is basic for national development and should be achieved by democratic processes. The Constitution of India has derived some of its inspiration from the Constitution of this country, including the Bill of Rights. We have a written Constitution with a federal structure of government and an independent judiciary. No doubt there are many divergences, as is only to be expected, but all I want to stress is that the basic objectives of the two Constitutions are the same. One important feature of our Constitution which has earned widespread appreciation is the absence of any discrimination against a citizen on grounds of religion, color, or caste. India is a secular state.

POLITICAL INDEPENDENCE

During our national movement, we derived inspiration from the early history of the American fight for independence, and we had the moral sympathy and support of many leaders of public opinion in this country. The principle of national self-determination enunciated by President Woodrow Wilson during World War I gave a stimulus to the movement for political emancipation in our country as in several other lands. During the interwar years, and particularly during the war period, the cause of Indian independence was supported by several eminent men and women in this country, including leaders in the Congress and in the administration. This co-operation has continued in the political, economic, and technical

spheres during the last seven years when a new India has been in the making.

TRADE AND MANUFACTURE

There has been growing economic interdependence between the two countries. Before World War II, the total trade between the United States and India was valued at about 200 million dollars per annum; it now runs to roughly 700 million dollars. Previously, India's trade with the United States was about 7 per cent of its total foreign trade; it is now nearly 20 per cent even after excluding import of foodstuffs. There have been significant increases in exports from the United States to India in cotton, machinery, oil and oil products, vehicles, and minerals such as sulphur. On the other hand, India supplies nearly 40 per cent of the manganese used by the steel industry in this country, 80 per cent of high-grade mica and a considerable quantity of castor oil (important for lubrication of high-speed aircraft), ilmenite (used for manufacture of special quality pigments and paints), cyanite (for making refractories), chromite, short-staple cotton, burlap, and shellac, as well as tea. It is of interest to know that both in 1952 and in 1953 the United States imported sufficient manganese from India to make 54,000,000 tons of steel, about half the total annual production in this country.

Again, during the last five years about twenty-five American firms have started or expanded manufacturing activities in India. These include the American Cyanamid Company, the Union Carbide and Carbon Company, the Firestone Tire and Rubber Company, Remington Typewriter Company, Otis Elevator Company, and other chemical and engineering concerns. Some of them are participating financially in Indian enterprises, others are collaborating technically, while still others are operating entirely on their own with American capital and management. The total American capital invested in India is about 100 million dollars. The most important example of this economic co-operation is the establishment of two oil refineries by the Standard-Vacuum Oil Company and the California Texas Oil Company, the former in Bombay and the latter in an eastern part of India, Vizagapatam, on the Bay of Bengal. As soon as these oil refineries are ready, along with another being built by the Burmah Oil Company of the United Kingdom, India will produce practically all the petroleum products that it requires. Although crude oil will be imported for the present, it is possible that in future such oil might be obtained in India itself as a result of drilling operations to be undertaken by the Standard-Vacuum Oil Company in collaboration with the government of India. This is probably the first instance in which an oil company of this importance has entered into a direct partnership with a foreign government. Merchant ships of both India and the United States are engaged in carrying important and often strategic goods between the two countries.

TECHNICAL AID

During the last four years, India has also been an active participant in schemes of technical co-operation and has received technical assistance from the specialized agencies of the United Nations and particularly from this country. Under the Point Four program, 101 Indian technicians have received training in this country and 105 American experts have gone over to India to assist in programs of agricultural extension, irrigation, health, education, fisheries, and so forth. In 1951, when India was faced by a serious drought, the United States gave a loan of two million tons of wheat of an aggregate value of 190 million dollars. I might add that India has already paid the full 7 million dollars of interest due on this loan by the end of 1953. Money realized by the sale of this wheat in India has been utilized for development projects, particularly for agriculture and irrigation. Let me also add that the amount of interest realized by the United States is going to be spent for educational purposes in India.

Moreover, because the United States has been conscious of our community of interests and aware of the vital importance of India's economic development, an Indo-American Technical Co-operation Agreement was made in 1952, under which a total of 160 million dollars has been allocated, principally for community development projects. Important private organizations such as the Ford and Rockefeller Foundations have also been extending material and technical help. Such assistance is a truer expression of co-operation between the United States and India than pious resolutions of mutual good will and treaties of "eternal friendship." I must point out, however, that the foreign aid we receive, although invaluable, is marginal and supplements our own efforts. Development programs are formulated by Indians themselves in consultation and co-operation with experts and technicians from abroad, where necessary; and the main financial burden of operating them is on the people themselves. Foreign aid can be acceptable to India if it is given with the object of furthering her economic development and not as an instrument of cold war. In order to produce the best results, it is important that economic aid and technical advice be given without creating a sense of inferiority in the recipient country or engendering any suspicions about the motives and objectives of such programs.

DIFFERING POLICIES

It will, therefore, be evident that there has been close relationship and growing co-operation in various spheres between India and the United States. And yet, if we read newspaper headlines and follow radio commentaries and listen to stray conversations, we hear only of differences and misunderstanding between our two countries; the inference would be that we are drifting apart. Why is this so? We must face this question frankly but calmly, without passion or prejudice. I do not expect to carry full conviction to you in what I am going to say, but it is enough if you appreciate to some extent at any rate India's point of view. Understanding of a different viewpoint does not necessarily imply agreement. What we want is more light and less heat.

I have already referred to the large area of agreement and understanding between the two countries. Our differences have arisen mainly in the international sphere and in respect of the choice of a foreign policy that would be most appropriate for the promotion of peace, particularly in Asia and Africa. These differences arise not because of any clash of interests or any struggle for leadership. Indeed, India does not aspire to any leadership even in Asia, nor has she any economic and territorial ambitions in any part of the world; the policies of the United States also are not designed with a view to building up an empire. Nor do our differences arise from any divergence of "ideological" approach. We believe in democracy both in spirit and as a technique for political and economic progress. We also agree that we should seek to prevent the disaster of a third world war and that all efforts should be directed to this end both in the United Nations and outside. But it is in the manner in which we should ensure peace and reduce tensions that there is a divergence.

Asian aspirations

Indians are of the view that there is inadequate recognition of the importance of Asia in the counsels of nations and we are distressed when we see attempts being made to settle Asian problems by ignoring the wishes and feelings of Asian countries. Asian countries no longer want to be the instruments for the ends of powerful nations. No lasting solution can be reached, whether it be in the Middle East or the Far East, if it does not take fully into account the aspirations and sentiments of the people of these lands. India desires nothing more than to bring to the consciousness of the Western world the new forces which are pulsating in Asia and Africa and which can be ignored only at peril to international peace and stability. This is no exclusive cult nor any transcontinental doctrine of "Asia for the Asians"; it is only a desire to develop our own systems and economies without domination from outside. We want to be friends, not satellites. Independent countries must be accepted as such, not as "camp followers" of countries with immense military and economic power. Enlightened opinion in this country recognizes this feeling and stresses the fact that the United States wants allies and partners. However, the attitude and policies of important Western countries are not always formulated in the spirit of what is called the "free world." Important Asian countries are often ignored in the United Nations and at conferences convened to discuss problems in Asia. Decisions so reached can only be regarded as impositions, which go against all the canons of freedom.

Colonialism

Closely related to this is the attitude to be adopted towards colonialism and racial discrimination. If colonialism is supported, perhaps for ulterior reasons, and undemocratic and unpopular regimes are bolstered up, how can the moral support of the peoples of such countries be elicited and their energies mobilized for democratic progress? Because of our struggle for freedom, people in our country have an instinctive sympathy with similar struggles in other countries, particularly in Asia and Africa. No structure for world peace can be built on the denial of freedom to countries and large masses of people. It is not without significance that countries like India, Pakistan, Burma, Ceylon, Indonesia, and the Philippines, which achieved independence after World War II, have successfully resisted subversive activities within their borders and are building up their own economies, while those countries which have been denied freedom are in a state of chaos and fall an easy prey to extreme doctrines and movements.

Who is the enemy?

The differences in the policies of the United States and India arise mainly from the fact that whereas to the United States the fight against Communism is the supreme issue to which all other problems should be subordinated, India holds that the real enemies of mankind are economic and social evils such as poverty and hunger and disease, racial discrimination, and domination and exploitation of weaker peoples by the powerful nations of the world. These problems would confront us even if the teachings of Karl Marx had not influenced Lenin and even though Mao Tsetung had not been the ruler of China. As Mr. Lester B. Pearson, the distinguished Secretary of State for External Affairs of Canada, has observed, "The conflict [between forces of Communist imperialism and free democracy] may not seem so simple to people who are preoccupied with the struggle for self-government and economic progress, millions of whom live under the recurring threat of starvation and who may be pardoned for thinking that hunger and servitude are worse enemies than Marxism." India's government and leaders, therefore, give the highest priority to "freedom from want." Mr. Chester Bowles, the former United States Ambassador to India, mentions in his *Ambassador's Report* that Sir Gerald Templer, the British general in charge of the war against guerillas in Malaya, told him: "Give me a hundred more divisions and I still couldn't destroy the Communists without the necessary reforms. My job is only 10 per cent military. The remaining 90 per cent is political and economic."

In other words, the theory and practice of Communism have to be studied as a historical process rather than as a malignant germ to be merely exterminated. So long as countries are not aggressive and have no extraterritorial ambitions or militant programs under ideological masks, no harm is done by peaceful coexistence and competition between different political and democratic systems. We believe, therefore, that the sounder method of ensuring stability and progress in the East is to give the common man the hope of a better and a fuller life, rather than to strengthen military defenses and put up bases which may only succeed in increasing tensions or even creating dissensions between countries in that area. In this connection, I cannot do better than quote what a distinguished American, Mr. Adlai Stevenson, said the other day in the last of his Godkin lectures at Harvard University. After pointing out that much of the world in Asia, Africa, and the Middle East was "trying to telescope centuries into decades" in the "drive" for industrial and technological development, he emphasized that a policy based on anti-Communism and military potency was not in the spirit of this drive and "will win few hearts." The challenge, he said, was "for us to identify ourselves with this social and human revolution, to encourage, aid, and inspire the aspirations of half of mankind for a better life, to guide these aspirations into paths that lead to freedom."

Military thinking

In this imperfect world of ours no country can afford to neglect its armed defenses, but it is well to remember that modern weapons have become so destructive that war has now ceased to be, if ever it was in the past, a solution of the differences and dissensions of nations. Two world wars have shown that war is no instrument for the attainment of social and economic objectives or even for the annihilation of systems which are regarded as evil. But now, the way to war is the surest path to disaster. It is, therefore, of vital importance that while military preparations are made, as a guarantee of self-preservation, everything humanly possible be done to ensure that such preparations do not produce the opposite effect by bringing us nearer to war. In other words, the climate of peace should be cultivated and extended by every means possible. The consequences of military thinking dominating political considerations are almost as disastrous today as those of neglecting essential military defense. As Mr. John Foster Dulles, the distinguished Secretary of State of this country, has observed in his book *War or Peace*, "Military needs are important, and a strong military establishment is a necessity. But we shall fail in our search for peace, security, and justice unless our policies, in reality and also in appearance, give priority to the hopes and aspirations for peace of the peoples of the world."

LACK OF UNDERSTANDING

The worst impediment in the way of full understanding and co-operation between our two countries is, I repeat, not any clash of interests or any differences in ideologies, not any subtleties of Oriental psychology or wiles of Occidental diplomacy, but plain lack of understanding. Indeed, during my stay in this country, extending over a year and a half, I have found that the American and Indian characters are similar in some ways. We are both informal, friendly, and hospitable—and also apt to be sensitive. But there are sharp differences too. The American mind is essentially an engineering mind: it is positive, constructive, and believes in continuous experiment, innovation, and action. The Indian mind is more contemplative: it is reflective, somewhat cautious, slow in tempo, believing in eternity rather than in a few seconds! There are radical differences in economic conditions between our two countries, and we have divergent traditions and customs. Both our peoples would benefit if each could imbibe some of the traits of the other. In India, there is great admiration for the high standards of life in America and there is eagerness to learn the techniques which have made this remarkable progress possible. In this task of improving the lot of our peoples we do not and shall not shut out light from other lands or reject the helping hand of a friend.

CONFIDENCE A SLOW GROWTH

Relationship between nations is a sensitive plant, never more so than today when there is frequently a tendency to treat any difference of opinion as almost an act of defiance. Mutual confidence is a slow growth, particularly between a country which has just achieved independence and has, therefore, pardonable sensitiveness and a country which is the most powerful in the world today through its immense financial and technical resources and which feels aggrieved that its unparalleled generosity in assisting the rehabilitation of countries from the ravages of war and in the development of economies of poorer lands is not adequately appreciated. What will maintain and promote good relations between our two countries is not gifts of money nor aid of arms but a sense of equality of status and a sharing of common objectives. It is only natural that Indo-American relations should be subject to all the strains and stresses which characterize relations between two free, independent, and friendly countries. But so long as the spirit of idealism which inspired your founding fathers and your great leaders guide you and so long as we are true to our cultural heritage and our faith in democratic values, we have nothing to fear.

His Excellency Gaganvihari L. Mehta, LL.D., Washington, D. C., is Ambassador of India to the United States. He was assistant editor of the Bombay Chronicle (1923–25) and manager of the Calcutta office of the Scindia Steam Navigation Ltd. (1928–47). Following India's independence he has been at various times president of the Tariff Board, member of the National Planning Commission, chairman of the Tariff Commission, president of the Indian Chamber of Commerce and of the Federation of Indian Chambers of Commerce, member of the Constituent Assembly, member of the Indian delegation to the International Conference on Trade and Employment, Geneva, and on the Governing Body of the Council of Scientific and Industrial Research. He is the author of The Conscience of a Nation (1932), From Wrong Angles (1935), and Perversities (1942).

American Policy Toward India and the Security of South Asia

By John D. Jernegan

THE subject of the relations between the United States and India is of deep interest to many of us and of great importance to us all. It is, of course, a subject of special concern to the Department of State.

First let me say that whenever troubled relations between ourselves and the Indians exist, this is no cause of concern to the Communists. There is little they would like better than to see friction between the two countries develop. They would like to see India and America alienated completely from each other. They are trying to accomplish just that right now. The Kremlin today is using all the propaganda devices in its possession to make the Indians feel that we are their enemies; that we represent a new imperialism; that we intend to dominate their economy; that we are bent on involving the whole world, including India, in a new world war; that what we hope to do and see in the area of the Middle East and South Asia is carefully calculated to go against Indian national interests.

These themes, let us admit, have not been selected at random. They have been chosen with the utmost care by the Soviets because they believe that these are the lines which are most likely to be believed in India.

What the Communists do and say, however, is not likely to have any very serious effect on United States–Indian relations; their strength in India is not sufficiently great. But we must frankly admit that today American relations with India are not so completely cordial as we should like to see them. There are various reasons for this. Partly it is a case of mutual misunderstanding arising out of the differing backgrounds of the two nations. Partly, however, our differences arise out of ordinary disagreements over the best ways to handle specific problems. We have, for example, disagreed over the attitude which should be adopted toward Communist China. Likewise, it took us a long time to reconcile our positions in regard to the Korean truce negotiations. Nor have we seen eye to eye over action to be taken in the United Nations regarding French North Africa and other questions involving dependent areas. I could name other instances of disagreement. The list might seem formidable and discouraging, but I hasten to emphasize that a similar list could be drawn up for almost any other major country in the world. Even with our best friends, and sometimes especially with our best friends, we are bound to have arguments.

MILITARY AID TO PAKISTAN

Many of our disagreements with India are now past history and, I hope, in the process of being forgotten. There is, however, one current problem which deserves special attention. It is the most recent to arise and a main source of concern in our mutual relations at the present moment. That is the American decision to extend military aid to Pakistan.

We made that decision for reasons well known to Americans, but sometimes misunderstood abroad.

This country and many others believe that our way of life is critically endangered by a predatory power which recognizes that the greatest threat to its existence is the very presence of democracy. Soviet Communism seeks to destroy us all, and we have ample reason to believe that domination of the Indian subcontinent is a part of the Soviet objective. It bears repeating that the actions of the Soviet Union prove beyond a doubt that it will use every means at its disposal, including war, to enslave us. Unless adequate measures are taken by the free nations acting together, it will succeed.

As the Kremlin's intentions became clear, the United States, as you know, in co-operation with other free nations, took far-reaching steps to meet the threat. These security measures included the North Atlantic Treaty and comprehensive arrangements in the Pacific area.

It has become apparent, however, that a power vacuum exists in the Middle East and South Asia. The countries of this region, largely lacking the resources necessary for a strong military posture, are also torn by other strains and stresses which sap their strength. Thus, we have the conflict between the Arab states and Israel, the Egyptian dispute with the United Kingdom over the Suez region, the tension between India and Pakistan over Kashmir. In addition, in many countries of the Middle East the economic and political situations have resulted in acute internal instability.

At the same time, this wide area remains of immense importance to us. It contains nearly a quarter of the world's population. It has tremendous resources, including oil, many of which are as yet untapped. It is a vital, strategic land, sea, and air route between East and West.

If this part of the world is to live in freedom, if it is to retain the capacity to develop its economy to its own best interests, and if its political institutions are to mature within an independent framework, we believe that it must have the ability to defend itself against aggression. The threat of aggression is ever present.

You will recall that early attempts to create a sound military system in the area failed. Both the idea of a Middle East command and a Middle East defense organization came to nothing for one good reason: both were born of initiative supplied by outside powers. As Secretary Dulles said when he came back from his trip to the Middle East a year ago, no collective security system can be imposed from without. "It should be designed and grow from within out of a sense of common danger and common destiny."

Until very recently, time stood still as far as defense of the Middle East was concerned, but various hopeful signs have begun to show.

First, the government of Pakistan asked the United States for grant military aid. This was a request which had to be taken seriously. The government and people of Pakistan are strongly anti-Communist. They have indicated their desire to stand and be counted with us in efforts to forestall the Kremlin's imperialism. In World War II, the history of the fighting forces from what is now Pakistan was a glorious one, as was that of the troops from what is now India.

India's fear

We were well aware, however, that the Indian government would dislike United States military aid to Pakistan. Its objections were carefully weighed. On balance, after considering them, it seemed clear to us that the consequences of this action feared by India would not develop. Indeed, we believe that as time passes India herself will see that her apprehensions on the subject were not justified.

During the lengthy debate in India while this matter was being considered by us, it became apparent that one motivation for India's opposition stemmed from fear that United States arms aid to Pakistan would be used against India. Therefore, when the decision was made by President Eisenhower to give military aid to Pakistan, he made it absolutely clear in his public announcement and in his letter on the subject to Prime Minister Nehru that the arms we would give could in no way be used in aggression without his taking appropriate action immediately, in accordance with his constitutional authority. The government of Pakistan has indicated to us that it accepts fully the definitive provisions limiting the end use of the aid.

Furthermore, we believe that if the military strength of the subcontinent is increased, it will serve to deter aggression from the outside.

A mind turned from war

Now on this point we differ with the Indian government. It has expressed the opinion that by this act the cold war is brought directly into the subcontinent. Very recently, in addressing the Indian House of the People, Prime Minister Nehru said:

There are two approaches to this question of war and peace. One is the approach of the feeling that war is almost inevitable and therefore one must be prepared for war. The other is that war must be avoided at all costs, if not at all costs, at almost all costs. The two approaches differ as everybody will see. Of course, nobody wants war—or very few people. And yet many people may well say, "We do not want war but how are you going to prevent it? War must come and therefore we must do this and do that." That is a legitimate approach. And yet if you lay stress on war coming you lose the battle for peace, and war is likely to

come because your minds have succumbed to the prospect of war coming in.

That is the danger of the situation: not that people want war, but many people seem to succumb to the idea of the inevitability of war.

Again, in the past, Prime Minister Nehru has put forward the idea of a "no war" area, of which India and presumably the neighboring countries, and perhaps others, would be a part.

I believe the reasons behind this attitude are many, and it is not possible for me at least to say which carry the most weight. They seem to include the following: (1) A feeling that India can best tackle her pressing internal problems if she avoids becoming involved in the "cold war" and that her influence can most effectively be exerted if she is not committed to either side. (2) A conviction that she only stands to lose by putting herself at least potentially in a position which might offend either the U.S.S.R. or Communist China, particularly the latter, and, at the same time, a reluctance to disassociate herself from the West. (3) A deep-seated fear and hatred of colonialism and imperialism and an identification of these with the Western powers, plus an awareness of the implications of Communist totalitarianism. (4) A feeling that moral weight exerted against war will present it from coming.

There are no doubt other motivations, and it may appear that contradictions exist in those I have just listed, but it seems to me that these, in varying degrees of importance, may help to explain attitudes and expressions which appear puzzling to many of us.

U. S. belief in collective security

We in the United States believe the cold war is already on the subcontinent, as it is in every other place in the world. It is there not through anything we or the other free nations have done, but through the actions and intentions of the Soviet Union, Communist China, and the other satellites.

One cannot lightly dismiss the lessons of aggression in Poland or Czechoslovakia or Korea. It could happen in the Indian subcontinent. If it does how will India defend herself—alone, or in the strong company of others who believe her independence should be guarded?

Collective security is the keystone of our foreign policy. In that concept, we think, lies the only hope of preventing another Poland or Czechoslovakia or Korea.

While the United States had under consideration the question of military aid to Pakistan, Pakistan and Turkey had been holding talks which resulted on February 19, 1954, in an announcement that they intended "to study methods of achieving closer, friendly collaboration in the political, economic, and cultural spheres as well as of strengthening peace and security in their own interest as also in that of all peace-loving nations." An agreement on these lines was signed at Karachi on April 2. The United States warmly welcomed this development, and its decision to extend military aid to Pakistan was made within its context.

Now, these matters have not made relations between the United States and India easy. On the problems of security, it may not seem that the two countries are likely to reach agreement in the near future. We believe we are right, and I am sure that the Indian government believes it is right. Indian leaders are as entitled to their opinions as we are to ours, and it is not profitable for either of us to try to impose our viewpoint on the other. But I do not concur with those who say that friendship is being destroyed between us. India and the United States are two

great democracies. We have more in common than we have in disagreement.

India after Partition

Following the partition of the subcontinent, India was faced with tremendous internal and external problems. There was the problem of unifying the nation into a single political entity from more than five hundred separate states. There was the problem of an already over-taxed economy being thrown further off balance by the partition itself. There was the problem of internal Communist activity. And finally, there was the problem of India's relations with her newly created neighbor, Pakistan.

While the new India moved quickly and effectively to meet some of its most pressing internal problems, the challenges were obviously too great to be overcome immediately. Further, there were and are forces trying to move against what the present government of India considers its peoples' best interests.

The Communists, for example, both those in the Kremlin and those in India taking their orders from the Kremlin, do not want a unified India. In India, as in other countries where they seek to gain power, they strive for disorder, disunity, and discontent.

We find, for instance, that the Communists consistently take the part of those who would weaken the power of the central government. They continually berate the concept of India's Five Year Plan. They belabor the slowness with which its benefits come. They, as happened in our own country during the depression, use the issue of unemployment to advance their aims.

However, Prime Minister Nehru's government has moved steadily forward to the solution of its problems. He himself has taken a strong anti-Communist position. It is clear that he recognizes the threat the Communists are to his country. At one time, he had about 7,000 of them in jail.

The general elections of 1951–52 which were held to form the government were a model of democratic procedure. About 106,000,000 people voted. Unlike the Soviet system, the Indian system gave them a wide range of parties and candidates to choose from.

Unification of the country, which many described as an impossible task, was accomplished swiftly and efficiently.

Faced with a fantastically low living standard, a desperate agricultural situation, the Indian government has taken bold steps to increase food production, to stimulate industry, and to increase India's foreign trade.

While progress has been made, there is a great distance left to travel. If the present economic program is successful, all well and good. If, however, the disruptive forces within the country gain strength and totalitarian efforts meet with increasing local successes, the countries of the free world will have cause for alarm.

U. S. SUPPORT OF INDIA

This possibility brings me to the heart of our feelings toward India. Regardless of our differences on foreign policy and security matters, what the United States is most interested in is a free, independent India following the route of her own choosing. It would be a major disaster if the freedom of India's government and people were taken away—a disaster from which the rest of the free world might never recover.

On our part, there are no hidden reservations or limitations in our relationship with India. We stand ready, as in the past, to help India where we can and in ways that she may desire. We shall do everything in our power to ensure that our relations produce noth-

ing but friendship and mutual benefit. We are confident that this is India's desire as well.

You will remember that the United States has long given aid and encouragement to India. In 1941, well before Indian independence, the two countries exchanged representatives. In 1942, Colonel Louis Johnson, President Roosevelt's personal representative with the rank of ambassador, participated in the unsuccessful efforts to work out agreement between the British and Indians on India's political future. Subsequently, the United States made known to the British government its views concerning its support of steps which might be taken toward fulfillment of Indian nationalist aspirations. At the same time, we made great efforts through the exchange of information, exchange of persons, and other formulas to ensure that America and our way of life be known to the people of India.

We welcomed wholeheartedly the measures taken toward real independence and the establishment in 1946 of an interim government and a Constituent Assembly to draft a constitution. In October 1946 the two nations exchanged ambassadors.

Following partition in August 1947, and as India began to exercise the rights and responsibilities of independence, the United States increasingly welcomed her active role in world affairs. We have been, for instance, happy to see the active part she has played in the work of the United Nations and its specialized agencies—although we have not at all times agreed with her position.

Economic relations

We have, further, taken a strong interest in the tremendous economic problems which face India. The average life expectancy is thirty-two years. About

75,000,000 each year suffer the debilitating and often fatal effects of malaria. India has a population density of 308 per square mile, compared to 54 in the United States, and her population is increasing at the rate of 5,000,000 a year. Her crop yields are desperately low. Famine is an ever present danger.

To help avert a desperate grain shortage in 1951, the United States Congress loaned India $190,000,000 to purchase 2,000,000 tons of wheat. Since 1951, our programs of technical assistance and special economic aid have been directed to supplementing the extraordinary steps being taken by the Indian government through its Five Year Plan to raise the living standards of its people. In 1952, our programs amounted to almost $53,000,000, in 1953 to $44,300,000, and in the present fiscal year to $89,000,000. Altogether, in grants and loans, the United States government has made about $390,000,000 available to India. We expect to continue this assistance. Under it, the United States is providing technical advice to India's Community Development Program, which is reaching 14,000,000 people in 22,000 villages. Indian leaders and technicians numbering in the hundreds have been brought to the United States for specialized training. Supplies and equipment are being provided farmers who cannot afford to purchase them. In addition, our funds are being used for direct assistance in economic development, industrial as well as agricultural.

Private American foundations are also playing an important part in these efforts. The Ford and Rockefeller Foundations are actively involved in helping improve living standards.

Thus, many, many Americans today are working daily side by side with Indians in the fundamental tasks of improving the lives of India's millions.

American private investment in India is substantial and contributes to a sounder Indian economy. Within the past year, for instance, we have seen a multimillion dollar oil refinery started in Bombay by an American company. India, in turn, has much to offer us economically. From India, we purchase large amounts of important industrial materials, including mica and manganese.

CULTURAL EXCHANGES

Outside the economic field, we find the ties of friendship being strengthened in other ways. A host of India's students and teachers and many of ours are continually being exchanged. These boys and girls and men and women, through the experience of daily living with their hosts, contribute greatly to good will.

India has a great cultural and spiritual heritage on which we can draw. As our two countries know each other better we can benefit more and more in nonmaterial as well as material ways. It has become a cliché to say that the West can learn as much from the East as the East from the West, but it is worth repeating nevertheless.

AREAS OF AGREEMENT

But what gives us the most hope for the future of our relations with India is the fact that there is no basic difference inherent in our respective philosophies of government. India has given the spirit of democracy a new strength. She has given, in the life of Gandhi, a new rallying point to all those who believe in the dignity of each individual. Both nations believe in freedom, in the individual, in his rights as an individual, in the commitment of democratic government to protect those rights. Our concept of democracy is the same. The necessity for protecting that democracy is mutually recognized. The way is open to friendly co-operation in efforts to build a better, more peaceful world.

Looking at the broad picture of our relations, there is much more to cheer than to induce despair. So long as we do not succumb to the doubtful luxury of carping and exasperation, the future is a bright one. The chief task is to build upon those areas in which India and the United States are in agreement and to strengthen them. We do not expect to agree on every issue. There are bound to be differences of opinion between two democratic states, but the basic principles on which we agree remain.

Let me repeat what I have already said: What the government of the United States wants above all is a free, independent, and democratic India. If it is an India which also agrees with the American outlook on international affairs, so much the better. We shall certainly work hard to reconcile our respective points of view, but it is the freedom, the independence, and the democracy of India that we consider essential and that we shall strive to support to the best of our ability.

John D. Jernegan, Washington, D. C., is Deputy Assistant Secretary of State for Near Eastern, South Asian and African Affairs. He has been a career Foreign Service officer since 1936, when he was appointed vice consul at Mexico City, serving also in Barcelona and Tehran, and as consul general in Tunis. During a tour of duty in the Department of State (1946–50), he was assistant chief of the Division of Near Eastern Affairs, chief of the division, and director of the Office of Greek, Turkish, and Iranian Affairs. He attended the Moscow Conferences of Foreign Ministers of 1943 and 1945.

The Quest for Security in the Middle East*

By Halford L. Hoskins

AMONG the more notable developments in international affairs during recent years are two which, taken together, give considerable character to the contemporary international scene. One is the evolution of what may be called a "new" Middle East. The other is the rapid growth of interest in the countries comprising this area on the part of the United States. It will appear, as we look into these developments, that American concern for this area is quite as new as any of the features which are characteristic of the new Middle East.

If we apply the expression "Middle East" to the lands adjacent to the eastern end of the Mediterranean Sea and extending thence to the borders of the subcontinent of India, we are referring, from the point of view of human culture, to the oldest countries in the world. Yet in several ways they are now to be counted among the youngest. Their newness is not to be measured by the elapsed time since they achieved independent status, even though this interval has been brief in every instance. It is rather to be gauged by the degree of maturity exhibited by their political and social institutions; by the type of judgment displayed by their political leaders in formulating and in executing public policy; by the extent to which genuine national patriotism has succeeded in uniting the various elements of the populations and in creating modern, viable nations. In terms such as

* In considerable measure this article is based on parts of a book, now in press, entitled, *The Middle East: Problem Area in World Politics,* to be published by The Macmillan Company.

these, the Middle East is young indeed, and for the most part still conspicuously immature.

THE "NEW" MIDDLE EAST

Evidences of newness abound on almost every hand. They appear in Egypt, where a monarchy nearly a century and a half old, without external support, could not survive a bloodless military *Putsch,* the authors of which yet govern *sans* constitution, popular mandate, or even mutual confidence. Similar evidences are to be observed in Syria, where for some years one military clique has succeeded another at frequent intervals without material advantage to the country. The royal regimes in Iran, Iraq, and Saudi Arabia have still to find practicable ways in which to apply great petroleum resources to the social and economic improvement of their peoples. Even in Kuwait, where a paternalistic sheik aims at the uplift of his indigent subjects, only a species of parasitism has been achieved. It is not yet clear what degree of sagacity the Knesset of Israel can bring to bear with sufficient promptitude on a series of problems whose solution is vital to that country's survival. Indeed, in the entire Middle East area only Turkey has reached the stage of political maturity requisite for stability in dealing with a difficult economic situation at home and with pressures from abroad due to its exposed position adjacent to the Iron Curtain.

Thus, except for a hard outer shell in Turkey, the countries of the Middle East must be described as essentially soft in a world—and especially in a strategic area—where softness is a constant temptation to great powers which regard aggression as a fitting instrument of state policy. "Softness" in the Middle East is the result of several contributing causes. Some of them are products of the physical environment. Not too much in terms of economic strength, political development, and material progress can be expected of a country much of whose area is inescapably arid, as in the case of Syria, the Hashemite Kingdom of Jordan, Saudi Arabia, or Iran, or mountainous, as in Lebanon or Yemen. Sudden wealth in the form of oil cannot quickly atone for the lack of other natural resources, such as arable soil, adequate rainfall, or deposits of the hard minerals of industry. Not a little of the underdeveloped character of parts of the Middle East is the result of centuries of Ottoman rule—a regime in which individual enterprise was regarded as subversive. To these factors might be added the influences of climate, age-old poverty, fatalistic philosophy, and even the external environment. For considering the position of the Middle East with reference to great power relationships, it is clear that the peoples of the area cannot hope to be left to develop their institutional life unhampered—or perhaps unhelped—by one or more of the powers whose interests are global in scope.

Barricade or Barrier

It is the position occupied by the countries of the Middle East quite as much as any intrinsic need for technical assistance or economic aid that accounts for the present interest of the United States in these underdeveloped nations. In a world where two power alignments of states are essentially at war, the Middle East forms either a barricade or a barrier to both power groups. In so far as the area serves to prevent access by the Soviet Union to the Mediterranean and the Persian Gulf—that is, to the sea lanes reaching to South Asia, southern Europe, and the greater part of the African continent—it figures as a barricade in defense plans of the free world. To the extent that it inhibits—or in time of war may inhibit—uninterrupted access of the Western powers to the southern shores of Asia, the eastern shores of Africa, and the British Commonwealth countries in Australasia, the Middle East is a potential barrier. It may well be observed, too, that the maintenance of dependable lines of free world communications through this area is not less essential in an air age than in one confined to surface travel. Even if Middle East refueling bases were not required, permission to cross national boundaries still is requisite. Few features of a strategic concept for the free world are more fundamental than maintaining a balance of influence throughout the Middle East.

Oil

The securing of lines of commercial intercourse with parts of the Middle East is not less consequential than the maintenance of other lines of communications, because of the part which petroleum plays in contemporary international relations. It is conceivable that in time to come atomic forces may in part supersede those now derived from petroleum. Meanwhile the industrial scene is dominated by petroleum derivatives. We represent an oil culture. Oil in the contemporary world is power. In a state of world affairs where war on a restricted scale now is in progress and one of unlimited scope might occur at any moment, oil as the first among the sinews of war possesses a significance beyond measurement in ordinary terms. Any optimistic outlook for the free world, in fact, rests on the availability to the United States, as the leader of the free world, of adequate supplies of petroleum at all times and under any circumstances.

It is the greatest of good fortune, therefore, that more than one-third of the world's oil resources, according to current estimates, lie within the Western Hemisphere and presumably—although not altogether certainly—will be constantly available to this country in time of peace or war. The satisfaction to which this circumstance might give rise, however, is gravely compromised by other considerations. One lies in the fact that even now, in time of relative peace and with no unusual handicaps on oil production, the United States consumes approximately two-thirds of all the oil used anywhere in the world. Undoubtedly in time of all-out war it would require more.

Another major consideration consists in the oil needs of Western Europe. The North Atlantic Treaty Organization, of which the United States was one of the principal architects, was created on the assumption that the defense of Western Europe is vital to the survival of the free world in the struggle with Communist totalitarianism. In this struggle European industry is counted on heavily to supplement that of the United States and Canada. But Europe does not rank high among the oil-producing areas and must be supplied mainly from extra-European sources. Inasmuch as the necessary quantities of oil cannot be drawn from Western Hemisphere sources without overtaxing those producing fields, the responsibility for European supply since 1948 has fallen principally on the sparsely populated oil-producing countries of the Middle East, whose minimal local oil needs and slight industrial development have represented complementary rather than competing demands.

In the uninterrupted continuation of the westward flow of Middle East oil the United States thus has an extremely important interest. This can be summed up in syllogistic form. The United States bears the principal responsibility for the security of the free world. The Atlantic Pact nations of Western Europe constitute the first line of defense of the free world. They can serve as a bulwark of defense only so long as they are well supplied with the sinews of industrial and military strength, one of the most essential of these being oil products. Oil in sufficient quantity for these needs, under conditions presently existing in the world oil industry, can be had only from the Middle East. Thus, in the interest of free institutions and possibly even its own survival, the United States faces the problem of establishing and maintaining in the Middle East conditions under which the defense of the area can be assured within reason and the flow of petroleum and petroleum products made secure under any easily imaginable circumstances.

U. S. AND THE MIDDLE EAST

It cannot be said that the United States has displayed a great deal either of ambition or of aptitude for the task of making sure of the westward orientation of the nations of the Middle East. Until World War II brought this country into some contact with Iran, Egypt, and North Africa, Americans generally knew and cared little about the area. The inevitable consequence was, on the one hand, an almost complete absence of interest and, on the other, a severe dearth of personnel fitted by training and experience to deal in a statesmanlike manner with Middle East questions as they might arise in the course of foreign relations. Inasmuch as the Middle East had occupied an important place in British foreign policy for at least a century and a half, there was much reluctance on the part of American officialdom, even after the close of World War II, to assume any direct responsibilities in this British sphere of interest.

Only as the decline of British imperial power and the importance to free world security of the Middle East came to be realized did the United States arrive at a more or less reluctant willingness to assume a measure of responsibility in the area. This was first manifested in relieving Britain of the burden of extending aid to hard-pressed Greece and Turkey. While this action proved to be of inestimable utility at a moment of crisis, it was clearly only a stopgap measure at a single crucial point in a contest that already had grown to global proportions. Free world security could on no reasonable grounds be regarded as having been attained by the setting up of the North Atlantic Treaty Organization for the defense of Europe or by assistance to Greece and Turkey. Security being indivisible, it would manifestly be of similar consequence to bring the Arab states, Iran, and Israel into a mutual defense system or at least to make sure of a preferential leaning toward the West in countries so strategically located.

For a task of this nature, as has been observed, the United States was poorly prepared. The measure of its unpreparedness is to be seen in the belief, prevalent but a few years ago and not by any means wholly dissipated today, that a spirit of mutual trust and interdependence could be induced, in countries so lacking as those of the Middle East in the elements of Western material culture, by means of the generous application of the Point Four concept. In keeping with this idea, programs of technical and financial assistance were developed and in due course were put into effect on a contractual basis in most of the Middle East countries. It is not requisite here to undertake an appraisal of the Point Four scheme as a means of improving conditions of life in so-called underdeveloped countries. In some parts of the Middle East the program undoubtedly has conferred benefits of one kind or another. It is essential to note, however, that in view of many of the circumstances prevailing in the area at the period when Point Four was launched, it could not justifiably have been expected to produce the attitudes anticipated in what we may call the political sphere within the critical period of a few years. A brief review of the main factors which have exercised a circumscribing influence on efforts to bring all of the Middle East within the range of a free world security system will help to explain the lack of important progress thus far.

BRITISH INTERESTS

In taking over certain of the responsibilities formerly regarded as lying within the British range of interest, the United States found itself heir to situations resulting from the long-time activities of Great Britain in the area. For many years Britain was the champion of the Ottoman Turkish regime. Parts of the Ottoman Empire—the sections now comprising Egypt, Iraq, Jordan, and Israel—for a varying number of years following World War I had been under direct British occupational or mandate control. British relations with Iran and with the princely houses of Arabia amounted to vested interests, some of which have not yet been surrendered. During the latter part of World War II Syria and Lebanon were beholden to Great Britain, having been freed from the Vichy French by British military action. Great Britain has been the internationally recognized protector of the Suez Canal, the principal member of the condominium for the Sudan, the liberator and sponsor of Libya. It still enjoys special privileges, including military base rights, by virtue of treaties with Egypt, Iraq, Jordan, and Libya.

At the same time, Great Britain was one of the founders of the North Atlantic Treaty Organization, and on this and other grounds was an indispensable partner in any scheme of defense of the free world. For these reasons, as well as for the sake of some measure of diplomatic collaboration from experienced hands, the United States, in establishing its own relations with Middle East governments, has been under the practical necessity of respecting the position still maintained by Britain in any part of the Middle East area. The inevitable consequence has been the transfer to the United States of a large portion of the suspicion and dislike that was attached to Great Britain as a "colonial" power by peoples still very conscious of their recent emancipation from British leading strings and hypersensitive, as are all young states, to any traces of influence of an imperialistic or restrictive nature. Thus the United States has been unable entirely to avoid involvement in some aspects of the British-Egyptian controversy over methods of closing out the Sudanese condominium and of making arrangements for Sudanese statehood. Similarly, this country has found it necessary to occupy the position of an interested party in the dispute resulting from Great Britain's refusal to evacuate the Suez Canal Zone, which it has occupied under rights acquired by treaty in 1936, on demand by Egypt. The acquisition by the United States of a major air base near Tripoli during the period of British military control of Libya also has been viewed askance in some of the Arab states.

Whereas the problems arising from association with Great Britain were inherent in any direct approach by the United States to the states of the Middle East and could not have been avoided altogether, others, perhaps quite avoidable, have sprung from United States behavior with reference to certain other situations and developments within the area. The part played by the United States government at the inception of the Zionist state of Israel, in the heart of the Arab world, is an instance particularly in point.

ISRAEL

In Palestine, Jews, Arabs, and miscellaneous Christian elements had lived together in comparative amity for many centuries under the various regimes that successively were ascendant in the lands east of the Mediterranean. The rise of serious internal discord in this Holy Land, ironically enough, followed the first stages in political emancipation from the rule of the Ottoman Turks. Under British administration, after World War I, it was the fate of both Jews and Arabs in Palestine to find themselves segments of two much greater groups already politically conscious of their religious and ethnic inheritances and imbued with nationalistic urges. Zionism, on the one hand, and pan-Arabism, on the other, inspired disorders within Palestine which came to assume international dimensions. The events of World War II, which created the need for the resettlement of hundreds of thousands of European Jewish refugees and further contributed to the rise of independent Arab states in the Middle East, rendered it essential, no doubt, that Palestine should be partitioned in some fashion into Jewish and Arab segments. It was one of the great misfortunes of the contemporary world, however, that this could not have been accomplished by the British mandatory regime or by the United Nations in a peaceful and orderly manner. The instant recognition de facto by the President of the United States of the state of Israel proclaimed by Zionist leaders upon the voluntary termination of the British mandate on May 15, 1948, the defensive strength subsequently manifested by Israeli forces in the Arab war already in progress, and the annexation by Transjordan of the remainder of Arab Palestine brought an end to the issue of partition. At the same time these developments gave a large measure of fixity to one of the most bitter of all international feuds—kept alive by the plight of more than 800,000 homeless, stateless Arab refugees driven from their former homes in Palestine, and marked by frequent instances of border violence and by a close Arab boycott of everything pertaining to Israel.

In this extremely unfortunate situation the United States on its own account is deeply involved and committed. In an over-all sense, it is involved as the power most responsible for the security of the free world. But in the Arab-Israel controversy, which has a direct bearing on that security, it is committed as a partisan not only by sponsorship of Israel at the time of its inception but also by extensive financial support thereafter, without which the Zionist state could not possibly have continued to survive. Consequently, with respect to the building up in the Middle East of a security system related to that which now applies to the North Atlantic and Mediterranean areas, the United States is compelled to proceed under a major handicap.

OTHER DIFFICULTIES

The Israel-Arab imbroglio is by no means the only serious obstacle to the building up of a security system in the Middle East beyond the confines of Turkey. Numerous other influences have contributed to the growth of an unpromising situation in the area. These include attitudes toward the West engendered by the grafting of modern nationalist sentiment on the ancient trunk of Islam. They spring from memories of earlier forms of European exploitation. In some measure they result from

envy of the advantages derived by Western countries from the utilization of Middle East oil resources. They stem, in part, from the countenance given by the United States and other members of the NATO group to France, for the sake of strategic air bases in North Africa, in its harsh efforts to restrain the nationalist aspirations of the Arabic populations in Tunis and Morocco. All of these and other difficulties less fundamental in character add up to the fact that most of the Middle East outside of Turkey cannot presently be counted upon to co-operate actively with the security system projected by the leading Atlantic Pact nations. Whether or in what way these handicaps can be overcome at all is a moot question.

INEPT DIPLOMACY

The elements touched upon as components in this unpromising situation are serious enough, but all too frequently they have been aggravated by inept diplomacy, the usual accompaniment of confused policy or no firm policy at all. It is not quite true, as critics occasionally have suggested, that the United States, influenced by but often disinclined to be guided by British policy, has had none of its own applicable to the Middle East. From the beginning of American interest in Middle East oil in the 1920's, if not earlier, there was something of an embryonic policy relating to the area. This waxed and waned in succeeding years according to the vagaries of political administrations at home and the incidence of crises abroad. After World War II there came a relatively rapid expansion of interest. From aiming broadly at the support of economic interests in the area, United States policy came to embrace political objectives, such as keeping a watchful eye on the activities of Communist agents, encouraging the strengthening of local governmental regimes, giving countenance to Zionist aims in Palestine, and, latterly, inaugurating aid programs not altogether innocent of political motives. Unfortunately, these aims have not always been consistent with one another and hence have not been parts of a whole. Indeed, down to the present, there has been no clear evidence that each of the American aims in the Middle East has entered as an integral part into basic United States foreign policy.

ANGLO-AMERICAN POLICY

In recent years, Great Britain has been in no position to make up for whatever deficiencies there may have been in American foreign policy. With the loss of control over the Indian subcontinent and the relinquishing of one position of vantage after another in the Middle East, coupled with serious economic problems at home and culminating in the surrender of a large measure of initiative to the United States, British policy in the Middle East has been halting and unsure. While British and American interests in the area now are fundamentally much alike, there has been considerable divergence in the methods chosen by the two powers for serving these interests. Absence on a number of occasions of a solid, united front has tended to undermine the really constructive programs jointly or severally undertaken in the area and to lower the confidence of Middle East political leaders in the wisdom and foresight of Western statesmanship. The lack of well-integrated allied policy—policy that does not appear to have arrived at a definite decision as to the course to be pursued should the presently uncommitted Middle East states refuse, at any stage in a defense emergency, to cooperate with the Atlantic Pact nations— goes far toward accounting for security problems in the Middle East area.

There is some evidence as time passes of an increasing measure of Anglo-American agreement on Middle East questions. As far as it goes, this is an excellent augury, for the Arab-Iranian states are not as yet definitely lost to the West. Temporizing cannot be continued indefinitely, however, without great risk of the dissipation of Western influence beyond recovery. Since neither Great Britain nor the United States is in a position to "go it alone," joint policy decisions of a consistent and enduring nature are called for and are not the less needed because they must take into account the diverse interests of other governments outside of the Middle East. But if time for decision still remains, what kind of decision is called for? What course is there but to continue to temporize—to hope that the "soft" nations of the Middle East will recognize their exposed position in time and that, in the interest of self-preservation, they will wish to have the United States or perchance Great Britain serve as their champion?

THE PRESENT TASK

It can only be answered that hope is a poor policy, or no policy at all, when time may be running out and when even the providing of economic and technical aid and conditional promises for the supplying of arms and armaments have failed to make partnership attractive. Possibly some formula has been overlooked that could win over the Arab nations, in particular, to the point of willing co-operation with the West. Thus far, search for that formula, because of the haphazard nature of the search, has been largely in vain. Obviously any attempt to make headway through the avenue of power prestige only undermines belief in the sincerity of any forms of aid supplied, whereas zealous efforts to build up friendly relations through forms of economic and social service or willingness to withdraw from positions of military strength only give the character of bluff to spasmodic demonstrations of power. Attempts to combine the two naturally savor of hypocrisy. So it is clear that those in whose hands lies the responsibility for the shaping of foreign policy face an unenviable task in the translation of long-range security calculations into policy for the Middle East. Any departure from more or less makeshift procedures requires decision in principle; decision in keeping with foreign policy as a whole; decision acceptable not only to the electorate at home but also to allies abroad.

Problems encountered in the contemporary Middle East thus constitute a challenge proportionate to the relationship of that area with its resources to the requirements for world security. That this fact is coming to be appreciated in the United States at last is suggested by a statement in the half-yearly report of President Eisenhower to the Congress on the Mutual Security Program under date of June 30, 1953. It said:

From the standpoint of defensive strength in the area of the Near East as a whole, the Mutual Security Program has achieved substantial, if partial, success. The substantial success lies in the greatly strengthened posture of Greece and Turkey. . . . The success is only partial because, although the area is still free of actual Soviet occupation, it cannot by any means be considered safe for the free world.

While the President's report was instinct with faith that the continuation of a program of good works and avoidance of any unwanted interference in Middle East situations, "so filled with high emotion and incendiary nationalism," would be likely to establish stronger ties with the free world, the absence of any specific allusion to that possibility might suggest a growing measure of uncertainty as to the outcome.

POWER POTENTIALS

While they are wary of the ways in which it may be applied, the peoples of the Middle East are extremely sensitive to the power factor in the outer world. They are not unique in this respect: power and its potential application invariably provide a basis of regard among nations when vital interests are at stake, but nowhere does this apply more illustratively than in the Middle East. The retreat of Great Britain from one position and another under nationalist pressures, the decline of enthusiasm for a common front among some of the members of the North Atlantic Treaty Organization, the degree of apprehension displayed by the United States at the growing military strength of the Soviet Union, all have contributed to a strong belief that the West has no monopoly in power. Since Middle East attitudes reflect not only current estimates of power potentials but quite as much the readiness to employ these potentials, the emphasis placed by the NATO powers in the past on purely defensive arrangements has tended to dim the Arab view of schemes proposed for a Middle East defense organization. Conceivably the "New Look" in United States military policy will modify this attitude in the Middle East.

Thus far, in undertaking to establish situations of strength in the Middle East, neither the United States nor Great Britain nor the two of them together with France, Greece, and Turkey and the African and Eastern Commonwealth nations have been prepared to move sufficiently from strength. Whatever may be the power potential of the United States and its NATO allies and associates in and beyond the Mediterranean, it cannot take the place of integrated, constructive, and consistent policy with respect to the Middle East. Even under the best of circumstances the allies will be hard put to maintain a substantial margin of favor and influence in the militarily "soft" yet strategically vital states of the area. The Middle East is so situated relative to the principal habitable parts of the world and bears such an important relationship to the balance of power among nations through its resources in petroleum that inevitably there will continue to be keen competition among rival power blocs for priority of influence in its constituent countries. In view of the fundamental needs and deficiencies of these countries, such competition almost certainly will continue to breed confusion and hesitation among the peoples of the area. Considering their long experience with the methods employed by great powers bent on consolidating their positions and advancing their national interests, there is little occasion for wonder that most of the states in this group, skeptical as to offers of friendship and protection and uncertain as to where the greater danger lies, prefer at the present juncture to seek refuge in neutralism. In seeking to provide for its own security as well as that of the rest of the free world, the United States thus is confronted with a challenge of a major order.

Halford L. Hoskins, Ph.D., Washington, D. C., has been senior specialist in international relations in the Legislative Reference Service of the Library of Congress since 1949. He has taught history at Trinity College (now Duke University) and Tufts College, was dean of the Fletcher School of Law and Diplomacy (1933–44) and director of the School of Advanced International Studies (1944–49), which he helped to organize, and during the war was consultant in the Department of State on matters relating to the Middle East. Recent works among his extensive writings are The Atlantic Pact (1949) and Middle East Oil in U. S. Foreign Policy (1950).

The Arab Commonwealth

By Abdul Monem Rifa'i

I SHOULD like, first of all, to set down here my deep gratitude and sincere appreciation for the letters that reach my office from American groups and individuals expressing their real interest in Arab views. Some write to me saying: "We are constantly hearing anti-Arab views, publicity, and propaganda, in the press, on radio and television, in the movies and at clubs and theaters, but the Arab voice is silent. You people seem to feel that as your cause is just and right, it needs no expression." As to this particular point, might I say parenthetically, "Yes, we still believe that right is its own defense." Actually there is no better mode of expression than to let the facts speak for themselves, especially when the press and the available publicity channels are reluctant to publish what these good Americans seek. Facts are the indisputable, concrete evidence of what is happening and what has happened in recent years in the Arab world, and these factual events form the very basis on which I am building my article. This article is not written by a professor or even by a student, but by a man who has witnessed facts and tries to describe them as they are.

However, an unrestricted discussion of the Arab countries or the Middle East, covering the various aspects of current life there, would greatly exceed the space allotted me in this volume. It may be advisable, rather, to present the major events in that part of the world and note their general indications and main features, and then to comment on the situation as a whole, a situation which is drawing the attention of the entire world. I shall naturally omit the long history of the Middle East with all its national developments and political movements, with all its rises and falls, with its huge background and its treasures. My intention is to concentrate on a new Middle East and on the main factors in its recent formation. Unfortunately for my speech and unfortunately for the present outlook in the Middle East, the situation is dark and gloomy. I should, in fact, prefer to write about the charm of the Middle East, the tranquillity of its life, the beauty of its nature, the purity of its sentiments, the nobility of its traditions, and the idealism of its morals and ethics. I would rather write of these things, of their importance and their effect upon civilization and humanity; or of Middle Eastern arts and their influence; or even of the economic possibilities and the opportunities for social reforms; but I am faced with pressing, bitter events that shift the direction of my thoughts. Therefore, let us come out of the bright American atmosphere, at least for thirty minutes, and live in the present atmosphere of the Middle East.

Developments in the new Middle East are characterized by several striking features.

AWAKENING NATIONALISM

First is the dominant will to attain freedom. The people of the Middle East are descendants of nations and races whose great empires and wide civilizations flourished throughout the world. They have great reservoirs of national pride and self-respect. Freedom to them is a fundamental principle of their life.

I still recall May of the year 1945,

when I was in Damascus, one of the oldest cities in the world, a city that has witnessed a long chain of conquests and glories. I still recall the seething masses of people, young and old, men and women, rushing from place to place; in revolt now against foreign colonial authorities and now against their own government, struggling desperately to attain their full freedom. The halls of the capital of the glorious Omayyad Caliphate echoed with the vehement voices of the crowds shouting for independence and liberty.

I was frequently reminded of that scene of Damascus in one of its awakenings during the last three years which I spent in Iran. There again I realized how deeply nationalism was entrenched in the people and how sincere and serious they are about it. There again I saw tens of thousands of people streaming through the streets and squares of Tehran calling for the realization of their national aspirations. That genuine desire for national sovereignty is dominant all over the Middle East, vivid and impressive wherever you go.

In Egypt, we all know how determined the Egyptians are to end the military occupation of the Suez Canal Zone and how the twenty-two million Egyptians are united in this national aim.

In Tunisia and Morocco, we are aware of the struggle for national freedom against the restraint of imperialism. I still remember on my visit to Tunis in 1947 how a man took me by the arm and said, "Brother, since you are visiting our country, do not forget to visit the tomb of our young national poet." I went to the tomb and to the humble little house in which the twenty-four-year-old Tunisian poet had lived, and I started reading, with great admiration, his excellent Arabic poems—poems that are memorized by the new Tunisian generation. It might be interesting to American scholars of political science to read one of these poems, translated from Arabic:

Oh my people!
I wish I were a forester to fell the trees
And leave the roots to perish in the sun.
I wish I were a flood to bare the graves
And clear them of their tenants one by one.
I wish I were a storm that I could roll—
And rage aloud the tempest in my soul.
Oh my people!
I will take me to the forest's solitude
And pass my days in desolate despair.
I'll rid your very image from my mind
And in forgetfulness I'll live and perish there.
I shall forget—and lose as much of you as I am able;
You don't deserve to taste my wine or even share my table.
Oh my people!
You are weak—asleep—you dwell in darkness,
Somnambulant you move not toward the light.
Therefore I leave to sing my songs
To birds that understand my plight.
For singing birds know better the words of Freedom's story,
And winging free they realize—awakening is glory.

THE ARAB NATION

The second significant feature in the Middle East is the tendency towards unity—unity among the Arab countries in particular and closer co-operation among the Middle Eastern countries in general.

The Arabs are in effect one nation, and unity among them is natural. For that unity, as well as for liberty, they rose up in 1916, and since then events have made them realize more and more the significance of their unity. Most of their states are, at present, members of the Arab League, an organization bound by a pact designed to develop further unities among its members. They are also associated in a collective security pact.

The Syrian Constitution states in its first article that Syria is an Arab state and that its people are a part of the Arab nation. The Jordanian Constitution states also in its first article that the people of Jordan are a part of the Arab nation. Every now and then we hear appeals from Arab governments and leaders for an Arab federation.

As there are social, political, and national motives toward unity within the Arab countries, similar factors motivate the Middle Eastern countries to strengthen co-operation and friendship among themselves. The countries in the Middle East, existing in one geographical zone which extends from the heart of Asia along the shores of Africa to the Atlantic Ocean, react uniformly to whatever fortunes and misfortunes may befall any one of them. I recall the huge and impressive demonstrations of the Pakistanis in Karachi in 1951, lasting several days, as they reacted sympathetically to the struggle that was taking place in Morocco. The countries of the Middle East form, as I see it, one social unit, developed, so to speak, into a "Middle Easternism" or even a "Middle Eastern nationalism," if the scholars of political science accept such a term! The solidarity of that area appears in endeavors to establish various forms of co-operation: a Moslem League, an Islamic High Governmental Meeting, an Islamic National Conference, an Inter-Islamic Economic Conference, a Middle Eastern Pact, or an Arab-Asiatic bloc.

This vast region, with its natural resources, strategic position, geographical association, and with all the other political, social, cultural, religious, and historical factors that unite its people, is bound to form sooner or later the third great political entity in the world, which will contribute more and more to the welfare of mankind and the progress of humanity. In fact, such a development might contribute substantially to international peace and stability.

PALESTINE

It is impossible to speak of the Arab countries in particular or the Middle East in general without mentioning the tragic problem of Palestine. The influence of this problem on the attitude of the Arab countries has a major effect on the stability of the Middle East. For us, it is a drastic fact that the Arabs of Palestine were driven out of the homeland in which they had lived continuously for fifteen hundred years. Recollections of violence and brutality rankle. The presence in neighboring Arab countries of hundreds of thousands of Palestinian refugees leading a wretched existence at an almost subhuman level is a constant irritant and focus of resentment. Furthermore, the Arab world believes with strong evidence that Israel is planning further expansion and is making military preparation to this end. The Palestine problem, therefore, should be solved on the basis of equity and justice for the purpose of attaining security and peace in the Middle East.

U. S. POLICY

These are the real factors in the development of the Middle East, and it is not possible to make an accurate appraisal of the situation in the Middle East without fully understanding them. They are, to be sure, generally well known by all students of international relations, but the role they play has often been distorted or misinterpreted. An interested group in America with substantial control over much of its information media has been successful in molding the views on the Middle East of a considerable portion of the American public, and has affected the formulation of government policy. What has been frustrating to most of the people of the Middle East is the striking absence, in America's Middle East policy, of its traditionally high principles with regard to the Arab national case, those principles which made America famous all over the globe and which are the basis of its international relations. It is essential that in order to succeed in building strong ties of friendship with the people of the Middle East the same lofty principles should be applied with regard to their problems. Unfortunately, however, the solution of the major problem, that of Palestine, is being directly hampered by United States aid to Israel, which increases the tension and complicates the just solution of this problem. However, no attitude shall be decisive in determining the dynamic growth and future development of the Middle East except that of the Middle East itself. The Arab countries with their fifty million Arabs, their extensive area, their substantial natural resources, will continue to progress and prosper, in spite of attempted disparagement.

In view of all these facts, it is in the interest of the United States of America to reconsider in part its Middle East policy, for the mutual advantage of the American people and the people of the countries of the Middle East.

His Excellency Abdul Monem Rifa'i, Washington, D. C., is Ambassador of the Hashemite Kingdom of Jordan to the United States. Prior to his present appointment he was for three years Minister in Iran and Pakistan. He earlier served as Under Secretary of Foreign Affairs, Chief Secretary of the Jordan government, and Acting Chief Secretary to the late King Abdullah.

The United States in the Changing Middle East

By N. Saifpour Fatemi

ROUGHLY, the region of the Middle and Near East stretches from the western border of Egypt to the western border of India and from the Black Sea and the Caspian Sea on the north to the Arabian Sea and the Indian Ocean in the south. This large and important area is today very vital to the defense of the free world. Its importance must be considered from three aspects.

Strategic Significance

The Middle East is a corridor between serfdom and freedom. It is also a bridge between three continents and has been through the ages a springboard for conquerors moving from west to east or coming from the east to conquest in the west. Its strategic position was as important in the time of Alexander the Great as during World War II. Throughout history, control of the Middle East has been the aim of practically every great empire. The area is a barometer of dynamic world forces. It was Peter the Great who believed that anyone who ruled the Persian Gulf and the Black Sea would rule India and Europe.

Since the beginning of the nineteenth century this region has been between the devil and the deep blue sea. British, French, and Russians plagued it all through the nineteenth century and the first half of the twentieth. Since the end of the war, the United States, in order to stop Russian aggression, has become the champion of the independence of the Middle Eastern countries. She has established air bases in North Africa, in Turkey, in Saudi Arabia and Bahrein. She has sent military missions, arms, and munition to several of the governments of that region.

In August 1951, President Eisenhower told the Senate's Armed Services Committee:

Turkey is only part of the great Middle Eastern problem—we should try to bring in the Arab world on our side. As far as the sheer value of territory is concerned, there is no more strategically important area in the world than the Middle East. This area is tremendously important in terms of what it could contribute for our whole effort. We should use our resources, our power, our organizational ability and above all, our leadership—to get some kind of organization that would rally all of them to go in with us.[1]

Economic Importance

Since 1908, when for the first time oil was discovered in Masjid-i-Sulaiman, in Iran, the British, Germans, French, Americans, and Russians have tried their best to obtain oil concessions in different parts of the Middle East. It is believed that its potential oil reserve is 80 billion barrels, 63 per cent of the world's known petroleum resources. The oil industry of one country, Iran, is as large as the entire estimated reserves, production, and refinery capacity of Russia and her satellites.[2]

The oil fields in that area produce enormously and at low cost. The wells drilled forty years ago in Iran are still able to produce at a rate of 8,000 barrels per well a day. In Iran eighty wells in 1950 produced 30,000,000 tons of

[1] *New York Times*, August 8, 1951.
[2] Mohammed Nemazee and S. Nakasian, *The Oil Forum*, March 1952, p. 93.

oil. In Iraq the average per well a day is estimated at 8,500 barrels and in Saudi Arabia at 12,000 barrels. It is interesting to compare this with the 11 barrels per well a day in the United States and 210 in Venezuela. It cost the Anglo-Iranian Oil Company less than $0.15 to produce a barrel of crude oil, against $0.70 in Venezuela and $1.70 in the United States.

All these wells of the wealth in the Middle East, are owned by five American companies—Standard Oil of New Jersey, Gulf Oil Corporation, Standard Oil of California, Socony-Vacuum Oil Company, the Texas Company; two British companies—the Anglo-Persian Oil Company and the Royal-Shell Company (there is also some Dutch interest in this company); and one French company. These eight companies, which enjoy a monopoly of production, refining, transportation, and distribution, send every day about 2,000,000 barrels of oil to markets all over the world. In terms of dollars the income from the oil in that area is well above 1,500 million dollars.

PEOPLE

Last and most important of all is the human interest. In this area from North Africa to the Indian border we have nearly 180,000,000 people. It has been called by Arnold Toynbee the heartland of Islamic civilization and its events reverberate from the rock of Gibraltar to the jungles of India, the steppes of Central Asia, and even the isolated plantations of Java and Sumatra.

U. S. INFLUENCES

Americans first came to this area in the middle of the nineteenth century, as educators, doctors, nurses, businessmen, and preachers of the gospel of truth and freedom. They helped the people and encouraged them in their fight against foreign exploiters and native despots, in their struggles against poverty, ignorance, disease, and tyranny. During the Iranian revolution of 1905–9, several young American educators fought on the side of the revolutionists and one of them gave his life for the freedom of the Iranians.

The American University of Beirut, Robert College in Istanbul, the American University at Cairo, the American Colleges in Tehran and Baghdad, dozens of high schools, and many hospitals, clinics, and libraries throughout the area are monuments to the lofty ideals of American humanitarianism.

In 1910 for the first time the Iranians turned to the United States for financial advice. The next year President Taft sent W. Morgan Shuster and five other American experts to Tehran to help the Iranians put their house in order. They accomplished such an excellent job that both the British and Russians were alarmed; they considered the work of the Shuster Mission harmful to the interests of their empires in Iran and, as a result, forced the mission out of Iran. On his return Shuster wrote his great book, *The Strangling of Persia*.

Then came Woodrow Wilson and his "Fourteen Points." He was called by the people of Eastern Europe and the Middle East "the Messiah of the West." His promises of self-determination for the colonial countries, of sovereignty, independence, democracy, and an end of the era of power politics, gave new life to an old world. His sincerity, honesty of purpose, and championship of the cause of oppressed nations undermined European imperialism and turned the tables on Communism. He strengthened nationalism and told the people of the Middle East that national sovereignty and independence, not Communism, would be the decisive factor. He condemned both European and Red imperialism and instructed his Minister in Tehran to tell the people of Iran that he was as much against the Anglo-Persian agreement as he was against the Russian invasion of the northern provinces. To him foreign domination and imperialism were intolerable. He could compromise neither with the British nor with the Communist exploitation and domination. This made him a savior in the eyes of many Iranians, Egyptians, Iraqis, and Syrians who were fighting for their freedom.

With the end of the Wilson era and the abandonment of the League of Nations by the United States, the Middle East was forgotten by the American people. Apart from Christian missionaries, a small group of businessmen, and a few oil companies, the people of the United States regarded the Middle East as a land of antiquities, of the Arabian Nights, of strange and backward people.

AFTER PEARL HARBOR

Then came Pearl Harbor. With the Japanese attack and Hitler's declaration of war against the United States, the Middle East became a vital area to America. Thousands of soldiers, technicians, pilots, and diplomats moved in. A Persian Gulf Command was established with headquarters at Khorramshahr and Tehran. At one time there were more than 70,000 American soldiers in Iran. By means of Iranian roads and railways, the Americans sent more than 6,000,000 tons of lend-lease goods to Russia. It was this help which saved Russia. During the Tehran Conference Stalin told Roosevelt, "If it were not for your help I do not know where we should have been by now."

Incidentally, rumors in Tehran were to the effect that in one of these meetings when President Roosevelt told Stalin that he could not send more lend-lease goods to Russia and that already he was under fire of some willful Republican senators, Stalin asked him how it was possible to be in power for ten years and yet have some Republicans in circulation. He was much astonished that they were not all liquidated.

Roosevelt's visit to the Middle East was a great experience for him. He could not conceive that people in a potentially rich region could be living in such abject poverty. He instructed General Patrick Hurley, his special envoy to Iran, to study the country's problems and report directly to the White House. In compliance with the President's instructions General Hurley prepared a comprehensive plan for economic and financial aid to Iran. He told the President how for the first time the resources of Iran could be developed for the benefit of the people of that country. He added that Iran had been exploited to such an extent that even the lend-lease goods coming from the United States had been sold to the Iranians by the English company, "United Kingdom Corporation," which "was keeping the money." Hurley asked the President for an independent American foreign policy in Iran. He believed that if Iran's two neighbors left her alone she could be encouraged to develop a "pattern of self-government and free enterprise."

Roosevelt replied to General Hurley:

I am thrilled with the idea of using our efforts in Iran as example of what can be done by an unselfish American policy. If we can get the right kind of American experts who will remain loyal to their ideals I feel certain that our policy of aiding Iran will succeed.

You are right that the distribution of lend-lease supplies throughout the Middle East should be taken over by our own people and I have let the Secretary of State know my views in this regard.[3]

[3] N. Saifpour Fatemi, *Oil Diplomacy: Powderkeg in Iran* (New York: Whittier Books, Inc., 1954), p. 210.

Subsequently there arrived in Iran from the United States a number of economic advisers, army officers to train the Iranian army and gendarmerie, and a few agricultural and health experts.

THE RUSSIANS IN IRAN

As long as the Western Allies were involved in the war against Germany and Italy they tolerated and even backed the highhanded Russian policy in Iran. With the end of the war the rift between the free nations and their strange bedfellow, Communist Russia, became clear. In Iran the gap became very wide, and it was there that the American "tough policy" towards Russia originated. When the Russians in 1945 set up the puppet government of Azerbaijan the American government protested, and at the Moscow Conference, Secretary Byrnes told Stalin that he was "seriously disturbed" at the prospect that the issue of the Russian evacuation of Iran and the separatist movement in Azerbaijan would be raised at the first meeting of the United Nations. He added that it was

exceedingly important that the great nations keep their pledges to the smaller powers. If Iran raised the issue at London it would be unfortunate. . . because, under the facts as we knew them and in view of our solemn pledge, we would greatly regret having to oppose the Soviet Union in the very first meeting of the United Nations and I hoped, therefore, that we could take action at Moscow that would forestall this possibility.[4]

Despite this threat and the complaint of Iran to the Security Council, the Russians kept their troops in Iran after the deadline provided in the Tripartite Pact. Following the withdrawal of the British and American troops the Russians sent some new troops to Iran and even

[4] James F. Byrnes, *Speaking Frankly* (New York: Harper & Brothers, 1947), pp. 119–20.

threatened occupation of the capital and overthrow of the government. All the pleas and protests of Iran and of the British and Americans were ignored, and the Soviet government made clear that it was not going to leave Iran alone.

By March 15, 1946, Washington, London, and Tehran were very much worried. No one could fathom the mystery of Russian intentions. No one could understand why the Russians were applying such pressure against Iran while the two main problems, the evacuation of Russian troops and the fate of the Azerbaijan government, remained unsolved. The great question everywhere was, What can the United Nations do to solve the Iranian problem?

There was no answer to this question even in Washington. The State Department, frightened by the turn of events in Iran, had instructed the Tehran Embassy to be ready to leave Tehran for the southern part of the country at a moment's notice. There were rumors that the government had decided to transfer the capital to Isfahan. In London the British government saw no solution to the problem.

The Russian conduct in Iran and Eastern Europe, at this time, convinced President Truman that the schism between Russia and the West was not bridgeable and that the United States could not compromise the principles for which she had sacrificed hundreds of thousands of her citizens. Therefore on March 21 he sent an ultimatum to Stalin, asking him to withdraw his troops from Iran or the "United States would put some more people in there."[5]

The Russian reaction to President Truman's ultimatum was prompt. At a time when many people expected the occupation of Tehran by the Russian troops, the Soviet government an-

[5] Fatemi, *op. cit. supra* n. 3, p. 235.

nounced that Iran would be completely evacuated within six weeks.

BRITISH AND AMERICAN POLICY

Then in 1947 came the Truman Doctrine concerning Greece and Turkey. The changes resulting from World War II and the support given by the United States encouraged the nations of the Middle East to revolt against Britain and France. Syria and Lebanon received their independence. The British were thrown out of Palestine. Iran, Iraq, and Egypt asked for the revision of their concessions and treaties with the British. Unfortunately, British concessions as usual were too little and too late. England did not understand the seriousness of the nationalist movement in the Middle East. She did not fathom the consequences of Iran's victory over Russia, the Truman Doctrine, the events in Palestine, the loss of India and Burma, and the effects of Point Four on the exploited and impoverished people of that area. Here for the first time a great power announced to the millions of poor people in Asia that she was prepared to help them without expecting anything in return. So far the people of the Middle East had experienced exploitation, concessions, domination of their countries by foreign loans and military pressures. After a hundred years of foreign exploitation the average income of the area is $75 per capita per annum, and in many countries 60 per cent of the people are illiterate. Point Four to these people is a continuation of missionary work with government support.

Britain did very little to readjust her policy in the postwar period. She did not heed the warnings and the advice of the Americans. The Iranians nationalized the property of the Anglo-Iranian Oil Company, and the Egyptians pressed hard for the evacuation of the Canal Zone. The good offices of the United States failed to dam the flood of nationalism and to bring about a solution of Iranian or Egyptian problems. It was from here on that the United States government was caught in the Middle Eastern dilemma. On the one hand the people of the Middle East blamed her for failing to help them against Britain and on the other the British censured American diplomats for interference in their area of influences.

The area is undergoing fundamental and rapid changes. It wants absolute freedom from the British economic and political domination, but the United States, which at one stage encouraged them to defy and resist Russian aggression and Communist imperialism, now is advising them to wait and not to upset the status quo, because any radical foreign or domestic change might play into the hands of the Communists, who are the immediate enemy. To the Middle East American foreign policy at this point looks like schizophrenia. The situation is well illustrated by the story of an Irish Municipal Council which voted three resolutions at one meeting.

They were: (1) Because the old jail is inadequate and collapsing, the jail should be torn down and rebuilt. (2) For the purpose of economy, the old materials in the jail should be used in the rebuilding. (3) The prisoners should be housed in the old jail till the new one is constructed. This is an exact description of what is happening in the Middle East.[6]

It looks as if the prisoners would have to stay in the old jail for the time being.

TODAY'S PROBLEMS

The United States today faces five vital problems in the Middle East: (1) the revolt of the people of North Africa

[6] Edwin M. Right, *The Threat of Soviet Imperialism*, edited by G. Grove Haines (Baltimore: The Johns Hopkins Press, 1954), p. 306.

against French colonialism; (2) the Anglo-Egyptian dispute; (3) the Arab-Israeli conflict; (4) the Anglo-Iranian dispute; (5) the poverty and backwardness of the area.

I shall not here elaborate on these problems or pretend that I have a solution to all these troubles, some of which have plagued the life of the people for fifty years. But before closing, I should like to make a few general remarks.

Most countries in Asia and Africa are going through two revolutions: one political and the other social and economic. The political revolution is against foreign domination, the social revolution is against interwoven poverty, disease, ignorance, and a corrupt ruling class. In the political revolution, nationalism, not Communism, is the decisive issue. Even the Communist groups in the area have to work under the guise of nationalism; otherwise nobody would listen to them.

The free world cannot be safe while vast reservoirs of poverty and colonial exploitation persist in Asia and Africa. For her own sake, just as much for the sake of those continents, the United States must find ways of solving the problems which threaten the peace and prosperity of the whole world. The old imperialism is certainly on its way out, and a new world quite different from that of the old is in process of being born. The revolutions, violence, pains, and pangs are indications of this new birth.

A CHALLENGE TO U. S.

The people of Asia and Africa expect understanding, help, and fair treatment from the United States and the Western European powers; reform, social justice, and consideration from their own ruling class. All Asia and Africa need a land program that calls for the breakup of feudal estates and their sale to the peasants, along the lines of a plan developed by the Shah of Iran. The rich people of these countries must be taxed and their capital used for the development of their countries. The land and income tax problems are the heart of the difficulties of Iran as well as of other parts of the Middle East.

The Western powers by now must have realized that stability in the Middle East can be achieved neither on the basis of military and economic pressure nor by an alliance with a few politicians who represent the groups defending the status quo, the feudal group, the landlord group.

As long as the changes in Iran and other parts of Asia are not extended to the masses of the people and as long as the grievances of these nations against the colonial powers are not redressed there can be no stability and security and no defense system in that region. Behind the defense system would stand hostile, ignorant, impoverished, and exploited people, to whom defense of democracy "is meaningless abstraction as long as it fails to cure or alleviate a basic malady—hunger." The events in China and Indochina must serve as an example of what may happen if the nationalist movements are not properly channeled and if something drastic and urgent is not done for the masses of the people.

The modern Middle East is a challenge to the United States and Britain. The new governments in Iran and Egypt have gone a long way toward co-operating with the British and even toward meeting some of their unreasonable demands. The Shah of Iran is doing his best to improve the lot of his people and is loved and admired by them. He has divided some of his estates among the peasants. He has devoted his untiring energy to reforms and improvements, but so far he has received very little support from outside or co-operation from the ruling class. The Shah presents an opportunity—an opportunity that is rare. He deserves the support of the people of the free world in his fight for economic freedom and in his struggle for reform and improvements in his country.

The strongest ground on which the United States and the free world can operate in Iran and the Middle East is by settlement of disputes through creation of a partnership and a common interest which will serve the interests of the people of the area first and foremost.

The people of the Middle East also expect the United States to develop an independent foreign policy in that area. They hope that you will speak to them in the language of Jefferson, Lincoln, Woodrow Wilson, Franklin D. Roosevelt, and Eisenhower. They are tired of the language of Palmerston, Disraeli, Joseph Chamberlain, Curzon, Jules Ferry, and Delcassé. They request that the United States in her relations with the Middle East avoid the pitfalls of British and French power politics. They pray that no foreign power will influence your high ideals and lofty principles. Your system of government and your way of living can win the hearts of the people of the Middle East, provided that you approach them directly and without the influence of your imperialistic friends and allies.

Let me remind you in conclusion of the words of a great revolutionist and an excellent reformist, Thomas Jefferson, who said:

I have no fear but the result of our experiment will be that men may be trusted to govern themselves without the masters; should the contrary of this be proved, I should conclude either that there is no God, or that he is a malicious being.

Let us all help to prove that Thomas Jefferson was right and that the people all over the world can be trusted to govern themselves without Russian, British, or French masters.

N. Saifpour Fatemi, Ph.D., Teaneck, New Jersey, is a member of the Department of Oriental Languages and Literatures, Program in Near Eastern Studies, at Princeton University. He has at various times served as editor of a leading newspaper in Tehran, member of the legislature in Isfahan, Mayor of Shiraz, Governor General of Fars, and member of the Parliament of Iran. He has also represented his country in the United Nations—as delegate to the UNESCO Conference in Cleveland, member of the Mossadegh mission to the Security Council, member of the Iranian Delegation to the General Assembly, and adviser to the Iranian Permanent Delegation. He is the author, among other works, of A Diplomatic History of Persia, 1917–1923 (1952) and Oil Diplomacy: Powderkeg in Iran (1954).

Book Department

ASIA

FAIRBANK, JOHN KING. *Trade and Diplomacy on the China Coast: The Opening of the Treaty Ports, 1842–1854.* Vol. I, text, pp. xiii, 489; Vol. II, notes, pp. 88. Cambridge, Mass.: Harvard University Press, 1953. $7.50 each volume.

This is an excellent account of the establishment of modern treaty relations with China from the first Anglo-Chinese war to the inauguration of the "foreign" inspectorate of the maritime customs. A distinctive feature of the volume is its attention to the Chinese documents and to the interpretation of events "in Chinese terms."

Within the brief period of twelve years the early treaty and treaty port system reached the point of breakdown as had the Canton system before it. The author does not follow the new difficulties to the second war; he ends his account with the inauguration of the inspectorate which he regards as the key institution (p. 462) in the new relations which were being worked out.

The general reader, if he can be induced to look into a work that seems highly specialized, will be rewarded by a beautifully drawn picture of the early negotiator for the Manchu Court, Chi Ying, whose effort was to bring the British barbarian under civilized control by a real sugar plum or two (p. 105) but chiefly by the sugar plums of trade. He will find, also, a neat exposition of the double hypocrisy of the opium trade of the time and may reflect upon the difference in the blinders worn by the Chinese and the British officials. He will find a lively description of the confusion at Shanghai during the Taiping rebellion.

The historian who undertakes to deal adequately with early Chinese-Western relations must be more than historian; he must be anthropologist, sociologist, political scientist, economist; and he can hardly avoid, if he has any imagination, an excursion into the philosophy of history as well. He must perform services of analysis and generalization beyond any narrow call of duty. The author accepts this with good courage, and his generalizations demand attention especially in the present state of Sino-Western relations.

He finds his significant generalizations in the fields of politics and diplomacy rather than in that of trade. There is, for example, a tantalizing reference (p. 297) to the extension of tea production in China but no examination of the nature of the industrial or economic organization which was soon to prevent China from meeting

Indian competition in a growing world market. The general effects—and possibilities—of trade are not explored, which may be accepted as further evidence that the chief importance of the early trade lay in the diplomatic and general international relations of the country.

The Chinese imperial system, which the author rightly considers one of the world's great political achievements, was the empirical fact and the theoretical concept into which, from the Chinese viewpoint, the new relations with the West had to be fitted. This was done, as the author sees it, by taking the Westerner into the system. The adjustment to the Manchu-Chinese dyarchy took the form of the inspectorate of customs and a "synarchy" came into existence. The institutions of the Chinese system were, and may still be, tough and adaptable. Thinking along these lines leads to the conclusion that the theory of imperialism is "not the only avenue of approach" (p. 468) to the problem.

Generalizations of quite a different sort seem at times to be on the point of formulation. There is reference (pp. 22, 468) to a landlord-gentry-scholar-official league against the peasantry in an agrarian-bureaucratic state. This seems to point in the direction of class struggle and to be inconsistent in its implications with the powerful traditions of the Chinese system.

If these powerful political traditions may be called Confucian, the current situation may be put into some such questions as these: Is a neo-Confucian solution of the political, social, and economic problem of China a possibility? How might China's relations with the West and with Russia fit into such a solution? By these questions exactly a century is spanned, from 1854 to 1954.

C. F. REMER
University of Michigan

SWISHER, EARL. *China's Management of the American Barbarians: A Study of Sino-American Relations, 1841–1861, with Documents.* Pp. xxi, 844. New Haven, Conn.: Far Eastern Publications, Yale University (for the Far Eastern Association), 1953. No price.

This handsome volume, the second monograph in the series sponsored by the Far Eastern Association, breaks new ground in the study of Sino-American relations and prepares the way for Western research on a new level of sophistication and control of the sources. One of the pioneers in the American study of nineteenth century China through Chinese sources, Professor Swisher here presents translations of 546 Chinese documents, most of them *in extenso* and few of them ever before available to the non-Chinese-reading researcher. They make available from the archives of the Manchu emperors the basic and originally secret documentation of the Chinese side of Sino-American relations in the fateful decades from 1841 to 1861. Though published in a photo-lithographed edition of the originally secret imperial compilation in 1930 and since then referred to by many scholars, the content of these documents has never before been so fully laid forth in English.

Professor Swisher's introduction gives the fullest account yet available of how these documents came into being and how they are related to other Ch'ing archives and publications. Of these 546 documents he finds that 19 have hitherto been available in English and that less than 200 of them are available in Chinese in other collections than the special one on foreign affairs which is here translated (the *I-wu shih-mo* series). Mr. Swisher began the process of selection and translation at Harvard in 1933, and continued it in Peking in 1937–38 and again in 1947–48. The results as now published, with a full complement of the necessary scholarly apparatus, form a landmark in the long and arduous process of understanding Chinese institutions and their functioning in foreign affairs.

Professor Swisher contributes three initial chapters on the handling of Chinese foreign affairs, the Chinese personnel involved in dealing with the United States, and the attitudes of Chinese officialdom toward this country in the middle decades of the nineteenth century. He then supplies introductions to the fourteen chapters in which the 546 documents are arranged, followed by a glossary of Chinese personal names with biographical notes (55 pages), foreign names with their Chinese equivalents (18 pages), geographical names identified (18 pages), and a full bibliography and index.

These research materials could have been made available only through extensive subsidy as well as unflagging persistence on the author's part. They give us for the first time a rough equivalent of the documentary publications from Western government archives which have formed the basis of so much research in international relations. Until further similar volumes can be made available to Western scholarship, it will remain impossible to bring China fully on to the Western academic stage. Political scientists and students of modern China and American foreign policy now have at hand a really significant segment of Chinese archival material, of sufficient bulk and scope for fruitful analysis.

J. K. FAIRBANK
Harvard University

ALLEN, G. C., and AUDREY G. DONNITHORNE. *Western Enterprise in Far Eastern Economic Development: China and Japan.* Pp. 292. London: George Allen & Unwin (distributed in the U. S. by The Macmillan Company, New York), 1954. $4.50.

The authors of this book have set forth a running account of the part played by Western enterprise in the economic development of China and of Japan and have drawn some interesting contrasts in the response of these two countries to the Western intrusion. The greater part of the book is devoted to China and to a description of the course of Western enterprise from a primary interest in trade for the sake of obtaining special products from China to the subsequent emphasis on the import into China of Western goods and the gradual development of ancillary enterprises to obtain and regulate the export products. Finally, an account is given of the attempt to modernize not only the industries, but the banking, the shipping, other transportation, and mining, and to establish public utilities. It details the political obstructions and the innate Chinese resistance to the invasion of Western enterprise and describes the defeats and fail-

ures encountered. Much detailed research has gone into this part of the book, but, as the authors have said, the greater part of their data has been obtained from Western sources. The problems are thus seen through Western eyes, and no new light is thrown on the enigma of why China resisted so tenaciously and Japan entered so eagerly into Western ways. The emphasis is upon the Westerner and his difficulties, and not upon the Chinese problem and the destructive impact of industrialization upon what had been a very highly developed economy. The result is a rather unsympathetic treatment of the Chinese scene.

The second part of the book describes the rapid modernization of Japan, the significant but relatively small part played by the foreign merchants in the reorganization of Japan's trade and industry, and the vital part of the government in initiating the change and creating the atmosphere in which Japanese enterprise was able to grasp control of its own industrialization, utilizing the "expertise" of the foreigners without being dominated by them. The section on Japan is the better analysis of the two. It is written with more sympathy and with much more understanding than is the Chinese section. This difference is probably due to the senior author's more intimate knowledge of Japan.

The authors plan a second volume on this theme covering Malaya and Indonesia, thus providing a number of mutually contrasting environments in which to study the impact of the West and the policies pursued in these so-called "undeveloped" regions.

JOHN E. ORCHARD
Columbia University

KIRBY, E. STUART. *Introduction to the Economic History of China.* Pp. ix, 202. London: George Allen & Unwin (distributed in the U. S. by The Macmillan Company), 1954. $4.25.

This book by Dr. Kirby, Professor of Economics and Political Science at the University of Hong Kong, is described by its author as follows, "the present treatise does not purport to give an account or narrative of the Economic History of China, but only to assess the importance of the subject, the position it has reached, its problems and prospectives of development. Incidentally, it presents a very wide bibliography of the subject" (pp. 62–63). As such, it is the first work of its kind in a Western language. The Introduction also contains a sound basic thesis, "that China must be viewed in terms of the interplay of a large number of forces," internal and external (p. 166). In contrast, the reader is repeatedly warned against the dogmatic interpretation in terms of class struggle.

The main contribution of the book lies in its summary of a considerable number of Japanese studies on the economic history of China. The extensive references even include Japanese translations from the Chinese and Western languages. The bibliography in these non-Japanese languages, however, is much less comprehensive and not always up-to-date. For instance, I find references to my early articles in Chinese up to 1937, but no mention of my more recent publications in English. The section on the last millennium is particularly disappointing. The author fails even to mention such leading economic historians as Ch'üan Han-sheng on the Sung dynasty (960–1279), and Shimizu Taiji and Liang Fang-chung on the Ming dynasty (1368–1644). In addition, the book is marred by occasional erroneous or misleading statements concerning historical facts, and by numerous mistakes in the romanization of Chinese characters. Thus the usefulness of this *Introduction* is appreciably reduced.

Referring to the periodical *Shih Huo* ("Food and Money," published 1934–37) which was devoted to Chinese economic history, Dr. Kirby remarks, "The contributions are very varied, but the magazine was under Marxist auspices and influence from its inception" (pp. 16–17). As a contributor to the periodical, I never heard anything about its Marxist auspices. Actually, it represented a trend to turn away from Marxist influence because its emphasis was on documentation rather than schematization. This misinterpretation probably arose from a lack of knowledge regarding the whereabouts of its editor, T'ao Hsi-sheng, who is in For-

mosa, because, in another place (p. 24), T'ao is cited along with Kuo Mo-jo as an outstanding example of present leaders of Marxist thought in Communist China. This kind of misrepresentation appears careless and irresponsible.

LIEN-SHENG YANG
Harvard University

MURPHEY, R. *Shanghai—Key to Modern China.* Pp. xii, 232. Cambridge, Mass.: Harvard University Press, 1953. $4.50.

This timely and well-documented study, enriched by the author's personal knowledge and experience, tells the story of the rise of Shanghai from a fishing settlement in the fourth century A.D. to one of the world's greatest cities and ports. When it fell to the Japanese in 1937 the population was estimated to exceed four million, and in tonnage entered and cleared the port ranked sixth or seventh among the world's ports. Although fortunate in suffering but little from either bombing or destruction by land forces it has since remained, if not at all times in a state of siege, at least cut off from the great channels of international trade which gave it birth and sustained its greatness.

In nationalist hands for four years from 1945, the Communist armies took Shanghai on May 27, 1949, and found themselves in possession of a great western-type city, the chief manufacturing center of the country, and its main gateway to the outside world. At first there was clearly an intention to reorient the city's life—that it should look inland. Signs are not lacking that second thoughts have prevailed and Shanghai is being refaced (witness the gardens along the Bund) to present a model of Chinese Communist enterprise to the outside world.

The author concludes, in a study singularly free from any political, national, or racial bias, that this former bridgehead for the penetration of China by the West is more likely to grow than to decline because of its new function as a catalyst in the changing economic relations between China and the world.

Shanghai's modern skyscraper office-blocks and hotels are built on concrete rafts replacing former pile foundations. Underneath are a thousand feet of alluvium; to the east Whangpoo Creek connected with the great Yangtse River forms a natural and dredgeable, if restricted, harbor. It matters little that the village once on the seaward margin of the great delta is now the city from which the open sea becomes sixty feet farther away every year. The story of the complex foreign settlement on Chinese soil, a western outpost in an eastern world, is a fascinating one. From Treaty port (1842), British settlement, French concession (1849) to famed International Settlement Shanghai had the best and the worst of the West. Law and justice attracted immense numbers of Chinese residents, but prostitution and vice flourished. All that is now history.

L. DUDLEY STAMP
London School of Economics
and Political Science
University of London

THOMAS, S. B. *Government and Administration in Communist China.* Pp. v, 150. New York: Institute of Pacific Relations, 1953. $2.50.

The research program of the Institute of Pacific Relations has presented studies on the development and features of Communist movements in Asia since the end of World War II. Reports have been published on Japan, India, Indochina, and Malaya. The Institute now adds *Government and Administration in Communist China,* written by S. B. Thomas, a Research Associate of the Institute and a graduate of the East Asian Institute at Columbia University. This well-footnoted and timely book contains chapters on the rise of the Chinese Communists to power, the return to the cities and the United Front policy, the formal program and constitutional structure of the "People's Republic of China," the role of the army, "Middle Parties," mass organizations and impact of the Sino-Soviet tie, the local government network and developments in national minorities, land reform, "suppression of counter-revolutionaries," and the major movements of 1953. The Appendix includes a report by the Central Committee of the Communist Party on "Struggle for Eradication of the Passive Attitude and Unhealthy Conditions in Party Or-

ganizations" and an editorial from a leading North China newspaper, "Our Thanks to the Soviet Union for Her Great Help."

The author asks some sagacious questions in an effort to assess the future of communism in China. To what extent will the land reform program give the Communists continued support from the peasantry? Can the Communists rapidly train capable technical-economic cadres in numbers large enough to meet the needs of a growing modern industrial economy? Can Moscow furnish sufficient technical aid and material support for this expansion? What will be the fate of the private businessman after the "struggle for nationalization" of all enterprises? Will the "old type" intellectual find it possible to co-operate with a regime hostile to his way of living and thinking? Will the Communists be successful in forcing their dogmatic ideologies into the minds of the tolerant Chinese? How much resistance will be offered by the devotees of ancient Chinese culture? Will there be an eventual emergence of a specific "Chinese Communism"? Will the Communists be able to reconcile Chinese nationalism with the more recent "proletarian internationalism"? And lastly, how will the strength of the new government and its hopes for industrial modernization be affected by military commitments, as laid down by the planners in the Kremlin?

Some of these questions have been answered. Others have been left for the muse of history to contemplate.

THOMAS E. ENNIS
West Virginia University

WRIGHT, ARTHUR F. (Ed.). *Studies in Chinese Thought.* Pp. xi, 317. Chicago: University of Chicago Press, 1953. $4.00.

Made possible financially by a grant from the Ford Foundation, this beautifully printed and relatively low-priced volume is at the same time an outstanding example of sound scholarship. Most of the eight authors are American born and trained The book is, therefore, happy evidence of the recent advance in Sinology in the United States and a welcome augury of still better things to follow.

The book is made up of essays which

cover much of the vast range of Chinese thought. Through the first five of them is to be had a more than cursory introduction to the course of the philosophy of China. Other essays deal topically with various aspects of the subject, including the types of symbols which display the influence of philosophy and religion in Chinese art and the problems of interpreting Chinese thought in categories familiar to the Western mind, of translating Chinese terms into Western language, and of putting Western thought into Chinese. The longest essay is a sketch of the history of Chinese thought by Professor Derk Bodde, translator of Fung Yu-lan's *History of Chinese Philosophy* and a specialist in his own right. The survey is from the novel interpretative approach of the interplay of harmony and conflict throughout the centuries. There is a fresh study of Neo-Confucianism. This is followed by one on "knowledge" and "action" since that stimulating mind of the Ming, Yang Yang-ming, which article pays especial attention to Chang Hsüeh-ch'êng (1738–1801), heretofore little noticed by American scholars. The second longest chapter, quite properly, deals with the more recent scene and the tensions produced by the inroads of thought from the Occident.

The volume makes no pretense of being a well-rounded account of all the vast range of Chinese thought. For example, only incidental mention is made of the massive Chinese Buddhist literature and the reaction of the Chinese mind to that faith, a field in which the editor has unusual competence. However, no better single volume on Chinese philosophy has been written in this country.

KENNETH SCOTT LATOURETTE
Yale University

BELOFF, MAX. *Soviet Policy in the Far East, 1944–1951.* Pp. viii, 278. New York: Oxford University Press, 1953. $4.00.

Similar in approach to the author's earlier work (*The Foreign Policy of Soviet Russia, 1929–1941*), this book provides a chronological account of Soviet policies in East and Southeast Asia from the Yalta Conference to the fall of 1951.

About one-third of the study is devoted to Soviet relations with China and the Chinese borderlands (Outer and Inner Mongolia, Sinkiang). The remainder deals in chapters of about equal length with Soviet policies in Japan, Korea, and Southeast Asia. Joseph Frankel, a specialist on the countries of Southeast Asia has written the latter section (covering Indonesia, Vietnam, Malaya, Burma, Thailand, and the Philippines) and has assisted the author generally with the analysis of Soviet and other research materials.

Mr. Beloff has been careful to maintain scholarly objectivity in his day-by-day account. Even when discussing as controversial and hotly debated a subject as the Soviets' role in the Communist seizure of power in China and the current relationship between the two regimes, the author is remarkably free of parti-pris. He considers it his primary task to present in logical sequence all the available factual evidence, leaving to the reader the task of synthesis.

In some respects, however, the writer has gone beyond this self-imposed role of chronologist. A brief introductory chapter raises some of the issues facing anyone who attempts to analyze Soviet strategy in Asia. In the process, Mr. Beloff has occasion to dispel some widely held misconceptions about Soviet policies. He neither believes in the existence of "a single masterplan conceived in advance for expanding the area of Soviet control to cover the entire Far East" (p. 1), nor, on the other hand, does he hold the notion that Soviet policy-makers operate entirely independent of Communist illusions about the external world: we must expect Soviet policy "to have its own inner logic and coherence" (p. 3).

Mr. Beloff and Mr. Frankel have carefully gathered the many small pieces of evidence from Soviet and other literature. But the author would be the first to admit the inadequacy of available Soviet source materials, especially in so far as factual information is concerned. On many vital questions several equally valid theories can be maintained. There is not sufficient evidence on hand to establish clearly the nature of the relationship between the Chinese Communists and the Soviet government, nor can we, with any degree of certainty, assess the relative importance of the several factors which may have entered into the decisions to strip Manchuria of its industrial potential or to launch the Korean attack.

Despite these obvious limitations imposed upon the author by circumstances, he has provided us with a very useful and much-needed book. The publication of new materials, in the future, and the completion of specialized studies (such as those devoted to the Russian-trained Asian Communists) may eventually further illuminate some of the problems under discussion. For some time, however, Mr. Beloff's study will remain indispensable for the student of Soviet and Asian affairs.

The value of the work is enhanced by a selection of appended diplomatic documents (regarding China, Mongolia, and Korea) and an index. A map would have been desirable.

PAUL F. LANGER
University of Southern California

KOLARZ, WALTER. *The Peoples of the Soviet Far East.* Pp. xii, 194. New York: Frederick A. Praeger, 1954. $4.50.

In Russian the term "Potemkin's village" is used to denote an impressive façade masking a far-from-imposing reality. No term could be devised which would more accurately describe Soviet policy toward national minorities. Granted on paper a considerable measure of autonomy, these minorities are in reality ruled by a Moscow-centered trinity of party, bureaucracy, and secret police.

This generalization is especially applicable to the Soviet Far East—the region lying east of Lake Baikal. The enormous distance of the Far East from European Russia and its adjacence to the North Pacific, once dominated by a hostile Japan and now by a hostile United States, guarantee it the closest supervision from Moscow.

The general nature of the steps taken during the past fifteen years toward the control and development of the Soviet Far East are well known: the establishment of military and industrial bases, the double-

tracking of the Trans-Siberian Railway and the building of other lines, the development of the Northern Sea Route along the Arctic coast, the efforts to render the region more nearly able to feed itself, the encouragement of immigration, and the like.

Somewhat less known is the impact of these trends upon the non-Russian peoples —Yakuts, Buryat Mongols, Chinese, Koreans, and others—most of whom inhabited the region before the advent of the Russians three centuries ago. In *The Peoples of the Soviet Far East* Walter Kolarz, a journalist and recognized authority on Soviet affairs, has subjected this impact to a highly critical examination. Drawing on a wide range of Soviet writings, he demonstrates the existence of a program of sovietization much more thoroughgoing, although perhaps less crude, than the Russification in effect under the Czars. An officially sponsored immigration of Russians has inundated the indigenous peoples and has virtually robbed them of their cultural identity and of their political and economic liberty.

Unlike many writers on Soviet Far Eastern policy, Mr. Kolarz appears to have taken some trouble to familiarize himself with the Far Eastern context of his subject; he presents, for example, an able summary of the Sovietization of Outer Mongolia. A very minor slip is the introduction of a notorious quondam warlord of Manchuria, known to English-speaking students as Chang Tso-lin, by the Russian form of his (Chinese) name, Tchan-Tso-Lin (p. 133).

Mr. Kolarz deserves great praise for his treatment of an obscure but important topic.

HAROLD C. HINTON
Georgetown University

WHEELER, MORTIMER. *The Indus Civilization.* (*Cambridge History of India,* a Supplementary Volume.) Pp. xi, 98. New York: Cambridge University Press, 1953. $3.75.

When the first volume of the *Cambridge History of India* was published in 1922, it contained nothing about the Indus civilization. The discovery of that phase of Indian history, so revolutionary of our knowledge, was first publicly announced by Sir John Marshall in the *Illustrated London News* of September 20, 1924, and was based upon excavations at Harappa in Southwestern Punjab and Mohenjo-daro in northern Sind. Since then these two sites have been further excavated, Chanhu-daro in central Sind has had a season of excavation, and various exploratory surveys have been made in western and southern Sind, Baluchistan, parts of the Punjab, and western Rajasthan. There has been a large volume of scientific publication of materials, discussion of the various cultures discovered, comparison with other known cultures of the third and second millennia B.C. in Western Asia, and comparisons and contrasts with later Indic materials.

This volume is a summary and appraisal of our knowledge by Sir Mortimer Wheeler, formerly Director General of Archaeology in prepartition India, later archaeological adviser to the Government of Pakistan, and himself the excavator at Harappa for several seasons, where he made notable amplifications of our knowledge. The book is meant to be, and is, a factual account of the Indus civilization—that is, of the most important of the cultures discovered there, called the Harappa culture. It has an ordered discussion of chronology, climate, the villages of the hills, and the cities of the plain, and it endeavors to give a picture of agriculture, commerce and industry, defense, arts and crafts, religion, and finally the dating.

So far as we can say now the maximum opening-date is 2500 B.C. and the closing date is the arrival of the Indo-Aryans, for which Sir Mortimer is willing to accept a time around 1500 B.C. This would give the Harappa civilization a life of a millenium, which may possibly be pushed farther back in time if it ever becomes possible to reach virgin soil at the principal sites. The author rarely goes beyond his data to speculate; for example, he treats more circumspectly than some other archaeologists the references to forts and the fort-destroying deeds of the god Indra which appear in the Rig Veda. He stays practically neutral on the two tiny statuettes

found at Harappa, whose period has been widely debated. He has not, it happens, noted the charming bronze dancing girl found at Chanhu-daro belonging to the Museum of Fine Arts, Boston, not mentioned in Mackay's published report. The script he flatly, and rightly, considers still unread. He resists well the temptation—irresistible to some others—to give over-interpretations to the religious material.

The book is a well-written lively, reliable description, a much-needed addition to the great *Cambridge History of India.*

W. NORMAN BROWN
University of Pennsylvania

VIVEK. *India Without Illusions.* Pp. viii, 216. Bombay: New Book Co., 1953. Rs. 4.4.

One of India's greatest national assets is her family of newspapers. Two or three of the English language dailies must rank among the twenty finest in the world. Readers of the Indian press will discover a rare freshness and vigor of analysis and a standard of prose excellence that compare favorably with the world's best. Columnists, editorial writers, and reporters often come from the ranks of the higher civil service, the universities, executive levels of business, and professional literary circles. The result of their combined efforts in news writing is first-class journalism.

The book under review contains a series of articles written by "Vivek," one of India's most distinguished scholar-journalists. The columns appeared in the *Times of India* (Bombay and New Delhi) between December 1950 and June 1953. A new series by the same author (now using his proper name, A. D. Gorwala) will be found currently in the *Statesman* (Calcutta and New Delhi). The Vivek collection has been divided into two sections: one containing articles stressing issues in foreign affairs; the second dealing with matters of domestic concern. Although each statement is short, the compendium read as a whole has a unity of constructive criticism that points out the social philosophy of the author.

Vivek will never be accused of being reticent to speak his mind. Indeed, if anything, he reflects a capacity for unveiling political and economic weaknesses, whether at home or abroad, with a brilliant, brittle, epigrammatic style that must annoy those actually charged with governmental responsibility. As a former civil servant of acknowledged experience and skill, Vivek knows whereof he speaks when dealing with the process of translating aspirations into laws and laws into action. It may be for this reason that the articles on domestic affairs carry with them more of an aura of authenticity than those that concern themselves with international relations.

However, Vivek propounds a thesis on foreign affairs relating to India that should be read along with the pronouncements of Prime Minister Jawaharlal Nehru. Vivek feels that India has erected a democratic political philosophy in her Constitution that demands not only domestic fulfillment, but also support of democratic ideals abroad. These ideals may manifest themselves in the encouragement of self-determination among colonial peoples; India's Constitution also implies a devotion to the cause of freedom that would bar giving aid and comfort to totalitarian regimes— of whatever variety and wherever found.

There are insights of significance on every page of this small book. It is best suited for those who have a grasp of the main outlines of contemporary Indian affairs. For them, Vivek's book is always provocative and is often wise.

RICHARD L. PARK
University of California
Berkeley

BRECHER, MICHAEL. *The Struggle for Kashmir.* Pp. xii, 211. New York: Oxford University Press, 1953. $5.00.

We are indebted to a young Canadian scholar for this useful guide through the many ramifications of the Kashmir question—the central problem in dispute between India and Pakistan and one of the great uncomprehended controversies in contemporary international relations.

Nearly one-half of the book is devoted to an analysis of the discussions on the Kashmir question in the Security Council of the United Nations, and of the proposals of the United Nations Commission for India and Pakistan, of General McNaughton as "informal mediator," and of the two mediators appointed by the Council, Sir Owen Dixon and Dr. Frank Graham. From the beginning the UN efforts to assist in the settlement of the dispute went awry. For example, as Dr. Brecher points out, the United Nations Commission for India and Pakistan (not for Kashmir, be it noted) "laid the ground-work for much future misunderstanding by obscuring the issues in its practice of endless clarification." Such insights are happily frequent in this book; but they are seldom presented with equal facility of expression.

The response of India and Pakistan to the various UN efforts, Dr. Brecher reminds us, "was determined by their basic outlook on the origin and nature of the dispute," and by "the basic disagreement on first principles." He makes some half-hearted suggestions for future UN action, but he sees more hope in direct negotiations between the two countries immediately concerned.

Dr. Brecher's survey of the situation in Kashmir before and immediately after partition is brief and rather superficial. His chapter on "The Importance of Kashmir to India and Pakistan" might be read with profit by those who wonder why the two nations are so concerned about this remote area. His final chapter sets the dispute in the broader context of general Indo-Pakistan relations. He has some interesting and rather uncritical comments on fundamental changes in the State of Jammu and Kashmir since 1947. He attaches great significance to the land reform program, which was indeed spectacular and sweeping; but he does not even question whether the program has achieved the results claimed for it.

Although he refers to events as recent as the riots in Jammu in March 1953, he gives no hint of the political crisis, already bubbling beneath the surface, which led to the dismissal and arrest of Sheikh Abdullah five months later. In his opinion most Kashmiris "favour the continuation of the present pro-Indian Government." He notes "the universal respect and admiration for Sheikh Abdullah" (at least, as he did not add, in the Valley of Kashmir), and he reports that many Kashmiris told him that "where the Sheikh goes, we go." Well, "Sheikh Sahib" is now in "protective custody." His fall from power must be an added source of confusion and bewilderment to thousands of the humble folk of Kashmir who thought of him and the "New Kashmir" as one.

Dr. Brecher has written an intelligent and objective book, based on a careful study of the pertinent documents and on first-hand observations in Kashmir, and in India and Pakistan. Unfortunately the book is unattractive in appearance and bears an outrageous price.

NORMAN D. PALMER
University of Pennsylvania

BISSON, T. A. *Zaibatsu Dissolution In Japan.* Pp. xi, 314. Berkeley: University of California Press, 1954. $5.00.

The term Zaibatsu has been variously defined to mean "money clique," "oligarchy of wealth," "concentrated business wealth," and so forth. It is the term applied to leading Japanese families, such as Mitsui, Mitsubishi, Yasuda, Sumitomo, Asano, and others, which had very extensive holdings in banking, industry, and trade until 1946.

Over three centuries ago Mitsui, Taketoshi, renounced his samurai status to open a pawnshop and sake and soy-sauce brewery in Echigo during the Genwa era (1615–1623). In 1722, the house of Mitsui developed a written set of rules and regulations, which with occasional revisions, controlled the actions of the eleven Mitsui families until it was abrogated in 1946. Under this code, the personal as well as the business lives of Mitsui members were subjected to regulation by a family council dominated by the head of the main family. Marriage, divorce, adoption, and other personal matters were so controlled, no less than the handling of corporate investment, savings, and profit distribution or reinvestment. A vast commercial and industrial empire grew out of the pawnshop and sake plant, encompassing banks, mining, shipbuilding, manufacturing, and an extensive network of world trade. At its peak the Mitsui combine employed 1,800,000 persons in Japan and about another 1,000,000 in the Far East and the rest of the world.

T. A. Bisson tells the story of the Occupation's efforts to dissolve these combines. His study outlines the position held by the Zaibatsu families and their methods of controlling their business empires. It examines the alternative policies open to the Occupation in dealing with the all-pervasive combines. It shows how the Occupation authorities finally arrived at a dissolution policy and how this—the most ambitious antitrust operation in history—was carried out. Finally, it summarizes, up to 1952, the results and implications of actual decrees and legislation.

The question of these semi-feudal business oligarchies posed a significant question for United States policy. Was it possible to transfer to Asia the free enterprise climate of the United States? The United States decision to break up the entrenched system of concentrated business power represented one of the most ambitious projects of the Occupation. How successful was the experiment?

In Bisson's judgment the U. S. policy decision to dissolve the combines was unrealistic from either an economic or political point of view. From an economic point of view, dissolution and fragmentation meant less efficiency, higher production costs, less ability to compete in essential world markets. From a political point of view Bisson holds that nationalization would have been a preferable policy to dissolution. Nationalization, he believes, would have preserved the advantages of large-scale operation, and it would have had the organized political support, which the dissolution policy lacked. He indicates that the Social Democrats favored nationalization rather than dissolution. "In choosing dissolution instead of public ownership . . . the Occupation weighted the odds against the one party through which liberal political as well as economic change might have been achieved."

Just how nationalization would have fared in the face of the split between Right Wing and Left Wing Socialists and just why transferring the bulk of Japanese banking and industry from the Zaibatsu to the Kanbatsu ("official cliques," or "entrenched bureaucracy") would have advanced the cause of democracy in Japan, Mr. Bisson nowhere explains. In surveying the results under the course the Occupation followed, he finds "disturbing questions about the effectiveness of dissolution," and notes that "by 1952 the combines were again emerging. Dissolution of the top holding companies had struck at the networks of subsidiaries, but the blow was not fatal."

JEROME B. COHEN
College of The City of New York

BLAKESLEE, GEORGE H. *The Far Eastern Commission, A Study in International Cooperation: 1945 to 1952.* (Department of State Publication 5138, Far Eastern Series 60.) Pp. v, 239. Washington, D. C., 1953. 70 cents.

When an eminent historian and expert in international relations is associated with the making of political history by serving in his country's government and subsequently, with access to all documents, prepares a comprehensive review which is published by his government, we are likely to have a document with unusual authority on the one hand, and the kind of objectivity we expect from historians on the other. Dr. George H. Blakeslee's record of the work of the Far Eastern Commission is such a document. He was political adviser to the Chairman of the Commission, member of the United States delegation to the Commission, and United States representative on its Steering Committee throughout the life of the body from 1945 to 1952. Hence the authority of the study; of Dr. Blakelee's place as a historian nothing need be said. His aim is to give an account of the Commission from the point of view of international cooperation. He does not hesitate to bring out clearly the strains and stresses which developed.

The Headquarters of the Commission were throughout its existence in Washington. It paid only one visit to Japan in December 1945—January 1946. It never achieved satisfactory liaison with the Supreme Commander of the Allied Powers, and as time went on and the viewpoint of the United States with regard to the Occupation changed, friction between the United States and the members of the Commission was frequent.

The Commission's terms of reference represented a compromise between the views of the United States and of the other Allies. It had authority to formulate policies. On the other hand the United States government had special rights and privileges. The Supreme Commander was American and "the sole executive authority for the Allied Powers in Japan," tending as Dr. Blakeslee says "to act in accordance with the views of the United States Government." In the Commission the United States could veto any policy with which it disagreed. Moreover it could issue interim directives to the Supreme Commander on "urgent matters," an elastic concept which was embracing. These directives were subject to review by the Commission, but this right was abridged by delays in submitting them. "The broad rights of the Commission and the specific rights of the United States government together created a condition of political instability." Friction became serious from the time when the Japanese Constitution began to be discussed.

Nevertheless, Dr. Blakeslee records that in the First Period, during approximately the first two years of the Commission's history, the United States and the Commission as a whole worked well together. Forty-six policy decisions were made by the 11-nation Commission, mostly unanimously. This was a period in which the United States and other members were in agreement on the Occupation, and the United States government respected the rights of the Commission. In the second period the United States government had changed its position: Japan was to pay no reparations and, in view of the delay in a peace treaty, should be given rights it would have obtained by the treaty. These positions were opposed by other members of the Commission. Dr. Blakeslee says "The task of passing judgment on . . . the respective positions . . . is rendered perplexing by the fact that judged by development of events and provisions in the Treaty of Peace, the United States was in general correct in the positions it took since these were later accepted by other members of the Commission." It is sometimes necessary to accept what cannot be changed.

A. VIOLA SMITH

New York City

ELSBREE, WILLARD H. *Japan's Role in Southeast Asian Nationalist Movements, 1940 to 1945.* Pp. vii, 182. Cambridge, Mass.: Harvard University Press (for Institute for Pacific Relations), 1953. $3.25.

The Japanese developed in their Greater East Asia Co-Prosperity Sphere policy what they justly considered a brilliant scheme for harnessing the nationalist, anticolonial movements of Southeast Asia to their war effort as well as for extending their own empire. In order to win this support, however, they were compelled to unleash nationalist forces which in the end turned—or would have turned, if not for the end of the war—as surely against themselves as they had been against the Western powers. Thus while the Japanese thought of themselves as using the nationalists for their own purposes, in the end it was the nationalists who had used Japan to advance their own goals of independence and unity.

How the Japanese came to be the used instead of the users is analyzed by Mr. Elsbree in his stimulating and readable volume through an examination of the course of the Japanese Occupation of the colonial countries of Southeast Asia. The book would have gained a good deal if Mr. Elsbree had had available to him as adequate materials for the other countries as he had for Indonesia, his most detailed case example. Also, some important perspective might have resulted from a parallel treatment of Thailand, which is significant for the very reasons it was excluded from the analysis, namely, that it was not under the direct control of a Western power and that its nationalism was not necessarily anti-Western. However, it is to be hoped that Mr. Elsbree and others will deal with these problems with the fullness they deserve at some other time.

The Japanese plan ultimately failed for several reasons. First, the Japanese themselves were not of one mind in their approach and ultimate intentions in the area. The nationalists were able to exploit these differences—between Tokyo and the field, between higher and lower headquarters, between politically and militarily-minded officials—for their own benefit. Thus the Japanese were never able to apply a uniform, monolithic pressure on the native peoples. Second, in order to win their support in the first instance against their Western masters, it was necessary to make concessions to the demands and aspirations of the nationalists in the fields of government employment and responsibility, armed forces, education, and mass media expansion which, in the end, developed the skills, organization, self-confidence, military power, and *esprit* that enabled them to stand up to the Japanese as well. Third, as Allied pressure on the Japanese increased, the Japanese came to need the Southeast Asians more than the Southeast Asians needed them, and they had to make increasingly greater concessions for continued support or even non-opposition.

Although the nationalist leaders for their part differed enormously in their estimate of and attitude toward the Japanese (some believed in Japan's "destiny," some believed her good intentions, some hoped to use them, some were motivated only by hatred of their colonial overlord or of the white man or of the West) they all followed a course of pressing on the Japanese for more and more freedom and sovereignty. In the light of Mr. Elsbree's analysis, the differences between the "puppets"—the Ba Maws and the Laurels—and the "anti-Fascists" take on the proportion of tactical rather than principled issues. Finally, towards the end of the war, the nationalist forces proved strong enough to assist in expelling the Japanese and to challenge the return of European rule with varying degrees of success.

There is much that the West can learn from the experience of the Japanese in Southeast Asia. Many Americans have come to know by now that the problems of the Occupier are pretty much the same all over the world, whether it is the Japanese in Southeast Asia or the Americans in Japan and Germany. We shall also have to learn that however steady and powerful a pressure we exert on Southeast Asia—in spite of our undoubted moral rightness—the end historical result will be conditioned, if not largely determined, by the needs, aspirations, understanding, and character of the Asians themselves.

HERBERT PASSIN

Ohio State University

LEACH, E. R., and RAYMOND FIRTH. *Political Systems of Highland Burma: A Study of Kachin Social Structure.* Pp. xii, 324. Cambridge, Mass.: Harvard University Press, 1954. $7.00.

Professor Leach has written an important book based on his contacts with the Kachin peoples of northern Burma from 1939 to the end of World War II. The first seven months of this period he spent in the village of Hpalang in the Namkham-Bhamo area doing anthropological research and mastering the Jinghpaw language. His first hand observations were supplemented later by wide reading in European language sources. The author breaks new ground not only in describing the confused social organization of a people hitherto little known, but also in his methodology. He rejects the idea of hypothetical norms prevailing in an assumed stable social structure in favor of reporting actual behavior in concrete situations. He discovered that social structure among the Kachins varied widely from community to community and from time to time in the same community and that the inconsistencies present were the essentially significant aspects in explaining Kachin society.

Traditionally, the hill-dwelling Kachins supplemented their meager livelihood from *taungya* cultivation by levying commercial toll or military blackmail against their more prosperous and less belligerent Shan neighbors. From time to time a Kachin chief (*duwa*) established hereditary predominance and attempted to imitate the feudal-type domination of the Shan chief over a limited valley area capable of wet-rice cultivation, and in rare instances a *duwa* actually turned Shan. Almost in-variably, however, such a presumptuous Kachin chief alienated his restless followers, who having plenty of hillside room in which to roam threw off his incipient feudal yoke and reverted to a primitive semi-anarchistic order which recognized no class distinctions or hereditary clan superiority. Kachin society thus tended to oscillate between the loosely organized democratic (*gumlao*) structure and the better integrated hereditary feudal-type (*gumsa*) system of dominance by a chief possessing ritualistic and lineage claims to superiority. Mr. Leach cites the multi-tongued (9 languages among 130 family units) village cluster of Hpalang as an example of an unstable *gumsa* community rent by factional rivalry, which was deterred in 1939 from reverting to *gumlao* status only by the marked preference of the British administration for the more orderly chief-centered *gumsa* system.

Although the Kachin situation seems to be fairly comprehensible on political and geographical grounds, the author has buttressed his interpretation by a plethora of technical anthropological data. In fact, Mr. Leach labors his sectarian arguments with professional opponents almost to the point of annoyance. The book will nevertheless stand a long time as a scholarly and realistic contribution to the understanding not only of the Kachins but also of the political and social institutions of old Burma. Particularly noteworthy is the similarity between the authority of the *gumsa duwa* and that of the Burman *myothugyi;* the systems of land tenure are similar and also the overriding importance of social status and symbols of rank. Leach challenges Luce and other Burman experts by questioning the assumption that successive waves of Tibeto-Burman peoples have migrated into the Irrawaddy valley in historic times. He thinks that the Burmese are probably the descendants of the ancient Pyu (second and third centuries A.D.) and that the Kachins have resided in northern Burma for many centuries.

JOHN F. CADY

Ohio University,
Athens, Ohio

INTERNATIONAL RELATIONS AND WORLD GOVERNMENT

MACMAHON, ARTHUR W. *Administration in Foreign Affairs*. Pp. 272. University, Ala.: University of Alabama Press, 1953. $3.50.

This book is the outgrowth of a series of lectures which Professor Arthur W. Macmahon, Eaton Professor of Public Administration, of Columbia University, gave at the University of Alabama under the auspices of the Southern Regional Training Program in Public Administration.

The first chapter deals with "The Concert of Judgment," "the ultimate concert of advice as it bears upon and emerges in decision." High among those who affect this concert are the Joint Chiefs of Staff, who are given power by Congress, not as militarists, but due to our deep worship of the expert, government being "believed to be incurably amateurish" by comparison. It is noted, nevertheless, that there can be "defensive militarism." The increasingly powerful role of the national Security Council and the minor influence of the Cabinet are described.

Recent developments in our "Department of Foreign Affairs" trace the expansion of units for economic analysis and negotiation, for the council diplomacy of the United Nations, "intelligence" research and the operation of informational and economic programs. These functions seem to Macmahon to belong in the State Department, and he is not persuaded that the 1953 Reorganization Plans which established a separate Foreign Operations Administration to handle most of them are the last word.

The chapter on "Field Structure for Foreign Programs" contains excellent discussions of the administrative aspects of NATO (North Atlantic Treaty Organization), the very powerful United States Special Representative in Europe, the European Coal and Steel Company, the European Defense Community, and other regional developments.

There is a penetrating discussion of the complex subject of interdepartmental coordination and a final chapter on Personnel for Foreign Affairs, which considers the arguments for and against maintaining the traditional separation between the State Department and the Foreign Service. Problems of personnel selection are examined, including the need for area training.

These lectures reveal a deep knowledge of the intricate processes of public administration which should delight the expert in that field. They are at the same time easily readable by the layman. There are apt figures of speech and touches of Macmahon's urbane humor, as well as illustrations useful to the general student of foreign affairs.

D. F. FLEMING
Vanderbilt University

MANGONE, GERARD J. *A Short History of International Organization*. Pp. ix, 326. New York: McGraw-Hill Book Company, 1954. $5.00.

This is an important contribution to the teaching literature in the field of international relations. The author, who is on the political science staff of Swarthmore College, brings a fresh approach to his subject in that he concentrates his attention on the broad historical factors which impel the seventy-odd states of the world to associate with one another in formal international organizations.

Despite the historical approach, the work should not be mistaken for a history in the strict sense. In fact it is this reviewer's opinion that the book is mistitled; its reception may suffer accordingly, since most courses in international organization are planned for a functional approach. Actually the work is well suited to text use in such a course, or in a broader course in international relations (in which some supplementary reading might be required). The historical material is chiefly found in the first four chapters, dealing with international organization before Napoleon, in the nineteenth century, and with international law. The remainder of the book is almost exclusively concerned with the contemporary pattern of world organization. There is a chapter each on the League of Nations, the United Nations, International Administration, Regional Organizations, and the Future of International Law and Organization.

Following each chapter, the author has included a brief appendix, which includes extracts from germane documents. This material has been selected with great care and the extracts carefully edited to compress the most meaningful passages within a limited space. Although the average documentary appendix for a given chapter is only about five pages in length, the author has managed to give the reader a look at some 33 documents in all.

A colorful style and a practical notion of the limitations on international organization characterize the book. Well-written throughout, it repeatedly emphasizes the role of power politics in relation to organized efforts to cope with the many problems of modern world society.

OLIVER BENSON
University of Oklahoma

BROOKINGS INSTITUTION. *Major Problems of American Foreign Policy, 1954.* Pp. x, 429. Washington, 1954. $2.00 paper; $4.00 cloth.

The most significant feature of this volume is its approach rather than its subject matter. The authors treat each problem as a government official responsible for policy formation would deal with it, considering the relationship of the immediate problem to the total world situation, to domestic conditions in the United States and elsewhere, and to the basic principles and objectives of American foreign policy, and analyzing and weighing alternative solutions in the light of these factors.

Illustrative of this approach is "A Problem Paper on the Soviet Threat," which presents a "predecision analysis," designed to "demonstrate a method of preparing the ground for decision," by including material which "breaks off with an analysis of issues and alternatives" (p. 347). Thus the student is encouraged to follow the process normally pursued by policymakers but is left to make his own choice among possible courses of action.

Substantively, Part One deals with key developments in international relations from July 1952 to September 1953 and surveys "the form and substance of pos-

sible negotiations" between the West and the Soviet Union. Part Two reviews the influences which frustrated efforts to preserve the unity of the wartime allies and traces the evolution and crystallization of the principles and objectives of American foreign policy, showing how attempts to apply them to specific situations are conditioned by domestic and foreign pressures. Part Three explores major problems confronting American policymakers at the beginning of 1954, first in the realms of politics, economics, military affairs, relations with the United Nations, and the Cold War, and second by regions and their national components. The text closes with the problem paper on the Soviet threat.

The impact of Soviet expansionism on American postwar actions, and even on the evolution of fundamental American principles, objectives, and methods, is apparent throughout the book. The authors regard 1954 as a potential turning-point, at which "the Soviet Union, either by design or in consequence of internal pressures created by Stalin's death, appeared to be seeking to relax international tension," thus confronting the United States with "the possible need to re-examine over-all relations with the Soviet Union" (p. 110) and other powers. Washington bears also partial responsibility for determining whether the United Nations is to be "a coalition of the free world" or "a universal organization of states" (p. 181).

The authors have provided excellent bibliographical guides to both primary and secondary sources.

AURIE N. DUNLAP
Lehigh University

VISSCHER, CHARLES DE. *Théories et réalités en droit international public.* Pp. 467. Paris: Éditions A. Pedone, 1953. 2,500 frs.

Urging the friends of international law to face frankly the extensive political elements within it, Professor Visscher in this volume roundly condemns theoretical systems like those of the Vienna School which divorce law from politics. He advocates instead that every effort be made to integrate our constantly growing knowledge about international politics with the traditional doctrines of the law. The former Judge of the International Court of Justice (1946–52) strikes a number of chords familiar to Americans who quite frequently in recent years have heard and played the symphony of "realism" in international relations. Reality to Prof. Visscher, however, does not prescribe jettisoning international law because it functions poorly. He condemns equally the legalist who divorces international law from politics and the specialist in international relations who "sins for his part by failing to understand . . . [that] law is a normative discipline; [that when] one speaks of norms, he speaks of precepts, and that precepts should never be confounded with facts" [translation by reviewer].

He urges his colleagues not to devitalize the law by cutting it off from either the facts of international life or from the "moral inspiration" which alone can raise the conduct of international affairs out of the jungle. He recognizes that an international community does not yet exist, but he speaks of it as one of the "civilizing ideas" which operates slowly and despite eclipses as a positive force generating social and political change. So too he characterizes the embryonic European Defense and Political Communities as "premature" and void of adequate spiritual and political bases, but he still sees in federal principles great possibilities for organizing international life in the future.

This treatise is in four parts. Part One describes international power politics and how the state system has developed since 1648 and treats historically and analytically theories of the state and international law from Machiavelli to Kelsen. Part Two considers the general relations between power and law in international affairs and how ideas of "sovereignty" and "vital interest" hamstring the United Nations and prevent the international community from developing. In the third and major portion of the work the author examines the principal rules of international law, effectively demonstrating in how few areas states are prepared to abide by detailed codes and how often international legal prescriptions are unrealistic. Finally, M. Visscher describes and deplores the limited

role the international Courts have played in settling international disputes.

This treatment of international law will not make happy those "legal theoreticians who ensconce themselves in a purely juridical vision of the world" or "certain writers who abandon themselves . . . drunkenly to a totalitarianism of politics." It will, however, challenge those who believe that there is a place in reality for values, law, and organization and a place in law for reality.

RICHARD N. SWIFT
New York University

VAN DER VEEN, GAELE. *Aiding Underdeveloped Countries Through International Economic Co-operation.* Pp. 200. Delft: Naamloze Vennootschap W. D. Neinema, 1953. No price. Written in English.

Heer Gaele Van der Veen has undertaken the important task of tracing the evolution of "outside" aid to underdeveloped areas from the fifteenth century to the Colombo Plan and Point Four. This University of Amsterdam study succeeds in calling attention to the real difficulties inherent in attempting to implement what the Economic and Social Council (ECOSOC) in 1951 recommended to the United Nations as a moral duty.

This moral duty flows from the "legally qualified duty" of the less advanced nations to bring to fuller development economic possibilities in their territories. Dr. Charles Malik, the Lebanese delegate, put this question to the Council during its eighth session: "If the international community was of the opinion that the economic backwardness of a given region constituted a real danger, was it not in duty bound to intervene in the interest of the country itself as well as in the interest of the world-community as a whole?" (pp. 12, 169). An affirmative answer might serve as a rationalization for the unilateral imperialism of the First (fifteenth to eighteenth century) and Second (eighteenth to twentieth century) Periods of imperialism. The author has recognized this possibility in his conclusions with respect to each Period. (He finds that during the First Period the West European states did not even take the trouble to rationalize their motives. Their ideas of national interest were enough. Only Vitoria, Gentili, Grotius and a few others were in open opposition).

The author hopes that technical and financial assistance will be based increasingly upon moral principles. Most states have abandoned laissez-faire in undertaking tasks of rehabilitation in the social field within the state. "But regarding the extent of this state-task there is often a wide and fundamental difference of opinion" (p. 174). How much more so in the international field? Point Four appropriations have been small; they have been cut, and they have been infused with military aid. The program is no longer "new" and it never has been "bold."

Space does not permit more than mention of the special case of Japan (whose development created an international menace), the impact of Wilsonian self-determination, the mandates system, and the history of the slave trade. Heer Van der Veen has important observations in these and other related fields.

The study is exceedingly well documented. Over two hundred titles are included in the Literature. There are 631 citations. Frequently used abbreviations are listed, from Bank to WHO. There is a minimum of statistics. Almost half of the study is a history of ideas concerning international co-operation, international law and cultural diffusion.

ROBERT ROCKAFELLOW
University of Rhode Island

Humanism and Education in East and West: An International Round Table Discussion Organized by UNESCO. Pp. 224. Paris: United Nations Educational, Scientific and Cultural Organization, 1953. $1.50.

As part of its program of developing closer intellectual and moral ties between East and West, UNESCO, at its Fifth Session, authorized an international round-table discussion among thinkers and philosophers. The conference was held from December 13 to 20, 1951, at Parliament House in New Delhi. The government co-operated fully in the arrangements, and prominent Indians took a leading part in the deliberations. The heart of the conference was a round-table discussion in which twelve eminent scholars from various countries participated.

The volume under review constitutes a report to the public of the deliberations that took place. It includes: a succinct review of the round-table discussions together with a summary of the conclusions and recommendations; the major addresses delivered by the Indian notables; and a series of essays, written by the participating scholars, incorporating ideas expressed in preparatory papers and views developed in the round-table discussions. The appendix contains a clearly formulated "basic document" which was drawn up by the UNESCO secretariat as a guide to the discussions and which provides an analysis of underlying problems.

The essays written by the participants in the round table form the main part of the book. These scholarly presentations provide a good introduction to the philosophical and religious systems of the Eurasian world. Hardly any aspect of Indian, Moslem, Classic, or Christian philosophy is left without some reference to it. Although to some extent the old stereotype of the East as representing high-minded contemplative spirituality and of the West as reflecting an aggressive scientific materialism finds an echo, the general trend is to emphasize the common ethical, philosophic, and religious aspirations within the variety of cultural systems. A number of the writers stress the fact that today the differences within each cultural system are greater than the differences between the East and the West as a whole. One point is repeatedly brought out—that the catastrophies of the twentieth century did not arise as a result of conflict between the two types of civilization but from "uncivilized minorities within a single culture." Dr. Radhakrishnan, in his opening address at the round-table conference, did not miss pointing out that Marxist Communism and the opposition to it were both characteristic products of Western civilization.

Besides the general question of the relation between the civilizations of the East and the West, two issues in particular occupied the attention of the participants of the round table: the significance of the scientific movement and the impact of democracy on life and education. Here, too, vestiges of traditional views as well as strong defense of the modern outlook were in evidence. One statement went so far as to decry science as responsible for all the evils of industrialism and militarism. But most of the speakers pointed out its importance for the improvement of living conditions in Asiatic countries. And there was even one speaker who defended science as an avenue to spiritual truth! In discussing democracy a European "brahmin" joined with a philosopher of the East in expressing skepticism of the ability of "the new masses" to absorb higher education. One Indian speaker exhibiting "a somewhat Platonic fear of democracy" sketched an ideal community of three classes along lines of *The Republic*—or was it a reflection of the caste system? But there were others, from India as well as from other countries, who emphasized the importance of a common education for the people and who recognized the significance of equality of educational opportunity in the development of a democratic social order. A point that received emphasis was the part that universities could play in the training of teachers for the common schools.

Seen in the perspective of the complex economic, political, and ideological problems that must be dealt with in the effort to advance East-West unity, the UNESCO conference seems, perhaps, no more than a wisp of straw in making the bricks for the edifice of world peace. But in these troubled times, surely, we should welcome every action, even if it is but a gesture, that may lead to closer co-operation.

I. B. BERKSON
College of the City of New York

CALVEZ, JEAN-YVES. *Droit international et souveraineté en U.R.S.S.* Pp. 299. Paris: Librairie Armand Colin, 1953. 800 fr.

The title of this book gives an insufficient idea of its scope. It is in reality a treatise on the various theories of inter-

national law current in the Union of Soviet Socialist Republics since the Russian Revolution, and an analysis of elements of Soviet practice to indicate what positions have been taken. The author explains that he selects "sovereignty" for emphasis only because since the emergence of Vyshinsky it has been the keystone of Soviet doctrine. In its name various positions have been taken on the international scene. The author then discusses a good many of those positions.

Being in the nature of a treatise, the book discusses the Soviet views on sources of international law and correctly indicates the Soviet predilection for treaties. The author notes the reliance of Soviet diplomats on the nineteenth-century principles of international law, but points out that this is not a mark of conservatism but rather of the usefulness at the present stage in Soviet development of those principles in seeking to obtain the ends of Soviet foreign policy. He understands the influence of dialectic materialism upon Soviet conceptions. He considers that to a Soviet jurist the old form may appear changed when used for current purposes.

One may quarrel not with basic facts but with emphasis. For example, there seems to be underemphasis of the political factors in the discussion of the 1944 grant to Soviet republics of the right of foreign representation. The Yalta record is referred to as indicating political considerations, but the whole operation is considered as an "original" development in international law. The Stettinius memoirs leave no doubt that no one argued international law, but that Stalin wanted a group of votes in the new United Nations organization then in process of formulation, and Roosevelt countered with a compromise, under which only two of the Republics received seats even though the legal status under the Soviet constitution was made the same for all sixteen.

The errors of fact are few, largely in the description of individuals. The author confuses the two Trainins. One was the director of the Institute of Law and the legal theoretician, while the other has been a leading criminologist and in that capacity attended the sessions establishing the charter for the Nuremberg tribunal. The author calls the voices which began to appear in print in the 1940's "young voices." He mentions Krylov and Durdanevsky in particular along with Kozhevnikov. The latter was young at the time, but the other two were well on in years, appearing as new voices only because they had previously been in eclipse because of what seems to have been considered to be a lack of complete Soviet orientation.

In summary, this book presents an accurate account of theory and a valuable compendium of information to place alongside such general books as those of Taracouzio. There is some stimulating speculation in the conclusion. The author understands the role Soviet international lawyers are called upon to play in advancing the cause of their country's foreign office. For those foreign authorities who have failed to understand this relationship the book will be especially valuable.

JOHN N. HAZARD
Columbia University

UNITED STATES GOVERNMENT AND HISTORY

HOLCOMBE, A. N., et al. *The Gaspar G. Bacon Lectures on the Constitution of the United States, 1940–1950.* Boston University. Pp. x, 541. Boston: Boston University Press, 1953. No price.

This distinguished potpourri consists of the ten Bacon lectures on the Constitution delivered at Boston University from 1940 to 1950. Six of the contributors are political scientists, two are historians, one is a practicing lawyer, and one is a former Supreme Court Justice. There are as many approaches to the Constitution as there are commentators, but perhaps the most striking characteristic is the number of contributors who do not go on the assumption that the Constitution is what the Supreme Court says it is. In several of the lectures the Supreme Court is scarcely mentioned. This healthy trend is exemplified in Leonard White's fascinating picture of the formative practices in public administration under the

Federalists, or Louise Overacker's study of presidential campaign funds. Again, Carl Swisher in the 1947 lecture discusses the postwar Constitution, not in terms of Supreme Court decisions, but in terms of the broad trends in relations between Congress and the President, and the developing powers of those "rivals of government," business corporations and labor unions.

Inevitably, however, the Supreme Court does receive its due. Two pieces deal in judicial biography. Henry S. Commager contributes a masterful vignette of Joseph Story, and Charles Fairman draws on his research into the life and times of Justice Bradley in an attempt to answer the question, what makes a great Justice? Former Justice Roberts comes closer to the present with a review of recent tendencies which he suggests have taken us far from the original constitutional "blueprint" towards a condition of "statism."

Two of the lectures may have more relevance to present problems than the rest. While much has happened since 1943, when Robert Cushman lectured on some constitutional problems of civil liberty, what he has to say on free speech, the Negro and the Constitution, and the Japanese evacuation is illuminated by his usual good sense and clear thinking and is still good reading.

The 1950 lectures by Harrison Tweed offer some explanation of the American Bar Association's current effort to amend the Constitution relative to the Supreme Court. Their proposals, which have now reached the stage of congressional discussion, would fix the size of the Supreme Court at nine, compel retirement at 75, disqualify any member of the Court as a candidate for President or Vice-President until five years after leaving the Court, specifically confirm the power to declare acts of Congress unconstitutional, and guarantee the Court's appellate jurisdiction in all cases arising under the Constitution. The goals sought by these proposals will probably be approved by most students of the Constitution, but there will be less agreement that a constitutional amendment is required to freeze a present consensus into the Constitution. The American Bar Association's ill-starred venture with the

Bricker Amendment has left its competence to advise on such problems somewhat in doubt.

C. HERMAN PRITCHETT
University of Chicago

CAHN, EDMOND (Ed.). *Supreme Court and Supreme Law.* Pp. ix, 250. Bloomington: Indiana University Press, 1954. $4.00.

Crisis and contempt are not strangers to the Supreme Court. In the course of its career that tribunal has known the pain of self-inflicted wounds, of which the deepest was the Dred Scott decision. More than once it has weathered the defiance of the Executive. President Roosevelt's threat to "pack" the Court in 1937 is the most memorable instance. On that occasion cynics observed that a switch in time saved nine. A distinguished federal judge was reminded of Jonathan Wild, who, Fielding relates, would have ravished a certain damsel "if she had not, by a timely compliance, prevented him." The President's popular following was large, the damage to the Court's prestige was measurable, but the moral of the tale lay in its ending: the public rallied to the Court's support.

Here was a vivid illustration of the public's respect for the Court—a respect which sometimes, among laymen at least, borders on reverence. Indeed, in the survey of prestige ratings for professions and occupations, conducted by Professor Hatt several years ago, Supreme Court Justices took first place.

This prestige of the Court rests upon its extraordinary power of judicial review. It was in *Marbury* v. *Madison,* decided in 1803, that the Court first asserted that power and established itself as the final arbiter of the meaning of the Constitution. Nor is it new learning that causes this celebrated case to be denounced as usurpation by some and welcomed as a national blessing by others. Only four years ago one of the Justices, writing in a law journal, spoke of the case in these hallowed tones: "Upon this rock the nation has been built." More recently a leader of legal education haled the case as "one of the most significant and dramatic developments in the history of our country."

Denouncer and enthusiast alike will agree that the sesquicentennial of *Marbury* v. *Madison* is an appropriate time for appraisal and stock taking. This book is a symposium dedicated to that end. It is an interesting and worthy contribution to the subject of judicial review. The contributors are, and speak the language of, lawyers, but all readers may pursue these pages with pleasure and profit, though they may disagree with many of the views expressed. Justice Hugo Black has expressed warm praise for this work.

There are six contributors, all authorities in constitutional law. Five are teachers in our law schools: Bishoff and Cahn, New York University; Frank, Yale; Freund, Harvard; and Hurst, University of Wisconsin. The sixth is Mr. Charles P. Curtis of the Massachusetts Bar.

In the first part of the book are found six short papers, read at meetings at New York University Law School, together with the spontaneous and unrevised discussion following each paper. The second part of the work is comprised of four comprehensive articles, one by each of the last four contributors named above. Each article, like each paper, is addressed to a particular phase of judicial review. An informative historical introduction (Chapter 1), supplied by Mr. Cahn, the editor, completes the undertaking.

One of the items here mentioned is the growing tendency of the Justices to pick up their pens and write off in several directions. The "spawning" of dissenting and concurring opinions proceeds at an alarming rate and weakens confidence in the Court. Of the 92 cases decided in 1952, for example, there were unanimous opinions in only 23.

Current interest in civil liberties makes Mr. Frank's article on Review and Basic Liberties (Chapter 5) very timely. Those who regard the Court as a champion of civil rights will find challenge in some of the conclusions here reached, not the smallest of which is the assertion that "courts love liberty most when it is under pressure least."

BERNARD F. CATALDO
University of Pennsylvania

TUNC, ANDRÉ, and SUZANNE TUNC. *Le Système constitutionnel des États-Unis d'Amérique.* Vol. I: *Histoire constitutionnelle.* Pp. viii, 507. Paris: Éditions Domat Montchrestien, 1954. 1,800 fr.

Rarely does an American historical scholar pick up a foreign book about his country without fear and trembling, and more rarely still does he put it down with a feeling of complete satisfaction. So few and far between are volumes like Alexis de Tocqueville's *Democracy in America* or Lord Bryce's *American Commonwealth* that when one receives a study of their distinction, one is overjoyed. It is no exaggeration to state that the work before us belongs to a very select class.

André Tunc, Professor on the Faculty of Law at Grenoble, and his wife spent several years in the United States studying the American legal system and acquiring experience in the service of the International Monetary Fund. To say that they have a command of their material would be a gross understatement; they have mastered it to such an extent that they produced a synthesis of American constitutional history which is an important contribution to the subject. For French readers this work is of especial importance, for nothing of its kind is presently available to them. Furthermore, this volume contains excellent bibliographies of American history in general, as well as of American law, and it has an index which will serve as a useful guide to those Americanisms which are so baffling to foreigners. I know from experience how important it is to have ready definitions of "yellow dog contracts," "featherbedding," and "scalawags."

SHEPARD B. CLOUGH
Columbia University

HARRIS, JOSEPH P. *The Advice and Consent of the Senate: A Study of the Confirmation of Appointments by the United States Senate.* Pp. xii, 457. Berkeley: University of California Press, 1953. $5.00.

This admirable book is one of those rare studies of American government which will make a reader wonder why nobody ever did this before. At any rate, nobody will have to do it again soon, for Professor Harris and his research assistants seem to have gone into every conceivable aspect of the problem from Washington to Eisenhower.

This book is also one that needed to be written, both because of the intrinsic importance of its subject and because it is the best study so far to appear of the amendment of the Constitution by custom and usage. All students of American government are familiar with the fact that the Senate has in reality (though not in words) amended the Constitution to restrict the President's power to nominate, with some exceptions, to those persons who are recommended to him by the senators from the state of the nominee's residence; but surely few can be familiar with the widespread ramifications of the practice. "Senatorial courtesy" began in Washington's administration, and it has carried down to date. It has helped to preserve the Byrd and other machines. It has kept some of the very best nominees from confirmation.

Where senatorial courtesy is not involved, it is apparent from Professor Harris' study that strong Presidents have generally had the most trouble in getting their nominees consented to; that persons of pronounced convictions who have written or spoken on public questions "are likely to face difficulty in being confirmed"; that "several of the most sensational contests in the Senate have risen over the nominations of Jews to high office"; that pressure groups are often able to stop a nominee they do not like in the Senate, when the President can resist their efforts; and that the Senate will refuse confirmation for strictly partisan reasons: "In the 1948 session, when the Republicans were confident of victory at the forthcoming election, 11,122 nominations were returned to the President without any action by the Senate."

The five chapters in this book on the cases of Louis D. Brandeis, David Lilienthal, and Leland Olds would stand alone as case studies in American politics. These cases also show that any man must really be devoted to the public service to risk the ordeal that these men went through.

Perhaps the nadir of advice and consent was reached when Senator Bilbo spent hours of the Senate's time, and filled up pages of the *Congressional Record,* with his objections to the nomination of a judge who had, years before, sentenced Bilbo to prison and to a fine of $1,000.

DAYTON D. MCKEAN
University of Colorado

WHITE, LEONARD D. *The States and the Nation.* Pp. xi, 103. Baton Rouge: Louisiana State University Press, 1953. $2.75.

The Latin maxim, *multum in parvo,* aptly characterizes this slender volume by Leonard D. White. Originally given as the Edward D. White Lectures on Citizenship, *The States and the Nation* has now appeared under the imprint of the Louisiana State University Press.

The temper and theme of this book is set by its frank avowal that "A federal system implies a partnership, all members of which are effective players on the team, and all of whom retain the capacity for independent action. It does not imply a system of collaboration in which one of the collaborators is annihilated by the other." Three trenchant sections or individual lectures sustain this argument. The various lecture titles carry their own impact and suggest their individual scope: (1) The March of Power to Washington; (2) The Strength and Limitations of the States; (3) The Next Quarter Century.

Along the way specific policies looking towards the attainment of a dynamic federalism make their appearance and receive forthright presentation, dispassionate yet positive in tone and language. So far as Professor White has a program to offer it compasses these chief points. The states can recover their early role in the federal union if it should be found possible to return to them some functions and activities now carried on or financed in whole or in part by the federal government. Conditions now attached to federal grants-in-aid may be modified so as to afford the states greater freedom as to ways and means of action. The states might help themselves by wider and more effective use of interstate compacts. Lastly, they might

avoid further limiting federal legislation in emerging policy fields, says Professor White, by vigorous and energetic use of those powers they now possess.

Fundamentally judgment of any book must proceed from the purpose and objective to which its author sought to dedicate his work. In terms of his own basic premises, Professor White has done a competent job. His argument has been set forth clearly, and can scarcely be mistaken for that which it is not. Absent is a sense of fanatical fervor—either panegyric or diatribe—while realism infuses his presentation and makes mature consideration of his specific proposals essential. At the point of acceptance or rejection of these suggestions, each person of course becomes a free agent. But *States and the Nation* should be read.

CHARLES W. SHULL
Wayne University

MCCORMICK, RICHARD P. *The History of Voting in New Jersey: A Study of the Development of Election Machinery, 1664–1911.* Pp. xii, 228. New Brunswick, N. J.: Rutgers University Press, 1953. $5.00.

The search for more effective ways of determining the voters' verdict is an unending one, and if the details of election procedure seem tedious to the non-specialist, the search itself is vital to the functioning of representative government. In our federal system, valid generalization on this as on many subjects is impossible without careful studies of individual states; such a study Dr. McCormick has now provided for New Jersey.

The book is divided into seven chapters: the proprietary period (1664–1703), New Jersey as a royal colony (1703–1774), the Revolutionary era (1774–1788), the early national period (1789–1838), the four decades from 1839 to 1876, the late nineteenth-century years of corruption and reform (1877–1899), and the Progressive era (1900–1911) culminating in the election measures of Woodrow Wilson's governorship. On each period Dr. McCormick gives us a little of the economic and political setting, a description of the election machinery and the changes made in it, and some indication of the way it worked in practice. Statistical tables show the number of voters who went to the polls each year from 1789 to 1900, and their proportionate relation to the total electorate.

The contrast between today's highly regulated election machinery and the casual methods of the eighteenth century is illuminating. Election officers might close the polls arbitrarily to favor their own party, voting places were sometimes as much as sixty miles distant from outlying areas, the polls were kept open for days at a time, and voice voting rather than the ballot was the rule. Yet the system worked smoothly on the whole, and New Jersey's freehold suffrage was liberal for the time.

Since colonial days, there have been two main lines of development: "the extension of the suffrage to ever wider segments of the population," and "the gradual emergence of an ever more detailed body of regulations" to govern the actual conduct of both general and primary elections. In the process political parties, originally ignored by the law, came to hold a highly regulated and therefore a thoroughly official position.

Dr. McCormick finds that the motivations for these changes were much more practical than theoretical. Lawmakers almost never attempted to justify particular suffrage requirements on the basis of principle, and in the long struggle to make the voting process efficient and convenient, motives of honest reform and partisan advantage were inextricably mixed.

RANSOM E. NOBLE, JR.
Pratt Institute

HYMAN, SIDNEY. *The American President.* Pp. 342. New York: Harper & Brothers, 1954. $4.00.

This is a very interesting and almost unique publication. It is not a traditional or legalistic discussion of the powers of the President as outlined in the Constitution nor is it a development of these powers. It is more of an exposition of the political process involved in the election and activities of the President as well as the relations of the President to the people and the other divisions of the government. It might very accurately be called the un-written constitution of the Presidency. It deals with matters not treated in other publications on the President and too little known or understood and possibly more vital than the dry bones of the constitutionality of the powers of the office of the President.

It is in this field of extraconstitutionality that the author makes a significant contribution. It is the red-blooded President as the director of the greatest nation on earth in both foreign and domestic affairs that is discussed and not the grandmama type of Whig King misnamed by the Constitution. It is not the titular type of executive which the Whig scheme of political organization provides for and which is really its chief contribution to practical politics but a world figure exercising semiroyal powers with almost the destiny of the free world as his responsibility. Whereas Jefferson said there would come a time when all Europe would be interested in the election of the American President, it is now mankind. So it has happened that a President of a string of loosely associated provincial states along the Atlantic Coast has become practically a popularly elected monarch of a unified nation whose foreign policy materially involves the peace of the world. While it was once Rome and later Britain that ruled the civilized world, it is now America, with this important difference—that its object is peace and self-government for all peoples.

The President as a candidate to succeed himself as well as the candidate of the opposition is discussed in all of the ramifications of a presidential campaign. The pros and cons of the various proposals for nominating presidential candidates as well as the different suggestions as to the methods of electing presidents are considered in a fresh and convincing manner.

The two-party system as an agent of democracy in phrasing and settling political issues and finally uniting the nation in a *modus vivendi* is especially emphasized as the most practical and satisfactory political process that has yet been devised. But for this system the nation would undoubtedly fall apart. The party system possibly does more than the Constitution to maintain national unity.

The President as an artist is presented in a contrast between Jefferson and Madison. Madison, whose work in the Federal Convention made him famous, who was quite as much the father of the Republican party as Jefferson, who had had eight years of experience in executive matters as Jefferson's Secretary of State, and who in his Federalist papers showed a most thorough understanding of the problems and workings of modern governments, when confronted with the task of the presidential office was almost, if not actually, a failure. Which is more important as a qualification for the office of President—to be an artist in politics or a scholar? Was this the difference between Hoover and Franklin D. Roosevelt? Anyway, this is an interesting basis for the comparative study of American Presidents.

The President's roles in self-defense, as manager of social justice and prosperity, and as director of war and peace are shown to be important roles of his office. The reorganization of the executive is critically examined, and important suggestions are made. This book is an informative supplement to the literature on the Presidency.

C. PERRY PATTERSON
University of Texas

WEBSTER, NOAH. *Letters of Noah Webster.* Edited by Harry R. Warfel. Pp. xlvi, 562. New York: Library Publishers [c. 1953]. $7.50.

To later generations of Americans, Noah Webster came to be known as the man who set the pattern for the American language, and made his name synonymous with the word "Dictionary." But to his contemporaries he was something far different. They knew him, to be sure, as a man who was uncommonly conscious of his importance as a lexicographer and grammarian, with a special penchant for disposing ruthlessly of all critics and criticisms. But they knew him also as rather more than an amateur scientist, one who wrote and published *A Brief History of Epidemic and Pestilential Diseases,* as the author of a *History of the United States,* as editor of a revised version of the Bible, and above all as a commentator on politics who wrote letters,

generally unsolicited and sometimes unappreciated, to such individuals as Samuel Adams, James Madison, Benjamin Franklin, George Washington, Timothy Pickering, Thomas Jefferson, Oliver Wolcott, Rufus King, John Jay, and Daniel Webster.

In politics Noah Webster was a conservative of the first magnitude; furthermore, he identified his opinions with high principle, and felt called upon to castigate his opponents as unmitigated rogues. His letter to Thomas Jefferson, written in October 1801, expressed well the sentiments of extreme anti-Jeffersonians; but with hardly a change it would have satisfied anti-Jackson men equally well in 1829, or anti-Roosevelt men in 1933. Webster's unofficial definitions of the words Republican and Democrat still make interesting reading. "Republicans," he said, are "the friends of our Representative Governments, who believe that no influence whatever should be exercised in a state which is not directly authorized by the Constitution and the laws." But a Democrat is "a person who attempts an undue opposition to or influence over government by means of private clubs, secret intrigues, or by popular meetings"; or, more simply, just "an opposer of administration generally" (p. 208).

These letters supplement and reinforce Warfel's biography of Webster, published in 1936. They range the whole gamut of Webster's interests, his efforts to obtain copyright laws, his theories about the yellow fever, his views on history, education, agriculture, manufacturing, and the reform of the alphabet, his replies to his critics, and his political observations. His long letter to John Pickering should be of interest to all students of language, and for the social and political historian nearly every letter has a point. The editing is painstakingly done, and is reinforced by both an index of words and a good general index.

JOHN D. HICKS
University of California

BETTS, EDWIN MORRIS (Ed.). *Thomas Jefferson's Farm Book: With Commentary and Relevant Extracts from Other Writings.* Foreword by Francis L. Berkeley, Jr. (Facsimile 179 pp.). Pp. xxiii,

552. Princeton, N. J.: Princeton University Press, 1953. $15.00.

Thomas Jefferson, while a man of many interests, was both a Virginia plantation owner-operator and a countryman of distinction. He loved his ancestral acres, his home, and the environment in which he was born, lived, and died. However, he was much more than a farmer in the ordinary sense. Monticello, as a place where new ideas were being tried out and Arthur Young's *Experimental Agriculture* was carefully studied, was perhaps more than any other farm or plantation of its time the forerunner of agricultural science and the agricultural experiment station of today. Jefferson's remarkable imagination, curiosity, and scientific instincts, coupled with his capacity for careful observation and accurate record-keeping and note-taking, make him very important in our history of scientific agriculture and rural life. Thomas Jefferson for more than fifty years kept two notebooks close at hand in which he carefully recorded or casually jotted down observations and notes about horticulture and farm management.

Thomas Jefferson's *Farm Book* is a companion to the previously published *Garden Book*. Both were edited by the same author and published by the Princeton University Press under the auspices of the American Philosophical Society of which Jefferson was at one time president. This volume begins with a brief but excellent introductory essay by Francis L. Berkeley of the University of Virginia Library, which gives the historical setting and the significance of the *Farm Book*, particularly in relation to plantation economy of the time. The major part of the volume naturally divides into two parts: First, a facsimile of Thomas Jefferson's *Farm Book*, and, second, "a commentary and relevant extracts from other writings." For a period of 52 years, 1774–1826, Jefferson jotted down in clear, legible handwriting all kinds of notes and memoranda such as inventories, accounts, bits of handy information, and so forth, in connection with his two plantations, Monticello and Poplar Forest. The facsimile reproduction is excellent and for all practical but non-sentimental purposes the general reader or the meticulous

scholar might just as well have the original in his hands. The second part, which contains the "commentary and relevant extracts from other writings," is of great significance and importance.

The *Farm Book* standing alone is fragmentary and incomplete and does not have much of value except as source material for the research scholar. Dr. Betts, the editor, is professor of biology at the University of Virginia and is the foremost student of the agricultural and horticultural phases of Jefferson's life and activities in Monticello. He has carefully examined all the available letters and other material of Jefferson. He selected and organized this material under topical headings which relate it where possible to the *Farm Book*. Each topic is introduced by a critical explanatory statement.

This edition of Thomas Jefferson's *Farm Book,* with the letters and commentary, is both an important source book and a contribution to biography. It will be of particular interest to students of the life and personality of Jefferson, to agricultural and other historians who are concerned with plantation agriculture, and with the emergence of scientific agriculture. To the "countryman" this is a classic for those who live in the country and enjoy and appreciate its historical literature.

M. L. WILSON
U. S. Department of Agriculture
(Retired) Washington, D. C.

ROOSEVELT, THEODORE. *The Letters of Theodore Roosevelt.* Vols. VII and VIII: *The Days of Armageddon,* 1909–1919. Edited by Elting E. Morison et al. Pp. xiv, 816; viii, 817–1621. Cambridge, Mass.: Harvard University Press, 1954. $20.00.

This is the fourth and the last two-volume set of Theodore Roosevelt's letters to appear under the editorship of Morison and his associates. During the period that the editors were preparing their earlier volumes, all the unpublished letters from Roosevelt to Henry Cabot Lodge were closed, but later Henry Cabot Lodge, Jr. made available to the editors the letters written between 1884 and 1906. Lodge and Roosevelt were the closest of life-long friends, and they were constant associates in politics, excepting only the Bull Moose years. It would seem, therefore, that until the full correspondence between Roosevelt and Lodge has been made available to scholars, there will remain a great deal to be revealed concerning the influence of these two men upon each other and of their tactics and strategy in relation to other men and the issues.

The letters published in the two volumes under review represent perhaps less than one tenth of the total available for the period covered, but scrupulous and painstaking care in their selection and extended and illuminating comment in the editor's footnotes, including explanations of the matter on which Roosevelt was writing, give the selections high value. In them Roosevelt reveals himself as an eager, joyous, and successful big game hunter, a fairly prolific contributing editor, candidate for President (1912), a hater and often an unfair critic of Woodrow Wilson, a champion of the Allies long before the United States entered the First World War, a would-be division commander in that war, an inordinately proud father (his four sons and son-in-law were in the service, and his son Quentin was killed), and a skeptic regarding world organization and peace plans.

By no means the least significant contribution of these volumes is found in Appendix V, "A Note on Method and Materials," by John W. Blum. The note evaluates the principal sources in such a manner as to be of the greatest possible aid to other Roosevelt scholars and students of his time. Furthermore, the author supplies an additional aid by indicating certain collections which one might assume to be sources but which, in fact, are not rewarding. The Manuscript Collections, some two hundred, are listed in Appendix VI, those being italicized that proved most useful to the editors. The editors would be the first to agree that the basic Roosevelt scholar must go beyond these eight volumes of letters, to the materials the editors combed and other sources, for definitive study of one of America's most versatile and engaging men. But the scholar will nevertheless find the Morison collection of great value, and the general reader and student will find it revealing, interesting, stimulating, and at times amusing.

CLAUDIUS O. JOHNSON
State College of Washington

PRESSLY, THOMAS J. *Americans Interpret Their Civil War*. Pp. xvi, 347. Princeton, N. J.: Princeton University Press, 1954. $5.00.

Professor Pressly has written an interesting and valuable book. It is a survey of the literature relating to the origin and character of the Civil War. In the first third of it there is laid a good foundation in a detailed study of what the protagonists themselves had to say about the war both during its course and after it was over. Upon this is built an account of the subsequent treatment of the subject by the historians both amateur and professional. The turning point in the story is reached with the work of James Ford Rhodes and the rise of academic historiography. In this Professor Pressly very rightly sees the prevalence of a nationalist school of thought. But its conclusions have subsequently been challenged by students dominated successively by the influence of political radicalism, a revived Southern sectarianism, and an extreme abhorrence of war. Professor Pressly thinks that today there are signs of a new synthesis; and his books ends with a discussion of the extent to which this has been achieved by Professor Nevins in his study of the *Ordeal of the Union*.

It is, of course, extremely difficult at so short a range to see things in a true perspective. And it may be that not all those whose work is here discussed will look in the long run as large as they do now. It is the case, to an extent greater perhaps than Professor Pressly allows, that historical interpretation is cumulative. It does not follow, because historical understanding is relative and not absolute, that all we can look for is a mere fluctuation of equally valid but incoherent versions of past events. To accept this would be to make less than full use of a familiar and well-established scientific procedure. No hypothesis comprehends all the evidence. Every pattern has its discards. But every scrap of evidence discarded is a challenge to the adequacy of the accepted pattern; and historical, like scientific, progress consists in enlargement of the hypothesis to comprehend more of the facts. In this point of view a charge, hinted at on page 299, may be preferred against a good deal of recent work that it has consisted too much of debate and too little of investigation. For it is to be expected of new viewpoints not merely that they should put in a new light what is already familiar, but that they should make intelligible some of the evidence that has hitherto been left aside.

H. HALE BELLOT

University College, University of London

WOODMASON, CHARLES. *The Carolina Backcountry on the Eve of the Revolution: The Journal and Other Writings of Charles Woodmason, Anglican Itinerant.* Edited with an Introduction by Richard J. Hooker. Pp. xxxix, 305. Chapel Hill: University of North Carolina Press, 1953. $5.00.

Charles Woodmason spent only about two decades of his life in America, yet in that brief span he managed to live two almost opposite lives. From 1752 until December 1765, Woodmason was a fairly successful planter, land-speculator, and minor office holder. From the fall of 1766, at the completion of his visit in England, until late in 1774, he was an Anglican clergyman. Most of his clerical duties were performed in the backcountry of South Carolina. His private journal, for parts of the years 1766, 1767, and 1768, three of his sermon books, a few letters, and numerous miscellaneous writings have been preserved. They are here collected and published for the first time.

This volume consists of an introductory essay and three parts. The first section contains the Journal; the second, Woodmason's miscellaneous writings on "Society and Institutions of the Backcountry"; and the final part includes the writings of this frontier clergyman in regard to the South Carolina Regulator movement. Here again can be noted an interesting ambivalence. In the first two sections, the reader is almost overwhelmed by the bitterness with which this Anglican clergyman denounces the Baptists and Presbyterians, exposes the lack of morality among the frontier people, and reveals the barrenness of life in the Carolina Piedmont. In the last section, however, Woodmason is the apologist and defender of the political rights of these same people. More than any of his contemporaries, he verbalized the situation and fought for a redress of grievances.

Professor Hooker has done a laudable job of editing these documents. His introductory essay evidences a staggering amount of research into the life and activity of Woodmason. He presents the result of this labor in such form that the reader senses the importance of the material that is to follow and becomes interested in the writer. The introduction to part three—the Regulator Documents—is a superb essay which explains the movement, establishes its place in our national history, and clarifies the way in which the South Carolina Regulators differed from their more famous namesakes in North Carolina. Throughout the sources, explanations and cross references abound.

He who reads this volume must, of course, balance Woodmason's violent language with a knowledge of his intense prejudice. Having done this, with the editor's help, many readers will find that they have gained new insight into frontier conditions and problems. In addition, it seems safe to say, many readers will have been intrigued by the personality of Woodmason and by the passions and the contradictions which drove him with such intensity toward frustration and unhappiness.

RALPH ADAMS BROWN

Cornish Flat, New Hampshire

PATRICK, REMBERT W. *Florida Fiasco: Rampant Rebels on the Georgia-Florida Border, 1810–1815.* Pp. x, 359. Athens: University of Georgia Press, 1954. $5.00.

Among the components of the United States of America which have a Spanish background none is more venerable than Florida (unless Puerto Rico is included). Yet Florida's history has probably been less explored than the histories of Texas, New Mexico, and California. Capable local historians are industriously writing Florida history, however, as this and other recent works on the subject demonstrate.

Professor Patrick's thorough and well-written volume deals with the efforts of the United States government and its frontier citizens to seize Florida from Spain—or rather the Floridas, for at this time there was both an East and a West Florida. The efforts failed, but they are no less interesting on that account. West Florida was occupied during the period, but was not ceded by Spain until East Florida was also ceded by the Treaty of 1819, ratified two years later.

Professor Patrick roundly condemns the United States for most of its Florida policies. "For more than a quarter-century," he declares, "the United States used diplomacy, intrigue, chicanery, force, and war in its march on the Floridas. . . . The encouragement and consequent repudiation of eager, patriotic George Mathews was indefensible. In their cavalier treatment of him the president [Madison] and secretary [Monroe] acted as autocrats casting aside and denoucing a faithful servant to save themselves embarrassment. By invading the territory of and making war on a friendly power [Spain] without the consent of Congress, President Madison followed in the steps of Old World dictators. The ideals of the young American republic were forgotten as his desire for the Floridas overcame his sense of justice" (p. 303).

It is well to remember, however, that the United States was not only suffering injury from the Napoleonic Wars but was also gravely disturbed by the fear that its security would be threatened by the seizure, sooner or later, of these adjacent Spanish possessions by England or some other strong European power. And it should also be recalled that national unity had long been threatened by the machinations of Spain, England, and France in the Floridas and in the Old Southwest. Approval of these Florida policies and procedures not only by Madison and Monroe but by Thomas Jefferson, Henry Clay, and many other leaders of the time may not justify them, but it tends to create a presumption in favor of their reasonableness in view of the grave circumstances in which they occurred.

It was the United States Senate that re-jected the policy of territorial acquisition by aggression and checked Madison, Monroe, and their advisers in their plans of conquest. "Eventually," says Professor Patrick, "the United States acquired the Floridas by fair negotiation. Title to the provinces resulted from a negotiated treaty and not from trickery and force" (p. 304). But the garrisons of the United States were never withdrawn from West Florida after 1814, and Andrew Jackson invaded East Florida in 1818. Spain may be said, therefore, to have negotiated under duress and to have ceded these provinces very reluctantly, after pleading in vain for British support.

The author has used a great variety of sources, both published and in manuscript, and has told his story with evident zest. Two secondary works which he does not refer to in his notes or mention in his bibliography, Frank Updike's *Diplomacy of the War of 1812* and J. Fred Rippy's *Rivalry of the United States and Great Britain over Latin America,* might have given him a firmer grasp of the broader diplomatic aspects of the problem; and a map would have enabled the reader to follow the details of his narrative with greater ease.

J. FRED RIPPY

University of Chicago

ALDEN, JOHN RICHARD. *The American Revolution, 1775–1783.* Pp. xviii, 294. New York: Harper & Brothers, 1954. $5.00.

This volume is the second in "The New American Nation Series" edited by Henry Steele Commager and Richard B. Morris. It contains in a clear, concise style many of the findings of students of the American Revolution during the half century since Claude Van Tyne's volume in the original "American Nation Series" edited by Albert Bushnell Hart.

In keeping with recent trends in scholarship, Dr. Alden finds that George III was not a monstrous tyrant, discovers no hard and fast line between the Radicals and Conservatives, praises the Second Continental Congress for its achievements, and is inclined to believe that the Articles of Confederation were mostly good. He seems definitely convinced that Silas Deane sold secrets to the British, doubts that a Conway Cabal ever existed, believes the number and intellectual importance of the Loyalists have been exaggerated, and omits the Galloway Plan for colonial administration and conciliation.

Although it appears hard for him to do so in some passages, he confesses the movement for independence was inarticulate before the fall of 1775. He admits that the philosophy of the American Revolution was based on earlier philosophies and precedents. Yet, in his opinion, the Americans combined them in a way that made them liberal—even progressive. Consequently, Jefferson's Declaration, the supreme summation of their views, has revolutionized history.

Dr. Alden is prudently cautious in following the lead of writers who have seen in the land reforms of the Revolutionary generation the development of a more equitable distribution of land. But he seems a little too exuberant in his statements about more liberal voting laws when the colonies became states, and he errs in stating that a Virginian had to own five hundred acres of undeveloped land to possess the ballot. The amount was fifty acres, the same under the state government as under colonial law. Dr. Alden probably is also on shaky ground when he implies, at least, that the western population of Virginia was more equitably represented in the new state government than it had been under the colonial regime.

The most disappointing feature of the book is, in my opinion, its scant and oversimple treatment of revolutionary propaganda and of the intellectual, moral, social, and economic phases of the period. Its most excellent aspect is its splendid description of military campaigns, analyzed mainly from the standpoint of commanders and strategy and, consequently, not overly burdened with detail. The undocumented statement that Massachusetts instructed its delegation in the Continental Congress to vote for independence in January, 1776, is rather startling, since Elbridge Gerry wrote a letter to James Warren, dated March 26, 1776, in which he suggested that the General Court of Massachusetts send such instructions. Gerry was one of the representatives of Massachusetts in the Congress. Disconcerting, too, are the assertions that the delegates of South Carolina and Georgia were sent similar instructions by their governments on or before April 5, 1776. Leading historians of those states have not mentioned such forwardness in the independence movement.

ROBERT L. HILLDRUP
Mary Washington College
University of Virginia

MOORE, GLOVER. *The Missouri Controversy, 1819–1821.* Pp. xi, 383. Lexington: University of Kentucky Press, 1953. $6.00.

The Missouri Compromise is imbedded in American history as thoroughly as George Washington or Christopher Columbus, and it has come to be considered as much a matter of fact as either of these. Therefore, what could there be new about these Missouri Compromises (for there were really two, or even three, before the question was settled), and why should one write a whole book on the subject? Would it not be retelling a twice-told tale? Professor Glover Moore, who teaches history at Mississippi State College, thought that the story was worth a book and that in fact the whole tale had never yet been told. And anyone who will read this interesting and well-written book will likely agree with the author.

The first debate over the admission of Missouri in the early part of 1819 produced little or no comment outside of Congress, and only by propaganda meetings designed to induce Congress to prohibit slavery in Missouri was the question made mildly exciting to the country as a whole. As the question became more involved during the next two years, the country began to take more notice; but even so, people in general were still more concerned with what could be done about the hard times produced by the Panic of 1819. So, though the dispute sounded to Thomas Jefferson like "a fire bell in the night," and it seemed to John Quincy Adams like "a title-page to a great tragic volume," yet the general public failed to take alarm.

But Professor Moore would not have it

understood that the Missouri Controversy was not important. Indeed, it was of vast importance, for it was not a flash out of a clear sky; it brought to the surface a tension which had long been growing between the North and South. And it also gave almost perfect proof that from that time to the outbreak of the Civil War there was to be little or nothing new under the sun in the American political struggle over slavery; for in this controversy appeared the clear outlines of the abolition crusade, the secession threat, Seward's higher law doctrine, Douglas' squatter sovereignty panacea, the Wilmot Proviso, and the threat of political parties based on geography.

Professor Moore has bolstered his book with the results of an impressive amount of research upon a couple of dozen collections of manuscript correspondence, more than a hundred newspaper files, and various pamphlets and books.

E. MERTON COULTER
University of Georgia

MOORE, GUY W. *The Case of Mrs. Surratt.* Pp. xi, 142. Norman: University of Oklahoma Press, 1954. $3.00.

Although this small volume of little more than a hundred pages, which examines the truth of the complicity of Mrs. Surratt in the assassination of President Lincoln, is distinctly a piece of historical research, it should make a wider appeal than merely to scholars of the Civil War period; it should hold interest for the students of political science, and, indeed, for all lovers of justice.

Interest in the case cannot, of course, be as keen today as it was at the time of the conspiracy trial, or immediately thereafter when doubts began to be entertained as to her guilt. However, it is never too late to try to establish the truth, and, as far as history can do it, to right a wrong.

Unfortunately, the author is able to reach no definite conclusion in regard to the justice of Mrs. Surratt's execution. He is properly careful and objective in weighing evidence, recognizes that secondhand evidence is difficult to evaluate (p. 10, note 42), has checked statements from one source with other sources wherever

possible, and accepts the fact that secondary evidence is not definitive. The conclusion reached is cautious: "there was and is a reasonable doubt" (p. 105), and again the author explicitly speaks of "the death of a woman whose guilt was never more than a guess" (p. 118).

Many questions, which would naturally arise in the mind of the reader, even if the author did not raise them, are still left unanswered, and there is little likelihood—barring the improbable event of the discovery of further documentary proof—that further research will resolve these questions. The author has made a thorough investigation of all available materials, both manuscript and printed, as is attested by the footnotes and bibliography.

The organization is simple and straightforward: the background and life of Mrs. Surratt is given briefly and the *dramatis personae* of the group in her boardinghouse on H Street in Washington introduced. The involved, protracted controversies ever since her death are reviewed and the evidence produced at the trial painstakingly weighed, upon which evidence the conclusion—so far as a conclusion is drawn—is based.

The style is simple and clear and touched with dramatic vividness. Several illustrations are used to dramatize a book so filled with drama that it scarcely needs such a gruesome illustration as the Execution of the Conspirators (facing p. 84). For those who can enjoy the newspaper account of the actual execution, a photostat of the *Constitutional Union* for July 7, 1865 is reproduced (facing p. 116), though in so small a type as to be difficult to decipher. A map of Washington to show the relative location of her house to Ford's Theater and other key points in the drama is mildly helpful.

ELLA LONN
Goucher College

DORRIS, JONATHAN T. *Pardon and Amnesty Under Lincoln and Johnson.* Pp. 460. Chapel Hill: University of North Carolina Press, 1953. $7.50.

Almost thirty years ago Professor Dorris began his study of amnesty and pardon in the reconstruction period. The historians of that period have waited with anticipation for his promised book on this tremendously important subject. If it has been a long time coming, Dr. Dorris can plead, in addition to the usual professorial excuse of the press of other duties, that he had to perform a truly massive job of research. He can also say that he wanted his book to be, when it appeared, as nearly definitive as he could make it and that definitive books on significant subjects are not made in a few years. And he has produced what should stand as the classic account for a much longer period than it took him to complete his research.

Here is the story, told with as much detail as even the specialist could ask for, of pardon and amnesty under Lincoln and Johnson and of the long struggle of the former Confederates to regain their rights and privileges. By far the greater part of the book is concerned with the policies of the two Presidents and with their radical opponents, but the narrative goes down to 1898, when the last disabilities imposed during reconstruction were finally removed. Among the topics treated by Dr. Dorris are: political prisoners, military oaths, pardon attorneys, pardons for the rich, pardons for civil leaders, presidential and congressional amnesty, and pardon and amnesty in the courts. Wisely he decided to highlight his essentially legal account by relating case histories of representative Confederates who sought pardons: Lee, General Ewell, General Howell Cobb, John H. Reagan, Clement C. Clay, and others. A chapter is devoted to Jefferson Davis, who refused to ask for a pardon, although others interceded for him.

All of the subject matter in this book, it should be noted, is difficult and tricky stuff. This is constitutional and judicial history, hard to research and digest and harder to present in comprehensible terms. Dr. Dorris' volume is not one to curl up with for a long evening, but it is as readable and as interesting as a book of this kind can be. Much of its human interest results from the fact that the author had access to the revealing and intimate letters in the Amnesty Papers in the National Archives. He seems to be the only historian who has used them.

Professor Dorris is sympathetic to the South and to the Southern view of reconstruction, perhaps overly so. Nevertheless, he concludes that the clemency of the government during and after the war was in the best tradition of American justice and democracy.

T. HARRY WILLIAMS
Louisiana State University

WENDT, LLOYD, and HERMAN KOGAN. *Big Bill of Chicago.* Pp. 384. New York: Bobbs-Merrill Co., 1953. $4.00.

REID, ED. *The Shame of New York.* Pp. xii, 235. New York: Random House, 1953. $3.00.

These tales of two American cities in the twentieth century will not make any American proud of the record of our municipal government. The first book is history, the second an account of contemporary New York, with the vice, crime, and crooked politics there portrayed still presumably continuing.

Big Bill Thompson has been dead these ten years. He left, at the age of 77, over two million dollars, two-thirds of it in old-style currency stuffed into safe deposit boxes. Where he got that money has never been explained. He left more, however: an immense city debt, a record of astonishing corruption, gangsterism, and demagoguery. At the height of his power, he and his political mentor, Congressman Fred Lundin, had such a thoroughly organized political machine that it was called the Thompson Tammany. While Thompson ranted about King George, Lundin from his hotel room took care of graft, patronage, and strategy; until the break came between them, Lundin hoped to make Thompson President, and the William Hale Thompson Republican Club had a war chest of over $100,000 for this purpose. As it was, not only was the government of Chicago in their control, but Governor Len Small and other state officials were their men as well.

Persons who are today horrified at the attacks on schools, teachers, textbooks, and libraries might well remember that it was William Hale Thompson who showed this way to get votes. One of the chief issues in his third (and successful) campaign for mayor was his attack upon the schools and their "un-American" textbooks. While Thompson shot off his verbal fireworks about the schools, Thompsonites on the school board were robbing the schools of millions of dollars. Although he succeeded in his immediate objective, Thompson's attack on the schools plagued him for the rest of his life and made "Chicago the object of ridicule and laughter all over the world." This may be cold comfort to the victims of current attacks, but it is still something to hope for.

Somehow the account of the antics of Thompson does not seem as funny or as sympathetic as the same authors' *Lords of the Levee* on Hinky Dink Kenna and Bathhouse John Coughlin. His clowning now seems disgusting, his corruption merely repulsive. The voters who, over and over, re-elected him deserve a share of the blame for those incredible decades of Chicago politics. Their behavior seems today depressing.

Anybody who thinks that, with Thompson gone, it can never happen again should read Reid's book on New York. Here are the same vice and crime, the crooked police, the political tie-ins, the gangster-selected judges—all the elements of the scene in Thompson's Chicago except for the blatant demagoguery. The political and gang murders in New York seem to be about as numerous as those in Chicago, but they appear to be committed less spectacularly. Probably the amount of graft has been just as great; Reid says that the Brooklyn police received twelve million dollars a year over several years in gambling protection alone. Much of what Reid recites is familiar to people who followed the Kefauver and other investigations of recent years. Much of the rest is unsupported—perhaps unavoidably—by anything except the author's own assertions.

Both of these books suffer from the newspaperman's dislike of documentation. A hundred times a reader may wonder, "How do they know Thompson thought that, back in 1927?" The most complicated conversations of conspirators are put down word for word as if the authors had been sitting in the room, not merely taking notes, but accompanied by a court

stenographer who got every name, initial, and dollar figure. It is not always possible to tell what is real and what is merely possible or hypothetical, to distinguish what was said from what might have been said.

DAYTON D. McKEAN
University of Colorado

FREIDEL, FRANK. *Franklin D. Roosevelt: The Ordeal.* Pp. 320. Boston: Little, Brown & Company, 1954. $6.00.

This second volume of Dr. Freidel's biography covers from January 1919, when Franklin Delano Roosevelt was still Assistant Secretary of the Navy, through his attack of poliomyelitis in 1921, his long uphill fight for health, and finally his election in 1928 as Governor of New York State. In smooth, colorful narrative, derived from diffuse and complex materials handled with critical selectivity and sustained perspective, Dr. Freidel has closely interwoven biography and history.

After F.D.R.'s resignation from the Navy and his subsequent defeat in November 1920 for the Vice-Presidency, he entered every activity which might bring him advantageous recognition, including work on national Democratic party policy. Dr. Freidel asserts that the number of causes he espoused, the mass of his methodically prosecuted correspondence from New York with party figures over the country, and his prolonged championship of Alfred E. Smith for the Presidency—all reflect his own fixed purpose to become President. He fortifies this interpretation by following the movements of Louis McH. Howe, F.D.R.'s secretary and member of his household, a wily, indefatigable political manipulator, obsessed with making F.D.R. President.

Dr. Freidel, no hero-worshiper, emphasizes F.D.R.'s apparently discreditable handling, as Assistant Secretary, of disputes with high naval officers concerning penal and other problems affecting Navy personnel; exposes his ethically questionable appearance as a lawyer before the Navy Department representing a concern for which he had formerly, as Assistant Secretary, procured favorable departmental action; and discloses some weird financial ventures and promotions in which F.D.R. invested time and money.

But, throughout, F.D.R. is contagiously alive, warm, and appealing; immature and superficial, even into his forties, about public questions, yet intuitively, if shrewdly, pursuing justice and decency; in domestic affairs, a dualistic disciple of both Carter Glass and Al Smith, and in foreign relations, a follower of the Woodrow Wilson vision.

Dr. Freidel gives us gripping drama in the preludes and scenes of the 1924 national Democratic convention, where Smith, pushed by F.D.R., deadlocked with Mc-Adoo on the issues of religion and liquor control, so that John W. Davis was nominated. The final chapter's stirring account of how F.D.R., the cripple, was dragooned by Smith into running for the New York governorship in 1928 and gallantly won his "Victory by a Hair's Breadth"—the definite upward turning point in his career—leaves us eager for the next volume. If, in the four still to come, Dr. Freidel can hold the quality of this one, we can well expect the work to have permanent pre-eminence.

LOUIS B. WEHLE

New York City

ECONOMICS AND INDUSTRY

BURNS, ARTHUR F. *The Frontiers of Economic Knowledge: Essays.* Pp. xi, 367. Princeton, N. J.: Princeton University Press (published for the National Bureau of Economic Research), 1954. $5.00.

This volume is a collection of essays, all of which have already appeared in one form or another. Those of Part I have been published as the Annual Reports of the *National Bureau of Economic Research* for which Dr. Burns was responsible from the time he succeeded the late Wesley C. Mitchell as Director of Research of the Bureau in 1945 until he was granted a leave of absence in 1953 to become chairman of President Eisenhower's Council of Economic Advisers. Those of Part II consist of eight items made up largely of

prefaces to earlier Bureau publications, journal articles, full-dress book reviews. The latter group of papers range in time from Dr. Burns's essay on "Long Cycles in Residential Construction" originally published in the *Economic Essays in Honor of Wesley Clair Mitchell* in 1935 to his review of J. R. Hicks's *Contribution to the Theory of the Trade Cycle* which came out in the *Journal of Political Economy* in 1952.

No formal development is to be expected in a miscellany of this sort. Nonetheless an essential unity and coherence is given by the cumulative effect of repetition of two or three leading ideas which make the book a treatise on the scope, method, and achievements of empiricist economics, as well as a convenient source of otherwise scattered writings.

The underlying leitmotif is methodological. To push the frontiers of economic knowledge beyond their present limits, what is needed, according to our author, is emphasis on the painstaking collection and organization of facts prior to the elaboration of explanatory systems. The lifework of Wesley Clair Mitchell, to whom a moving tribute is paid, and the continued labors of the Bureau, particularly on business cycles, exemplify this procedure at its best. Notable progress has been made in defining the phenomenon of business cycles in realistic terms—all this in the hope that out of the close and ingenious study of empirical data, somehow a satisfactory theoretical elucidation will come, at least a more satisfactory one than that given by Keynes or Hicks, for example, whose models are vitiated by assumptions, such as that of a practically constant consumption function or that of a constant investment coefficient, for which there is no empirical justification. It is, however, to be observed that Wesley Mitchell, for all his heroic labors, never got beyond the first half of his program, which he was wont to symbolize in the Marshallian phrase, "The Many in the One," but neither his work nor that of his associates and successors has yet given us a clue to "The One in the Many." Perhaps a little more attention to Alfred Marshall would help, particularly to Marshall's admonition that while "the economist must be greedy of facts, . . . facts by themselves teach nothing." Not that Dr. Burns is unaware of this, for the principle is clearly invoked in his penetrating review of Dr. Nourse's *American Capacity to Produce.*

The National Bureau of Economic Research is to be commended for republishing Dr. Burns's recent papers, for their value as a collection lies not only in the methodological and analytical developments of interest to the economist, but also in the discussions relating to economic policy which are of interest to the political scientist and to the bewildered citizen seeking to clarify current issues.

WILLIAM JAFFÉ
Northwestern University

BENNETT, M. K. *The World's Food: A Study of the Interrelations of World Populations, National Diets, and Food Potentials.* Pp. vi, 282. New York: Harper & Brothers, 1954. $4.00.

Reviewing a thousand years of population growth, Bennett concludes: "I hope that I have shown convincingly that consumption levels had risen over a large fraction of the population, that calorie consumption per capita cannot have fallen, that, again over a large fraction of the population, diets had become more diversified in composition, that famine from natural causes had fallen from its status as a nearly universal risk to a status of risk to a much diminished fraction of the swollen population of today."

Part II deals with the American national diet and how it has changed since the years just preceding World War I, and Part III reviews the food consumption in the various parts of the world today and food management as it was developed during the recent war.

The United States spends nearly one-fourth of total disposable personal income for about 1500 pounds of food per person per year. Since the days before World War I, the total poundage has risen but calorie consumption has fallen by about five percent. The consumption of carbohydrates and of proteins has been reduced, but the consumption of milk, vege-

tables, fruit, and eggs, and thus of calcium, iron, and the major vitamins has increased. Grain products and potatoes together provide about 27 per cent of our total calories; formerly they provided 42 per cent.

Part III deals with international comparisons. Here Bennett makes extensive use of the Food Balance Sheets which have been assembled by FAO (the Food and Agriculture Organization of the United Nations), though he challenges the accuracy of many of the figures which are contained in them, as well as the standards from which deficiencies are measured. He insists that large proportions of the world's population were not short of calories before the war or in recent years. A part of the disagreement is due to the use of different standards. Bennett is concerned with the point at which bodily weight can be maintained; the FAO standards on the other hand are concerned with diets which will promote health. He finds that per capita national income tends rather strongly to determine the degree of national dependence on cheap, starchy staples, though dietary habits and preferences play a strong role as well.

With a persistent search for the facts and a skeptical approach to generalizations, as well as to the bridges which have been constructed over the many gaps in the existing body of facts, he presents in highly readable form the results of many years of painstaking research. He has no causes other than getting at the facts; he scorns the emotionalism that surrounds much current discussion of the relations of population and food supplies and what to him is the "sterile arithmetic" of projections of present trends into an indefinite future. He offers no solutions to the problems of feeding the world's growing population. But his contribution to the thinking about these problems comes from the clear presentation of these problems, of his point of view, and of his findings.

CONRAD TAEUBER
U. S. Bureau of the Census

CHAMBERLAIN, NEIL W., and JANE METZGER SCHILLING. *The Impact of Strikes: Their Social and Economic Costs.* Pp. viii, 257. New York: Harper & Brothers, 1954. $4.00.

In an earlier study, *Social Responsibility and Strikes,* Professor Chamberlain of the Labor and Management Center of Yale University devised a method for measuring the cost of strikes in terms of their impact upon the various publics affected, including consumers, industrial users of the struck product, and suppliers of the struck firm. The procedure thus worked out is reproduced in this volume, which applies the technique to seventeen strikes in the coal, railroad, and steel industries and obtains comparative scores for each strike.

In thus attempting to reduce the effect of strikes to quantitative terms the authors must make a number of assumptions at critical points, as they must often fall back upon impressionistic judgments because no data are available. Nevertheless they have sought to get the most reliable figures available, and have shown considerable ingenuity in combining the various effects of strikes into a mathematical formula. The authors take account of the cultural necessity of the product, the period of time that existing stocks will last, and the extent to which other products can be substituted. From all these an urgency rating is derived; and this in turn, in combination with the number of persons affected, yields a score for the strike. Each strike is rated as of a particular day, usually the last day that it was fully in effect.

The authors are greatly concerned with the implications of their findings for public policy. They conclude that some strikes are serious, not because they withhold final products from consumers, but because they deprive employees in related industries of employment income. They criticize the drawing up of lists of industries in which strikes are forbidden or in which government is empowered to intervene—typically on the ground that the products or services are vital to consumers—as a limited and faulty approach to the problems presented by major strikes. They argue for administrative flexibility in the control of strikes, and offer their strike rating procedure as an aid to sounder judgments than are presently made.

This volume represents an important contribution to the study of strike effects.

Both in its method of analysis and in its effort to quantify, it marks a substantial advance over the mere listing of industries whose continued operation is thought vital enough to justify governmental intervention.   JOEL SEIDMAN
University of Chicago

HARBISON, FREDERICK H., and JOHN R. COLEMAN. *Working Harmony: A Summary of the Collective Bargaining Relationships in 18 Companies.* Case Study No. 13 in series "Causes of Industrial Peace under Collective Bargaining." Pp. xii, 64. Washington, D. C.: National Planning Association, 1953. $1.00.

This is an excellent summary by Frederick H. Harbison, Executive Officer of the Industrial Relations Center, University of Chicago, and John R. Coleman, Assistant Professor, Industrial Relations Section, Massachusetts Institute of Technology. As in all of these studies by the National Planning Association, the principal question is, what makes collective bargaining tick? And the answers are found in the attitudes of management and unions toward one another; attitudes of trust, of accommodation, of informality, and of constructive collective bargaining. There may be fighting, but it is principally the conflicts of conference and debate.

The reader will be swayed by alternate feelings of optimism and pessimism; optimism when he sees peaceful relations growing and their beneficial effects upon both companies and unions; pessimism when he notes upon what fortuitous circumstances peaceful relations come about, and upon what slender threads they continue to be maintained. Since harmony does not come about naturally, and, in fact, there are powerful pressures moving both sides toward the area of struggle, the reader is struck with what appears, at first, to be the inconsequential things that ultimately have important effects. Take, for example, the joint union-management safety committees in plants. These committees perform an important service in safety work, but the most important effects are indirect, in that they teach the parties to work together, and they grow to know one another better. So it is with other joint committees; the principal benefits are indirect. Or take the example of harmonious relations between management and the principal officers of a union; at first sight this appears ideal, but the very circumstance of harmony may lead to a revolt within the union, with charges of class collaboration, however unwarranted, against the incumbent officers. The settlement of grievances is another example; the formal contract procedures are not so important as is the development of informal communication and consultation in the area of problem-solving.

Throughout the summary, the reader is impressed with the highly significant role of management in the development of harmonious relations. The initiative on many points is with management. The unions' requests are basic in the presentation of problems, but it is most frequently from the side of management that the suggestions of co-operation, informal consultation, and of accommodation initially arise. This may be a product of fairly recent history in which many unions were struggling for existence; in any case, the burden appears to be thrown upon management, in very considerable degree, to have the ideas, the imagination, and the initiative, to move into the realm of harmonious industrial relations.

FREDERICK L. RYAN
San Diego State College

FLORENCE, P. SARGANT. *The Logic of British and American Industry: A Realistic Analysis of Industrial Structure and Government.* Pp. xvi, 368. Chapel Hill: University of North Carolina Press (and Routledge and Kegan Paul, London), 1954. $5.00.

The reports of the various Anglo-American Productivity Teams which visited the United States in recent years stand as a landmark to the thoroughness with which members of these groups surveyed American manufacturing processes and managerial procedures. The competence with which the investigators summarized their findings is indisputable, yet the Teams' recommendations have not had wide implementation in Great Britain, largely because of important differences between the British and the American working climate, business philosophy, and management technique. Although the work of the Productivity Teams continues, now under the aegis of a new body, the complex question of how to introduce the best and most adaptable production and management methods in Great Britain remains relatively unsolved.

This dilemma, solution of which has vital reference to British prosperity, has been analyzed recently by several economists. Probably the most detailed consideration of the subject to date is presented by Professor P. Sargant Florence in his study, *The Logic of British and American Industry: A Realistic Analysis of Industrial Structure and Government.* An American citizen, Professor Florence has been Professor of Commerce at Birmingham University since 1929, and in 1940–41 he served as Consultant to the United States National Resources Planning Board.

After presenting pertinent information concerning the prevailing size of industrial firms and the pattern of industrial location in Britain and America, Professor Florence interprets the facts in basic terms, such as technical requirements and consumer habits. The contrast between the two countries is discovered mainly in certain social attitudes and motivation, while unexpected similarities are found in industrial structure and government. A wealth of statistical material is presented in easily digested tables.

In what Professor Florence calls the political science of industry, certainly one of the most important issues discussed is how to educate and recruit outstanding young people for business management. "Educational institutions," he argues, "should make it possible for the fittest of the new generation, whatever their class, to prepare for the profession of business government, and thus allow inborn ability plus training plus experience to supply leadership for a new, more efficient, more logical industrial order."

This argument is sustained by a recent editorial in *The Times* which stated, in part, "British business needs a larger share of the ablest men and women trained by the universities whether as technicians or as managers and directors." Reference should be made to Colonel L. Urwick's brilliant discussion of the whole problem in the report he wrote for the British Specialist Team on Education for Management. Many able observers of the contemporary scene contend that business and financial procedures cannot improve in conception and execution in Great Britain, and indeed in the Commonwealth, unless the range of the managing director, the industrial accountant, the personnel administrator, and the works manager is expanded by higher education.

Professor Florence's book explores this topic in a highly professional manner, and affords adequate discussion of many questions involving labor-management and company-government relations in Britain and America. It should stimulate thought and research on both sides of the Atlantic. The reviewer recommends it especially to those persons whose interests lie in the organization and function of business enterprise, and in the implications of industrial growth and efficiency for national prosperity and international security.

MARY E. MURPHY
Los Angeles State College of
Applied Arts and Sciences

HARRIS, MARSHALL D. *Origin of the Land Tenure System in the United States.* Pp. xiv, 447. Ames: Iowa State College Press, 1953. $7.50.

The author of this study feels that there is a "serious lack of usable information about the forces that influenced the evolution of the present tenure system" in the United States, and that no adequate study exists of "how basic tenure principles were developed." He offers this study which is intended to help "to determine the processes through which the land tenure system of the United States became what it was at the time of its emergence, just prior to 1800." He is concerned with the "changes made in the land tenure system prior to establishment of the national government"; and the "forces, factors, conditions, and situations that brought about these changes and finally secured their recognition." Despite these statements it is clear that the author was more interested in bringing together material from various scattered sources than he was in re-examining this enormously complex problem.

The book is made up of twenty-one chapters arranged as follows: One chapter is devoted to a discussion of the nature of land tenure, two discuss the English feudal system, and two more are required to examine the national claims in American and colonial charters in general. Four chapters are then given over to a discussion of the several types of English colonial organization, followed by a chapter examining the relation of the original grants to the colonial tenure systems. The acquisition of title to Indian lands is disposed of in the next chapter. This is followed by six chapters which summarize the various means by which title to land was transferred to individuals and the nature of such titles. The remaining four chapters consider the emergence of the national land system, the factors which influenced the land system, the impact of the Revolutionary War, and the relation of the colonial developments to the United States land policies.

Students of American history will find here very little that is new. The book is legalistic, synoptic, slow-paced, sometimes not wholly clear. The acquisition of land engaged the lively, unremitting, and often scheming attention of hosts of colonists and of many of their countrymen at home, but the author manages quite successfully to keep his book from reflecting anything of this ceaseless, often passionate, pursuit. However, within the limits suggested, he has provided an orderly and usable handbook on the origins of the American tenure system.

VERNON CARSTENSEN
University of Wisconsin

NURKSE, RAGNAR. *Problems of Capital Formation in Underdeveloped Countries.* Pp. vii, 163. New York: Oxford University Press, 1953. $3.00.

Ragnar Nurkse's very readable book discusses the underlying economic realities of capital formation and points out that, whether the institutional framework be capitalist or socialist, development requires that some economic resources be used not for immediate consumption but to increase capital equipment, that is that society "save" and "invest." To Nurkse the presence in the underdeveloped countries of much underutilized manpower makes theoretically possible an increase in total output—hence a development regimen in which consumption is held constant, with the increased manpower engaged in expanding productive capacity, rather than the more Spartan regimen with consumption actually reduced, as under the classic assumptions of full employment and no technological change. But Nurkse oscillates between a static equilibrium analysis, which highlights low consumer demand as an important obstacle to capital formation (because it deprives the individual businessman of the inducement to invest), and a more dynamic treatment of the development process in which high consumer demand becomes an obstacle to capital formation.

Since development is a process which itself generates within business the demand for capital as well as the supply of funds initially from within business (under socialism investment and savings are even more intimately joined), the reader is led to ask, whether it would not be more fruitful to focus on the sociopolitical forces which in fact condition the initiation of the development process rather than on the surface reflection of this process in current saving and investment.

Nurkse, recognizing that underdeveloped countries often have a cultural environment less conducive to the emergence of economic enterprise, accords greatly expanded functions to the state. But the state is, after all, the product of the same cultural environment (so it too needs a metamorphosis). Furthermore the governments of underdeveloped countries are subject to great pressure to expand immediate consumption. Nurkse attributes this pressure to growing awareness of advanced living standards but still thinks it possible for the state to undertake saving, that is to limit consumption, while leaving much of the actual process of investment in private hands. But, even if such a procedure were to accelerate development, would such a distribution of immediate sacrifices and

privileges be politically viable in the era of the welfare state?

Nurkse gives underdeveloped countries sound advice on the necessity for complementary action on the home front if foreign loans are to be effective, and he helpfully clears away many familiar misconceptions regarding commercial policies in relation to economic development. Unfortunately, Nurkse's bland view of the nature of imperialism may lead readers in newly sovereign countries to dismiss this useful book.

HELEN LAMB
Massachusetts Institute of Technology

CZERWONKY, HUGO E. *Freedom from Insecurity.* Pp. ix, 198. Washington, D. C.: Public Affairs Press, 1954. $3.50.

Mr. Czerwonky, an engineer, who since 1933 has been employed by various federal government agencies, has given us a panacea for a multitude of economic evils. This book is reminiscent of Henry George's *Progress and Poverty* to the extent that the solution is simple and is based primarily upon a tax scheme.

The solution, according to Mr. Czerwonky, is the creation of "a society wherein widespread work opportunity persistently prevails." This society would be brought about by the adoption of the maximum-jobs principle of taxation, two-way bargaining, and amendments to the Federal Reserve Act.

Under the maximum-jobs principle of taxation, the federal government would rely almost entirely upon a manufacturers' sales or excise tax on all finished consumer goods. This tax policy would maximize the private savings available for investment, thereby creating maximum work opportunity and competition between employers for the services of wage and salary workers. In such a climate of ever-widening industrial activity, our present labor relations structure would be unnecessary. All labor relations would be governed by individual contracts of employment, a system which is labeled two-way bargaining. The workers, management, and the public would all be protected "because of the umbrella of widespread work opportunity which would continuously prevail." The Federal Reserve Act would be amended so that the

Board of Governors could synchronize the flow of dollars to the flow of consumer goods, thereby eradicating instability within our economic system.

If his program should be adopted, he recommends abolition of unemployment insurance, placing old age pensions on a pay-as-you-go basis, and the allowance of a credit for charitable contributions to the full extent of the federal estate tax. He claims that the adoption of his program would, among other things, eliminate the need for minimum wage legislation, eliminate the discrimination in pay between men and women, eliminate racial discrimination, bring about lasting peace, and make the farmer permanently prosperous.

Although the arguments advanced are supported principally by the repetition of commendatory expressions and promissory representations, Mr. Czerwonky points the finger of "economic illiteracy" at the Congress, the entire nation, and even at the economists. Naturally, it is claimed that the fault lies with our educational institutions.

ROBERT L. PATRICK
Louisiana Polytechnic Institute

BULEY, R. CARLYLE. *The American Life Convention, 1906–1952: A Study in the History of Life Insurance.* 2 Vols. Pp. xxx, 680; viii, 681–1397. New York: Appleton-Century-Crofts, 1953. $15.00.

It is hard to believe that there exists no book on the history of America's biggest business, life insurance. All we have are some books on the history of individual companies and on certain phases of life insurance. Therefore, the two volumes by the Indiana University professor, R. Carlyle Buley, fill a gap and are highly welcome, because the American Life Convention, holding almost 97 per cent of the legal reserve insurance in force in the United States and Canada, "plays a vital part in the study of all phases of life insurance, in the influencing of practices and policies, and in the protection of more than 90,000,000 policyholders."

Part I, in its 247 pages, contains a clear history of life insurance from its beginning, about 2,000 years ago, up to the organization of the American Life Convention in the year 1906, almost 100 years after the first commercial company in the United States for life insurance business exclusively had been organized and about 75 years after our life insurance was on the eve of its first great advance by mutuals.

In contrast to the highly concentrated first 247 pages, the following 885 pages, covering the years 1906–1952 of the American Life Convention, offer an abundance of details. The list of papers read before the Convention covers 110 pages, the index almost 100. Also the bibliographical notes are excellent. The same is true of the statistical data, year by year. Much of the association's business is conducted in the annual meetings. Thus, the author had to present the volumes to a large degree as a chronicle.

Founded for the betterment of business methods and the protection of common interests and common rights, the American Life Convention's sphere of activity is much broader. It is an organization to "accumulate facts, disseminate information, further education, abolish abuses, eliminate unsound competition, adjust controversies, establish good will, promote confidence, expose frauds, safeguard investments, prevent venal and misguided legislation, and protect policyholders." Furthermore, the American Life Convention played an important part in "one of the most constructive accomplishments of the century in the field of life insurance," the construction of modern mortality tables. The various sections of the Convention show the great variety of problems life insurance has to deal with: economy, law, taxation, actuarial science, medicine.

It is to be hoped that the two excellent volumes will put an end to the deplorable fact that life insurance is ignored by writers of American history books, even when presenting our economic and social development.   ALFRED MANES
St. Petersburg, Florida

CHILDS, MARQUIS W., and DOUGLASS CATER. *Ethics in a Business Society.* Pp. x, 191. New York: Harper & Brothers, 1954. $2.75.

This little book was inspired by the several studies arranged for by the Department of Church and Economic Life of the National Council of the Churches of Christ of the United States of America. These studies covered in general and very broadly the relation of religion to economics. The authors state in the Foreword: "What we have written . . . is not a part of the study series itself but rather our interpretation and reflection on all the materials we have used. We have undertaken to present in as readable a form as possible some of the results of the churches' effort to relate the seemingly unrelated parts of our society."

Ethics in a Business Society is more than a summary or digest of the Church series. The authors have drawn from other sources, have added valuable historical perspectives, and have given more unity than was possible in some of the Church series. They paint in broad perspective the really serious problems facing us today, such problems as the following: growing insecurity; the problem of freedom and individualism in an age of giant business; the achievements, real and spurious, of machine technology; the churches' attitude toward imperialism, slavery, and poverty; Marx's "fake religion"; the character and incentives of business leaders; and the alleged spread of corporations and of monopoly. The authors' view of our present status is judicious and properly not very optimistic.

This little book, with all its religious side lights, might well be called "social economics." It is well and interestingly written —one of the most significant books I have read recently. It would be most worthwhile reading for students, and, I venture to assert, even for most economists.

JOHN ISE

University of Kansas

SOCIOLOGY AND EDUCATION

GILLIN, JOHN (Ed.). *For a Science of Social Man: Convergences in Anthropology, Psychology, and Sociology.* By Howard Becker, John Gillin, A. Irving Hallowell, George Peter Murdock, Theodore M. Newcomb, Talcott Parsons, and M. Brewster Smith. Pp. vii, 289. New York: The Macmillan Company, 1954. $4.00.

This book contributes importantly to the co-ordination of theoretical positions among the behavioral sciences. The seven authors are evenly divided between anthropology, sociology, and psychology. Each writer is already noted for his cross-disciplinary contributions. Each is asked to consider the relation of his discipline to one or the other of the three fields of inquiry. No brief review can do justice to the richness of the resulting papers. Unlike many compilations that result from solicited contributions, this volume has coherence and consistently high quality.

Murdock, as an anthropologist, believes that sociology is methodologically and scientifically more sophisticated than anthropology but "that the total body of verified theory which has resulted from sociological research compares unfavorably with anthropology in unity, generality of application, in sheer quantity and in potential significance for the integrated human science of the future" (p. 26). M. Brewster Smith as a psychologist provides a penetrating discussion of the interplay between his field and anthropology, a sharp appraisal of culture and of personality as concepts, and the directions from which convergence between the two fields may be expected. Parsons presents views that bear on the theory of action that has become associated with his name and which embraces major notions derived from psychology, sociology, and anthropology. Becker and Hallowell are respectively concerned with scholarly historical resumé of the interplay between sociology and anthropology and between psychology and anthropology. These are useful statements although somewhat less creative and imaginative than the other contributions. With a clarity that is relatively rare in the theoretical writings of social scientists, Newcomb presents a model for constructive collaboration between the sciences of social man that avoids dangers of reductionism but does not reject the idea of levels or of specialization. Gillin, in addition to a foreword, has written the final chapter. It summarizes and restates the position of the authors in terms of the human organism, human behavior, grouping, culture, social structure, personality, symbolization, and communication. It also enters a plea for more rigorous theory building in the social sciences and for better teaching of the "theory of theories" in the logico-deductive-empirical system of thought.

As might be anticipated, the authors are on the whole singularly without crotchets. They build constructive bridges between disciplines and deal rigorously with meaningful problems. This book is not easy reading, but it is a must for anyone concerned with the theoretical frontiers of that science of man whose development in the last decade has been so rapid and fruitful.

CORA DU BOIS
Institute of International Education
Washington, D. C.

CHRISTIE, RICHARD, and MARIE JAHODA (Eds.). *Studies in the Scope and Method of "The Authoritarian Personality": Continuities in Social Research.* Pp. 279. Glencoe, Ill.: Free Press, 1954. $4.50.

The subject of this second volume in the *Continuities* series is the unwieldy but seminal book on prejudice and personality by T. W. Adorno, Else Frenkel-Brunswik, D. J. Levinson, and R. N. Sanford (Harper, 1950). After an introduction by Miss Jahoda that places the book historically, chapters by contributors follow in neat "con" to "pro" order. The argument runs, in caricature, something like this: The California investigators should have studied something different in the first place (E. A. Shils); their methods were totally inadequate for what they did study (H. H. Hyman and P. B. Sheatsley); yet their principal findings have in the main been confirmed in subsequent research (R. Christie). Harold Lasswell's chapter, which follows, is more concerned with his well-known schema for political motivation than with the authoritarian personality, but he apparently accepts the California findings without criticism. In the concluding piece, Else Frenkel-Brunswik considers the book and subsequent related research from the standpoint of a participant.

In his chapter "Authoritarianism: 'Right' and 'Left,'" Shils is obsessed with a valid point: that "right" and "left" no longer pose the polar antithesis that ordered the ideological politics of the nineteenth century; that, specifically, if Fascism and Nazi Germany were authoritarian, so are Communism and Soviet Russia. He finds serious fault with the study in that it was not designed to expose the authoritarianism of the left. Undoubtedly the research bears the marks of a pre-Cold-War intellectual climate rather than a post-McCarthy one. But arriving at its focus on the pre-Fascist mentality from an initial and continuing concern with American anti-Semitism, it could hardly have been expected to throw much light on Communist authoritarianism.

The detailed methodological critique by Hyman and Sheatsley, on the other hand, is exemplary as an intellectual exercise in the analysis of research design and inference. One might wish that the authors did not take such relish in their double-barreled critical volleys, but one can only admire the virtuosity of the performance. They prove their case: that *The Authoritarian Personality* did not prove its case.

Christie judiciously assesses several of the book's principal themes in the light of evidence since accumulated. Verdict: While the exact nature and dimensions of authoritarianism remain obscure after the wealth of research stimulated by the book, its conclusions are probably pretty close to the mark for a first approximation. But situational and group membership factors, he holds with Hyman and Sheatsley, are more important than the California authors thought.

One has only to read Frenkel-Brunswik's final chapter to grasp what may have seemed elusive in the earlier sections, why the book created such a stir and warrants this symposium. Here are the same qualities of theoretical subtlety and research imagination that marked the best of the earlier volume. Granted that *The Authoritarian Personality* falls short as definitive research, how much the richer it has left the whole field of social behavior!

M. BREWSTER SMITH
New York City

MEAD, MARGARET (Ed.). *Cultural Patterns and Technical Change*. Pp. 348. New York: Columbia University Press (for UNESCO), 1953. $1.75.

Programs of Technical Assistance potentially open opportunities for social scientists to guide cultural change. This manual demonstrates the eagerness of some social scientists to assume such guidance, the relevance of their interests for the task, and the present immaturity of their knowledge.

The book reflects differences among three groups: (1) the Economic and Social Council of the United Nations, anxious to induce rapid economic development in "under-developed" countries; (2) the World Federation for Mental Health, sponsor of the book, aiming to improve "mental health" among all peoples; and (3) anthropologists espousing a doctrine of cultural conservation. Differences among these three groups are most evident in the introduction and conclusions of the book.

Between introduction and conclusions, however, are three chapters of independent worth. First come studies of "whole cultures"—Burma, Palau, Tiv of Nigeria, Greece, and Spanish Americans of New Mexico. The last two are written from new materials. Next follows a summary of some 300 reports on success and failure in efforts to change agriculture, nutrition, child care, health, industry, and education in various other cultures. Finally there is a brief catalogue of psychodynamic processes likely to operate in situations of induced change. None of these three chapters is closely connected with any other or with the initial or concluding generalities.

Since the generalities of the book are but slightly connected with each other or with a body of fact they sometimes express conflicting biases. The anthropological introduction argues, for example, that cultural integration should be preserved at all cost. Any change liable to affect traditional values should be made with caution. Values are said to give "continuity" and "meaning" to life; change of values is difficult for individuals, producing tension and mental illness. But psychological statements in the book indicate that tradi-

tional values in a culture may conceal "obsolete" and psychically "harmful" practices. "Sometimes," the psychologists warn, it may be necessary to alter "the whole structure of belief." Momentous cultural changes may be induced with psychic ease if motivations are correctly manipulated.

These and other apparent contradictions blunt the advice of the book and obscure its wisdom. It may be doubted, too, if the patronizing views put forward concerning the elites of the underdeveloped countries will encourage those elites to request the assistance of social scientists. As an exposure of current chaos in social scientific fact and opinion, the book may rather serve as a challenge to the social scientists themselves.

McKIM MARRIOTT
University of California
Berkeley

VERNANT, JACQUES. *The Refugee in the Post-War World*. Pp. xvi, 827. New Haven: Yale University Press, 1953. $6.00.

The refugees are distinctly a modern phenomenon. In earlier eras, exile was the fate reserved for the political elite; only the leaders, by choice or compulsion, found it necessary or desirable to leave their homes in the aftermath of unsuccessful war or revolution. Even the greatest disturbances in the wake of the revolutions of 1789 or 1848 produced relatively few emigrees.

Since the First World War, however, displacement of a vast part of the civilian population has been an accepted consequence of war. The settlement of 1918 left hundreds of thousands unable or unwilling to return to the places of their birth; and the peace of 1945 brought the numbers of such displaced persons to the millions. In part, these displacements were due to the impact of nationalistic ideas, often tinged with racism; in part they were the product of a political situation in which the masses were more consequential than ever before in determination of the control of the state. Even in countries in which democracy did not prevail, new circumstances forced commitments on thousands of people from which they found it difficult, under altered conditions, to extricate themselves. As a result, the problem of the refugee has assumed ever larger proportions and presents a continuing challenge to modern society.

A long tradition of "asylum" has offered some sort of privileged status to political fugitives. Refugees, furthermore, have exercised a claim upon the humanitarian sentiments of the West; these displacements, like famines or earthquakes, have customarily been occasions for the display of international solidarity. And the refugees, by their numbers and their connections, are a strategic factor of no mean importance. For all these reasons, their fate has been a subject of concern to the League of Nations, the United Nations, and other international organizations.

The present study undertaken on behalf of the United Nations High Commission for Refugees by Jacques Vernant, with the aid of a Rockefeller grant, is the indispensable handbook for understanding the problems of the refugee. It contains a meticulously accurate summary of all the available information on the question. It focuses its attention upon the period since 1939 and particularly upon those groups under the care of the United Nations; but it covers also the surviving groups of displaced persons from the First World War. By its comprehensive scale and its thoroughness, this study supplants all others.

The work opens with a general consideration of the international problem and of the agencies involved. It proceeds to an analysis of the various groups of refugees, by nationalities. The most substantial section of the volume then follows: a place by place analysis of 39 countries in which refugees are presently found. Under each country is included a history of the immigration, an analysis of the legal and administrative position of the newcomers, and some consideration of their economic and social situation.

As might be expected, the book is more valuable for the information it contains than for the tentative conclusions it reaches. Given the marked differences of circumstances, generalizations as to the state of the newcomers must necessarily be tentative and circumscribed. Nevertheless, this does not in the least diminish the utility of the work, which will serve students of international migration for years to come.

OSCAR HANDLIN
Harvard University

COHEN, ELIE A. *Human Behavior in the Concentration Camp.* Translated from the Dutch by M. H. Braaksma. Pp. xvi, 295. New York: W. W. Norton & Company, 1953. $5.00.

The author of this volume is a Dutch physician who was a war prisoner of the Nazis from August in 1942 until liberated by Americans in 1945. He was held in the concentration camp Amersfoort, Netherlands, for nearly two months, transferred to the transient camp for Jews at Westerbrook, Netherlands, and then shifted to the notorious concentration camp Auschwitz, Poland, where for some fifteen months he experienced all of the horrors that accompanied the extermination program that was carried on there, involving gassings and other forms of extermination of Jews that appear to have run as high as 500,000 a month.

This book, however, is not a personal narrative nor an emotional indictment of German treatment of the prisoners. It is, rather, an objectively analytical study of human reactions to camp existence, devoid of any trace of sentimentality, although illuminated from time to time by personal references that have direct bearing upon the data that are presented. One of its contributions is the systematic presentation of relevant materials that have been carefully combed by the author.

There are four major divisions to the work. An initial chapter provides a documented background concerning the organization, administration, and purposes of the concentration camps, with attention to the devices of extermination that were used. Then follows material on medical aspects of life in the camps, mortality, nutrition, diseases, and sections on medical experiments on prisoners. There is a wealth of carefully correlated material. The longest section, and by far the most valuable, is on the psychology of the prisoner: the stage of initial reaction, the process of adaptation, and the stage of resignation. The pages bristle with hypotheses many of which, as the author would admit, call for further research analysis. The importance in the adaptation process of the previous conception of life in the camps is stressed, and especially significant appear to be the hypotheses with respect to the role of "spiritual" values, broadly defined, in survival. In all of the analysis, the author draws heavily upon the concepts of Freud and interprets the prisoners' behavior in the light of them.

Having described systematically the behavior of the prisoners, Dr. Cohen seeks to understand the psychology of the S.S. members who administered and largely policed the camps. A quasi-cultural approach to the problem mingles with an interpretation of group psychology that is not entirely convincing or satisfactory. Yet the attempt to apply Freud's principles is carried through consistently. In any event, the human reactions are minutely described, and these descriptions have value for social science; even the interpretations may lead to more adequate explanations of the observed behavior. Certainly the mechanisms that are involved are not circumscribed by the electric fences of the concentration camp. It is the larger relevance of Dr. Cohen's material to the every-day world in which we now live that gives the book especial significance.

MALCOLM M. WILLEY
University of Minnesota

ROGOFF, NATALIE. *Recent Trends in Occupational Mobility.* Pp. 131. Glencoe, Ill.: Free Press, 1953. $4.00.

This is the most significant study on occupational mobility since Davidson and Anderson's *Occupational Mobility in an American Community.* The primary contribution of this work is methodological, for unlike most earlier studies, an attempt is made to measure the amount of occupational mobility which occurs independently of the mobility caused by changes in the occupational structure. The significance of the study is heightened because trends in occupational mobility and origins (from

fathers' occupations) are studied for two periods (1910 and 1940) in a rather representative industrial city (Indianapolis). Despite limitations imposed by the source materials (marriage licenses which asked for applicant's occupation and that of his father) certain trends are clear:

(1) There has been almost no change in a generation in the chances of avoiding occupational inheritance; (2) The most probable occupational destiny of males is their father's occupation; (3) Occupational destiny depends increasingly on the worker's social origins or his father's occupation; (4) The barrier between white-collar and manual work is the most difficult to penetrate over a generation; (5) Least amount of occupational inheritance is found among sons of skilled workers; (6) Sons of farmers find it increasingly difficult to become white-collar workers; (7) Occupational inheritance is lowest among Negroes since, irrespective of origin, they are usually forced into unskilled or service occupations; (8) Sons of foreign born suffer little or no job discrimination; (9) Younger men are increasingly less inclined to be occupationally mobile.

Rogoff's findings that deal with older workers, sons of foreign born, and farmers must be considered tentative because these groups are not adequately representative of similar groups in other communities. Further, Rogoff displays a tendency to overstate the differences between her findings and those reported by earlier studies. Despite the significant methodological refinement, one is struck more with the replication of findings. The most important criticism of this excellent study is the general lack of interpretation of the findings. No attention is given to changes in the general social structure of the United States or changes in the industrial structure which may account for changing patterns of occupational mobility. Failure to do so limits the general applicability of the findings, or a consideration of probable future trends in occupational mobility.

WILLIAM H. FORM
Michigan State College

SPELLMAN, HOWARD HILTON. *Successful Management of Matrimonial Cases.* Pp.

ix, 306. New York: Prentice-Hall, 1954.
$5.65.

There is a belief in some quarters that
"respectable" lawyers shy away from divorce suits in much the same manner that
respectable police officers avoid petty dis-
orderly-conduct cases. In both instances
the feeling persists that such interpersonal
wrangles are beneath the dignity of the
law—that there is much more important
work to do; let us get on with it and leave
the domestic squabbles to be handled by
those with nothing better to do. Mr.
Spellman's book does much to discredit
this point of view. The author feels that
"The greatest personal tragedy in our
modern society is divorce." But he feels
just as strongly that the state has a vital
interest in every divorce proceeding. Between these two often-conflicting perspectives—the wishes of the litigants and the
interests of the state—a balance must be
struck, and it is here, says the author, that
the divorce lawyer is instrumental. And
the stakes are high enough to concern all
of us.

Mr. Spellman does not criticize existing
divorce laws, nor does he preach for an
extension of the family court—and on
these two counts alone his book is marked
as "different." Written for the general
public as well as for lawyers who handle
divorce cases, the volume is incisively presented. It is likely that practicing lawyers
will find in it a wealth of practical material, since, in effect, the author has written
a procedural handbook rather than a routine legal reference work. However, it is
just as likely that the general public will
find it no more intriguing than other books
dealing with specialized law.

Social scientists interested in the family
field—especially those who, though dis-
satisfied with current divorce philosophy,
are not convinced that the family court is
a necessary panacea—should find the volume rewarding, and irritating. Rewards
lie in the author's repeated and crystal-
clear statements as to what the divorce law
is and what the law means. Collusion,
connivance, condonation, and recrimination
are thoroughly covered, as are separation
agreements, pleadings, and preliminary motions. The section dealing with the in-

vestigation of marital "misconduct" is the
best this reviewer has yet come across,
even though a disproportionate amount of
space is devoted to the loops and twists
of the New York State adultery requirement. On the other hand, estoppel, inter-
locutory decrees and rights of remarriage,
appeals, and out-of-court settlements are
largely ignored. Throughout, the author
annoyingly uses the term "foreign" to refer
to out-of-state divorces. It is also somewhat disquieting to discover, upon checking citations, that side by side with scientific and legal references are several allud-
ing to *The Ladies Home Journal, Colliers,
Look,* and *Cosmopolitan.*

All in all, the author's approach is refreshing. To anyone who is at all familiar
with actual divorce proceedings, it will be
evident that what divorce lawyers actually
do in the handling of divorce suits is many
leagues removed from what Mr. Spellman
says they should do. He says they should
follow the spirit of the law as well as the
letter. He says it forthrightly and without apologies, thereby imparting a sense
of dignity to the legal aspect of divorce—
a dignity which apparently the legal practitioners would sell down the river.

WILLIAM M. KEPHART
University of Pennsylvania

GLASS, D. V. (Ed.). *Introduction to
Malthus.* Pp. x, 205. New York: John
Wiley & Sons, 1953. $2.75 (London:
Watts & Company, 1953. 10s 6d).

The core of this little book consists of
three short papers which, though separately rather self-contained, form a unity
in that they are concerned, respectively,
with the background, the essence, and the
modern implications of Malthus' theory of
population. The papers are: "The Historical Context of the Essay on Population" by H. L. Beales; "Malthus and the
Limitation of Population Growth" by D.
V. Glass; and "Malthus in the Twentieth
Century" by Alan T. Peacock. These papers are followed by a classified bibliography, "A List of Books, Pamphlets, and
Articles on the Population Question, published in Britain in the period 1793 to
1880," compiled by J. A. Banks and D. V.
Glass. The list "is intended to cover the

genesis and course of the Malthusian controversy in Britain. While the list is extensive, it does not claim to be complete. . . . The period covered begins with Godwin and ends shortly after the establishment of the Malthusian League" (pp. 81–82). Perhaps partly because the bibliography closes with 1880, the paper by Peacock at the close of his article lists some citations of recent works on the economics of population.

The volume ends with reprints of two compositions by Malthus that are seldom seen. "The first is *A Summary View of the Principle of Population,* originally published in 1830, and consisting of the larger part of Malthus's article on 'Population' which appeared in the 1824 Supplement to the *Encyclopaedia Britannica. . . .* The second is Malthus's *Letter to Samuel Whitbread,*" the first edition of which was published in 1807. In this letter, "Malthus stated in clear and explicit terms his views on poor relief, views which, both his supporters and his critics agree, powerfully influenced the course of Poor Law reform and coloured the attitude to the social services in general for a century or more" (p. ix).

The purpose of this book is of modest character. "It is not the purpose of the three introductory papers to do more than serve as a stimulus to further study. The reader will not therefore find in those papers a general analysis of the development of population theory or of the relationship between theory and policy. Certain broad views of the writers are, however, evident. First, population theory cannot be discussed without reference to the nature of a particular society, for population is not itself an independent variable. Secondly, to believe, as we do, in the importance of population as a factor in economic development does not thereby involve subscribing either to Malthus's theory as a statement of long-run principles, or to his proposals for social and economic policy. Finally, if there are no grounds for complacency—especially in considering the short-run relation between population growth and economic progress in under-developed countries— . . . [neither] is there justification for hysteria" (p. x). CLYDE V. KISER
Milbank Memorial Fund

STOTT, D. H. *Saving Children from Delinquency.* Pp. x, 266. New York: Philosophical Library, 1953. $4.75.

The main concern of this essay, as the author names it, is explicitly to set forth the fact that delinquent behavior is engendered most largely by emotional disturbances and frustrations. He is a psychologist primarily interested in the personality development of children. As a Research Fellow having a grant from the Carnegie United Kingdom Trust, under which he earlier published *Delinquency and Human Nature,* his aim, he states, is to bring about greater awareness of what he himself has learned about the emotional health needs of children—awareness on the part of social workers, probation officers, and others responsible for the care of children, including parents.

Though Stott's thesis, written in terms of a common-sense approach, is sound, valuable, and to a considerable extent applicable everywhere, his outlook is narrowly insular. In repeatedly speaking of "a new science of personality psychology" he gives credit to no earlier exponents of the points he stresses and he seems unacquainted with the great volume of research and other material which, over many years, has been contributed in this country to his main theme. Then, he curiously omits even mention of the noteworthy London Institute for the Scientific Treatment of Delinquency—this perhaps because he may regard the work there as being tinged with what he scornfully terms Freudian occultism.

After chapters on generally recognized principles that should in family life and in the school and the community offer bases for the prevention of delinquency, considerable space is devoted to the treatment methods of the Approved Schools. These methods, the results, and the backgrounds of boys committed to such Schools has been the subject of a special research study by Stott, from which he has learned much that appears in his book, but he fails to give any information whatever concerning the organization of these Schools and their unique place in the British scene.

(For the sake of the American reader who is handicapped by this lack of background material, the reviewer can supply some orienting facts gained for the most part during a study of the remarkably fine Borstal system for the treatment of older youthful offenders. In Britain there are no institutions corresponding to our state correctional schools for juvenile delinquents, but, developed largely from many old small endowed institutions for the care of needy and delinquent children, there are about 150 now-designated "Approved Schools." These vary considerably in size, and the equipment of some—for example in trade training—is very good. They are all under private and often capable management, but the Home Office keeps close supervision over them and grants considerable subsidies. They receive delinquents from the ages of 8 to 15, all of whom are committed by the lay judges of juvenile courts, whether or not always for definite terms one is not sure. Nowadays, the allocation of cases is not, as formerly, left to the judge, but rather is undertaken according to ages and needs by three classification centers, of which Stott writes approvingly.)

Stott gives sound suggestions for Approved Schools' personnel regarding treatment and better understandings of emotional health needs, suggesting that the 50 to 60 per cent of satisfactory after-conduct could be greatly increased.

In an appendix he offers, as a necessary preliminary to treatment by psychiatric social workers and probation officers, criteria for diagnoses to be made by them. They really should be practicing psychologists, he says, utilizing the principles of "modern personality psychology." The diagnostic criteria are related to the primary human needs for emotional attachments and acceptance and for recognition as an individual with a status. These and the subheads of reactive tendencies are not newly formulated. Though in much of this a certain naïvete is revealed, we can believe that many a probation officer might profit by reading the book. The trained psychiatric social worker will find it rather unrewardingly elementary.

WILLIAM HEALY

Clearwater, Florida

RUCHAMES, LOUIS. *Race, Jobs, & Politics: The Story of FEPC.* Pp. xi, 255. New York: Columbia University Press, 1953. $3.75.

Fair employment practice legislation may receive its first real test if the present "recession" becomes a depression. Seven states, beginning with New York and New Jersey in 1945, followed by Massachusetts, Connecticut, Rhode Island, Washington, and Oregon, and several cities, including Minneapolis, Philadelphia, Cleveland, and Pittsburgh, have passed legislation with sanctions. To date, these state and city fair employment practice commissions have been able to assist the integration of Negroes and other racial, religious, and national origin minority peoples in a wide variety of occupations in business and industry. The commissions have relied almost entirely on private "conference, conciliation and persuasion." They have handled more than 5,000 cases, and only about five cases have reached the public hearing stage.

In his preface the author states, "The purpose of this study is to present a comprehensive picture of the effort to achieve fair employment practices through government intervention. It includes a description of the origins, history, and impact upon discrimination of the President's Committee on Fair Employment Practice, created by the late President Roosevelt in 1941; an evaluation of state and municipal fair employment practice legislation; an analysis of the relationship between fair employment practice legislation and other social problems; and the history of the movement to achieve permanent fair employment practice legislation on a national level."

Of the four aspects listed above, Ruchames has done an excellent job on the President's wartime Committee. Less than one-fourth of the book, however, deals with the three other topics. The book is weakest in its treatment of state and municipal commissions. The fifteen-page discussion of these bodies is superficial. The analysis of the last two topics is adequate.

The greatest importance of the President's Committee, as Ruchames states, "lies in the stimulus it gave to the movement for permanent FEPC legislation." By his thorough examination of the President's Committee, the author has made a signal contribution to our knowledge of the struggle of Negroes and other minorities for an equal chance. Although in recent years discrimination in employment has been reduced, it is still a tragic fact of American life that millions of Americans— Negroes, Jews, Mexican-Americans, Oriental-Americans, Puerto Ricans, American Indians, and others—are subjected to one of the worst kinds of injustice, job discrimination.

Gunnar Myrdal in *An American Dilemma* called for a great educational offensive against discrimination and segregation. During the 1940's that offensive began to gather force in employment. With so much to be done on other fronts—housing, schools, churches, and public accommodations—we can ill afford any slackening of effort on the basic job front.

FRANK S. LOESCHER
Philadelphia, Pennsylvania

HAVIGHURST, ROBERT J., and RUTH ALBRECHT. *Older People.* Pp. xvi, 415. New York: Longmans, Green and Co., 1953. $5.00.

Older People represents the first attempt to present an integrated statement of the characteristics, situations, and needs of America's older adults in what the publisher appropriately calls an introduction to social gerontology. Following an identification of the problems peculiar to older people and a chapter on attitudes toward them, the book deals with their happiness, health, economic security, work and leisure, family relations and living arrangements, friends, and participation in organized community life.

Part I, the first half, describes the older population on the basis of national data with somewhat more detailed analyses based on material collected in Prairie City, a small midwestern town which was the subject of intensive study. Part II is a more thorough presentation of Prairie City data. Instruments for measuring public opinion toward the roles of older people,

the roles played by older people, and older people's attitudes and adjustments are presented and discussed in three appendixes. Data collected by the University of Chicago's Committee on Human Development from various samples of older people with the aid of these instruments are used with good effect in both the national and local analyses.

Perhaps the principal conclusion one obtains from the book is that there is tremendous variation in society's attitudes toward older people and their proper roles and in their own interests, circumstances, and adjustments. In general, society appears to approve continued activity even to a greater extent than do older people themselves. A curious circumstance revealed by the Prairie City data is that many older people withdraw from activity even though activity and good adjustment are positively correlated.

There is also evidence that popular thinking is ambivalent or in a stage of transition with regard to such matters as family relationships and responsibilities, continuance in the work force, acceptance of financial assistance from the community, and persistence in political leadership roles.

In the chapter "A Personal and Social Philosophy of Old Age" and running through the book there is strong implication that the later years should become a period of increased personal satisfaction to be achieved largely through broadened social consciousness and citizenship responsibility, and that community attitudes and facilities must provide an environment that encourages good adjustment and continuing usefulness.

CLARK TIBBITTS
U. S. Department of Health,
Education, and Welfare

MEANS, JAMES HOWARD. *Doctors, People, and Government.* Pp. viii, 206. Boston: Little, Brown & Co., 1953. $3.50.

Among the numerous publications on social organization of medical care, Dr. Means's book stands out for two reasons. It is a statement of convictions gained in almost thirty years of experience as hospital physician, teacher of clinical medicine, and research worker. It is written for the general reader in an effort to "stimulate the formation of an enlightened public opinion" on the problems to be solved in improving and extending medical care.

Like a number of earlier writers on this subject, Dr. Means believes that the American people are entitled to the best possible medical care at the lowest price consistent with high quality and that they "are not now getting it." He advocates prepayment plans "which afford benefits directly in the form of comprehensive service," compensation of physicians by salary, and group practice of medicine; endorses "government aid to both education and research" as indispensable to continued progress; and makes a strong plea for "a threefold attack from a very broad base embodying government, private, and community elements." These are ideas which have been advanced and debated time and again ever since the publication of the classic report of the Committee on the Costs of Medical Care in 1932. How they can be translated into a practicable plan of action by evolutionary process is a question yet to be answered.

Although Dr. Means has no new suggestions to offer, he has nevertheless made a noteworthy contribution to the literature on the social and economic aspects of medicine. He has assembled widely scattered material and presented it in a clear and readable manner. He has analyzed the available facts with a discerning mind and a keen eye for basic issues. And he has stated his conclusions with sincerity and courage. His book has all the earmarks of a crusade. It is certain to be attacked by those who refuse to listen to honest opinions and criticism. It should be studied by those who are genuinely interested in the continued adaptation of medicine to social needs and uses.

FRANZ GOLDMANN
Harvard University

MILLER, PAUL A., and ASSOCIATES. *Community Health Action.* Pp. 192. East Lansing: Michigan State College Press, 1953. $3.00.

The general public is more and more concerned with problems of medical care, whether the need for the extension of health facilities or the pressing problem of how to meet the rapidly increasing cost of medical care. This little book focuses on community endeavors to develop health facilities. It deals with the attempts of citizens in small communities to acquire hospital facilities and public health services, and to a lesser degree with co-operative prepayment plans for medical care. It contains a factual report of what really happened when people in small communities co-operated to secure better medical care for themselves. Six regions of the United States were studied to compare the differences in community action.

The study was based on carefully drawn up and tested questionnaires sent to local health departments in communities of less than 7,500 population where community action had been initiated since 1940. These were followed by field visits by a research team to five carefully selected communities in different regions.

The book is about an idea—that health is, in part, an enterprise of a community. It is also a book about a process—that of employing community resources for gains in good health.

Perhaps it is not strange that there was more interest in hospitals (and more successful efforts to acquire hospitals) than in either public health services or in prepayment plans. Credit was given to the financial support from federal resources under Hill-Burton legislation. Undoubtedly this aid and stimulation has helped tremendously in the efforts to secure good hospital facilities in small communities. Businessmen in the communities studied were certainly more interested in hospitals than in public health services or prepayment plans. There were 218 successful community efforts to acquire hospitals, 51 recently organized local health departments, and evidence that 18 co-operative prepayment plans will be employed in the communities covered by the questionnaires. Prepayment plan organizations apparently required longer periods of discussion before any action was initiated.

This book gives clear evidence that to move from an idea to an accomplishment requires that some one or some group

channel community readiness into purpose-
ful action. Discussion of the variety of
sponsorship, the conflicts encountered, the
organizational methods used, public relations techniques, the ways of persuading
key people, and the contrasts between
projects should prove helpful to other
communities embarking on similar under-
takings. The findings of the study serve
to stake out some guidelines for future
planning toward major health goals in
small communities.

MARIETTA STEVENSON
School of Social Work
University of Illinois

BALLOU, RICHARD BOYD. *The Individual
and the State: The Modern Challenge
to Education.* Pp. xxviii, 305. Boston:
Beacon Press, 1953. $4.50.

The morale of American education has
been so shaken in the past half-dozen years
by concerted attacks from demagogues and
similar self-appointed saviors that it is of
special importance to have books such as
Dr. Ballou's widely read by parents, prospective teachers, and others likely to be
disturbed by the present babble of tongues.

For Dr. Ballou takes his stand squarely
on the side of the finest traditions of an
enlightened democracy, and of the crucial
role which education plays in their preservation and development. The heart of his
interpretation lies in his analysis of three
interrelated problems, all of them as old
as educational philosophy itself, yet each
just as indispensable as it ever was: the
meaning of human knowledge, the nature
of human purpose, and the components of
personality. Despite occasional concessions
to eclecticism, the author for the most part
offers a naturalistic and liberal solution to
all three problems.

His conception of knowledge opposes
absolutism and finality, and supports an
experimental approach that insists upon
the self-correcting and tentative character
of truth. His discussion of the role of
dissent, as basic to this approach, seems
unnecessarily general, however. He never
deals forthrightly with the heart of the
issue today, which is, of course, how far
and under what conditions we should allow
educators to maintain heretical political

views in both words and actions. A careful reading of the policies of, for example,
the American Civil Liberties Union and
the American Association of University
Professors might have benefited Dr. Ballou.

His insistence upon the need for strong
and clear purposes is a healthy corrective
to an overemphasis on process and method
which have been fashionable among liberal
educators. Here, again, the argument could
have been made more definite: the *kind* of
future that education ought to strive for,
especially those sociocultural dimensions
adequate to a technological and revolutionary age such as our own, is paid only
the most cursory attention. Nevertheless,
it is gratifying to find a stress upon the
future at all—a needed counterbalance to
another recent overemphasis by liberal educators upon the past and present as the
chief foci of education.

Dr. Ballou's theory of personality reveals
the strong influence of Gestalt psychology.
Three aspects are developed: the biological,
the aesthetic, and the psychical, each fused
with the other two. The only serious
question to be raised here is whether anything like enough attention has been paid
to the social pole of the personality equa-
tion. The influence of pioneers like George
Herbert Mead in social psychology or of
Alfred Kroeber in cultural anthropology
seems to be negligible in the author's
thinking.

After assessing the strengths and weaknesses of American schools over the past
fifty years, the book concludes with an
overview of "critical perspectives for educational institutions" and "the promise of the
future: insights for teachers." Here Dr.
Ballou offers many suggestions for improving both policy and program, all of them
admirable if also largely familiar, sometimes vague, and occasionally overcautious.

The title of the volume is perhaps unfortunate. A great deal of attention is
properly paid to the individual, but too
little to the theory and practice of the
modern state. Only a few words are devoted to such questions as federal aid and
control of education, to the growing pressures of organized religion upon the state
and its schools, to the conflict between
national sovereignty and world govern-

ment, or to other thorny problems of current political philosophy. The subtitle, however, is entirely relevant, and Dr. Ballou is both earnest and praiseworthy in his effort to measure up to it.

THEODORE BRAMELD

New York University

CANTOR, NATHANIEL. *The Teaching–Learning Process*. Pp. xvi, 350. New York: Dryden Press, 1953. $2.90.

The title of this book is an artifice or an expedient. It actually deals with only one method and one that is applicable to only a fraction of the curriculum and not with the teaching and learning process as the title implies. In spite of this semantic exaggeration it is a challenging and possibly an important book.

The formal requirements of the school situation tend to foster insecurity, fear, dominance, and hostility in the minds and hearts of teachers. In spite of any possible justification for these attitudes they tend to provoke similar responses from the pupils; consequently teaching and learning are often frustrated. How can the situation be changed? One partial answer is for teachers to recognize their contribution to this frustration. By using group therapy Professor Cantor has demonstrated that teachers can be led to recognize their culpability, confess their guilt, and alter to a considerable extent their attitudes and practices. Since this book is a mirror that reflects pedagogical blemishes, the careful reader can also participate in this soul-cleansing process. In fact, it is probable that teachers who read this book appreciatively will treat their pupils more humanely. By stressing feelings rather than intellect, attitudes rather than knowledge, and freedom rather than authority the author writes in the tradition of Rousseau and thus becomes also a liberator of children.

The book suffers from two faults all too common in educational writing—the implication of newness and the straw-man device. Long ago St. Augustine observed that talking, even when it eventuates in communication, is not teaching, and listening is not necessarily learning. Professor

Cantor has arrived at the same conclusion. He is not content merely to pull out the worm of truth; he accompanies the act with cackles of discovery, splutters of excitement, and cluckings for attention, admiration, and agreement.

After a pointless introduction by Professor Stephen Corey, the author takes over and wages a furious battle with "disconnected subjects," "unrelated data," "isolated facts," and other non-existent enemies. He refers to "genuine" and "actual" learning in such manner as to imply that there are two categories—"learning" and "actual learning." He draws up an indictment of twelve or fifteen counts against parents, schools, and teachers. After this arraignment it is rather easy to agree that whatever the author proposes will be an improvement over the situation as described.

Pages and pages are devoted to the meanderings, confessions, and testimonials of Lila, Mabel, Stella, Cora, Harry, Gregory, Philip, Bert, and a dozen other seminar participants. They rejoice over the absence of imposed assignments and exult in the uniqueness of their experience. "The kind of thing we are doing isn't done in colleges" (p. 8). They slowly rid themselves of self-consciousness, become accustomed to the rare atmosphere, and confess their personal and pedagogical sins. Through discussion and contemplation some of them achieve humility, patience, and high resolves, virtues that are transferred to their classrooms.

In spite of these faults and some vain repetitions of the obvious, the book is a fresh, vigorous, and helpful demonstration of one method of dealing with one segment of teaching. Stodgy, formalistic, and aggressive teachers should read this little book and consider its moral.

EDGAR B. WESLEY

Stanford University

The Teaching of the Social Sciences in the United Kingdom. Pp. 140. Paris: UNESCO, 1953. No price.

Described in its preface as a guide for prospective students and visitors to British universities, UNESCO's booklet opens with a chapter by Sir Ernest Barker on "The General Organization of Universities and of other Institutions for the Promotion of Higher Learning." This is followed by five chapters on the teaching of economics; political science; sociology, social anthropology, and social psychology; international relations; and on legal education, which is largely outside the universities. A four-page "Universities Reference Table" which is appended lists the principal curricula and degrees offered in each field in each institution.

Most American students and scholars will learn with some surprise that "only six of the [nineteen] British universities (and four of these six in Scotland) are anterior to the nineteenth century," and that nine of the nineteen are "creations, in their present form, of the twentieth century."

Since about 1920 British universities have offered advanced degrees, usually with the title of doctor of philosophy; but according to the author of the chapter on economics "first class" standing in the honours examination for the B.A. degree is still generally regarded as a stronger qualification for an academic post than possession of the Ph.D.

Sir Ernest remarks that "there has been an uneasy stirring of late . . . reflected in a demand for what is called 'synthesis' "— a revolt against traditional specialization paralleling the current American demand for "general education." However, the specialization which has characterized British higher education appears to be something different from the vocational orientation which is common in this country. For example, although a diploma in public administration is offered by many universities, we are told that this does not signify "specialist qualification." A competitor for entry into the Civil Service must stand on an equal footing with candidates whose degrees are in other fields.

A student looking for courses to meet his particular needs, interests, and capabilities will not find in this booklet the detailed information he requires; nor will a reader in search of more than superficial understanding of the organization, philosophy, and methods of British social science teaching. But both will find here a very helpful introduction to the educational institutions and curricula of another country.

ELBRIDGE SIBLEY
Social Science Research Council
Washington, D. C.

PHILOSOPHY AND RELIGION

JASPERS, KARL. *The Origin and Goal of History*. Pp. xvi, 294. New Haven: Yale University Press, 1953. $4.00.

To review in brief compass this work of compressed meaty essences by a world renowned existentialist is impossible. Apart from expressing gratitude that it has been made available with unusual speed by translation from the German original of 1949, I shall therefore confine myself to noting its general scope and content. In time it runs from the uncertain distances of prehistory to the indeterminate reach of the future. Analytically its range is from technology to deity. Its themes are simple. The first major leap of humanity toward self-consciousness and historical consciousness took place in the Axial Period. That sudden and inexplicable spring forward took place independently yet along the same lines in three different regions and cultures, which founded the great world philosophies and religions in a brief span of centuries preceding the Christian era.

Thereafter in the West a peculiar rationality and confidence in life led to a special development which, though one-sided and incomplete, produced both political liberty and science and technology. The outcome, the industrial order, places us at the beginning of the second great period, universal and unified in space as well as in concept: the factual, as well as the conceptual, unity of mankind today is inescapable. Its effective ordering is imperative. The alternatives are world conquest marked by force and fear, or world organization under federal law. Unfortunately, the corruptions of rationalism, the positivist debasement of technological insights, and the inadequacies of spiritual and humanist vision tend to sap energetic courage and to hamper the concomitant realization of a universal ordering together with liberty and human dignity. Aware of history, we tend to look backward on it, rather than to project it. We need a conscious penetration and depth whereby to unite tradition, present, and future; and, conceiving real unity, to create it. We need proper awareness of the primacy of the person, the nature of God, and the meaning of man. We need awareness also, through history, of the limits of history and of the need to overcome history, by means of the open society of questing and confident human spirits.

Such, in bare bones, are some of the theses, almost caricatured by compression, of an enormously rich and suggestive work, which casts light not only on the meaning of man's historical adventures and on issues metaphysical and ontological, but also on the root social and political problems of our day, on the meaning of the alternatives confronting us, and on the potentialities of a great human future in which the second great step in the realization of humanity may be fully taken.

THOMAS I. COOK

Johns Hopkins University

HARDING, D. W. *Social Psychology and Individual Values.* Pp. 184. London: Hutchinson's University Library, 1953; New York: Longmans, Green and Co., 1954. Text $1.80; trade $2.40.

Concisely and modestly written, this excellent and judicious English volume will, I earnestly hope, be widely read in our country. Its arguments are sustained by the admirable temper of "animated moderation." In it, all that is valuable in the skills of English moral science is lucidly brought to bear upon the vexed intricacy of the interaction between persons and the groups in which they enjoy or suffer membership. The emphasis is not merely upon mechanisms and typologies, but invariably also upon moral costs and opportunities.

The following appear to me to be timely and refreshing features of Harding's essay. A revindication of man's social nature is attempted; in the main, I think it succeeds by neat refutations of all attempts to "deduce" social behavior from nonsocial roots. Especially refreshing is the rejec-

tion of the "straw man" theory of instincts so often flogged in American texts without any espousal by Harding of the view that moral conduct is all "learned" or "imposed" upon amoral "needs." Crucial effects of childhood training and the cultural variability of socialization processes are freely recognized without drawing the unwarranted consequence that moral validity and innovating responsibility are thereby nullified. Cultural variability is correctly appreciated as settling no normative issues but as supplying only possible alternatives whose costs and compatibility upon proposed borrowing must be faced. A sensitive discussion of the services of subgroups goes far to quiet the fears inspired by those who obsessively speak of the horrors of undifferentiated mass society. With a sure hand, the frequent neglect by social scientists of the study of the conditions of creative autonomy is demonstrated. The calm discussion of the ways in which social feeling and sentiment can and must often be frustrated is balanced by an equally calm appreciation of the advantages of industrial society for the average man, advantages so often cavalierly contemned by the reforming, literary intelligentsia.

No effort is made to evade the need for social invention in the areas of status, leadership, and competition, for the obsolescence of old institutions in these areas cannot, as Harding points out, prevent the emergence of analogous problems even in the welfare state. A brilliant discussion of the meaning of normality (in many ways the best thing in the book) in terms of irrelevance of motive and coherence of personality is ethically evaluated with precision and tact. Everywhere there is perceptive notice of the required maximizing or minimizing or mediating procedures for dealing with the inevitable conflicts of two or more social desiderata.

Harding's book is both stimulating and tranquilizing for any social scientist. This reviewer would look forward to the author's comments, in a later edition, upon the related work of S. de Grazia, Parsons, Weber, the American game theorists and economists who are interested in the quantification of maximization and minimization problems of human choice, and upon the newer French cultural philosophers who often write discerning social psychology under the head of "metaphysics." As for the general American reader who has recently been acutely interested by the books of Kinsey and Riesman on related topics, Harding's book will do much to save him from the dilemma of a façade of calculation combined with moral dullness or aesthetic vision in which fantasy tends to replace rational estimates.

HENRY A. FINCH
Pennsylvania State University

WOOLF, LEONARD. *Principia Politica: A Study of Communal Psychology.* Pp. 319. New York: Harcourt, Brace & Company, 1953. $5.00.

This is the third volume of the series originally entitled *After the Deluge* and prompted by the author's shock at the First World War and his failure to understand its causes. He sought understanding in an historical analysis beginning about 1789. At the year 1848, however, his subject matter became history of which he himself was a part. Instead, therefore, of continuing the chronological method, he shifted in this volume to the analysis of ideas, mainly of freedom and authority and the corresponding modern institutions of democracy and authoritarianism.

Woolf considers the important changes in his time to be changes in the material environment, the intrusion of politics into everyday life, a marked increase in social instability, and vigorous challenges to traditional values. It is the last of these which is Woolf's special concern, with reference, of course, to the other three. He isolates and dignifies such concepts as "individual freedom and initiative, humanity, cooperation for social ends, justice and social equality, truth and reason," and shows that such values, first worked out both in theory and practice by the Greeks, are the very meaning of democracy: they define the value of democracy's free and rational individual. They also define civilization. They are values which are "there," they are objective, and they are discerned and chosen by all men free to discern and choose.

Further, "the ordinary man is right in judging implicitly that the happiness which he gets from the free enjoyment of his ordinary and private process of living, his way of life, is the thing which privately, socially and ethically has intrinsic value. And the value is in life and living . . . not in myths, nightmares and abstractions. It will be found in the thoughts and feelings of individuals, in their reactions to cricket or truth, to football or beauty, in their homes or among their friends, not in the state or churches or 'society' or work or sin or salvation."

Woolf's theme is not new, nor is it demonstrable, as he well knows. But if he is not right, so much the worse for mankind. And if he is right, it bears constant restatement. Woolf's contribution lies in his particular and very able examination of traditional Western rationalism and idealism in relation to modern irrationalisms and authoritarianisms, whether political or religious. "The values in an authoritarian society are fundamentally wrong and the longer it exists the more corrupt they become." Consequently totalitarian dictatorship is not a viable form of government for the twentieth century—the viability of democracy requires a fourth promised volume.

My one criticism is of Woolf's failure to consider the value potential in the organic type of state. Russia doubtless is an authoritarian state with a strong force component, but it is also somewhat an organic state.

LESLIE M. PAPE
Pennsylvania State University

LONG, EDWARD LEROY, JR. *Conscience and Compromise: An Approach to Protestant Casuistry.* Pp. 166. Philadelphia: Westminster Press, 1954. $3.00.

Compromise is here interpreted as a form of casuistry. The author recognizes that casuistry is in bad repute. But this disfavor is due to certain evil uses of casuistry, notably by Jesuits and pharisees. The Jesuits used casuistry to evade moral demands, says the author, while the pharisees tried to specify every requirement of the moral law down to details fitted to every situation. These mistaken practices must not blind us to the moral necessity of interpreting high ideals in such a way that they can guide conduct in concrete situations where the practical alternatives of action cannot possibly conform perfectly to the ideal. Such interpretation is what the author means by compromise or casuistry.

Mr. Long is not concerned with ethics and moral conduct in general but with Christian living. "We are interested in that dialectic of Christian experience by which a person comes to terms with the Christian imperative on the one hand and the situation in which he lives on the other" (pp. 15). The standard by which the Christian lives has not been set up by human wisdom nor discovered by the human mind, says the author. It is given by God and "cannot be . . . watered down." Yet the Christian imperative cannot be dismissed because it seems impossible of complete attainment. Men must do what they can to live by it in each concrete situation. This is the problem to be solved by casuistry.

Love is the moral imperative for the Christian, says Mr. Long, and this love is to be measured by the teaching and example of Jesus who made the neighbor's claim for love as great as the self's claim and the claim of God greater than both. "Christian love is the unstinting love of every possible neighbor for the sake of service to God, a love that seeks its only reward in the joy of faithful obedience to God. Such a love can love even those who persecute it and can rejoice even when falsely maligned by those whom it seeks to serve" (p. 47).

The reviewer is compelled to question this claim, which runs through the book. Can anyone love another out of obedience to a command, for the sake of service to God and for the joy of obedience, and not because of what is lovable in the neighbor? I have seen people trying to go through the motions of love in this manner. It did not seem good to me.

HENRY NELSON WIEMAN
Houston, Texas

SMYTH, F. HASTINGS. *Sacrifice: A Doctrinal Homily.* Pp. ix, 149. New York: Vantage Press, 1953. $2.75.

In these times many Protestant Christians are looking for ideas that will hold their faith together. They are being invited by those who work from the background of the Protestant Reformation to consider such unifying ideas as "the old and new covenants," "the apostolic preaching," and "the biblical philosophy of history."

It might be well for such Protestants to look at the volume under consideration here. Father Smyth is an Anglican with deep Catholic convictions. To him the central unifying idea of Christianity is the idea of "sacrifice," an idea which reached its culminating expression in the sacrifice of Jesus Christ, the Incarnate Son of God.

The author begins with notions associated with sacrifice in primitive religions. Everywhere men have sought "to prepare something within their world which is desirable and worthy . . . to be conveyed to their god." The god has then been believed to respond by returning something of the gift with his own life infused into it, revitalizing his worshipers for their tasks.

The Law of Israel reveals the quest for sacrifices without physical blemish; and the Prophets reveal the quest for sacrifices without moral blemish on the part of the donors of the gifts to God. But because of the Fall, all human sacrifices were infected by sin. They were never able to penetrate the barrier between man and the Holiness of God. They "bumped, as it were, against the floor of heaven and recoiled upon men to spread a sense of failure and disaster."

This impasse was broken in the fullness of time by Christ, whose unique accomplishment was that He offered himself as a sacrifice without defect or imperfection. He presented Himself deliberately for crucifixion; and the Resurrection and Ascension were the marks of His breaking through the barrier which hitherto had separated man from God.

The Church is the socially extended body of Christ upon earth, made possible by His ascended life, and His presence now at the right hand of God. The Church's vocation is to continue His sacrificial mission of taking the things of earth and offering them to God. To take the material things of this world, offer them sacrificially to God, and then use them in co-operative love for one's fellowmen becomes the vocation of the individual members of Christ's body.

Father Smyth believes that this kind of Christianity contains the only answer to the materialistic propaganda of Marxism. True Christianity to him has always been more materialistic and more communal than the Christianity of the Reformation.

JUSTIN WROE NIXON
Colgate Rochester Divinity School

LEE, E. G. *Christianity and the New Situation.* Pp. 157. Boston: The Beacon Press, 1954. $3.00.

More adept at raising issues and problems than at solving them, this is an interesting book even though not a particularly satisfying one. The author, who is the editor of *The London Inquirer*, begins his discussion by pointing out the present day coexistence of the religious and secular orders. This coexistence is the "new situation" in which the worldly world with its values lives side by side with the religious world and its values. This live-and-let-live condition contrasts with the previous situations of the Church in the world.

The subsequent discussion is the author's proposed prescription for exploiting this new situation for the benefit both of religion and of the secular order. But nowhere does the discussion really get to the crucial issues. It comes out rather as a further analysis of the general human situation made from a self-styled point of view which, valuable as it may be in its own right, is difficult to relate to any of the main streams of interpretative thought found today in either the secular or the theological thought worlds.

To be sure, the alert reader will find in this book many helpful insights and many suggestions which reflect ideas generally part of the current scene, but the reflection is unconscious rather than articulate. There is a good treatment of the relationship of meaning and historic fact, one which is essentially in agreement with contemporary theological thought. There is a similar treatment of the relationship of cultural symbol and religious reality and a valuable analysis of the breakdown of lawful standards in contemporary culture. There is a call to belief in God made on what actually are existentialist grounds. Yet nowhere is the real nature of secularism understood nor the relationship of secular to religious knowledge carefully examined, nor the respective roles of each defined.

Perhaps the failure of the author is a result of his having set for himself too prodigious a task; yet we should hope it is not an altogether impossible one. What the author calls for is at least a conversation, if not actually a rapprochement, between secular learning and religious thought. Such a union can come, of course, only if secular learning ceases to be guided by an alternative secular "faith" and listens to religion and if theological learning takes adequate account of autonomous secular knowledge and resists current efforts to make of itself an esoteric system divorced from communion with the world of earthly knowledge. This book does not see these issues as explicitly as we must in order to develop the kind of working unity for which it rightly calls.

EDWARD LEROY LONG, JR.
Blacksburg Presbyterian Church and
Virginia Polytechnic Institute

MOODY, JOSEPH N. (Ed.). *Church and Society: Catholic Social and Political Thought and Movements, 1789–1950.* Pp. 914. New York: Arts, Inc., 1953. $12.00.

As the editor explains in his introduction to this volume, its scope is "strictly limited." Its theme is "the relation of Catholics to the major secular forces of the period 1789–1950." Two of these forces are explicitly considered, namely, the modern secularized state and the modern economic system. The treatment is organized on a geographical basis. The editor and a dozen collaborating authors discuss their theme, first in relation to the papacy, and then in relation to seven specific countries or groups of countries. As the title promises, both Catholic thought and Catholic movements are included. Official statements by popes and bishops, declarations by various groups and organizations, as well as the writings of individual authors, serve as sources for the exposition of Catholic social thinking. Most of the sections of the book end with an appendix of documents, giving excerpts from important sources. Many significant social movements are considered, but it is interesting to note that Catholic labor movements are singled out for particular emphasis. The editor is a professional historian, and most of his collaborators have followed his lead in placing their material in its relevant historical perspective.

Collaborative works usually show a certain unevenness of treatment, and this one is no exception. Edgar Alexander's section on Germany runs to 259 pages; with its own introduction and table of contents, it amounts to a book within a book. In contrast, Spain has only ten pages, and Italy receives only incidental treatment. Belgium is included, but Holland is not. There is a section on Latin America, but nothing on Canada. Within each section, too, there are noticeable differences of treatment. Thus the section on the United States is confined to a discussion of the Catholic contribution to the American labor movement, whereas the section on Germany is very full and comprehensive. The book as a whole is thus selective, rather than inclusive. Within its limits, however, it is an excellent book. Its authors are competent, and they write clearly and interestingly. They try to be objective, and they make no obvious effort to gloss over the more unflattering aspects of Catholic social history. Probably most readers, like the present reviewer, will disagree with their interpretations here and there. Yet all in all they do succeed in showing how the Catholic attitude toward the modern economic and political situation has crystallized since the time of the French Revolution; and this, after all, was the original purpose of the book.

PAUL HANLY FURFEY
Catholic University of America

NOBLE, VERNON. *The Life & Times of George Fox: The Man in Leather Breeches.* Pp. 298. New York: Philosophical Library, 1953. $6.00.

The Society of Friends celebrated its Tercentenary in North England in the summer of 1952. As a part of that celebration, Vernon Noble was asked by the British Broadcasting Company to prepare a dramatic presentation for the air. In the course of duty his interest was sufficiently captured by the founder of the Society of Friends, George Fox, that he went further in his studies and has produced this interesting and valuable addition to Quaker literature. It has the great advantage of being written by someone who is not an adherent of the Society and who comes to the topic with a freshness but with an active interest.

As a good dramatist, he sets his stage well for his characters. The divine right of kings was being challenged. Who was the true head of the church—the King, or the Archbishop of Canterbury, or the Pope, or the Presbyterians, or the Baptists, or the Independents? Besides these "respectable" groups there were such extremists as the Grindletonians, the Anabaptists, the Ranters, the Muggletonians, the Behemists, the Manifestarians, the Sabbatarians, the Millenaries, the Traskites, the Fifth Monarchy Men, and others.

It was into this political and religious climate that the Society of Friends was born. The founder, George Fox, was the son of a workman, himself a craftsman, who lived largely by the work of his own hands. Naturally introspective as a growing lad, he consulted with his priest but got most unsatisfactory advice. The use of physic was proposed; marriage was suggested. All the while he himself was reading the New Testament and comparing the teachings of Jesus with what he saw going on among churchgoers about him, and feeling deeply disturbed. The author places emphasis on the young convert's reaction to religious and political practices about him more than he does on the influences of the mystical sects whose teachings and literature he knew. Jakob Boehme, Hans Denck, Brethren of the Common Lot, and Theologia Germanica— all products of earlier mystical sects—have been shown, especially by Rufus M. Jones, to have deeply influenced George Fox. He was a part of the mystical strain of Christianity in contrast to the institutional and clerical emphasis of the church.

In the face of bitter persecution for heresies, the sect Fox founded increased to nearly 60,000 during his short life and played no small part in the struggle for religious liberty in England and America.

CLARENCE E. PICKETT
Philadelphia, Pennsylvania

COMMONWEALTH OF NATIONS

LE BOURDAIS, D. M. *Nation of the North: Canada since Confederation.* Pp. x, 270. New York: Frederick A. Praeger, 1954. $5.00.

After disposing of the history of the preceding century in two introductory chapters, Mr. Le Bourdais divides the period subsequent to confederation into three eras, each dominated, in a way that would be impossible in the United States, by an outstanding statesman. Macdonald, Laurier, and King had, all three, a steadfast determination not to allow any consideration whatever of principle or emotion to deflect them from policies essential to the preservation of Canadian unity. This story of their success is, therefore, concerned in the main with political history.

Mr. Le Bourdais, journalist rather than trained historian, presents a compact, yet comprehensive and readable narrative. It includes many shrewd appreciations of the *dramatis personae* of Canadian life. The author has his likes and dislikes. Particularly in respect of the later years, when the account becomes more and more journalistic, he writes as an observer "indebted only in a very general way to other writers."

The proportions are good, though slightly distorted by interest in boundary disputes and distaste for problems of constitutional law. It is too optimistic to say that "nothing has been set down which cannot be documented." For instance, the people whom the author describes as Hindus were excluded by Orders-in-Council, sometimes of doubtful validity, and not by an amendment to the Immigration Act.

Omissions are inevitable, yet some are curious: the Chinese Immigration Act stopping immigration from China; the part played by Mr. Meighen in persuading

Britain to terminate the Japanese alliance; Canadian insistence that the Statute of Westminster should not enable Canada to amend its constitution; the Rowell-Sirois Commission; wartime friendliness with Russia and its eclipse in the spy trials.

Mr. Le Bourdais is to be congratulated on his sincerity, his fairness to others, and the frankness with which he discloses his predilections. But the sum of these qualities is not objectivity. Is it entirely consistent to reproach Great Britain for a timid appraisal of the risks of hard bargaining with the United States over boundary questions in 1783, 1814, and 1903, or with Russia in 1825, and then to disparage imperialism and approve Canadian reluctance to support its quarrels in other parts of the Empire? Is it quite fair to contend that conscription was unnecessary and unwise in Canada in World War I because the United States, which did conscript, could produce the necessary soldiers?

H. F. ANGUS
University of British Columbia

FALARDEAU, JEAN C. (Ed.). *Essais sur le Québec contemporain.* Pp. 260. Quebec: Les Presses Universitaires Laval, 1953. No price. 6 chapters in French, 6 in English.

In June 1952, a group of scholars met for two days at the University of Laval to discuss *"les répercussions sociales de l'industrialisation dans la province de Québec."* This volume represents the results of their deliberations. As in all such collections of papers by different authors, there is no central theme running throughout this book, yet it nevertheless has a surprising sense of unity which reflects the careful planning of the original symposium and the skillful bringing together in the final chapter by the editor of the main conclusions of the various papers.

Beginning with the chapter on the history of industrial development, the papers seek, perhaps more than anything else, to show how what is happening today in the province of Quebec is related to the general economic development of the North American continent. The insularity of the society of French Canada is recognized, but an attempt is made to see it in perspective. Industrialization is not something wholly antipathetic to the social values and institutions of the local society, a development which inevitably must result in destroying all that is precious in the culture of the French Canadian. As Falardeau shows in his chapter on Changing Social Structures, industrial growth is resulting in far-reaching adjustments in the social institutions of French Canada, but the local society is not a passive partner in the changes which are taking place. Commerce and industry have roots deep in the history of Quebec, and, if modern large-scale industrial organization is making demands upon the society very different from the kind made by earlier, simpler forms of industry, the problem of the society of French Canada is not essentially different from that of the society of North America as a whole.

Space makes impossible any examination in detail of the views set forward in the various papers. This reviewer could readily find some things to quarrel with. But any such criticism would be intended to give emphasis to the general excellence of this volume. It marks a distinct contribution to an understanding of one important sector of our North American society. One can look forward to further detailed studies of problems which here could only be discussed in general terms.

S. D. CLARK

University of Toronto

CAIGER, GEORGE (Ed.). *The Australian Way of Life.* Pp. xvi, 158. New York: Columbia University Press, 1954. $3.00.

This volume is one of the first of a series being prepared under the auspices of the International Studies Conference, at the request and with the financial assistance of UNESCO (the United Nations Educational, Scientific and Cultural Organization). It includes discussions of the Australian family, educational systems, political, economic, and religious institutions, and foreign policy. Unfortunately, however, these separate contributions do not add up to the Australian way of life.

Though one can hardly agree with Sir Frederic Eggleston that Bernard O'Dowd is the greatest of Australian poets, this is a minor criticism of a contribution which starts the book at a level of brilliance it never again reaches. There are insights, as at the end of Mr. Henderson's article on religion, but we must first travel through much detail. There is Professor Alexander's competent essay on foreign policy; but these do not redeem the whole. The bare bones of factual outlines are there, but little interpretation.

However, this lack of depth may be a reflection of the subject. Some of her writers, particularly the poets, have explored the spiritual dimensions of Australian life, but the average Australian does not share their curiosity. In the social realm there is a similar aimlessness. And growth is stunted by the hardened conflicts of labor and management.

At the conclusion of his description of economic institutions, the late Professor Wood poses the question whether the Australian-managed economy will achieve "ever-normal and equalized material rewards." It is interesting to note that the objectives are not greater productivity and a higher standard of living, but normalcy and equality. And he goes on to assert that Australian economic institutions are now almost adequate for these purposes.

But others in Australia, notably Sir Douglas Copland and Sir Frederic Eggleston, have different opinions. They have asserted that administration has not proved equal to the tasks laid upon it. They deplore the failure of the state to devise methods of administration involving a devolution of authority. And they note that where adequate delegation was made, as in some of the earlier Victorian State enterprises, pressure groups have been successful in breaking down their independence and, by asserting parliamentary control, have inhibited enterprise.

Yet, there is encouragement in Mr. Henderson's comment that "the nation is aching and agonizing for social reconstruction." Habitual attitudes must, he says, be broken by "heroic personalities trying to create a new situation out of apparently nothing." It is time, he concludes, to turn both outwards and inwards, to wider social loyalties and greater spiritual depth, from the cultivation of gregariousness to the development of personality. This is a new theme for Australia, and its appearance may be a sign of a transformation of ideals —from a level mediocrity to a varied maturity.

EDWARD LITTLEJOHN
Detroit, Michigan

BAILEY, SYDNEY D. (Ed.). *The Future of the House of Lords. A symposium.* Pp. 180. London: Hansard Society, 1954. 10/6d.

This is an extremely lucid and valuable little book which will be especially welcomed by teachers of political science. Its comparative survey of second chambers, its descriptions of the opening of Parliament, of the giving of the Royal Assent to legislation, of prorogation, of procedure and standing orders, and of the place and function of the House of Lords both as the second chamber of the legislature and as the highest court of appeal for the United Kingdom of Great Britain and Northern Ireland are models of brevity, clarity, and precision. This book also has the merit of printing in its appendix the forms of parliamentary writs in current use, the Parliament Acts of 1911 and 1949, and excerpts from committee and conference reports on House of Lords reform since 1908, which are not easily available elsewhere.

The editor admits in his introduction that his distinguished group of contributors (Lord Campion, Sir Albert Napier, Lord Pettrick-Lawrence, F. W. Lascelles, Walter Elliott, P. C. Gordon-Walker, Viscount Hinchingbrooke, and the Archbishop of York) have not, for the most part, written about the future of the House of Lords, and it is indeed true that many readers would wish to learn more of various schemes of reform and their prospects of future adoption. Nevertheless, perhaps the best lesson to be derived from the perusal of these essays is an appreciation of the possibilities of the adaptation of this institution to varying conditions from age to age within its ancient framework of hereditary privilege and ecclesiastical preferment. The saving grace of today's House is that most of its less competent members stay at home and its ecclesiastical members do not attempt to be politicians. In a truly "reformed" House, every member, "representing" something either by election or appointment, would, whatever his abilities, be in constant attendance, and, if any ecclesiastics were admitted, they could hardly express the Christian conscience on the great problems of the day with the force, authority, and dignity which historic tradition gives to the present bench of bishops.

There are many delightful and useful tidbits of information scattered through this symposium. Temporal peers may sit in but not speak from the bishops' benches on the right of the Throne, a rule once forgotten by the late Lord Birkenhead much to the amusement of his friends. We learn how the determined opponents of the admission of women to the House successfully marshalled their forces to prevent that issue from being considered separately on its merits apart from the broader issues of general reform. We are reminded that the Lord Chancellor's sole function as presiding officer is to put the question from the Woolsack, that he may speak like any other peer (but not from the Woolsack), that he has a vote but no casting vote, and that the House keeps itself in order by virtue of its Order of 1626 on "asperity of speech" in which "all personal, sharp, or taxing speeches" are to be "forborn." These and other usages dear to the House testify to the force of tradition. Nevertheless there is hope; the house has just changed its ancient rule by which a tie vote meant failure of any motion, whether framed positively or negatively. Henceforth, no proposal for the rejection or amendment of a bill shall be agreed to unless there is a majority in favor of such rejection or amendment (p. 91).

HOLDEN FURBER
University of Pennsylvania

RICHMOND, HERBERT. *The Navy as an Instrument of Policy, 1558–1727.* Edited by E. A. Hughes. Pp. 404. New York: Cambridge University Press, 1953. $12.00.

·In the field of maritime history the work of Admiral Mahan has exerted an influence far beyond the borders of his own country and the span of his own lifetime. The impact of Admiral Richmond's learning on the world is less evident and significant; for one thing his books were a slower and less inspired creation and lacked, moreover, the drama of a new approach. Nevertheless, the lessons Richmond taught on the meaning of sea power based on materials not always available to Mahan are certain to outlive the battleships in which he served. Richmond was that rare kind of seaman (and a distinguished seaman) who obtained, by hard service in library and record office, that disciplined judgment and technical skill which go to make up scholarship.

The Navy as an Instrument of Policy is a straight narrative history (a large part of which has been told before) of military operations at sea, designed to reveal the development of the Royal Navy as a decisive instrument of national power. Military strength forms the main thread of the argument, and the battle is vital to the theme; but the author strengthens his conclusions by emphasizing the contributions of politics, diplomacy, and land operations to the final result. The narrative begins in the days of Henry VII, when the Navy's primary function was to assure safe passage of the Army to France. The Elizabethan Age provided a period of gradual education; statesmen were slow to grasp the importance of controlling sea communications in the interests of national security. Drake's organized offensive against the Spanish overseas Empire illustrated how naval warfare might affect the result of a struggle on the European continent; and on the basis of Mediterranean operations during the period of the early Stuarts, Richmond contends that English statesmen were beginning to perceive, dimly perhaps, that the Navy was "an instrument capable of affecting the course of European affairs by means other than warfare upon commerce" (pp. 67–68). He confesses that his evidence "is as a straw only, showing a breath of wind in a new direction . . . ," and he might well have argued that the statesmen of the Commonwealth were the first to glimpse, during the First Dutch War, the full implication of mastery of the sea. In his view, however,

only during the Second Dutch War (following the Restoration) did the elimination of the main enemy fighting force become the basic naval strategy of England. Yet, he admits that the English fleet was "expressly specified" as Tromp's primary objective in 1652 (pp. 105, 110), and Tromp's basic principle of smashing the enemy's main fleet certainly inspired not only an equally offensive spirit, but a strategy of concentration on the part of the English.

There is a brief and cogent discussion of the rise of French naval power under Richelieu and Colbert. France, because of the demands of her army, possessed at sea neither the audacity nor the recuperative powers of Holland, and although the material loss inflicted at La Hogue in 1692 was not greater than that suffered by the English at Beachy Head (1690), France abandoned finally her policy of command of the sea and proposed henceforth not to use her navy to crush the enemy's fighting forces but to employ it in squadrons against English commerce.

Full and accurate footnote references were never Admiral Richmond's forte, and an editor's eye, however eagle-like, could hardly discover every error or omission of name, place, and date, of which there are many. (One of the more obvious slips is the repeated spelling of Captain Vetch as 'Ketch'—pp. 353–354.) Both the list of sources and the index are flimsy, but only a very ill-conditioned reviewer could refuse to rejoice at the posthumous publication of the last work of a master.

GERALD S. GRAHAM
University of London

MABILEAU, ALBERT. *Le Parti libéral dans le système constitutionnel britannique.* Pp. viii, 354. Paris: Librairie Armand Colin, 1953. 1,100 fr. No. 47, "Cahiers de la Fondation Nationale des Sciences Politiques."

The author, a French admirer of British democracy, tolerance, and individualism, has analyzed the decline of the Liberal party which was long their chief exponent. The first section of his book, which covers the years 1906–1922, dates the decline from the great electoral triumph of 1906, because it also brought the Labour party to the House of Commons. Then war, for which liberalism was ill-adapted, led to feuds and a disastrous split; it left the Liberal party no longer on equal terms with the Conservative and even surpassed by a new rival for whose rise to power it was in large part responsible. It had prepared the way for the Labour party's progress by the Parliament Act of 1911 which breached a fortress of tradition; the payment of members of Parliament and the permission for a political levy on trade unionists made Labour financially viable; the democratization of the suffrage in 1918 provided the potential Labour voters. It spoke well for British honor that a party should abandon political advantages in the national interest, but in the two-party system, as the Liberals discovered in 1922, there was place for only one party of movement. The author contends that these social and constitutional facts, rather than the Lloyd George–Asquith feud, destroyed the Liberals as a party of government. He does not speculate as to what might have happened had they possessed a Sir Robert Peel to provide the leadership and program demanded by the situation.

The last two sections cover thirty years of steady decline. The constitution operated against the Liberals, for power bypassed the center party and alternated between the greater rivals to right and left, while the system of single-member constituencies caused it, the minor party, to suffer disproportionate loss in the electoral returns. The Labour party's wisdom in refusing alliances was vindicated by the fate of the Liberals, whose unequal bargains and coalitions with the Conservatives resulted in heavy losses. Since the election of 1935 the party has been only a "party of opinion" with a handful of members in the Commons and a steadily weakening organization in the country. In dying, however, the Liberal party enjoys a triumph of a kind; the author examines the major parties and, except for a bit of class consciousness here and there, he concludes that both are "liberal," and that, since liberalism has become a national tradition, the party has lost its reason for being.

CARL F. BRAND

Stanford University

COLLIER, ADAM. *The Crofting Problem.* Pp. xv, 191. New York: Cambridge University Press, 1954. $5.00.

The crofting problem of the Highlands and Islands of Scotland is that of a sparse, old subsistence agricultural culture of 130,000 souls situated on the fringe of a heavily populated industrial country. The terrain is, by the general standard of Britain, poor and forbidding, and social organization is not developed to the urban level of much of Britain. Public administration which originates from urban conditions is largely incompatible with the needs of a relatively primitive, communalistic culture. The clan system broke down in the eighteenth century; no other effective leadership has taken its place. Rapidly rising population up to 1840 (and in the Outer Hebrides till 1911) caused many problems and much hardship. The subsequent rapid fall in population has brought its own problems, social and economic. Standards of husbandry and diet have deteriorated; the desire for a higher standard of living is strengthening. That is the crofting problem.

Adam Collier was a Scottish economist with a reflective, sociological turn of mind. The present book, full of meat and admirably edited by A. K. Cairncross, represents Collier's much interrupted attempt to investigate the problem with thoroughness and in a scientific spirit. He was killed in a mountaineering accident in 1945, so he neither finished his book nor satisfied his own curiosity.

Collier's chapters on the New Economic Revolution, the Role of the State, the Regional Income of the Highlands in pre-War Years, will stand for a long time. Nobody else has reached such authentic quality in these fields; his chapter on the Decline of Population is accurate as a summary but has been superseded by a much more detailed study by R. S. Barclay in the West Highland Survey, 1944–50, a body which the reviewer directed and in which it was hoped that Collier would have participated in major fashion. *West Highland Survey* is at present in the press; although it represents a much fuller investigation than Collier, as a one-man outfit, was able to tackle, it is complementary to this remarkable work of one man and will not in any way swamp it.

The chapter What can be Done? shows Collier's lively interest and curiosity in fields which were not his. If he was perhaps a little too optimistic and believing, the fault should not be set against him, for he died a young man. Collier in due course would probably have brought anthropology into the study of economic problems of marginal peoples. Here, he was just feeling his way, and the reviewer feels sure that experience would have caused him to modify his thoughts. The strength of the book is in Collier's firm grasp of refractory data.

The map appearing as an end paper is inadequate to the needs of the book.

F. FRASER DARLING
Malmesbury, Wiltshire, England

SLAVIC COUNTRIES

FLORINSKY, MICHAEL T. *Russia: A History and an Interpretation.* 2 vols. Pp. xvii, 628, xxiv; viii, 629–1511, xxv–lxxvi. New York: The Macmillan Company, 1953. $15.00.

There have been a sufficient number of bad short histories of Russia in recent years for one to be grateful when a good one appears. Professor Florinsky has spent many years on the study of Russia's history since he left the country in which he grew up. He writes from personal understanding of both Russia and the Western World, as well as from knowledge of written sources in both Russian and Western languages. This book deserves a wider circulation than its high price is likely to give it, not only in America but in Europe and Asia too.

At a time when historical studies are more overshadowed by political passions than they have ever been since serious historical study has existed, the author has bravely maintained scientific standards of honesty. This is even more necessary in the history of Russia than of other countries. The attempt to project the controversies of the present into the recent and distant past has, in the case of Russian

history, assumed almost Orwellian proportions, and this, it must unfortunately be admitted, not only behind the Iron Curtain. We have the increasing chauvinism of Soviet historical writing—for which it is important to blame not the historians themselves but the Party bosses who force them to write as the Party wishes. We have the view, so popular with some German and Germanophile writers, that there is throughout Russian history a continuous tradition of aggressiveness, different in kind from the aggressiveness of other nations, and that in the present century the two World Wars were the work of Pan-Slavism. We have the view, widespread in Western Europe, that the Russians are barbarians "incapable of valuing liberty." Whether put forward by sorrowing liberals, pitying the poor irredeemable savages, or by haters of liberalism, contemptuous of "the masses" in Russia or elsewhere, the result is similar. Professor Florinsky does not subscribe to these or kindred theories. At the same time he escapes another snare for historians, that of Olympian superiority to moral considerations. Moral factors are as relevant to history as other factors. In writing for example of Ivan the Terrible, Professor Florinsky shows himself fully aware of this. That it should be necessary to commend Professor Florinsky for observing standards which a few decades ago were taken for granted by western historians is distressing. But the commendation is deserved.

This long book is readable and clear. Most book reviewers nowadays assume that the reading public is not capable of absorbing more than about one fact in every fifty pages, and that any author who fails to provide his readers with prefabricated ideas on every page is failing to do his duty. Whether the majority of readers really have such tastes, the present reviewer doubts. And if they do, then authors should ignore them. Readers of Professor Florinsky will have to use their mental facilities, but the task is made as little arduous as is compatible with scholarship.

The relative emphasis to be given to different periods and different factors in the history of a great nation is a matter on which few can ever agree. Professor Florinsky has made his own choice, and his long experience and knowledge entitle him to respect. Some may argue that the Middle Ages do not receive enough space. The first five hundred of Russia's thousand years of history get only one tenth of the space. But as the interest of the author and of most of his readers is likely to be in more recent periods, this can be excused. More serious is the very scanty treatment given to the Orthodox Church and to religious dissent and sects, especially in the last centuries. Among the factors which moulded the Russian intelligentsia, from which in time the radical and revolutionary leaderships emerged, surely the Orthodox cultural tradition was one of the strongest. Another gap is the problem of nationalities. In the nineteenth century about half (at the 1897 census 56 per cent) of the population of the Empire were non-Russians. The national movements of the subject peoples receive only a few scattered pages or paragraphs, and the social and political problems within the non-Russian areas are barely mentioned at all. On the other hand some subjects seem to be treated at too great length. The Eastern Crisis of 1875–1878 has 40 pages. It has been exhaustively discussed in the books of Sumner, R. W. Seton-Watson, Rupp, and others, and Mr. Florinsky has no essential new contribution to make. The First World War, up to the February Revolution, gets 70 pages. This too has been fully treated before, not least in Mr. Florinsky's own work *The End of the Russian Empire.*

These are however matters of opinion. They are criticisms of an admirable enterprise, which can be warmly recommended to those who wish to learn some Russian history.

HUGH SETON-WATSON
University of London

STEVENS, LESLIE C. *Russian Assignment.* Pp. xv, 568. Boston: Little, Brown & Company, 1953. $5.75.

This large and delightfully written book by Vice Admiral Stevens, our Naval Attaché for a little more than two years in Moscow when the cold war was just be-

ginning, is an important addition to the fast growing body of literature on the Soviet Union. Written in the form of memoirs, the book is replete with keen notes and observations on the multiple phases of Soviet life: literature, theater, play-writing, book-printing, museums, moving pictures, fishing and flying, living conditions, concentration camps, women's lot as laborers, and of course the life of the diplomatic corps in that "golden land" held firmly "in the golden hands of the people."

At the present juncture of world affairs, however, the book is most important in its graphic, almost daily account of the tests and trials of our embassy personnel. The author could have had, as subtitle, the "decline and fall of our prestige in the Soviet Union," for while arresting and informative details of many significant events are given, yet all through it this disturbing fact, the sudden—almost catastrophic—fall of our prestige overshadows all else. For instance, the embassy quarters are leased on an annual basis, "but the renewal of leases is always a time of troubles." Every Russian employee of the embassy is required to report back to his government "on everything he can regarding foreigners—their interests, their characters and abilities, and what they are up to" (p. 20). When an official of the embassy is jailed and we try to elicit information about the case, the Soviet Foreign Office "would not even discuss the case with Durbrow [our Minister-Counselor]" (p. 98). The embassy has difficulties in importing supplies needed there. And when permits for importing are issued, then the imported articles are held in customs house. Next the embassy is informed "that everything which has been piling up for the last eight or nine months must be cleared out within ten days or it will be confiscated" (p. 253).

General Carter, our Military Attaché, and several assistant attachés were watching some planes practicing. Red Air Force officers told them that they could not do that. Our attachés were told to accompany them to the airfield headquarters; General Carter refused, and Red officers kept his diplomatic card. Subsequently it took several weeks to make an appointment with proper officials "to discuss the matter" (p. 350). At the end of a year in Moscow Durbrow told the author that 1937 was regarded as the worst year for foreigners in Russia, but that this past year (1948) "far surpasses it." Finally, in mid-1949 when his tour of duty was over the author could say (in Lermontov's words):

"Farewell to you, unwashed Russia,
Land of slaves, and land of lords."

The Admiral knew the Russian language and made very effective use of it at all times. His book, along with General Deane's *Strange Alliance* (1947), and General Smith's *My Three Years in Moscow* (1949), should have a distinct and deserving place on any selected list of books on the subject.

A. O. SARKISSIAN
The Library of Congress

DEUTSCHER, ISAAC. *The Prophet Armed: Trotsky, 1879–1921.* Pp. xii, 540. New York: Oxford University Press, 1954. $6.00.

The Prophet Armed is the third in an ambitious series of biographies of Stalin, Trotsky, and Lenin, undertaken by Isaac Deutscher. One book on Stalin's life and one on the effect of Stalin's death made clear the framework of Mr. Deutscher's political thought and approach to his three protagonists. The present volume tells the story of Stalin's great opponent, from Trotsky's birth in 1879 to his apogee in 1921, when, as the powerful Commissar of War, he had just brought the Civil War to a triumphant end. A sequel, *The Prophet Unarmed*, will recount Trotsky's downfall and murder. A biography of Lenin will complete the trilogy.

In the two Stalin books Mr. Deutscher made clear his belief that the Russian Revolutions of 1917, particularly the Bolshevik seizure of power, were historically necessary and progressive. His criticisms of Joseph Stalin were made in general human terms ("cruel," "despotic," "barbarous"), but these methods were "forced" upon the dictator by the backwardness of his land and people. Only "totalitarian

methods" could have industrialized, modernized, and collectivized Russia's industry and agriculture. Moreover, by his methods, Stalin so raised the level of Russia's economy and mass culture that, by the time of his death, he had made Stalinist totalitarianism historically unnecessary and outlived.

In *The Prophet Armed* Mr. Deutscher no longer argues but takes for granted the soundness of this approach. The minority seizure of power in November 1917, of which Trotsky is the hero, was only the "necessary" sequel to the overthrow of czarism in March. All those who thought otherwise—liberals, democrats, and democratic and agrarian socialists—are treated by the author as wrongheaded, base, perverse, historically myopic. The author is aware of the fact that minority seizure of power and holding of power against the will of even the peasants and workers made totalitarianism inevitable, but both the seizure of power and the totalitarian methods are "justified" by history. Only the "utopian illusions" of Lenin and Trotsky that they might use democratic methods or be bailed out of their dilemma by a revolution in the West are subject to Deutscher's criticism, since the hindsight, which comes from having lived longer, enables him to see that these were illusions. But it is these illusions which make Trotsky into a tragic hero.

Despite this unpromising moral and intellectual framework, *The Prophet Armed* is a moving and compassionate book. The cold reluctance of Deutscher's apologetics for Stalin are forced upon him by the dogmatics of his political position. But his life of Trotsky is done *con amore*. The writing takes on deeper dimensions. The research is more thorough, his protagonist more self-revealing. The tragedy of the conflict between the protagonist's dreams and the consequences of his deeds is deeply felt and ably presented. Only at the very end does the cold apologist return to hint that "when next the Prophet Unarmed is contemplated, the question will arise whether a strong element of victory was not concealed in his very defeat."

BERTRAM D. WOLFE
Brooklyn, New York

WARTH, ROBERT D. *The Allies and the Russian Revolution from the Fall of the Monarchy to the Peace of Brest-Litovsk.* Pp. vii, 294. Durham, N. C.: Duke University Press, 1954. $4.50.

This book produces a rather strange effect of simultaneous remoteness and nearness of the events it relates. Basically there is little that this book adds to what we already know; yet I consider the work a valuable contribution, for it deals with a subject that deserves continuous repetition since public memory is short lived. The subject of this work is the year of turmoil in Russia, March 1917 to March 1918, and the diplomatic fiasco which the Allies suffered in their futile endeavor to tame the events. Since western diplomacy can easily repeat the same follies it becomes absolutely necessary to refresh periodically our memory by reading a book such as this one.

To illustrate, take, for instance, the ill-famed "forgotten peace" of Brest-Litovsk. The subject has been adequately covered by J. W. Wheeler-Bennett. Warth devotes to the same subject a graphic chapter; it contains no startling revelation, yet by reading the account one regains useful insights into Communist tactics and policies. The overtones of the cold war are easily detected on every page.

The book serves other purposes: it reminds of the importance of understanding the peoples to whom we appeal through means such as the Voice of America, urging them to follow our way of life. It revives the memory of Allied blundering policies during the fateful four months following the November revolution, due to the abysmal lack of intelligent information. One cannot escape a sense of remorse at the staring poverty of imagination which the world press or the Allied leaders had demonstrated in evaluating the November revolution. Leading newspapers presented the occurrence as a "freakish happenstance which would be remedied when 'reason' and 'sanity' reasserted their rightful heritage in the affairs of man." According to the press the revolution was carried out by "fanatics and anarchists" led by Lenin whose real name was Zederbaum, his comrades a mere handful of German-Jews in the service of the Kaiser. One magazine traced the entire affair to the "cabals of Geneva and Stockholm."

Gullible Allied statesemen were ready to buy sensational documents that presented the crudest forgeries, such as the Sission documents. It is a source of melancholy thought that a student of history such as President Woodrow Wilson should have been easily persuaded by Mr. Creel to accept the obvious forgeries as authentic sources. Dr. Warth aptly cites an "impeccably anti-Bolshevik commentator" who summarized the episode as a reminder that a state of war and a paralysis of critical faculties seem to march together.

Dr. Warth's book should be the desk copy of our policy-forming officials. It should be read by many Americans who seek to form intelligent political opinion concerning many of our crucial problems emanating from the presumably "passing incident" that occurred on November 7, 1917, when the scum came to triumph, as the *Journal des débats* had reported the November Revolution.

ANATOLE G. MAZOUR
Stanford University

CAROE, OLAF. *Soviet Empire: The Turks of Central Asia and Stalinism.* Pp. x, 300. New York: St. Martin's Press, 1953. $5.00.

Soviet Empire, which deals with a very important part of Asia and of the Soviet Union, is composed of three essential parts. The first two treat of "The Muslim Period and the Tsars" and the transition, 1917–1924, from czarist control to Soviet domination of Central Asia. Part III, which is of special interest, deals with the contemporary scene, under the general title of "Soviet Pressures." It is concerned with the problems of Nationalism and the Soviet Colonial Empire, Russianization, Collectivization and the Suppression of Nomadism, Industrialization and Public Works, Soviet Central Asia during World War II, and the general problem of Deviationism.

Sir Olaf's volume is not a product of personal experience or of profound original research, but it is an important volume because the author has brought conveniently together into a single volume a great deal of material from the appropriate and available sources—what should be known about this highly important area. Readers will find of special interest, perhaps, his remarks about the problem of self-determination and the so-called "higher right of the dictatorship of the proletariat" in Communist jargon on this subject. But the other material in the volume is of equal interest—such as that on industrialization in Central Asia and the economic exploitation of the Turki and other elements in the area. Moreover, the chapter on World War II is of particular interest because of evident attitudes in the area, as reflected by the surrender of thousands of Red Army soldiers from Central Asia and the Nazi attempt to exploit these people.

Sir Olaf's volume is not only very well written, it is also well documented, with an extended bibliography of materials from Russian, Soviet, and Turkish sources, among others, for assistance in further research and study on this problem. In addition, there are four black and white maps which indicate the physical characteristics of the area, trace the Russian advance in Central Asia, mark the railway network, and demonstrate the linguistic distribution. It may well be hoped that the volume will have a wide reading.

HARRY N. HOWARD
Arlington, Virginia

LEITES, NATHAN. *A Study of Bolshevism.* Pp. 639. Glencoe, Ill.: Free Press. $6.50.

Four years ago Dr. Nathan Leites of the Rand Corporation published a slim volume entitled *The Operational Code of the Politburo* (McGraw-Hill, 1951), as part of a study undertaken for the United States Air Force. He sought, in the tradition of Machiavelli, to reduce to general precepts the political strategy and tactics of the power-holders in the Kremlin. The effort was unsuccessful. Machiavelli as a practical diplomat was concerned with what Princes do. Leites, as an ivory-tower scholar, is concerned with what they say and write, with little regard to their acts or to the arena of their deeds. In a futile

effort to reduce Communist ideology to Communist strategy, he failed to illumine either.

In the present volume, compiled with Gargantuan labor and suffocating documentation, he has expanded his earlier effort into a mountain which brings forth not even a mouse. His titles are intriguing: "Push to the Limit," "If Pays to Be Rude," "Avoid Adventures," "The Denial of Accidents," "The Irrelevance of Truth," "The Danger of Vagueness," (37 "dangers" are listed), "The Profits of Pressure," "The Legitimacy of Retreat." Each section consists of small quotations strung together from Communist classics and Russian literature, embellished with brief comments.

The result, alas, is wholly unreadable, uninformative, and stupifying. Every quotation is quoted out of context and is therefore meaningless, save to the reader who happens to know the context. The resulting jumble is utterly lacking in analytical or predictive value. This is a pity, for Dr. Leites is an earnest and intelligent researcher, trying seriously to grapple with an important problem of analysis and interpretation. It is a sad commentary on the "social science" here exemplified that its practitioners cannot distinguish between ideologies and policies and succeed in reducing both to nonsense and boredom. The effort is comparable to explaining the politics of the medieval Papacy by verses from the New Testament, the diplomacy of the Ottoman Empire by excerpts from the Koran, or the military strategy of Napoleon by quotations from Rousseau and Voltaire. This effort "to portray the spirit of the Bolshevik elite" portrays nothing, reveals nothing of any spirit save pedantry, and tells us nothing of value about the Bolshevik elite. Fortunately, it is not representative of contemporary social science but only its *reductio ad absurdum.*

FREDERICK L. SCHUMAN
Williams College

GERSON, LOUIS L. *Woodrow Wilson and the Rebirth of Poland, 1914–1920: A Study in the Influence on American Policy of Minority Groups of Foreign*

Origin. Pp. xi, 166. New Haven: Yale University Press, 1953. $4.00.

The subtitle of Mr. Gerson's book promised a study of the little-known effects of activities of pressure groups on American foreign policy. It is too bad that this promise was not fulfilled. Of the 137 pages of text only six (pages 60–66) deal *stricto sensu* with the subject. The documentation of this part is limited to a few items from the Wilson archives and some earlier published documents. The rich material buried in the archives and libraries of the Polish National Alliance of America and the Polish Roman Catholic Union of America (both in Chicago) still remain untapped. Any serious study of this subject should not omit them. This omission makes Mr. Gerson's presentation incomplete: the work shows, in a quite fragmentary manner, the reaction of Wilson to the political pressure of the American Poles without indicating the strength of this pressure, the efforts behind it, and the means through which it was applied. Thus, an evaluation of causes and effects, of successes and failures of this pressure is impossible.

This, however, is a comparatively minor deficiency in Mr. Gerson's book. The bulk of the volume deals with a characterization of the large group of Americans of Polish descent and the internal politics of this group during World War I, and with the diplomatic history concerning Poland during this period. The author has brought out the crucial role of President Wilson and Colonel House in these events. He has also attempted to deal with the intricate problem of changing political orientations among the Poles in their homeland. Lack of knowledge and understanding of this subject, evident from erroneous use of source materials, is responsible for the essential errors in Mr. Greson's book. For instance, by confounding "a certain Doctor Paderewski," mentioned in Pilsudski's writings as a representative of the National Democratic Party, with Ignace Paderewski, Mr. Gerson produced an utter confusion in the presentation of events (pp. 105–106). A more careful study of the sources would have prevented the confusion and the erroneous conclusions. Out of this mistake arose another: Mr. Gerson in several instances presents Ignace Paderewski as a representative and mouthpiece of the National Democratic Party, to which the artist and prime minister never belonged.

Another error exemplifying negligent research and lack of knowledge of contemporary Austro-Polish developments is not less damaging to the book: on page 20 Mr. Gerson quotes an excerpt of a document annexed to the Bilinski diaries. The document in the Bilinski book contains a printing error: its date, instead of 1918, should read 1916. The text of the document is preceded by a reference to the page of the diary where it is discussed. A better knowledge of Austro-Polish developments and a glance into the text of the diary would have saved Mr. Gerson from repeating the error and from drawing an incorrect conclusion. Another Bilinski document was also quoted without consultation of the diary and led to additional false conclusions (p. 20).

Mr. Gerson had a good idea in replacing the usual bibliography of the subject by a *Bibliographical Essay* (pp. 140–146). However, the books discussed prove that he did not exhaust the available sources. The books on the American Poles are limited to a few monographs in the English language and a single book in Polish. The other pertinent writings in the Polish language, especially those originating during, and dealing with, the years 1914–1919, are completely ignored. He writes, "There are no works which deal exclusively with the Polish problem at the Peace Conference." Then he goes on to quote, "for the Polish point of view," a single volume by Smogorzewski. He is unaware of the existence of a four-volume collection of Polish documents relating to the Conference (*Acts and Documents concerning Poland at the Paris Peace Conference*, Paris, 1920–26, in Polish, parts in French and English) and an excellent book by the Secretary General of the Polish Delegation, Stanislaw Kutrzeba (*The Congress, the Treaty, and Poland,* Warsaw, 1919, 198 p., in Polish). There exist still other titles referring to special questions at the Conference.

Lack of space makes it impossible to bring out here all the errors, misinterpretations, and other shortcomings of this volume. It is amazing to see how these deficiencies could have been overlooked in a Ph.D. dissertation and unobserved by the publishers of a serious historical series.

W. S. SWORAKOWSKI
Stanford University

VUCINICH, WAYNE S. *Serbia Between East and West: The Events of 1903–1908.* Pp. x, 304. Stanford, Calif.: Stanford University Press, 1954. $4.75.

Through the use of the primary (also secondary) sources in several languages, especially the much neglected Serbian materials, Professor Vucinich has given us a significant picture of domestic political changes in Serbia during the period under study, and the impact these changes had upon the foreign policies of the Great Powers of Europe as well as upon Serbia's own foreign relations. This book, the product of years of painstaking effort and meticulous scholarship, represents an important contribution to historical research in a field which has received little attention in the English-speaking world.

From this careful study it is evident that the Serbian revolution of 1903 was not primarily a struggle between two dynasties. The conspiracy to assassinate the King and Queen and the plan to restore the Karageorgevich dynasty did not originate in Karageorgevich circles. Popular discontent with and hostility toward King Alexander Obrenovich was widespread, especially after his marriage to Queen Draga, a widow and a commoner, when not "a single general was willing to accept the post of war minister in the cabinet." His father had admonished Alexander that should he go through with his marriage plans "the dynasty could never recover from it," adding that he would be "the first to cheer the Government which shall drive you from the country, after such a folly on your part."

Professor Vucinich devotes considerable space to a discussion of Serbian politics and government in the period following the assassination of the childless Obrenovich royal couple and the coming to the throne of Peter I in 1903. From these pages there emerges a picture of a developing democratic parliamentary order, characterized by freedom, dynamic political parties, and a constitutional monarch. This is a long forgotten or little appreciated fact. By comparison with Tito's tyranny, the Serbia of King Peter I was a model democracy.

Also, in these pages one finds a detailed account of the "divide and rule" policy practiced in the Balkans by the Great Powers. Although Austro-Hungary seems to have excelled in this respect, Russia apparently was not far behind. And some British actions are not free from censure. In treating this whole problem, the author presents significant data on a number of Balkan questions (e.g., Macedonia), together with a great deal of historical information on the developing Great Power controversy in the Balkans during the years preceding the period with which this work is primarily concerned.

Last, but not least, note should be made of the first-rate documentation which characterizes this book, together with its excellent bibliography and the detailed index.

Experts may disagree with some of the author's conclusions, but they cannot deny that this work is a real contribution to historical scholarship.

ALEX N. DRAGNICH
Vanderbilt University

KOUSOULAS, DIMITRIOS G. *The Price of Freedom: Greece in World Affairs, 1939–1953.* Pp. xi, 210. Syracuse, N. Y.: Syracuse University Press, 1953. $4.00.

Those who love the cradle of democracy should read this small book—a concise and good summary of the foreign and domestic affairs of modern Greece during the most trying period of her existence. Dimitrios Kousoulas, who in his teen age lived in Greece and took part in the underground fight against the German invaders as well as in the civil war against the Communists, unfolds a terrible story of international rivalries focused around his beloved native Greece as well as around the other

Balkan countries—Albania, Bulgaria, Rumania, Turkey, and Yugoslavia.

For a hundred years after her emancipation from Turkish domination in 1830 Greece was plagued by internal dissensions and international complications. Not unlike her own mythical Sisyphus, this modern nation with ancient glory was rolling a huge stone—the "Great Idea" of the restoration of the medieval Byzantine Empire under the scepter of the modern Greek King—up to the top of the steep hill, and always it escaped her hands and rolled down to the bottom again. At last, in 1930, her great statesman, Eleutherios Venizelos, had the courage to scrap the whole idea; and, after five centuries of enmity, Greece and Turkey became friends as well as neighbors.

During those later years the Greek people had to cope with a domestic military dictatorship, the unsuccessful Italian fascist aggression, the successful subjugation by the German Panzer Divisions, the ravishes of the various underground resistance groups that fought with frightful brutality less against the German invaders and more against one another for supremacy, and, after its liberation from the German occupation, a bloody civil war between the Communists and the anti-Communists.

Yet, thanks to the Churchill-Stalin "Percentage Agreement"—providing that Great Britain should have 100 per cent predominance in Greece while the Soviet Union should have only 75 per cent predominance in Bulgaria, Hungary, and Rumania—the subsequent intervention of the United Nations Organization, and especially the Truman Doctrine and American help, Greece managed to preserve her independence.

Disclaiming the intent to express sympathy for authoritarian regimes of any form, the author momentarily departs from his remarkable impartiality in order to praise the dictatorial regime of General Metaxas, which was established by royal decrees abolishing the political parties, dissolving Parliament, and suspending the constitutional Bill of Rights—although admitting at the same time that the said Regime of August Fourth (1936) was unpopular with the liberty-loving Greek people and that the apparent weaknesses of that regime virtually invited the Italian fascist aggression.

Moreover, the author has no sympathy for Greece's two-party system, the Liberal party (Venizelists) and the Populist party (Monarchists). He blames the latter for having undermined the efforts of the great Venizelos to bring about the realization of the "Great Idea" and the Liberals for having discredited the great prestige of the Greek Government-in-Exile during the German occupation and thus frustrated the Greek territorial claims at the peace parleys.

It seems to this reviewer (a United States citizen of Bulgarian origin, who had in his teens a gruesome experience with such "Balkan politics") that these charges are baseless and unfair, for the author himself gives plenty of evidence that the reaching for the Byzantine rainbow in the 'twenties as well as the achievement of the Greek territorial claims in the 'forties was beyond Greek control. History teaches us that a state, great or small, invites disaster if it is divided against itself into two factions, "patriots" and "traitors."

THEODORE I. GESHKOFF

New York City

WESTERN CONTINENTAL EUROPE

PÖLNITZ, GÖTZ FREIHERR VON. *Fugger und Hanse: Ein hundertjähriges Ringen um Ostsee und Nordsee.* Pp. xiv, 236. Tübingen, Germany: J. C. B. Mohr (Paul Siebeck), 1953. DM 11,50.

Professor Götz von Pölnitz, whose brilliant two-volume biography of *Jakob Fugger* was reviewed in these pages in January 1953, gives in his present book the first authoritative and comprehensive survey of the Fuggers' struggle with the Hansa over economic power in its economic-political "Raum" in northern and eastern Europe. The conflict lasted from 1500 to 1600 and spanned the most interesting years in the life of Jacob the Rich (d. 1525), the time of Anton Fugger (d. 1560), his nephew, and of the latter's successors in "the epoch of the decline" of both the Fugger company and the Hansa.

Von Pölnitz devotes roughly half of the 132 pages of text to Jacob Fugger's successful penetration of the Hanseatic sphere of interest. The principal elements of this early phase of the Fugger-Hansa struggle he outlined in the biography of his hero. But in this work the author has fully expanded the account on the basis of the rich material contained in the "Sources and Explanations" of the second volume of the biography and of other hitherto unpublished documents. For the period after 1525, covered in the second half of the text, von Pölnitz has drawn on materials which he and his collaborators have so far collected for "the history of Anton Fugger." As the author makes clear, the entrance of the Fuggers into the maritime trade in the Baltic and the North seas was part of the sixteenth century expansion and of wide encroachment of southern German business firms upon the Hanseatic sphere of influence. But when Jacob Fugger first penetrated this area the classic period of the Hansa's power was long past; it now concentrated entirely upon preserving the position already achieved. The Fuggers were the most successful challengers of this monopoly; through their extensive system of "political finance" they secured the support of the Church and the ruling princes against the Hansa, which enabled them to invade its "powerful economic strongholds."

Fugger und Hanse is not purely economic history, however; it is essentially a study of the political and cultural development of sixteenth-century Germany and Europe. And the Fugger-Hansa conflict is discussed within the context of this development which embraced the great religious schism (Reformation), the rise of national states and economies, the virtual disintegration of the Holy Roman Empire, and the shift of the center of political power to the Atlantic coast, particularly to England. Von Pölnitz shows with admirable lucidity how these momentous changes in the political and cultural structure of Europe perniciously affected both the Hansa and Fugger interests, ending in the simultaneous descent of the contestants.

As a study of Fugger business activities in a specific area, the volume makes a welcome addition to the meager number of such investigations and thus enriches the literature on this famous Augsburg family and its unique business organization. Moreover, it is an important contribution to the history of Europe in the sixteenth century. The book contains 19 pages of bibliographical notes, an 8-page index of persons and places, and 17 selected documents which are published here for the first time. Also, it should be noted that the work appears in a new series of studies on the Fuggers which is being edited by Professor von Pölnitz.

ARTHUR LEON HORNIKER
Washington, D. C.

SCHACHT, HJALMAR. *76 Jahre meines Lebens.* Pp. 692. Bad Wörishofen: Kindler & Schiermeyer Verlag, 1953. DM 19,80.

76 years of my life is Schacht's autobiography, first published in *Revue*, a German illustrated weekly. The book's easy style, the often jovial approach of its author, and the many illustrations are sure to make it popular. Schacht portrays himself as an earthy type, a rugged individualist who was always ready to speak his mind.

Great intelligence, an excellent education, and ambition were the main ingredients which enabled Schacht to rise. He is at his best when he illustrates his exceptional ability to reduce economic principles to simplicity and when he describes his readiness to apply them to the root of the problem despite the opposition of special interests. His roles as currency administrator at the end of the inflation and later as Reichsbank President gave him ample opportunity for a stalwart course.

Schacht entered politics as one of the founders of the left-of-center German Democratic Party. Later, his more conservative and nationalistic views led him to oppose the Weimar Government's policy of fulfillment. Schacht resigned from the Reichsbank presidency in 1930, primarily because of his opposition to the payment of reparations and the unsound policy of foreign loans received by German communities, but returned to his old post under Hitler. He was acquitted at Nuremberg, and then held by German courts awaiting his denazification. Now the head of his own banking firm, Schacht is again the financial expert called upon by many governments.

Schacht's historic role will continue to arouse moral judgments which differ from his own. He was quite obviously attracted to Hitler. An ambivalence of loyalty and opposition to the Führer expresses itself long after he recognized Hitler's duplicity. This cleverly written book could not convince this reviewer that Schacht was not rationalizing his participation in the Hitler cabinet when he says that he tried to exert a moderating influence from within. Surely Schacht must have realized that his role in Hitler's government not only furnished it with the financial know-how it needed, but also lent it prestige and a camouflage of moderation. To Schacht's credit, it should be noted that he was on occasion outspoken and courageous in his opposition to Nazism and Hitler's war policy. His attitude finally led to his detention in concentration camp after the July 1944 coup. But he does not explain convincingly why he continued as a Minister without Portfolio when dismissed from his old post in 1939. Similarly, in 1937, when every minister received the Nazi Golden Party Emblem, he accepted that decoration, though he had by that time set his course against Nazi rowdyism. Another minister (Eltz v. Rübenach) returned his and resigned.

Toward the end the reader is estranged by Schacht's dependence on the *argumentum ad hominem*, his distortion, and vindictiveness against those whose views of his part in Hitler's rise differ from his own. For those who cannot so glibly dismiss the disastrous consequences of the Hitler holocaust over Europe, Schacht's oblique treatment of the basic moral problem makes this book another in a series of sad commentaries on our time.

ERIC H. BOEHM

Historical Abstracts
Vienna, Austria

WHEELER-BENNETT, JOHN W. *The Nemesis of Power: The German Army in Politics 1918–1945.* Pp. xvi, 829. New York: St. Martin's Press (distributors for Macmillan & Co., London), 1953. $12.00.

If you have time to read only one book on modern Germany and on the Germans, it should be this one. Not only is it a brilliantly written history and one of the best examples of Wheeler-Bennett's scholarship; it is also a guidebook for those who are seriously interested in preventing another German rearmament from once again losing for us the battle of the peace. A center of interest in this dramatic story of twenty-seven years is the German mind, and particularly the German military mind. The unraveling of the plot should aid considerably in answering the perplexing question: Why have the Germans contributed so greatly to western civilization and at the same time destroyed so much? How could the nation which produced Heine and Goethe and Hindenburg tolerate the "beasts of Buchenwald"?

The story begins—and ends—with unconditional surrender. For those who have lived intimately with the Germany of this period, dramatic moments such as the ill-fated Kapp *putsch*, the blood-purge of 1934, and the poorly planned attempt by certain army leaders on Hitler's life, in 1944, stand out as high spots in the tragedy. But even the narrative and analysis of less dramatic events and more plodding years are made alive. One of the most historically decisive periods is objectively analyzed in the chapter on the von Seeckt period, during the early Weimar regime. For when Kaiser Wilhelm II and his entourage crossed the Dutch border in 1918, the Army which had owed loyalty to its Emperor alone lost its political independence. Into this vacuum came General von Seeckt, who successfully avoided parliamentary control over the Army by the Socialists and who instead made of the Army the most powerful political factor in Ebert's and Stresemann's Republic. The first political step led to the second as von Schleicher, the intriguer, followed von Seeckt and as the Army looked on Hitler as one who could convert the worker from socialism to nationalism. But it was not long, as we see, before the Army's use of Hitler became Hitler's use of the Army.

The conclusion is inevitable that the German army aided greatly in the ascendancy of Hitler and the National Socialists and in the revival of German nationalism. Some of the parallels in the periods after 1918 and 1945 are ominous, and Wheeler-Bennett's masterpiece is required reading on current problems.

RALPH F. BISCHOFF
New York University

ANDERS, WLADYSLAW. *Hitler's Defeat in Russia.* Pp. xviii, 267. Chicago: Henry Regnery Company, 1953. $4.00.

Excellently introduced by an expert on Germany and the Second World War, Colonel (retired) Truman Smith (former United States Military Attaché to Berlin and German specialist in the Intelligence Division of the War Department General Staff from 1941 till 1945), this book shows thorough experience of modern strategy in the broadest sense of the word. Colonel Smith states, obviously with justification, that "General Anders attempts to answer in the present analytical study of the Russo-German war a number of questions and succeeds to the full, with amazing clarity and unanswerable logic." Based on seven maps, Hitler's military blunders and the German army's defeats are recalled. But far beyond being a technical book, it gives the hitherto unwritten story of an astounding misuse of military possibilities by stupid and criminal *psychological,* that is, *political* warfare. The chapters "German Policy in the Occupied Territories of USSR," "Treatment of Soviet Prisoners and of the Population of the USSR plus Partisan Warfare" disclose facts, which the writer of this review, then a German soldier in Russia, witnessed or learned about after the war.

Anybody interested in modern mass psychology should not miss the chapter about the "Eastern Volunteer Formations on the German Side," which amounted to more than 800,000 soldiers. He will agree with the author's remark, as does the present reviewer (who met these soldiers in action): "This movement was one of the strongest idealogical movements known in modern history." The picture is rounded by indispensable chapters on "Western War Supplies to the USSR," "the Results of Western Bombing of the Reich," and "the Tying up of German Forces in the West." The Conclusion gives the author's excellent estimate of the "Communist Strength in 1953" and a Bibliography, in which anybody who wants to deal further with this grim story will find, if not all, at any rate the most recent and important foreign publications.

It seems probable that Wladyslaw Anders will be counted one day among the great names of a free and independent Poland, as are Thaddeus Kosciuszko and Prince Jozef Anton Poniatowski. The reviewer would like to express the feeling that this sober study may one day be regarded as one of the beginnings on which Polish-German understanding can be rebuilt. This seems possible only in the very climate the book offers, rising above the understandable hatred resulting from the events of 1939—the unjustified German aggression toward Poland and the treatment of the vanquished Poles. The consequences of these days are still with us.

AXEL VON DEM BUSSCHE
Bonn am Rhein, Germany

GRAYSON, CARY TRAVERS, JR. *Austria's International Position, 1938–1953: The Re-establishment of an Independent Austria.* Pp. xvi, 317. Geneva: Librairie E. Droz, 1953. 15 fr. s.

The chief "text" for *Austria's International Position, 1938–1953* by Dr. Cary Travers Grayson, Jr., is from the Moscow Declaration of November 1, 1943, by the British, Soviet, and American governments: "Austria, the first free country to fall a victim to Hitlerite aggression, shall be liberated from German domination." The book is divided into five Parts: "The Austrian Question (1918–1938)"; "Under German Rule (1938–1945)"; "Allied Planning (1943–1945)"; "Under Allied Occupation (1945–1947)"; and "Victim of Cold War (1947–1953)." Except for certain passages, the first two Parts are mediocre or worse. It is inexcusable, for example, to include inaccurate dates (pp. 10, three instances; 24); to present an incorrect account of the immediate origins of the civil war of 1934 (p. 10); and to characterize L. Kunschak as a member of the "peasant wing" of his political party (p. 43).

On the other hand, because of the continuing efforts to distort and falsify historical fact, Grayson merits warm thanks for reminding his readers of the record of three former Chancellors of Austria. Seipel's influence was "anti-democratic"; he "encouraged" the Fascist *Heimwehr* (p. 7). Dollfuss "crushed socialism and democracy [and] created a Catholic-Fascist Austria" (p. 11). Schuschnigg helped Seipel and Dollfuss and became a "virtual dictator" (p. 11). Possibly of equal importance is the author's suggestion that if Schuschnigg had decided to fight Hitler in March 1938, "even if only on a small scale . . . Austria, at the end of the war, would have been" considered and treated like other fully liberated and "guilt-free" nations (p. 34).

The remaining Parts of Grayson's study were read by this reviewer with steadily rising enthusiasm. Any reader with interest in international affairs will find a compact account of many aspects of them —why Austrian resistance to Hitler has "been generally undervalued" (p. 50); why the decision at Potsdam to include German assets in eastern Austria among Russia's share of such assets was "absolutely contradictory" to the intent of the Moscow Declaration to re-establish an Austria "capable of finding economic security" (pp. 68, 79); why the author concludes that "Both East and West seem to realize that the complete collapse of Allied cooperation in Vienna would signify world collapse" (p. 172); and others. Specialists will particularly appreciate the reproduction of documents (pp. 180–300). Most praiseworthy of all are the author's masterly analysis of the diabolical cleverness and the brutal cynicism with which the Union of Soviet Socialist Republics utilized the Potsdam decision about "German assets," and his explanation of the justness of the Austrians' plea to be "liberated from their liberators."

CHARLES A. GULICK
University of California
Berkeley

SCHLESINGER, RUDOLF: *Central European Democracy and Its Background.* Pp. xiv, 402. New York: Grove Press, 1954. $5.00.

The title of Mr. Schlesinger's competent work is not quite appropriate. Mr. Schlesinger's discussion of *Central European Democracy and Its Background* is essentially limited to- but two of the several democratic forces that influenced democratic trends in Germany, Austria, and Czechoslovakia during the period under consideration, 1848 to 1938.

The book, learned as is the presentation, makes sorry reading. In spite of the libertarian spirit of the Central European political movements in the nineteenth century and of the high-powered ideological theses of German socialist theoreticians, the social structure of the Central European countries, with the exception of Czechoslovakia, escaped their impact and remained basically unchanged. The "sham constitutionalism," to use the author's term, as applied after World War I, was nothing more than an artificial framework without economic and social content.

The embryonic labor movements of Imperial Germany and Austro-Hungary battled against lack of political consciousness, for they themselves lacked political orientation; they were confused about their aims and uncertain of their place in a semi-industrial society. Ideological struggle among socialist leaders corroded the unity of the labor movement, and the trade unions were torn between the wings of radicals and mild reformists; thus, disunited and uncertain, they had to face the strong hand of the well-entrenched combination of Prussian junkers, the military and the industrial magnates in Berlin, and the ultraconservatives in Vienna. In the Austro-Hungarian Empire the labor movement suffered, in addition, from the contradictory national interests of its various components. When the pacifist convictions of the labor movement in Central Europe were put to the crucial test in 1914, they broke down for the cheap price of mere existence. Slogans on "the defense of the Fatherland" compromised its ideological standing and brought further confusion into the ranks of the socialist parties.

The story of impotence in leadership continued in the interwar period, now in the new setting of postwar opportunities. Ground between the millstones of right-wing and fascist political parties on one side and the unscrupulous agitation of Communists on the other, the democratic labor movement once again lost sense of direction. When the events in Germany in the early 1930's and in Austria in 1933–34 led to the inevitable clash between the forces of democracy and fascism, once again the democratic labor movement and organization succumbed.

Mr. Schlesinger concludes the story with the catastrophe of 1938, when the last democratic stronghold, Czechoslovakia, fell, though in this case the blame was clearly to be found not on the scene of home politics, but in Western Europe. If his study had included recent developments, he would undoubtedly have to add to the aggravating list of socialist failures the fact that the socialist parties in all countries west of Germany offered little resistance to the Communist onslaught and were completely absorbed by the Communist parties.

Thus we see confirmed once again, as we have during the past fifty years of the socialist movement, their perplexing inability to face history's challenge with adequate means.

It would be, however, one-sided to overlook the achievements of democracy in Central Europe, as it would be unfair to put the responsibility for its failures on any single party or movement. The international factors appear to have played a considerable, if not decisive, role in the debacle, though Mr. Schlesinger does not give them a proper place. A full appreciation of his book presupposes knowledge of the complex political, economic, social, and national picture of Central Europe as it developed during the last hundred years. As a specialized study, sometimes narrowly

conceived, it is to be highly appreciated for its research value in the little known area and even less known problem.

JOSEF KORBEL
University of Denver

OTHER COUNTRIES

WILGUS, A. CURTIS (Ed.). *The Caribbean: Contemporary Trends.* Pp. xxvi, 292. Gainesville: University of Florida Press, 1953. $4.00.

Not counting the Foreword and Introduction, this volume consists of twenty papers delivered at a conference in December 1952 under the joint auspices of the University of Florida and the Alcoa Steamship Company. These are grouped in five parts: economic 5, social 2, literary and artistic 4, political and diplomatic 4, and peace and security 5. A break-down of authorship shows the following distribution: by nationality, 7 Latin America, 1 Great Britain, 12 United States; by occupation, 12 government, 5 academic, 3 business. No one could complain that the coverage is not broad.

The character of the volume is better indicated by the word "trends" in the title than by the word "problems" which is stressed in the Foreword and occurs several times in the table of contents. When problems are discussed, the discussion is unilateral and long-range; little attention is paid to controversies that have been making the headlines, and there is no argument over pros and cons. For example, the index has only three entries under "Communism"; the only direct reference to the central problem of Guatemala, which has been shaping up rapidly since 1944, is an unexplained allusion to "the Guatemalan Government's harassment of the United Fruit Company" (p. 48); and the main discussion of United States investment and enterprise in the Caribbean area occurs in a paper characterized by its descriptions of Venezuela as "a shining example of the open door to private enterprise and foreign capital development" and of the record of the

United States oil companies in Venezuela as "spotless" (pp. 50, 51).

While all twenty papers have something of interest and value for readers curious about the Caribbean area, the two groups that average highest in caloric content are those dealing with economic and social trends, for most of these come to grips with specific long-range problems of the Caribbean area. Particularly noteworthy in this respect are the papers by Miron Burgin on economic development, Gilberto Loyo and Raúl Ortiz Mena on underdeveloped areas, Carl C. Taylor on land, and Francis Violich on urbanization in Venezuela. Papers of the same type in other groups are those by Fernando Rivera on the civil service and John and Mavis Biesanz on "Uncle Sam on the Isthmus of Panama—a Diplomatic Case History." Other papers which are of high quality do not possess this specific appeal in the same degree. For example, the excellent paper by R. S. Boggs on Caribbean ballads deals with the period of the Spanish conquest, and the papers by Harold Davis on political philosophies and by John C. Dreier, Luis Quintanilla, and Misael Pastrana on peace and security deal primarily with themes of general inter-American or Latin American interest and secondarily with the Caribbean area.

ARTHUR P. WHITAKER
University of Pennsylvania

KOTB, SAYED. *Social Justice in Islam.* Translated from the Arabic by John B. Hardie. Pp. viii, 298. Washington, D. C.: American Council of Learned Societies (Near Eastern Translation Program, No. 1), 1953. $3.00 paper; $4.00 cloth.

The highly useful project inaugurated by this volume promises to do yeoman service for our knowledge of the modern Near East. The language barrier here is particularly formidable. Neither the best informed Western works nor even a prolonged stay in the area itself can put students who do not know Near Eastern languages in touch with the true thinking and feeling of the people and acquaint them with the "grass-roots," attitudes of Near Easterners toward their problems. Now,

this series of translations sponsored by the ACLS can be expected to form a ready source of information on all shades of Near East intellectual activity.

Political and sociological scholarship in the Near East is frankly polemical and intensely partisan. Sayed Kotb's book, first published about 1945, is no exception. It is no objective exposition of the subject of social justice in Islam from the historical or sociological point of view. The author's purpose is to disprove frequent accusations that the contemporary Muslim religious authorities are opposed to social progress. At the same time, he intends to show that within its traditional framework Islam provides the basis for a perfect solution of all the social problems of the day.

Specifically, Sayed Kotb is concerned with the chronic problem of the grossly uneven distribution of wealth in his native Egypt. His solution, constituting the controversial nub of the work, is an attempt to prove that, according to Muslim legal thinking, "the property belongs to the society and is merely administered by an individual, so that when his stewardship is over the property reverts to its original ownership, the community (p. 106)." In this connection, the author emphasizes his opposition to Communism. He maintains that Islam is a force to be reckoned with in the political struggle between Communism and the West. In his opinion, the ideologies of both Communism and the West are identical, and both groups are united in their materialism. The spiritualistic ideology of Islam, he believes, remains the only possible alternative.

Throughout the book and its many interesting discussions, the Western reader will constantly ask himself two mutually related questions: Is this Islam? And is this kind of thinking influential in the Near East? In connection with these questions, it should be kept in mind that the recognized sources of Muslim law and theology are immensely rich in all kinds of sociological reflections and, in addition, are rarely satisfied with presenting just one side of any given problem. Sayed Kotb uses those sources skilfully and reinterprets them against a background that is more strongly molded by the ideals of the French Revolution than any other more recent current. His Islam never existed before the nineteenth century, but it is a legitimate reinterpretation of a great religion which is very much alive. Its influence may be minimized by many Near Easterners who have an entirely secular outlook. However, Sayed Kotb's ideas represent a definite continuity with the past and speak the language which the majority of Near East people still understand best. Thus, their actual and potential appeal must not be underestimated by anybody interested in the present and future of the Near East.

FRANZ ROSENTHAL
University of Pennsylvania

OTHER BOOKS

ABBOTT, [SISTER] M. MARTINA. *A City Parish Grows and Changes.* Pp. vii, 87. Washington, D. C.: Catholic University of America Press, [c. 1953]. $3.00.

ALLEN, CLARK LEE, JAMES M. BUCHANAN, and MARSHALL R. COLBERG. *Prices, Income, and Public Policy: The ABC's of Economics.* Pp. x, 418. New York: McGraw-Hill Book Company, 1954. $5.00.

ARNOLD, MAGDA B., and JOHN A. GASSON. *The Human Person: An Approach to an Integral Theory of Personality.* Pp. x, 593. New York: Ronald Press Company, 1954. $5.75.

AWAD, MAHMOUD M. *A Challenge to the Arabs.* Pp. 120. New York: Pageant Press, 1954. $2.50.

BAILEY, SIDNEY. *Naissance de nouvelles démocraties: Introduction et développement des institutions parlementaires das les pays de l'Asie du Sud et dans les territoires coloniaux.* Two reports. Pp. xiii, 200. Paris: Librairie Armand Colin, 1953. 650 fr.

BARBER, JOSEPH (Ed). *Diplomacy and the Communist Challenge: A Report on the Views of Leading Citizens in Twenty-five Cities.* Pp. vi, 46. New York: Council on Foreign Relations, 1954. 50 cents.

BATTISTINI, LAWRENCE H. *Japan and America: From Earliest Times to the Present.* Pp. x, 198. New York: John Day Company, 1954. $3.00.

BERTELSEN, AAGE. *October '43.* Translated by Milly Lindholm and Willy Agtby, with a

Foreword by Sholem Asch. Pp. x, 246. New York: G. P. Putnam's Sons, 1954. $3.00.

BLACKFORD, L. MINOR. *Mine Eyes Have Seen the Glory: The Story of a Virginia Lady, Mary Berkeley Minor Blackford, 1802–1896. Who Taught Her Sons to Hate Slavery and to Love the Union.* Pp. xxii, 293. Cambridge, Mass.: Harvard University Press, 1954. $5.00.

BOCK, EDWIN A. *Fifty Years of Technical Assistance: Some Administrative Experiences of U. S. Voluntary Agencies.* Pp. x, 65. Chicago: Public Administration Clearing House, 1954. $1.50.

BORTON, HUGH, SERGE ELISSEEFF, WILLIAM W. LOCKWOOD, and JOHN C. PELZEL (Compilers). *A Selected List of Books and Articles on Japan in English, French and German.* Pp. xiv, 272. Rev. and enlarged ed. Cambridge, Mass.: Harvard University Press (for the Harvard-Yenching Institute), 1954. $5.00.

BOSSARD, JAMES H. S. *The Sociology of Child Development.* Pp. xii, 788. Rev. ed. New York: Harper & Brothers, 1954. $6.00.

BRAINARD, HARRY G. *International Economics and Public Policy.* Pp. xiii, 706. New York: Henry Holt and Company, 1954. $6.00.

BRECHT, ARNOLD. *The Political Philosophy of Arnold Brecht: "That the dignity of man is to be respected in every individual."* Edited by Morris D. Forkosch. Pp. 178. New York: Exposition Press, 1954. No price.

BROOKES, EDGAR H. *South Africa in a Changing World.* Pp. v, 151. New York: Oxford University Press, 1954. $3.00.

BURNS, JAMES MACGREGOR, and JACK WALTER PELTASON. *Government by the People: The Dynamics of American National Government.* Pp. xxiii, 905. 2d ed. New York: Prentice-Hall, 1954. $8.65.

CALVOCORESSI, PETER, assisted by KONSTANZE ISEPP. *Survey of International Affairs 1951.* Pp. xii, 505. New York: Oxford University Press (for Royal Institute of International Affairs), 1954. $10.50.

CHINOY, ELY. *Sociological Perspective: Basic Concepts and Their Application.* Pp. vi, 58. Garden City, N. Y.: Doubleday & Company, 1954. 85 cents.

COLLINS, JAMES. *A History of Modern European Philosophy.* Pp. x, 854. Milwaukee, Wis.: Bruce Publishing Company, 1954. $9.75.

COMMISSION ON FOREIGN ECONOMIC POLICY. *Staff Papers Presented to the Commission on Foreign Economic Policy.* Pp. xv, 531.

Washington, D. C.: U. S. Superintendent of Documents, 1954. $1.75.

CREAMER, DANIEL, assisted by MARTIN BERNSTEIN. *Capital and Output Trends in Manufacturing Industries, 1880–1948.* Studies in Capital Formation and Financing, Occasional Paper No. 41. Pp. viii, 104. New York: National Bureau of Economic Research, 1954. $1.50.

CROMBIE, A. C. *Augustine to Galileo: The History of Science A.D. 400–1650.* Pp. xv, 436. Cambridge, Mass.: Harvard University Press, 1953. $8.00.

DAVIS, PEARCE, and GERALD J. MATCHETT. *Modern Labor Economics: An Analysis of Labor-Management Relations.* Pp. xviii, 659. New York: Ronald Press Company, 1954. $6.00.

DAY, CLARENCE ALBERT. *A History of Maine Agriculture, 1604–1860.* Pp. ix, 318. Orono, Maine: University Press, 1954. $2.50.

DONIGER, SIMON (Ed.). *Religion and Human Behavior.* "Pastoral Psychology Series." Pp. xxii, 233. New York: Association Press, 1954. $3.00.

ERICKSEN, E. GORDON. *Urban Behavior.* Pp. xiv, 482. New York: The Macmillan Company, 1954. $4.75.

FABIAN, ROBERT. *London After Dark: An Intimate Record of Night Life in London, and a Selection of Crime Stories from the Case Book of Ex-Superintendent, Robert Fabian.* Pp. 237. New York: British Book Centre, 1954. $3.50.

FAULKNER, HAROLD UNDERWOOD. *American Economic History.* Pp. xxiv, 816. 7th ed. New York: Harper & Brothers, 1954. $5.75.

FERGUSON, JOHN H., and DEAN E. McHENRY. *Elements of American Government.* Pp. x, 649. 2d ed. New York: McGraw-Hill Book Company, 1954. $5.00.

FRIEDMANN, W. (Ed.). *The Public Corporation: A Comparative Symposium.* Pp. vii, 612. Toronto, Canada: The Carswell Company, 1954. $10.00.

FRIEDRICH, CARL J., and ROBERT G. McCLOSKEY (Eds.). *From the Declaration of Independence to the Constitution: The Roots of American Constitutionalism.* Pp. lxviii, 71. New York: Liberal Arts Press, 1954. 75 cents.

GORER, GEOFFREY. *The Life and Ideas of the Marquis de Sade.* Pp. 244. Rev. ed. New York: British Book Centre, 1954 (originally published by Peter Owen, London, 1953). $3.50.

GRAYSON, HENRY. *Economic Planning Under Free Enterprise.* Pp. x, 134. Washington, D. C.: Public Affairs Press, 1954. $2.00.

GROVES, HAROLD M. *Financing Government.* Pp. xviii, 618. 4th ed. New York: Henry Holt and Company, 1954. $6.00.

HERTZLER, JOYCE O. *Society in Action: A Study of Basic Social Processes.* Pp. xii, 452. New York: Dryden Press, 1954. $5.25.

HROZNÝ, BEDŘICH. *Ancient History of Western Asia, India and Crete.* Translated by Jindřich Procházka. Pp. xv, 260. New York: Philosophical Library, [c. 1953]. $12.00.

INSTITUTE OF INTERNATIONAL INDUSTRIAL AND LABOR RELATIONS. *Labor, Management, and Economic Growth.* Proceedings of a Conference on Human Resources and Labor Relations in Underdeveloped Countries, November 12–14, 1953. Edited by Robert L. Aronson and John P. Windmuller. Pp. v, 251. Ithaca, N. Y.: New York State School of Industrial and Labor Relations, Cornell University, 1954. $2.00.

JAMES, PRESTON E., and CLARENCE F. JONES (Eds.). *American Geography: Inventory and Prospect.* John K. Wright, Consulting Editor. Maps by John C. Sherman. Pp. xii, 590. Syracuse, N. Y.: Syracuse University Press (for the Association of American Geographers), 1954. $6.00.

KAMIAT, ARNOLD H. *The Ethics of Civilization.* Pp. vii, 80. Washington: Public Affairs Press, 1954. $2.00.

KEIRSTEAD, B. S. *An Essay in the Theory of Profits and Income Distribution.* Pp. viii, 110. Oxford, England: Basil Blackwell (distributed in the U. S. by Augustus M. Kelley, New York), 1953. $1.75.

KNIGHT, HENRY. *Food Administration in India, 1939–47.* Pp. xii, 323. Stanford, Calif.: Stanford University Press, 1954. $7.50.

LEOPOLD, LUNA B., and THOMAS MADDOCK, JR. *The Flood Control Controversy: Big Dams, Little Dams, and Land Management.* Pp. xiii, 278. New York: Ronald Press Company, 1954. $5.00.

MAO TSE-TUNG. *Selected Works.* Volume One: *1926–1936.* Pp. 336. New York: International Publishers, 1954. $3.00. *Works* will be published in 5 volumes.

MARKHAM, F. M. H. *Napoleon and the Awakening of Europe.* In "Teach Yourself History Series." Pp. vii, 184. New York: The Macmillan Company, 1954. $2.00.

MERRIAM, CHARLES E., and ROBERT E. MERRIAM. *The American Government: Democracy in Action.* Pp. xi, 944. Boston: Ginn and Company, 1954. $6.25.

MITCHELL, ROBERT B., and CHESTER RAPKINS. *Urban Traffic: A Function of Land Use.*

Pp. xviii, 226. New York: Columbia University Press, 1954. $5.00.

MORGENTHAU, HANS J. *Politics Among Nations: The Struggle for Power and Peace.* Pp. xxv, 600, xxv. 2d ed., revised and enlarged. New York: Alfred A. Knopf, 1954. $5.75.

NORDIN, J. A., and VIRGIL SALERA. *Elementary Economics.* Pp. xv, 783. 2d ed. New York: Prentice-Hall, 1954. $7.95.

OGLE, MARBURY B., JR., LOUIS SCHNEIDER, and JAY W. WILEY. *Power, Order, and the Economy: A Preface to the Social Sciences.* Pp. xii, 852. New York: Harper & Brothers, 1954. $6.00.

OLIVER, HENRY M., JR. *A Critique of Socio-economic Goals.* Pp. 189. Bloomington: Indiana University Press, 1954. $2.50 paper; $3.00 cloth.

OMAN, CAROLA. *Lord Nelson.* Pp. 158. New York: The Macmillan Company, 1954. $1.75.

PARSONS, TALCOTT. *Essays in Sociological Theory.* Pp. 459. Rev. ed. Glencoe, Ill.: Free Press, 1954. $6.00.

PATTERSON, ROBERT T. *Federal Debt-Management Policies, 1865–1879.* Pp. xi, 244. Durham, N. C.: Duke University Press, 1954. $4.50.

PAZ-SOLDAN, C. E. *La Solidaridad de las Americas ante la Salud: Un Testimonio Personal.* Pp. 316. Lima: Biblioteca de Cultura Sanitaria del Instituto de Medicina Social de la Universidad de San Marcos, 1954. No price.

PENNINGTON, L. A., and IRWIN A. BERG (Eds.). *An Introduction to Clinical Psychology.* Pp. vii, 709. 2d ed. New York: Ronald Press Company, 1954. $6.50.

PEPINSKY, HAROLD B., and PAULINE NICHOLS PEPINSKY. *Counseling Theory and Prac-the British Isles: A Study of the Stone-* Press Company, 1954. $4.50.

PETERSON, SHOREY. *Economics.* Pp. xx, 827. Rev. ed. New York: Henry Holt and Company, 1954. $5.75.

PIGGOTT, STUART. *The Neolithic Cultures of the British Isles: A Study of the Stone-using Agricultural Communities of Britain in the Second Millennium.* Pp. xix, 420. New York: Cambridge University Press, 1954. $13.50.

PRICE, F. A. *Liberian Odyssey: "By Hammock and Surfboat"—The Autobiography of F. A. Price.* Pp. xv, 260. New York: Pageant Press, 1954. $7.50.

RAISIN, JACOB S. *Gentile Reactions to Jewish Ideals, With Special Reference to Proselytes.* Edited by Herman Hailperin. Pp. xxiii, 876.

New York: Philosophical Library, 1953. $7.50.

St. Lawrence University and Frederick A. Moran Memorial Institute on Delinquency and Crime, 1950–1953. Edited by Herbert A. Bloch et al. Pp. 197. Canton, N. Y.: St. Lawrence University, 1953. No price.

SAINT-YVES, LEONARD DE (Ed. and translator). *Selected Writings of De Sade.* Pp. 306. New York: British Book Centre (originally published by Peter Owen, London, 1953), 1954. $6.75.

SAYE, ALBERT B., MERRITT B. POUND, and JOHN F. ALLUMS. *Principles of American Government.* Pp. vi, 442. 2d ed. New York: Prentice-Hall, 1954. $6.35.

SCHICKELE, RAINER. *Agricultural Policy: Farm Programs and National Welfare.* Pp. x, 453. New York: McGraw-Hill Book Company, 1954. $6.50.

SETTON, KENNETH M., and HENRY R. WINKLER (Eds.). *Great Problems in European Civilization.* Pp. xx, 649. New York: Prentice-Hall, 1954. $7.65.

SHEEHAN, DONALD (Ed.). *The Making of American History.* Book 1: *The Emergence of a Nation.* Book 2: *Democracy in an Industrial World.* Pp. xi, 462; xi, 463–912. Rev. and enlarged ed. New York: Dryden Press, 1954. $2.90 each volume.

SNIDER, DELBERT. *Introduction to International Economics.* Pp. xix, 472. Homewood, Ill.: Richard D. Irwin, 1954. $6.00.

TATE, H. CLAY. *Building a Better Home Town: A Program of Community Self-analysis and Self-help.* Pp. xvi, 236. New York: Harper & Brothers, 1954. $3.50.

UNITED NATIONS, Department of Economic Affairs. *Economic Survey of Asia and the Far East, 1953.* Also issued as Vol. IV, No. 4 of the *Economic Bulletin for Asia and the Far East.* Pp. xiv, 161. Bangkok (distributed in U. S. by Columbia University Press, New York), 1954. $1.50.

——. *Economic Survey of Europe in 1953, Including a Study of Economic Development in Southern Europe.* Pp. xii, 314. Geneva: (distributed in the U. S. by Columbia University Press, New York), 1954. $2.50.

WEHLE, LOUIS B. *Hidden Threads of History: Wilson Through Roosevelt.* Pp. xix, 300. New York: The Macmillan Company, 1953. $4.00.

WILBUR, WILLIAM H. *Guideposts to the Future: A New American Foreign Policy.* Pp. xiv, 176. Chicago: Henry Regnery Company, 1954. $2.50.

INDEX

New and vivid insights into the troubled East

"A thorough, competent and extremely fascinating piece of political history."—THE AUSTRALIAN OUTLOOK

NATIONALISM AND REVOLUTION IN INDONESIA

By GEORGE McT. KAHIN, *Assistant Professor of Government, Cornell University*

HERE is the documented and unembroidered account of the events that have reshaped the political face of Indonesia. The history of Dutch rule, the policies of the Japanese during the occupation, the role of the United Nations, the attitude of the native Communists in Indonesia, the interplay of political parties, and the personalities of the native leaders are all shown as interlocking elements in the history of this national awakening.　　　*503 pp., 4 maps.* $6.00

A colorful, intimate account of people and new ways in Arabia

THE ARABIAN PENINSULA

By RICHARD H. SANGER, *Public Affairs Adviser of the Bureau of Near Eastern, South Asian, and African Affairs*

THE fast-changing Arab world of today is here described by a man who has lived and traveled widely in the Middle East. Bustling Jidda, the model farms of Al Kharj, the mines of the Hejaz, the royal palaces of Riyadh, the towns of the oil coast, as well as King Saud al Saud and the sheikhs, bedouin, and town people of Arabia come to life in this knowledgeable book.　　　*309 pp., 2 maps, 29 illus.* $5.00

"Perhaps the best introduction to the modern Middle East to appear in the post-war period."
—THE JOURNAL OF INTERNATIONAL AFFAIRS

THE MIDDLE EAST IN WORLD AFFAIRS

By GEORGE LENCZOWSKI, *University of California*

Recent developments in eleven Middle Eastern countries are systematically set forth.
479 pp., 8 maps. $6.00

Order from your bookseller or from

Cornell University Press
124 Roberts Place, Ithaca, New York

Kindly mention THE ANNALS *when writing to advertisers*

Kindly mention THE ANNALS *when writing to advertisers*

To Make Storage Available for New Volumes of

The ANNALS
4 VOLUMES FOR $1.00

- **No orders at sale price accepted after 31 August 1954**
- **Minimum order 4 volumes, 25¢ for each additional volume**
- **Shipping charges extra, unless payment accompanies order**
- **Sale restricted to paper-bound volumes listed below; for sale of cloth-bound volumes see previous page**
- **Circle your choice and detach**

WORLD AFFAIRS AND NATIONAL SECURITY

1. The Search for National Security (November 1951)
2. Moscow's European Satellites (September 1950)
3. Military Government (January 1950)
4. Peace Settlements of World War II (May 1948)
5. Making the United Nations Work (July 1946)
6. Agenda for Peace (July 1944)
7. Winning Both the War and the Peace (July 1942)
8. Defending America's Future (July 1941)
9. Billions for Defense (March 1941)
10. When War Ends (July 1940)
11. Refugees (May 1939)
12. Present International Tensions (July 1938)
13. The United States and World War (July 1937)
14. The Attainment and Maintenance of World Peace (July 1936)
15. Present Day Causes of International Friction (July 1929)
16. Some Aspects of the Present International Situation (July 1928)
17. Europe in 1927 (November 1927)
18. Some Outstanding Problems of American Foreign Policy (July 1927)

OTHER COUNTRIES

19. Postwar Reconstruction in Western Germany (November 1948)
20. Belgium in Transition (September 1946)
21. The Netherlands During German Occupation (May 1946)
22. Southeastern Asia and the Philippines (March 1943)
23. Social Problems and Policies in Sweden (May 1938)
24. An Economic Survey of Australia (November 1931)
25. Russia Today (March 1922)

GOVERNMENT AND POLITICS

LAW AND LAW ENFORCEMENT

MODERN SOCIETY AND SOCIAL PROBLEMS

ECONOMIC PROBLEMS AND LABOR

THE AMERICAN ACADEMY

3937 Chestnut Street
Philadelphia 4, Pennsylvania

YOUR NAME ....

ADDRESS ....

....

0534